MANCHESTER

an architectural history

MANCHESTER
UNIVERSITY PRESS

to Rosamund Kate

MANCHESTER

AN ARCHITECTURAL HISTORY

John J. Parkinson-Bailey

Manchester University Press

MANCHESTER AND NEW YORK

distributed exclusively in the USA by St Martin's Press

Published by Manchester University Press
Oxford Road, Manchester M13 9NR, UK
and Room 400, 175 Fifth Avenue, New York, NY 10010, USA
http://www.man.ac.uk/mup

Distributed exclusively in the USA by
St Martin's Press, Inc., 175 Fifth Avenue, New York,
NY 10010, USA

Distributed exclusively in Canada by
UBC Press, University of British Columbia, 6344 Memorial Road,
Vancouver, BC, Canada V6T 1Z2

British Library Cataloguing-in-Publication Data
A catalogue record for this book is available from the British Library

Library of Congress Cataloging-in-Publication Data applied for

ISBN 0 7190 5606 3 *hardback*

First published 2000

07 06 05 04 03 02 01 00   10 9 8 7 6 5 4 3 2 1

Designed in Apollo with Chianti display
by Max Nettleton FCSD

Typeset in Hong Kong by Graphicraft Limited

Printed in Great Britain
by Biddles Limited, Guildford and King's Lynn

CONTENTS

LIST OF FIGURES

Where no other source is given, photographs by Graeme McCaig

LIST OF PLATES

ACKNOWLEDGEMENTS

THIS BOOK would never have been written without the discussions I had many years ago with Alex Gordon PPRIBA, and with Peter Forbes and Robert Smart, who, in their days at BDP and mine in London, gave me so much enthusiasm for their profession.

The late Cecil Stewart's *Stones of Manchester* is still the best history of the architecture of Victorian Manchester – my debt to him and to the works of Dennis Sharp and Philip Atkins will be evident to anyone who has read about the architecture of the city.

I have to thank all those architects who, over the past few years, gave up precious time to answer my often intemperate questions about their buildings and their practices (in both senses): John Sheard, Cruickshank & Seward, especially, for sharing his insights; Neil Musgrove, Austin-Smith:Lord; David Barnes, Adrian Jackson, Ken Moth, Terry Davenport, and Simon Bedford, Building Design Partnership; Ian Chapman, John Lynch, Denver Humphrey and Justin Barnard, Fairhursts Design Group; Jack Bogle, EGS Designs; Andrew McDonald, FaulknerBrowns; Ian Finlay, Ian Finlay Architects; Alan Parry-Davies, Halliday Meecham Architects; Vic Basil and Andrew Robson, Holford Associates; James Stevenson, Hurd Rolland Partnership; Nicholas Johnson, Johnson Urban Development Consultants; Ian Savage and Jeffrey Varnom, Leach Rhodes Walker; Mike Greenwood, Leslie Jones Architects; Malcolm Brown and Matthew Goulcher, Levitt Bernstein Associates; George Mills, Mills Beaumont Leavey & Channon; Robin Derham, Barry Pritchard and Nicholas Thompson, Renton Howard Wood Levin Partnership; Roger Stephenson, Stephenson Bell; Barry Johnson, Thomas Worthington & Sons. All the views expressed are mine, not theirs, and I hope I have not traduced any of them too much.

There are others I have to thank for their help in attempting to unravel the city: Peter Budd of Ove Arup & Partners; Warren Marshall, head of the Urban Design & Conservation Group, City Planning Department; Marilyn Steane, lately of Eastside Regeneration; Robert Pugh, Regional Marketing Manager, John Laing Construction Ltd; Jeremy Michelson, Curator of the Manchester Jewish Museum; Peter Crockett, Property Manager, Morrison Merlin Ltd; Tania Hollins and Steve King, for informed discussions about the Gay Village; Peter Ferriday, who ought to have written this book, for he has forgotten more architectural history than I have ever learnt. A special debt of gratitude is owed to David Hilton, Plankeeper, City Architect's Office, not only for giving up so much of his time, but also for sharing so freely his considerable knowledge of Manchester's buildings.

For their patient assistance I have to thank the staff of the All Saints Library at the Manchester Metropolitan University and the staff of Manchester Central Library Local Studies Unit, who also gave permission to reproduce Slater's 1848 *Plan of Manchester and Salford* for the front end-paper. The back end-paper was reproduced from the February 2000 Superplan scale 1:2500 Ordnance Survey Map by permission of the Ordnance Survey on behalf of the Controller of her Majesty's Stationery Office, © Crown Copyright MC100031042. The map was provided by the Superplan Mapping Department at Waterstone's, Manchester. The Department of Environmental Development, Manchester City Council, kindly allowed me to use excerpts from the 1945 *Manchester Plan*. My thanks also go to the staff of the Slide Library at the Metropolitan University, and particularly to Steve Yates for having taken many of the photographs in this book. I am obliged to Professor Diana Donald for setting me off on the project, and to colleagues on my Departmental Research Committee for granting me a much needed sabbatical term as well as financial assistance toward the cost of the photographs.

I wish especially to thank Christopher Woodward for his close reading of the text, for his sagacious and scholarly comments and for his timely suggestions about the structure of the book, and Ray Offord, who is blessed with an eye for both detail and meaning. I am most grateful to Len Grant, the assiduous recorder of Manchester, for many of the colour plates and the remarkable photographs for the cover. I am indebted to all the staff at Manchester University Press, and particularly to Matthew Frost, without whose encouragement and enthusiasm this work would have faltered long ago. I owe the warmest thanks to Graeme McCaig, not only for taking on the task of photographing most of the buildings in the book, often at unsociable hours, but also for his long friendship and for making our walks around Manchester both enjoyable and revealing.

My deepest debt of gratitude must go to my wife Rosamund, for her steadfast encouragement, for putting up uncomplainingly with my bouts of ill-humour and her state of neglect, and, most important, for her consummate and constructive critiques of my work; without her help and support, this book would never have been finished.

J. J. P. B.

PREFACE

When we build, let us think that we build for ever. [John Ruskin, *The Seven Lamps of Architecture*, 1849]

THIS BOOK is an attempt to provide a history of Manchester, through its buildings, and of the buildings themselves through the cultural, social and political events of the periods in which they were built. The development of Manchester is dealt with chronologically rather than thematically, and each of the chapters is based around a particular episode or episodes which have had consequences on the built environment.

The book concentrates on the city centre, an area broadly within a half-mile radius from St Ann's Church, but there have been events outside the city which have affected it considerably and the boundaries of the book wax and wane to include them. The displacing, in the nineteenth century, of Manchester's inhabitants from the centre to the ring of inner suburbs and beyond also affected the subsequent infrastructure of the city. (The recent immigration into the centre is even now having another impact.) The Ship Canal and its docks and Trafford Park lie outside the political as well as the physical boundaries of the city, but their effect on Manchester at the turn of the twentieth century, and in more recent years, has been significant. For these reasons, Hulme, Salford, Trafford and Wythenshawe all have a brief mention; that they appear all too fleetingly is due not to conscious neglect but to lack of space. Much more work needs to be done on the history of Manchester's urban deprivation in the twentieth century. Salford, which had a formal existence before Manchester, deserves its own book.

This is not a guidebook but a history, and like all histories it is necessarily selective. Undoubtedly, there will be favourite buildings that I have failed to mention, but those that are included are representative of a period. If architects' names occur with regularity, it is because, at different times, they have built a lot in the city, and in the case of current architectural practices have been willing to share details of their buildings. I am only too aware that there are other architects who have contributed much to the city – the Manchester Society of Architects alone has 700 members – and to them I apologise for their exclusion.

In many ways the nineteenth century has been easier to write about; there is little disagreement about which buildings have been significant. More recent architecture is less easy. For many people the architecture of the 1960s and 1970s is an eyesore, to others it is as valuable a part of our architectural heritage as Georgian mills or Victorian warehouses. People either love or hate the Bridgewater Hall, some welcome the idea of bringing new life to the far end of Deansgate, others object to what they see as the misuse of the Great Northern Railway Warehouse. No one will object to the refacing of the Arndale Centre, but who knows how the buildings being erected today will be judged in ten or twenty years' time?

I have tried to write a book accessible to the general reader, and one that is not overly laden with either theory or jargon, though it is difficult to write about architecture without using the shorthand phrases of the discipline, and for that reason a brief glossary of terms is provided. It will be noticed that there are few illustrations of the early history of Manchester and progressively more images as the centuries progress. The concentration is consciously on extant buildings in an attempt to persuade the reader to go out and look at the buildings themselves. A gazetteer has been provided at the end of the book, and this, together with a large-scale A–Z, will, hopefully, be effective as a guide. All listed buildings – as far as I have been able to ascertain them – are included in the gazetteer, as well as a selection of other buildings. I should be pleased to hear of any errors of omission or commission.

A. J. P. Taylor wrote in 1957:

Manchester is irredeemably ugly. There is no spot to which you could lead a blindfold stranger and say happily: 'Now open your eyes.' Norman Douglas had a theory that English people walked with their eyes on the ground so as to avoid the excrement of dogs on the pavement. The explanation in Manchester is simpler: they avert their eyes from the ugliness of their surroundings.

Believe him not, for there are good and occasionally wondrous buildings in the city. If there is a word of advice it is to walk the streets looking up, for there are few dogs in the city and many marvels above the street line.

I

AD 70–1800

FROM THE ROMANS TO THE CANALS

Manchester, on the south side of the Irwel river, stondeth in Salfordshiret, and is the fairest, best buildid, quickkst and most populus tounne of all Lancastreshire. [John Leland, 1538]

THE ROMAN OUTPOST of Mamucium was established in AD 70 on sandstone bluff at the junction of the rivers Irwell and Medlock, on the major road from Chester to York, and over the next three centuries developed into a stone fortification. Outside this fort a small fortified town, or *vicus*, was established.[1] In AD 410 the Roman troops were withdrawn from Mamucium, leaving it in the hands of the Saxons, who renamed it Manigceastre. The Danes seized Manigceastre in 870, and from them comes the word *gat* meaning road or way, hence Deansgate and Millgate. By 920 Manceastre, as it was then known, had become a frontier town between Mercia and Northumberland, and Prince Edward the Elder placed a strong garrison there. At some time during the tenth century the town developed at the opposite end of Deansgate on a more defensible sandstone outcrop, at the confluence of the rivers Irwell and Irk, and here was established the church of St Mary, somewhere between St Mary's Gate and the site of the present Cathedral. Over the next hundred years the town grew around the parish church, and by 1028 Manchester was important enough to be designated one of the thirty-seven towns appointed by King Canute for the coinage of money.

In 1066 William the Conqueror granted an immense territory to Roger of Poitou, who bestowed the manor of Manchester on Nigellus, a Norman knight, and the manor, valued at £1,000, was made an honour within the hundred of Salford. In 1129 Albert de Gresley, Nigellus's son-in-law, gained possession of the manor, and his successor, Thomas de Gresley, the sixth baron, was granted the 'Great Charter of Manchester' in 1301 by which it became a free borough.* Thomas de Gresley surveyed his manor and found:

> There is a mill at Manchester, running by the water of the Irk, value ten pounds, at which the burgesses and all the tenants of Manchester, with the hamlets, and Ardwick, Pensham, Crummeshall, Moston, Notchurst, Getheswych, and Ancotes ought to grind, paying the sixteenth grain, except the lord of Moston, who (hopper free) pays the twentieth grain. And there is here a certain common oven, near the lord's court, value six shillings and eight pence, at which, according to custom, every burgess must bake.[2]

Thomas de Gresley died without issue in 1313, and his brother-in-law John de la Warre became Lord of the manor. His successor, Thomas West, the rector of Manchester, succeeded to the manorial rights in 1399, and in 1421 Henry V granted West a licence for the refounding of St Mary's as a collegiate church, dedicated to St Mary, St Denys and St George [1]. John Huntington, the rector of Ashton, was appointed as the first warden, together with eight priests, four clerks and six lay choristers, known as 'the guild or company of the Blessed Virgin in Manchester', and he rebuilt the choir, the first stone of which was laid on 28 July 1422. The third warden, Ralph Langley, built the nave during the 1460s and 1470s, and the fifth warden, John Stanley, Bishop of Ely, altered some of the earlier work.

In 1515 a Free Grammar School was founded by Hugh Oldham, Bishop of Exeter, and in 1520 the first school building was erected in Long Millgate just outside the present entrance to Chetham's College. The school was granted the income from the manor's mills in 1525 and the Court Leet reminded the inhabitants of Manchester in 1577 that if people stopped using the mills it would lead 'to the greate overthrowe of the saide school, which ys only founded and maynteyned by such comoditye'.[3] The Grammar School survived and removed to new premises in Fallowfield in 1931 (architects, Percy Worthington and Francis Jones).

By the sixteenth century the weaving of cloth was becoming important to Manchester. In 1524 there is a record of one Martin Brian, a great woollen clothier, living in Manchester, and in 1541 an Act of Parliament refers to the town as 'well inhabited for a long time, and the king's subjects well set a work in the making of clothes as well of linen as of woollen'. By 1552 Manchester was already identifiable as a cloth producer, and an Act of that year charged 'that all cottons called Manchester, Lancashire and Cheshire cottons [which were actually woollen], shall be in length twenty-two yards, and that all Manchester rugs, otherwise Manchester frizes, shall contain in length thirty-six yards'. By 1565 aulnegers, or parliamentary agents, were stationed at Manchester for stamping woollen cloth, and 1578 saw a large influx of weavers exiled from the Low Countries.

On 15 May 1579 the manor of Manchester was mortgaged by Thomas West for £3,000 to John Lacye, a London mercer, and the manor passed to Lacye by default in 1581. He in turn, on 23 March 1596, sold the manor for £3,500 to Nicholas

---

* Salford was granted a charter in 1230 which established its privileges long before Manchester's.

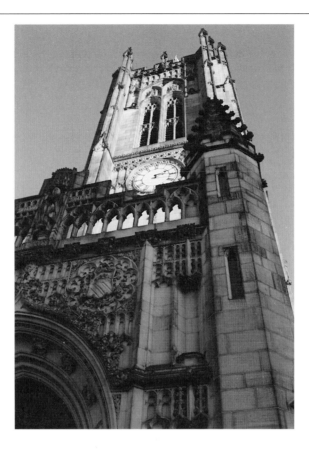

1] Cathedral, west tower

Mosley, the son of Edward Mosley of Hough End in Withington. Nicholas, who managed the London end of the family textile business, was an alderman of the Clothworkers' Company and was elected Lord Mayor of London in 1599, at which time he received his knighthood. Sir Nicholas retired in 1602, came back to Manchester and built Hough End Hall, the only extant Elizabethan mansion in Manchester. The Mosleys were to remain lords of the manor until 1835.

Another cloth merchant, Humphrey Chetham, founded the Chetham's Hospital and Library in 1635, and based them on the low Collyhurst sandstone buildings which had been the domestic quarters of the Collegiate Church. The hospital and library (arguably the first free public library in Europe) was incorporated by royal charter in 1655.

By 1641 Manchester weavers were producing both linen and cotton cloths, and Lewis Roberts's *The Treasure of Traffic* noted that:

> The town of Manchester buys the linen yarn of the Irish in great quantity, and, weaving it, returns the same again to Ireland to sell. Neither doth her industry rest here, for they buy cotton wool in London, that comes from Cyprus and Smyrna, and work the same into fustians, vermilions, dimities, and other such stuffs, which they return to London, where they are sold; and thence not seldom are sent into foreign parts, which have means on far easier terms to provide themselves of the first material.[4]

One year later Manchester became famous for quite different reasons, for, on 5 July 1642, the first blood of the Civil War was spilt between Charles I's troops, commanded by Lord Strange, and the Parliamentarians of Manchester. Four days later it was announced in the House of Commons as 'The beginning of Civil Warres in England: or Terrible News from the North'.

By 1653 Manchester consisted of Salford Bridge, Acres Field, the old and new Market Steads, and eleven streets: Market Stead Lane, Alport Street, Hunt's Bank, Meale Gate, Fennel Street, Toad Lane, Witthingreave, Hanging Ditch, Smithy Door, Mylve Gate and Mylners Lane. In 1673 an Act was passed to allow Sir Edward Mosley to acquire Hulme.

It was a political act in the early eighteenth century which changed the shape of Manchester, and moved the centre of the town from the mediaeval area around the Collegiate Church to what became St Ann's Square. Queen Ann had acceded to the throne in 1702, and Mosley's daughter, Lady Ann Bland, angered by the pro-Jacobite sentiments being expressed from the pulpit of the Collegiate Church, determined to erect a second church in the township from which pro-monarchist sermons would be preached. Parliament granted her leave in 1708 to enclose the open pasture land of Acres Field for the building of St Ann's Church [2], on the condition that the new square should be thirty yards wide to allow the holding of the 'Acres Fair' which had been held there since 1229.*

After the church was built, St Ann's Square quickly became the most fashionable part of town, and by 1735 the south side of the square, parts of King Street and Ridgefield were being built upon with elegant brick houses. St James's Square (so named by Jacobite supporters) was laid out in 1739 with large houses and gardens for 'respectable people' and in 1747 leases were granted for buildings to be erected on ground now bordered by Market Street, Cross Street, King Street and Mosley Street, and this, after St Ann's Square, was the first major piece of development in the town. In 1753 the lower part of King Street started to be built on.

Already in existence, at the end of Toll Lane (now St Ann's Street), was the Cross Street Chapel, Manchester's oldest Nonconformist place of worship. The Dissenters' Meeting House, as it was then known, had been erected in 1694 on a place called Plungeon Meadow, where had originally stood the town's ducking stool before its removal to Hanging Ditch. The Meeting House (whose congregation was Hanoverian in its politics) was gutted by a Jacobite mob in 1715, and was rebuilt with a grant of £1,000 from Parliament. The building was important to the town, for not only was Lady Bland a member of the congregation, many of Manchester's leading figures in the late eighteenth and nineteenth centuries came from the group of Unitarians who

---

* The Acres Fair continued to be held in the square until 1823, when it became such a nuisance that it was removed to Knott Mill (Castlefield) by Sir Oswald Mosley, a later lord of the manor. By 1876 the fair had become too large and created too much traffic congestion on Deansgate, so it was moved to Pomona Gardens until its cessation in 1877.

2] St Ann's Church,
St Ann's Square, c. 1712

worshipped in this chapel. The first Methodist chapel was built in Oldham Street in 1780, a Unitarian chapel in Mosley Street in 1789, and the first Catholic church in Mulberry Street in 1794, all later demolished and replaced by other buildings.

Daniel Defoe, in 1726, found Manchester 'one of the greatest, if not the greatest meer Village in England. It is neither a wall'd Town, City or Corporation; they send no Members to Parliament; and the highest Magistrate they have is a Constable or Headborough; and yet it has a Collegiate Church, several Parishes, takes up a large space of Ground, and, including the Suburb, or that part of the Town called [Salford] over the Bridge; it is said to contain about fifty thousand people.'[5] Defoe exaggerated the size of both towns, since the first enumeration of the population of Salford and Manchester in 1756 counted only 19,839 inhabitants. The wealth to create the 'greatest mere village' came from the manufacture of and trade in cotton, and so important had this commodity become that, in 1729, the first Cotton Exchange was built on St Mary's Gate at the expense of Sir Oswald Mosley.

An elegant Palladian version of an old market hall, with Ionic columns and pilasters, the building had an open ground-floor arcade and an assembly room above, but it was never popular with the merchants who were meant to use it. The area abounded with petty criminals and layabouts, it was inconvenient and filthy, and the approach to the Exchange and Market Place from St Ann's Square was through a narrow passageway so dark and dismal, even at midday, that it was called the 'Dark Entry'. By 1750 the merchants had stopped using the Exchange, preferring to negotiate in the street, or to meet in Lady Bland's Assembly Rooms above the passage between King Street and St Ann's Square (hence the name 'Old Exchange' written above St Ann's Passage). An Act of Parliament was obtained in 1776 which allowed the demolition of the Dark Entry buildings and the creation of Exchange Street, and so keen were the inhabitants to rid this fashionable area of its slums that £10,000 was raised by public subscription in two weeks. The Cotton Exchange was demolished in 1792 and its site marked by a post and pillars on which a clock was mounted. The clock never gave the correct time and was eventually removed.

To the west of the town, at the top of Market Stead Lane, the mid-eighteenth century saw the erection of Manchester's first purpose-built 'civic' buildings. Opposite Lever's Row (the first group of houses to be erected in what became Piccadilly) Sir Oswald Mosley owned a large grass plot fronted by a pond known as the 'Daub Holes', so called from the habit of people taking clay from the land for daubing their houses. Sir Oswald granted permission for this land to be used for a new hospital to replace the old Manchester Public Infirmary which had been founded in 1752 in a house in Garden Street, off Withy Grove. One condition of the lease was that the Daub Holes should be converted into an ornamental pond, and that the land must be open to the public for ever, on pain of it reverting to the Mosley family.

The foundation stone of the new building was laid on 20 May 1754, and the Infirmary opened in 1755 with accommodation for eighty patients.[6] Teaching of medical apprentices took place from 1757, making it the oldest teaching hospital in the provinces. In 1763, the adjoining Lunatic Hospital and Asylum were opened, and in 1781 Public Baths were added, with Matlock, Buxton and Vapour baths. Subscribers were allowed the use of the baths by all their family and visitors, but not by their servants. Persons bathing on Sundays paid double; patients at the Infirmary were never allowed to use the baths, they had their own. The baths were always unprofitable, and closed in 1847.

In 1792 a Dispensary was added to the site, and this, like the earlier buildings, was of unembellished red brick, baked from local clay. In front of the buildings was a gravel walk, bordered by grass and some trees, 'open to all orderly persons at proper hours', and the Daub Holes, which had been joined together to make an ornamental pond 615 ft long and 80 ft wide (the site was turned into sunken gardens in the 1930s). Other parts of the public garden lay between the Dispensary and Public Baths, laid out in serpentine walks with shrubs and flowers, and from these gardens the first hot-air balloon ascended in 1783, alighting at Cromford in Derbyshire.* In 1849 the Royal Manchester Lunatic Asylum moved to Stockport Etchells, seven miles from the city, into a hospital in the Elizabethan style designed by Richard Lane,[7] and the Manchester Royal Infirmary moved to its present site on Oxford Road in 1908 (architects E. T. Hall and John Brooke).

As a result of a disagreement between medical staff at the Infirmary, a lying-in charity was founded by Dr Charles White in 1790 in a house in Old Bridge Street, Salford, and it moved in 1796 to the Bath Inn in Stanley Street, Salford, opening as the 'Manchester Lying-in Hospital and Charity for the delivery of poor women at their own habitations'. The bar parlour became the Matron's room, the bar room the apothecaries' shop, the dining room became the board room and the other bars became the porters' and inoculating rooms. Under the Physician were three 'Men-midwives Extraordinary' and three 'in Ordinary'. Although the hospital was originally intended for in-patients, by 1814 poor women were seen only at home, and by 1815 the building had become too large for its pupose. In 1854 the Lying-in Hospital was renamed the 'St Mary's Hospital and Dispensary for the diseases peculiar to women and also for the diseases of children under six years of age'. St Mary's moved to Quay Street in 1856, then to Oxford Road in 1890 (on the corner of Whitworth Street West, into a building designed by Alfred Waterhouse, demolished in the 1970s), and to its present site on Oxford Road in 1970.[8]

In Aytoun Street there was a House of Recovery, a large plain brick building for the reception and 'recovery' of 100 fever patients rescued 'from the almost inevitable certainty of perishing, amidst the unavailing cries of their friends, and surrounded by uncleanliness, which in itself is sufficient, without any contagious principle in the disease, to scatter the seeds of Death around, and sweep whole families to the grave'.[9] Between 1796, when the building was opened, and 1815, 6,509 patients had been restored to health. Dr Kay noted that the House of Recovery had been effective in checking the spread of typhus. In 1855 the Infirmary took over the House of Recovery and the patients were transferred. A. Collie & Co. built a warehouse on the site in 1867 (architects, Mills & Murgatroyd), which was converted into the Grand Hotel in 1883.

At the top of Market Stead Lane (Market Street) stood Lever's Hall, the town residence of the Lever family. Market Stead Lane was part of the main London to Carlisle road and became a centre of the coaching trade, and in 1773 Lever's Hall was converted into the White Bear, a coaching inn. Coaches departed from the inn every Sunday, Tuesday and Thursday, arriving in London two days later. The house was demolished in 1904, having ceased to be an inn since the latter nineteenth century. At the rear of the White Bear, on High Street, was the Bridgewater Arms, another house converted to a coaching inn, offering accommodation for 100 persons, and this became the

---

* Mr Saddler's balloon ascent on 12 May 1785 from a garden behind the Manchester Arms Inn, Long Millgate (hence Balloon Street), is often erroneously given as the first.

centre of stagecoach traffic for Manchester from 1788 for forty years, before being demolished to make room for warehouses. The *Manchester Mercury* announced in January 1788 that 'the old London coach leaves Manchester every Monday, Wednesday and Friday, at 5 a.m. Breakfasts at Macclesfield. Dines at Derby at four p.m. Sups at Leicester. Reaches Northampton next morning at six, and the Swan, in Lad Lane, about eight the following evening,' a journey time of thirty-six hours. To Hull took twenty-four hours, to Birmingham seventeen, Sheffield via Buxton twelve, Leeds and Lancaster eleven, to Liverpool nine hours. On relaying the news of the defeat of Napoleon the *Traveller*, the *Defiance* and the *Telegraph* brought news from London in eighteen hours.

In 1770 there was only one stagecoach to London and one to Liverpool, and these ran only twice a week, but by 1816 there were seventy distinct coaches; fifty-four set out every day and sixteen others three times a week. Trade between London and the provinces was increasing rapidly, and hotels sprang up on Market Street and at the top of Mosley Street to cater for travellers. The Royal Hotel on Mosley Street was demolished for the extension of Lewis's in 1908; the Mosley Hotel in Piccadilly gave way to the Piccadilly Cinema in 1922. The Albion Hotel, on the corner of Oldham Street, was demolished for Woolworth's in 1928.

The land at present bounded by Oldham Street, Great Ancoats Street, Port Street and Piccadilly was owned by Sir Ashton Lever, who, in 1780, sold nine acres to a property developer, William Stevenson, after whom the square is named. Stevenson developed the square in an attempt to rival St Ann's Square, but it was well outside the fashionable part of town, and its greatest claim to fame was as a place of public oratory in the nineteenth century, when up to 10,000 people gathered in the square. Houses of the period can still be seen at 69–73 Lever Street (1787, Grade II) and 4–8 Bradley Street.

Away from the commercial area around Market Street other, more polite streets were being developed. In the 1770s St John Street, part of the Byrom estate, was laid out with houses for the gentry. This little road remains one of the few parts of Manchester in which Georgian houses can still be seen, though now given over to offices. Princess Street was created in 1772, George Street and Charlotte Street from 1788, and Hanover Street from 1792–93, all as fashionable streets, as indicated by their 'royal' names. Churches were being built in these areas to meet the needs of the fast-growing population, though, unfortunately, all of them were subsequently demolished as the centre of Manchester became depopulated and the churches lost their congregations. St Mary's, St Mary's Parsonage, built in 1756, was demolished in 1880; the site was never built on and is now Parsonage Gardens. St John's, Byrom Street, was consecrated in 1769 and was demolished in 1932, and the flower gardens on Byrom Street mark the site. St James's, St James Street, of 1786, was a handsome brick building with a small stone spire, and had the largest congregation outside the Collegiate Church. It was demolished in 1928. St Peter's, St Peter's Square, 1788–94, designed by James Wyatt, was demolished in 1906–07, and only the cross in the square marks its site.

For their corporeal needs country manufacturers ate at the inns around Market Place and Hanging Ditch, but Manchester men had no need of such places, since they lived near their place of business and it was their habit to eat at home. The first restaurant in Manchester, the Fountain Street Refectory, was not built until 1824, and even by 1838 there were only eighteen restaurants in the town, six of them on Deansgate. However, gentlemen did meet and conduct business in the many coffee shops, such as the Cobden Coffee House on Port Street, which, in the nineteenth century, became a hotbed of social reform and was visited by John Stuart Mill and the Earl of Shaftesbury. On Exchange Street was Day's Coffee House, where in the eighteenth century a group of twenty-four amateur flautists entertained the customers once a fortnight. It was from these musicians that the Gentlemen's Concert Orchestra was founded, and the foundation stone of their first Concert Hall was laid, in 1775, at the corner of York Street and what is now Concert Lane. The Concert Hall was large, 81 ft long and 30 ft wide, and could hold an audience of 1,200, and its opening, in September 1777, was celebrated by a three-day musical festival, probably the first in the country. In 1831 the concerts were removed to Peter Street, to a building designed by Richard Lane.

Following the passing of the Manchester Playhouse Bill in 1775, a licence was granted for the first Theatre Royal, which was opened on 5 June 1775 on the corner of Spring Gardens and York Street. Mrs Siddons and John Kemble were part of the stock company, and Stephen Kemble appeared there. The theatre was burnt down in 1789, but reopened in 1790 and survived under the successive names of the Amphitheatre, the Minor Theatre and the Queen's until it was demolished in 1869.

Spring Gardens gets its name from the spring which arose there until the Theatre Royal was built on the site, and which provided Manchester's main drinking supply for 200 years. When the theatre was demolished in 1869 the spring again came to light under the stage, about 15 ft below street level. During the alterations to the site the spring was drained, and no traces are left. Parr's Bank (Heathcote, 1902, now the Athenaeum) was eventually built on the site.*

On 6 May 1783 the foundation stone of the New Bailey Bridge was laid, and the bridge was opened in 1785. Constructed of stone, three arches spanned the river, with a smaller arch over the towing path to the Duke of Bridgewater's quay in Salford. The first bridge over the Irwell had been erected in 1365, and in 1368 there is mention of a chapel built upon 'Salford bridge'. Situated on the north side of the bridge, on the middle pier, the chapel consisted of two apartments, one above the other, and the lower chamber, in spite of being subject to frequent flooding, was used as a gaol until 1778, when the chapel

---

* At 9 Spring Gardens lived George Nicholson, printer and vegetarian, who produced in 1803 the first vegetarian cookery-book, a tract of recipes of 'one hundred perfectly palatable and highly nutritious substances which may easily be secured at an expense much below the price of the limbs of our fellow-animals'. In 1824 the Vegetarian Society was formed in Manchester, and on 22 July 1852 a vegetarian banquet was held in Salford Town Hall.

was removed for bridge widening.* On the other side of the bridge, on Stanley Street, the New Bailey gaol commenced building in May 1787, and opened for prisoners in April 1790. The outside walls were 120 yards long, and over the entrance was a Session Room for weekly and quarterly sessions, with adjoining rooms for the jurors, counsel and magistrates. Behind the lodge stood the prison, of 150 cells: a large building three storeys high in the form of a cross.[10] There were fifty-three workshops within the prison walls where unskilled prisoners would beat, pick and clean cotton. If committed for twelve months or longer, they were taught to weave. Shoemaking and tailoring were also taught, but, even in gaol, cotton was becoming king.

The prison was doubled in size in 1816, with the addition of a new semicircular cell block and workshops, a circular chapel, and the dreaded treadwheels or 'cockchafers' used for grinding corn. The expanded prison took up the whole of the land between New Bailey Street and Irwell Street. The prison was replaced by Strangeways Gaol (Waterhouse, 1869) and became Bailey Yard, a large railway goods yard. A new building for the Inland Revenue (Trinity Bridge House) now stands on part of the site.

By 1788 Manchester and Salford had a combined population of 50,000 people. In 1790 Oxford Road was opened southward from St Peter's Church, and in that year Manchester paid £11,000 in postage, a larger amount than any other provincial town. In 1791 an Act of Parliament was obtained for lighting, watching and cleaning the town, and a police tax of 1s 3d in the pound was levied upon the rents of houses to defray the expenses. Paid for by this rate, fifty-three watchmen paraded the streets nightly from 8.00 p.m. to 6.00 a.m. in winter and from 10.00 p.m. to 4.00 a.m. in summer. By 1793 Manchester had 600 streets, and by the end of the eighteenth century the town was lighted by 2,758 oil lamps.

From their houses in St Ann's Square or St John Street or King Street polite society could be conveyed in sedans to the Assembly Rooms on Mosley Street, which had opened on 20 September 1792. Here, behind a Classical portico, a wide staircase from Mosley Street led to an 87 ft by 34 ft ballroom, lit by three pendant and twelve wall chandeliers, and with seats upholstered in orange satin. The ten-person orchestra sat in a balcony over the front entrance. The rules were strict: gentlemen had to change partners every two dances, no couples were allowed to leave a dance before its conclusion, and no refreshments were allowed in the ballroom. During the season there were evening promenades at seven o'clock, 2s (10p) per person, tea included. The tea room was 54 ft by 31 ft, and adjoining it was a card room, the walls of which were covered with an opulent Chinese paper. Underneath the tea room, at the Charlotte Street end, and approached by a separate entrance from Back Mosley Street, was a

---

* A wooden bridge over the Irwell had been built in 1761 by a theatrical company who were performing in Salford and wished to provide better access for their Manchester patrons. It was named Blackfriars as a joke because Blackfriars Bridge in London was being built at the time. The present Blackfriars Bridge was designed by Thomas Wright in 1818 at a cost of £9,000.

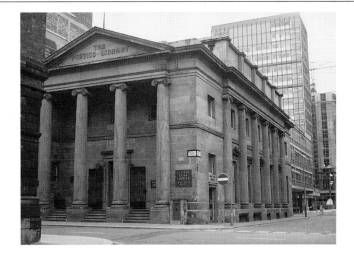

[3] Portico Library, Mosley Street,
Thomas Harrison, 1802–06

billiard room, open in summer at 8.00 a.m., in winter at 9.00 a.m., and closed at 10.00 p.m. On Sundays the room was open for newspapers, but not for games, and no alcoholic drinks were allowed at any time. Membership of the Assembly Rooms was by ballot, but attendance gradually fell off as it became more fashionable to live out of town, and in December 1851 the Assembly Rooms were sold by auction, for £9,000, to be replaced by warehouses.

In 1802, opposite the Assembly Rooms, the Portico Library was being built – the first Classical Revival building in the town. The venture was the brain-child of two businessmen, Robert Robinson and Michael Ward, whose intention was to set up a proprietary library, owned then, as now, by its 400 members. There was to be a library and newsroom for the papers from London and elsewhere, *The Times*, *Morning Chronicle*, *Lloyd's List*, *New Statesman* and the *Edinburgh Review*, as well as the three Manchester newspapers *Wheeler's*, *Harrop's* and *Cowdrey's*.

But where to turn for the inspiration for this novel building? In Liverpool the Lyceum Library and Newsroom in Bold Street was nearing completion, and its architect, Thomas Harrison of Chester (1744–1829), was already becoming a national name, notably for Chester Castle (1788–1822), arguably the best group of Greek Revival buildings in the country. In Harrison Manchester had one of the acknowledged masters of the Classical, who would design for the town one of the first Greek Revival buildings erected in the country, and at a time before 'Greekomania' had hit even fashionable London.

The portico, from which the library is named, is of four giant-order Ionic columns carrying an undecorated frieze and pediment [3]. The design is similar to the Temple of Athena Polias at Priene, which had been reproduced in *The Antiquities of Iona* by the Society of Dilettanti in 1769, and this was probably Harrison's source, for he had never been to Greece. At the side of the building, the seven bays are separated by attached Ionic half-columns carrying a plain entablature. Tall windows on the ground floor, alternately pedimented, and smaller square ones at the first floor, light the interior of the library. Built of Runcorn stone, the building cost over £7,000; the builder was David Bellhouse.

The interior is roofed by a saucer dome of timber with glazed lights, supported by segmental barrel vaults at each end and by segmental arches at the sides. The newsroom, lit by the dome on top of the building as well as from Charlotte Street, was 65 ft long and 42 ft wide. On the right of the Mosley Street entrance a large staircase led to the first-floor library, and on the left was a bar room. The library was the same size as the newsroom and being lit entirely by the dome was provided with bookshelves on all four walls. In the centre of the library was a gallery, 16 ft high, overlooking the newsroom and guarded by iron railings. The committee room on the same floor was 30 ft long, 16 ft wide and 16 ft high, and from the door of this room a back staircase led down to the reading room.

The library's chairman for many years was the Reverend William Gaskell, minister of the Cross Street Chapel. Its first secretary, until he left for London, was a young doctor at the Infirmary, Peter Mark Roget of *Thesaurus* fame. John Dalton was made an honorary member and was given free admission on the proviso that he would maintain the clock. The ground floor of the Portico was leased to the Bank of Athens in 1902 (and subsequently to Lloyd's Bank), and it was then that a floor was inserted at gallery level. It is now a public house, but the top floor still houses the Portico Library, entered by a doorway in Charlotte Street.

Behind the Portico Library, in a three-storey house on George Street, polite society could hear lectures by Thomas Percival, John Dalton, William Sturgeon or James Joule at the 'Lit and Phil'. The Manchester Literary & Philosophical Society was founded in 1781, and apart from the Royal Society, the Manchester Lit & Phil is the oldest extant institution devoted to scientific discourse. A founder of the Lit & Phil in 1781 was Dr Thomas Percival, in whose home in King Street the first meetings were held, and whose grandson was Benjamin Heywood, who dabbled in chemistry and became Lord Mayor, and who, with Mark Philips, created Queen's Park and Phillips Park. Dr Percival was also a founder of Manchester's unofficial Board of Health in 1796 (Robert Owen was also a member) which attempted on a voluntary basis to inspect and improve the dwellings of the poor, as well as dealing with the regulation of lodging houses, the provision of public baths, the cleansing of streets and the inspection and regulation of conditions and hours of work in cotton mills and factories. Percival's studies prompted Peel's Health and Morals of Apprentices Act of 1802. Lit & Phil members helped establish the Portico Library, the Royal Manchester Institution and Owens College.

For the great fancy dress ball, part of the Festival of Music of 1836, the Portico Library, the Assembly Rooms and the Theatre Royal were used to cater for the 5,000 participants; covers were built over Mosley Street and Back Mosley Street connecting the buildings together, and a temporary building was erected over Charlotte Street for refreshments. This Theatre Royal, the second of that name, was opened in June 1807 on the corner of Fountain Street and Charlotte Street, and built to a design by Thomas Harrison. The theatre was enormous, having its front entrance on Fountain Street, its rear entrance on Back Mosley (now West Mosley) Street and its width spanning from Charlotte

Street to the Garrick Arms public house – today the site is covered by two large office blocks, 50 Spring Gardens and Barnett House on Fountain Street. The theatre was far too large, and its lobby was converted into a warehouse, thus gaining much-needed rent for the company. Macready, aged sixteen, became manager of its stock company, both Mrs. Siddons and Joseph Grimaldi trod its boards, and Paganini played his violin there.

On 7 May 1844 the Theatre Royal burnt down, and the proprietors sold their rights to John Knowles, who demolished the Wellington Inn and Brogden's horse bazaar on Peter Street, and built another Theatre Royal to the designs of Francis Chester assisted by a Mr Irwin [4]. The third Theatre Royal opened on 29 September 1845, to an audience of 2,500 people. Charles Dickens, John Leech and George Cruickshank appeared there, and among the artistes were Fanny Kemble, Jenny Lind and Macready, and the young Henry Irving joined the stock company in 1860. The theatre became a cinema in 1929 and later a bingo hall. It then lay fallow and neglected until, in 1989, it became Royales Discotheque.

Thomas Harrison had not finished work in Manchester, and his third and most important commission was the new Cotton Exchange. In 1804 a number of old buildings belonging to Lord Ducie, in Market Place and Exchange Street, started to be pulled down and on 21 July 1806, the first stone of the new Exchange was laid [5]. Built, like the Portico Library, in Runcorn stone, it was rectangular, with an apsidal north front of three-light, arched windows. A pedimented hexastyle portico with fluted Doric columns opened on to Ducie Place, and there was a peristyle of giant-order (27 ft high) fluted Grecian Doric pilasters.

When the Cotton Exchange opened in 1808, 400 shares were issued at £50 each, and by 1815 the number of subscribers had grown to 1,600. Manchester

4] Theatre Royal, Peter Street,
Chester & Irwin, 1844

by then had consolidated its position not only as a cotton-producing town but also as the trading centre of the Lancashire cotton industry, and its role had been assured by the complex canal system which provided transport and communication links with its hinterland, and which had commenced with the building of the Bridgewater Canal forty-six years earlier.

In 1759, following the Bridgewater Act, the twenty-three-year-old Francis Egerton, third Duke of Bridgewater, started work on the canal between his coal mines at Worsley and Manchester. In 1760 a further Act was passed allowing Bridgewater to carry his canal on a stone viaduct some 38 ft over the river Irwell.[11] Such an engineering feat had not been attempted before, and it is said that his engineer, James Brindley, demonstrated to the parliamentary select committee a model made of cheese. Brindley's aqueduct was eventually replaced by a steel swing bridge during the building of the Manchester Ship Canal. The canal was opened to Cornbrook in 1763 and then to Castlefield in 1764, where it terminated in a giant cloverleaf weir at a junction with the river Medlock, thus ensuring a constant supply of water. The canal provided the town with coal at half the price it had cost by road, and a coal wharf was made by cutting back the sandstone bluff upon which the Roman fort had been situated (Beattie's coal depot closed only in 1975). Castle Street stood 20 ft above the canal, and in 1765 Brindley extended the canal by a tunnel driven into the sandstone bluff with a 22 ft shaft rising to Castle Street. A crane hoist was worked by a waterwheel driven by the river Medlock.

The Bridgewater Canal was extended to Runcorn in 1776, allowing easier shipment of cotton into Manchester and south Lancashire, by allowing the transfer of goods from seagoing vessels to canal boats, and in 1784 the first American cotton was imported into Manchester via the Bridgewater Canal. In 1777 the Bridgewater Canal, by way of the Grand Trunk Canal, joined Manchester to the Midlands and the south. In 1791 the Manchester Bolton &

5] Royal Exchange, Cross Street, Thomas Harrison, 1806

Bury Canal joined the Leeds–Liverpool Canal near Bolton. Castlefield, by 1794, was becoming an important centre of manufacturing as well as of trade, and there were vitriol manufacturers, dyers, cotton manufacturers and a log mill. The canals were not used only for the transportation of bulk goods; as the size of the town started to increase, they were used to bring in produce from the countryside, cabbages from Warrington, potatoes from Runcorn, pulses from Bowdon and fish from the Yorkshire coast. For these perishables fast fly-boats were designed, and for the transport of passengers packet boats made daily journeys.

Once steam machinery was installed in factories, coal became one of the most important commodities carried by the canals. In 1800 there were eighty-nine steam engines in the whole of Lancashire, Cheshire and Yorkshire. Thirty-two of them were in mills in Manchester, and, as Aston pointed out in 1816, these factories were hungry: 'One thousand spindles will perhaps be a fair average for each horse's power. A factory set in motion by an engine of ten horses' power will consume, including the stove, a ton of coals a day. From these data a calculation may be made of the coal consumed in the year by the engines of the different factories in Manchester. The result will be pretty nearly forty seven thousand, two hundred and twenty tons.'[12]

James Brindley built a series of warehouses from 1770 which by 1829 extended from the canal to Alport Street (Deansgate).[13] Earliest among them was the Duke of Bridgewater's Warehouse of the 1770s, built across the end of the Bridgewater Canal, with an opening, or 'shipping hole', provided so that goods could be loaded directly from barges on to the ground floor or raised, through counterweighted winches, through hatches to the floors above. The Duke's Warehouse was rebuilt after 1789 following a fire, though it was sub-sequently demolished in 1960.

These early warehouses were constructed with load-carrying brick walls and an internal timber frame supported on timber or cast-iron posts. Internally, the main beams carried timber joists on which floorboards were laid. Where the spans were greater than about 14 ft, square-section timber posts supported the main beams, or, more often, supported the length of one single beam running the length of the building, on which secondary beams rested. Wooden posts were sometimes replaced by cast-iron columns, especially on ground or base-ment floors where they might be subject to flooding, but cast-iron beams were less used in warehouses than in mills because of the concentrated floor loading, and because the warehouses were less of a fire risk. Occasionally, internal transverse walls (also known as cross-walls, or spine walls), running continu-ously from front to rear of the building on the lowest floors, were used to carry internal loads.

The Grocers' Warehouse, Castle Street, 1770–80, was originally owned by Henshall Gilbert & Co. (Hugh Henshall was James Brindley's brother-in-law), and then between 1811 and 1836 by the Manchester Grocers' Company. It was 63 ft long with five storeys on the quayside and four on Castle Street, and internally a cross-wall carried transverse wooden beams. There was originally one shipping hole for an arm of the Bridgewater Canal, and a second was added in 1807. The Grocers' was demolished in 1960, though parts survived. It was partly reconstructed in the 1990s, the canal basin was reclaimed, and the warehouse's waterwheel and hydraulic lift were reconstructed.

The Staffordshire Warehouse, the third warehouse on this site, adjacent to the present YHA, was eight storeys high with two large arched canal arm entrances which ran through the building. This had small round-headed windows, and loading loopholes on either side of the canal entrances. A five-storey extension was added to the west, and by 1848 it was extended eastwards with a two-storey arched construction for timber storage. There were two additional entrances and a tunnel for road traffic under Duke's Place some 20 ft above canal level. The Staffordshire was shared by a number of carriers, mostly of cotton and grain, namely the Shropshire Union, Faulkner & Green, and Kenworthy, who also had another warehouse on an adjacent arm of the canal.

Kenworthy's Warehouse, built before 1848 for their sole use, was five storeys high with two adjacent canal openings. It was of brick with small round-headed windows and loopholes at the ends of the building. The 2 in. floorboards on 16 in. joists were designed to carry heavy goods: the ground floor for oils, the first floor for shipping goods, the second and third for cotton, flour and grain, the upper floor for the storage of cotton, the lightest bulk material. The building was later demolished and only the paved floor remains.

Merchants' Warehouse is the oldest extant canal warehouse in Manchester, and dates from 1827–28 [6]. Brick, with small, round-headed windows with stone sills, with four storeys on the canal side, and three on the Castle Street side. There are two large arched shipping holes, edged with stone and with a central stone pier, on the canal side. There were also four loopholes on the canal side, and six on Castle Street. Internally, on the ground floor, six bays are divided by brick cross-walls at 23 ft intervals, carrying 12 in. by 8 in. wooden

6] Merchants' Warehouse, Castlefield, 1827–28

joists; the floors above are timber-framed. It was converted into studios and offices in 1996.

The Middle Warehouse of 1831 is five storeys of brick with small round-headed windows with stone sills. There are six loopholes on the quayside, three on either side of the two arched shipping holes. Above the shipping holes is a huge elliptical relieving arch which spans up to the fourth storey. The building was in use until the 1970s by the Bridgewater Department of the Manchester Ship Canal Company, and used to store maize products brought by barge from Trafford Park. It was restored for apartments and offices in 1992. (See [185].)

The New Warehouse on Slate Wharf was built before 1848. This was the last Castlefield warehouse to be built, and the largest, at 280 ft long, with six storeys and twenty bays. There were originally ten hoists, divided by pairs of round-headed windows, and the central six bays were surmounted by a double pediment over two shipping holes. Internally there were cross-walls with slotted iron columns supporting 12 ft 6 in. joists. It was demolished in the mid-1970s.

All these early warehouses were constructed of hand-made bricks, for mechanisation of the brick industry did not occur until the repeal of the Brick Tax in 1850 produced a growing demand for bricks. The Hoffman kiln (invented in 1858), which was fired continuously and could contain up to 40,000 bricks, reduced their cost considerably.[14] It was common practice, before the growth of canals and railways reduced the cost of transporting building materials, for ordinary buildings to be made of local materials – brick where there was clay, or stone where it was locally available. This, to a large extent, is what gave towns their architectural colour, if not their character. Manchester clays, because of the high iron content of the Triassic marls, give a redder-colour brick than, say, the grey-yellows of the south-east of England. The hottest reds, the 'Accrington Bloods' (introduced after the mechanisation of the brick industry), were bricks made from the very hard and particularly durable clays from the coal measures of Lancashire.

By the early nineteenth century the canals were allowing the cheaper importation of building materials, and in 1802 the Peak Forest Canal Company bought land in Ancoats for wharves, and bulk-shipped both limestone and lime at cheap rates from its quarries in the Peak District via the Ashton Canal. Samuel Oldknow of Mellor, who pioneered the manufacture of muslin, was the largest shareholder in the Peak Forest Canal, and his warehouse can still be seen at Marple locks, together with the lime kilns which were built into vertical rock face. Manchester's only surviving stone warehouse, of 1806, on the corner of Dale Street and Back China Lane, belonged to the Rochdale Canal Company, which probably carried the Millstone Grit sandstone from which it is constructed from the quarries at Swales Moor, near Halifax.

The Rochdale Canal, which opened in 1804, joined the Bridgewater Canal at Castlefield, providing a link, via the Calder & Hebble Navigation, between Manchester and Hull, and opened up Manchester to the eastern coast. Its main basin, however, was not at Castlefield but at Dale Street in Ancoats, where it joined the Ashton Canal. Major wharves and warehouses were erected in the area bounded by Great Ancoats Street, Dale Street, Port Street and Ducie Street, among them the Rochdale Canal Company Warehouse of 1836 on Upper Stanley Street and the Hall & Rogers Warehouse, of 1836, on Tariff Street. More important than these canal warehouses, it was here at the side of the Rochdale Canal in Ancoats that the first generation of steam-powered spinning mills was erected.

2

1800–40

THE OPEN TOWN

Look up and all around this place and you will see the huge palaces of industry . . . here is the slave, there the master; there is the wealth of some, here the poverty of most; there the organised efforts of thousands produce, to the profit of one man, what society has not yet learnt to give . . . From this foul drain the greatest stream of human industry flows out to fertilise the whole world. From this filthy sewer pure gold flows. [Alexis de Tocqueville, *Journeys to England and Ireland*, 1835]

IN 1782 there were just two cotton mills in and around Manchester, but within ten years fifty-two mills had been established in the town, and what brought the mill in from the countryside was the development of steam machinery and its application to the spinning mule – no longer were manufacturers reliant on fast-flowing rivers driving waterwheels. James Watt's steam engine had first been applied to spinning rollers in 1785, and by the 1790s Watt's engine was being used to drive spinning mules. Watt and his partner Boulton made a number of improvements in rotative steam engines, and before their patents expired in 1800 more than 500 of their engines were made and operating.

Richard Arkwright introduced a mill with steam power to Manchester in about 1782 in Miller Street, Shudehill (destroyed in 1940). This was Arkwright's largest mill and testifies to the growing importance of Manchester as a cotton-manufacturing town; the steam engine, however, was used only to raise water for a waterwheel. Peter Drinkwater was the first Manchester spinner to use a steam engine to power cotton machinery, and installed a Boulton & Watt rotary beam engine in his Piccadilly Mill in Auburn Street in 1790, increasing his output thirtyfold, though this engine was used initially only to drive the preparation machinery, the 144-spindle mules still being hand-operated.[1]

Even this hesitant introduction of steam power naturally enough caused great disquiet among the hand workers, and there was great fear of the loss of jobs from the potential mechanisation of the industry. When Robert Grimshaw of Gorton tried to set up a steam-powered weaving factory at Knott Mill in 1790, he was threatened and a few weeks later his mill was burnt to the ground. This may not have been a deliberate act of arson, for factories were hazardous places, lit first by oil lamps, and then after 1805 increasingly by gas lamps, and with short, inflammable cotton lintners in the air. The *Manchester Historical Recorder* notes at least one mill fire almost every year. Most of them must have been accidental, although one Thomas Armstrong was hanged at Lancaster for setting fire to a factory at Knott Mill on 20 September 1817. Nonetheless, after Grimshaw's fire, no other Manchester employer used steam power until the Murray brothers installed machines in their Old Mill in Ancoats eight years later in 1798.

Adam and George Murray came to Manchester from Scotland in the 1780s and set up a successful business as textile machinery manufacturers and cotton spinners, and the fine yarns spun in Manchester were sent back to Scotland for hand-loom weavers. In Ancoats, between 1798 and 1806, the Murrays erected four buildings around a central yard which contained, from 1804, a basin from an arm of the Rochdale Canal. These were the six-storey, eleven-bay Old Mill of 1798 on Union (now Redhill) Street, the oldest extant cotton mill in Manchester [7], the ten-bay Decker Mill of 1802, and, on the north side of the yard, the six-storey, twenty-two-bay New Mill of 1804. All these mills were powered by Boulton & Watt beam engines. In 1806 the Murrays added the

7] Mills, Redhill Street, Ancoats

four-storey Murray Street and Bengal Street blocks, mainly for warehousing. By 1818 the Murrays had 84,000 spindles and 1,300 workers. On the other side of Bengal Street the Little Mill was added in the 1820s (replaced by New Little Mill in 1908, in Accrington brick and powered by electric motors, probably the first of Manchester's mills to use electricity from the Corporation's mains), and the Doubling Mill and Fireproof Mill in 1842.

The Murrays' mills were typical of early purpose-built mills in Manchester, which were generally five or six storeys high and ten to twenty bays long, and wide enough either for two spinning mules to be operated back to back, or two side-by-side with a walkway between them. Like the early canal warehouses, the mills were also constructed of load-bearing brick, though the windows tended to be larger than storage warehouses, since as much light as possible was needed to help in the spinning operations. Few original windows remain, but generally they comprised small panes set in glazing bars with opening sections to control the humidity inside the mill, and such windows can still be seen at Quarry Bank Mill, Styal. Internally, the mills utilised fireproof construction of cast-iron columns supporting iron beams on which floorboards were supported. Because of the increased risk of fire there were separate rooms or buildings for processes like scutching, and when weaving sheds were added later in the century they were generally only one or two storeys high, since vibration from the looms could cause instability problems in taller buildings.

For many manufacturers such factories were too expensive at least until sufficient profits had been made, and spinning rooms were often set up in conveniently large buildings such as converted warehouses or stables. Two other Scots who came to Manchester in the late eighteenth century, James McConnel and John Kennedy, started as textile machinery makers in partnership with Benjamin and William Sandford, who put up most of the capital but left McConnel and Kennedy to run the business. Their first factory was in Stable (now Back Oldham) Street, 'and our capital not more than £600 or £700. Here we made machines for others as well as ourselves, putting up our own mules in any convenient garrets we could find. After some time we removed to a building in Canal Street, called Salvin's factory – from the name of the owner who occupied a portion of it himself, letting off the remainder to us.'[2] The partnership was dissolved in 1795, and McConnel and Kennedy formed a separate partnership, leasing a building in Shooter's Brook and renting part of a second building from Colonel Sedgwick for carding and drawing. During 1796 they rented another mill in Bengal Street.[3] In 1797 a 16 h.p. Boulton & Watt steam engine was installed, and later, in 1802, another of 45 h.p.

The year 1797 was a time of considerable hardship in trade, continuing into early 1798, and McConnel & Kennedy were forced to sell yarn at a discount. But by June 1798 trade had picked up considerably, imports increased and exports soared and 'in July, McConnel and Kennedy were able to boast that they had not a single bundle of yarn on hand due to large orders from foreign buyers'.[4] Sufficient profits were made to erect the Old Mill on Henry Street in 1799 (rebuilt as the Royal Mill in 1912) and the contractor, Geo. Wilkinson, in February, agreed 'to turn and temper the clay on Mr. M'Connel's own land near Ancoats Lane in Manchester and wheel it and make it into good kiln bricks upon Mr. Hope's land . . . and afterwards wheel and kiln the said bricks on the land that the clay now lies on, for the sum of sixteen shillings and three pence for every thousand made.'[5] Even here, they let off half the factory at a yearly rent of £375 in order to defray the building costs.

Such was the volatile nature of the industry that by the autumn of 1799, in common with many manufacturers, McConnel & Kennedy were overdrawn at the bank, and by December some of their dealers were complaining that they had been waiting eight months for payment. Two years later the firm purchased the deeds of five dwelling houses, and on the site started to construct their New Factory, though it was not completed until 1806, perhaps because of a shortage of money for building or equipping the mill. The factory had eight floors and covered an area of 650 square yards. Gas lighting was installed in 1809, the equipment coming from Boulton & Watt. In 1810 the Long Mill was added between Henry Street and Pickford Street (since demolished).

In the summer of 1811 there were many bankruptcies and firms were on short time or, like McConnel & Kennedy's, closed altogether. The production and export of cotton cloth had grown rapidly from the 1790s, but the expansion of the industry was taking place against a very uncertain market. The war with France meant that there was no permanent peace in Europe until 1815, and the cotton embargoes and eventual war with the United States kept American cotton intermittently from the British market until 1814. George Lee (of Philips & Lee of Salford, the third largest firm in the Manchester area), giving evidence to a House of Commons committee in 1816, thought that only one in five of Manchester's cotton mills remained in the hands of their original owners. George Smith, a Manchester spinner, giving evidence to the same committee, said 'that of thirty-two hand-loom calico manufacturers whom I know personally in the trade from 1812 to 1816, twenty-eight have failed'.[6] There were more great crises in 1819, 1825–26, 1836–37 and 1839–42, and Faucher recounted that in Manchester, in March 1842, 116 factories and mills had stopped working, 681 shops and offices had been closed and 5,492 houses were unoccupied. The value of mill buildings and machinery had lessened fully half.[7]

McConnel & Kennedy bought more land on Union Street from Colonel Sedgwick in 1815 on which to build another mill, but the erection did not start for another three years, perhaps owing to the on-going crises in the industry. James Lowe was commissioned in 1818 to construct the mill, McConnel & Kennedy supplied all the building materials, and the bricks were made from clay dug at Ancoats. The U-shaped Sedgwick Mill, of eight storeys, with a seventeen-bay front on Redhill Street, was completed in 1820, and in 1868 the Sedgwick New Mill was added on the north side – of five storeys and fifteen bays. This mill was used for yarn doubling, the increase in the use of doubling yarn being due to the growing use of the sewing machine. The last mills in the complex were erected in 1912; the Paragon and Royal Mills (the Royal Mill was renamed after a visit by King George in 1942), both of six storeys and nine bays, in Accrington brick with terracotta and sandstone details, and both with concrete floors supported by steel beams and cast-iron columns.

McConnel & Kennedy, in common with the Murrays and many of the other earlier manufacturers, made their own spinning mules. Crompton's mule had never been patented, and although the crude wooden mechanism he invented in 1779 had, by 1795, become a cast-iron machine, the tolerances were so loose that improvements in efficiency could be made relatively easily. Mules of 280 spindles could be made in 1795, and by 1832 improvements allowed up to 600 spindles per mule. John Kennedy had made significant improvements to the spinning mule, especially in the making of fine yarns, though by 1800 the firm had stopped making machinery for others and was concentrating on its own spinning activities. McConnel & Kennedy could spin coarse yarns if necessary, and their Old Mill could spin yarn down to No. 70 and even lower. However, higher profits were to be made from spinning fine yarns and they generally provided fine yarns (up to No. 230) to weavers and merchants in Glasgow, Paisley and Belfast. The difference between coarse and fine yarns was described by Aston in 1816, and his astonishing statistics make him worth quoting at length:

> The value of cotton yarn depends upon its length; it is distinguished by numbers, which bespeak the hanks in the pound. Thus No. 20 yarn, has 20 hanks; No. 100, has 100 hanks in each pound weight. Every hank is 840 yards long; so that one pound of cotton yarn, of No. 20, is 16,800 yards long; and one pound of No. 100, contains 84,000 yards. The finest yarn we have ever seen, was about 300 hanks; one pound of which was, of course, 252,000 yards (upwards of 156 miles long!). The average number spun in Manchester is supposed to be 100. The spindles in the different factories are about two millions, which each turn off, upon a fair average, ten hanks per week. It would be curious to carry the calculation a little farther, when we should find that the whole of the factories in Manchester spin threads, in one year, which, tied together, would measure the almost incredible length of 313,385,384 miles!! A length of thread sufficient to wrap round the earth, nearly twelve thousand times.[8]

By 1814 McConnel & Kennedy had nearly 79,000 spindles in operation (and the number increased steadily until 1914, when McConnel & Co. were turning 400,000 spindles). Their employees had increased from 312 in 1802 to 1,553 in 1833, 200 more than any other Manchester firm. McConnel & Kennedy's and the Murrays' mills employed between them 19.5 per cent of the total mill labour force in Manchester, but even their operations were to be beaten for size at Birley's Chorlton New Mill.

The Birley family had been 'putters-out' in Lancashire and moved to Manchester in the early nineteenth century, and in 1814 Hugh Birley* and his partners commenced building their complex of mills on the south bank of the Medlock, on Cambridge Street, Chorlton-on-Medlock. Their original mill of

---

* Captain Hugh Hornby Birley was a magistrate and one of the commanders of the Manchester and Salford Yeomanry at Peterloo, and he is recorded as having given the order for the yeomanry to charge the crowd. It is said that on the anniversaries of Peterloo radicals would gather outside his Mosley Street house and groan.

1814 was six storeys above ground and two below. There were twenty bays on Cambridge Street, with a six-storey block added in 1818 on Hulme Street and a corner block built between them in 1845. The 1814 mill is probably the earliest example of fireproof construction in Manchester, with cast-iron columns supporting cast-iron beams and brick vaulting. The roof, too, was probably originally iron-framed. The mill was powered by a Boulton & Watt 100 h.p. beam engine. Gas for lighting was manufactured in the basement, stored in three gasholders and circulated through the building via the hollow cast-iron columns. The mill buildings were connected by subterranean tunnels with iron tramways for speedier movement of goods. A large, 600 loom, weaving shed was added at the north end of the site in the 1830s, but was replaced in the late nineteenth century by Robert Peel & Co.'s finishing works. By 1840, Messrs. Birley & Co. employed 2,000 people and specialised in the spinning and weaving of coarse threads woven into cloths for the foreign market, and theirs was by then the largest mill in Manchester. In the 1860s, the site was taken over by Charles MacIntosh & Co. for the production of rubberised cloth.[9]

Mills like these were exceptionally large for Manchester: in 1816 the average firm employed just over 300 people, and the four largest firms employed 862, 937, 1,020 and 1,215 people respectively. It was also unusual to have factories dedicated to the use of one firm. In 1816 two-thirds of Manchester's cotton spinning firms shared part of a factory, and a single factory building might hold up to ten different firms, the rent being determined by the location of the factory, the number of spindles being turned and the amount of steam power required. McConnel & Kennedy wrote to a Scottish manufacturer who wanted to rent part of a factory: 'There are several situations here where rooms are let off with power to turn various kinds of machinery and the rent of course is in proportion to the power, and room for the purposes you mention would be about £22 to £25 per annum for 100 spindles. We presume about 350 spindles may require about one horse power.'[10]

The Beehive Mill in Ancoats was built for multiple occupation as three attached blocks on the south side of the Bengal Street arm of the Rochdale Canal. The main block was built in the early 1820s with an additional block of 1824 and a third block of 1848 (rebuilt in 1861 after a fire). The five-storey Jersey Street wing, added in 1824, was probably used for warehousing and storage. It had a novel fireproof construction of stone flags supported on a grid of cast-iron beams; there were no timber elements, and even the roof was supported on cast-iron trusses. The Brownsfield Mill, on the west side of Great Ancoats Street, has seven storeys and two L-shaped wings. Until the later nineteenth century there were two occupants in the cotton trade, but by the end of the century many smaller trades were using the building. It was in the loft of this mill, where his brother had a braces and surgical webbing factory, that Alliott Verdon Roe established the firm of A. V. Roe & Co. in 1910. Aeroplanes were sold for £450 with a five-mile flight guaranteed.

The early mills were not architect-designed but built by local builders, and the technical expertise was provided by firms like Boulton & Watt or by specialist millwrights. Manchester's spinners were fortunate in having on hand the services of William Fairbairn (1789–1874), one of the great engineers of the nineteenth century, and one of the greatest millwrights. As Andrew Ure remarked of mill engineering, 'It had been ably begun by Mr Watt, but, till it fell into the hands of Messrs Fairbairn and Lillie, the eminent engineers of Manchester, it was all too subject to the whims of the several individuals, often utterly ignorant of statics or dynamics, or the laws of equilibrium and impulse, who had the capital to lay out in building a mill.'[11]

Fairbairn moved to Manchester in 1813, and in 1815 gained an order for drive shafts from Adam and George Murray, 'who pleased with the product recommended him to their friends'. By 1817 he had set up in partnership with James Lillie as consultant millwrights, and in that year he was recommended to John Kennedy for engineering calculations at the Sedgwick mill, where 'I laid down all his plans for the new mill to a scale, calculated the proportions and strength of the parts, fixed the position and arrangement of the different machines.' This apparently enhanced the reputation of Fairbairn & Lillie, for 'we had now become engineers and millwrights of some consequence, and the complete and satisfactory execution of millwork established our characters as young men who were likely to introduce improvements in the construction of machinery, millwork and general mechanisms of other branches of industry.'[12] Moreover, their expertise was not limited to engineering; they even designed Stalybridge Town Hall in 1830.

The partnership was dissolved in 1832, when speculation in a cotton mill 'reduced their resources', and Fairbairn, thereafter, prospered. By the 1840s he employed over 2,000 workers in his works in Canal Street, Ancoats, and gave his workers a nine-hour day, unasked. He conceived the use of lighter wrought rather than cast iron for machine shafts, enabling an increase in speed from 40 r.p.m., to 300 r.p.m., he carried out some of the earliest tests on cast-iron beams, and, concerned with the safety of boilers and high-pressure steam, experimented with the riveting of boiler plates.*

The relationship between spinners and engineers was a close one, and was not limited to business. In 1824 Fairbairn, with Kennedy and Murray, led the founding of the Mechanics' Institute. Between 1855 and 1860 Fairbairn was President of the Manchester Lit & Phil, of which body Kennedy was also an active member. Fairbairn died on 18 August 1874 aged eighty-five; he apparently caught a chill on the opening of the new Owens College in 1870 from which he never recovered.[13]

As Fairbairn was important to the development of the structure of mills, so Joseph Whitworth (1803–87) was important to the improvements in their machines. After working in his uncle's cotton mill in Derbyshire, Whitworth joined the London engineering firm of Henry Maudslay in 1825, where he devised the first machine to produce a true plane surface. From 1833 he was in

---

* The *Manchester Historical Recorder*, 1875, noted boiler explosions occurring almost every year in the nineteenth century. On 2 July 1858, for example, there was a boiler explosion in the Atlas Iron Works, when seven people were killed and five seriously injured.

business as a toolmaker in Manchester from premises on Chorlton Street, and by 1840 he was able to produce tools made to an accuracy of a ten-thousandth of an inch, at a time when tolerances of a sixteenth of an inch was considered acceptable. He also invented Manchester's first road-sweeping machine in 1842. He was an early contributor to the Mechanics' Institute and gave the city the Whitworth Art Gallery and Park. Twelve years after his death the new street linking Deansgate Station with London Road Station was named after him.

In London, Whitworth had known Henry Nasmyth (1808–90), who had become Maudslay's assistant in 1829. After Maudslay's death in 1831, Nasmyth came to Manchester to start up an engineering firm. He was introduced, probably by Whitworth, to Edward Tootal, a merchant, of York Street, and to John Kennedy, who persuaded him to start business from a disused cotton mill at the corner of Dale Street and Port Street. After an accident with some machinery, which fell through the floor of the building into a glass cutter's below, he moved his business to Patricroft. His new Bridgewater Foundry (1838) was built with funds from Hugh Birley and his younger brother Joseph, who invested £4,883 in Nasmyth's business, and the Birleys sensibly insisted that the building should be designed to be convertible into a cotton mill in case Nasmyth's firm foundered. A year after moving into his new factory, Nasmyth developed his famous vertical steam hammer for making large forgings. (It was designed to make the 30 in. diameter paddle shaft for Brunel's steamship, the *Great Britain*, though the proposal was not carried out.) The hammer, which could strike a blow every second, unlike earlier tilt hammers, which struck one blow every few minutes, could still be operated with enough precision just to crack the shell of an egg.

Apart from the factories of Fairbairn, Whitworth and Nasmyth, other great iron foundries and engineering works ran from Shudehill to Great Bridgewater Street, mostly along the line of the Ashton and Rochdale Canals, like the Soho Foundry in Ancoats belonging to Peel Williams & Co. Here were a foundry, smithies, patterns makers and turners, all in a building 100 yards long. There were also other specialist machinery makers, spindle makers and calico printing machine makers. Dyeing, bleaching and chemical works, which required plentiful supplies of water, grew on the banks of the rivers, and by 1849 on the Medlock there were the huge Ardwick Bridge Chemical Company, the New Garratt Printworks, the Chapel Field Dye Works and the Ardwick Dye Works. Manchester's industry was rapidly diversifying and Manchester was beginning to be the provider of machinery, goods and services to the other towns of Lancashire and Cheshire.

As the century progressed and construction techniques improved (partly owing to Fairbairn's investigations into beams), steam engines were given more power (the first successful 'compounding' of a steam engine – adding a high-pressure cylinder – was by McNaught of Bury in 1845, and this subsequently became the standard engine of the cotton industry) and the industry tended to be consolidated in the hands of single owners, so buildings became larger, though it is in the mill towns of Lancashire, rather than in Manchester, that the biggest mills were erected. A typical building is the Brunswick Mill, Bradford Road, on the banks of the Ashton Canal, which was constructed in the 1840s by the ubiquitous builder David Bellhouse.[14] The main spinning block was of thirty-five bays, and of seven storeys alongside the canal, with a four-storey (originally three-storey) front block on Bradford Road used mostly for warehousing and offices. This was one of the largest mid-nineteenth-century mills in the country, and in the 1850s the mill contained 276 carding machines, twenty drawing frames, fifty slubbing frames, eighty-one roving frames and 77,000 mule spindles.

The growth of the spinning industry allowed a considerable expansion of the weaving trade, and the number of hand-loom weavers increased from 108,000 in 1788 to 240,000 by 1813. In 1813 there were fewer than 2,400 power looms in the country, for developments in the mechanisation of weaving lagged far behind that of spinning. Although Edmund Cartwright had invented the power loom in 1784, it was not until after the 1820s, following technical improvements by Radcliffe & Horrocks of Stockport and Roberts of Manchester, that it came into common use. As Bythell has said, 'The cotton weaving industry was not much affected by technological change until the 1820s, mainly because in the relatively primitive state of machine-making, it simply was not possible to produce an efficient machine at a cost which a manufacturer would be prepared to incur in order to enjoy the power-loom's expected advantage.'[15]

Whitworth's improved tool-making techniques allowed machines with closer tolerances to be made, and undoubtedly his work hastened the technical progress of the power loom. It is significant that by 1836 Manchester had more power looms than any other town in the country; the parliamentary returns of power looms show that, of the UK total of 117,151, Manchester had 15,960.[16]

The hand-loom weavers, naturally enough, saw their livelihoods coming under threat. In 1812 there were riots at Middleton on the introduction of power looms, and on 5 May 1829 there were further serious riots. The weaving factories of Mr T. Harbottle, Messrs Twiss and Mr James Guest were attacked and their contents entirely destroyed and that of Mr Parker was burnt down. By the 1830s the hand-loom weaver had all but disappeared, and this is hardly surprising given the abject levels of pay. Hand-loom weavers in the 1830s could earn on average between 5s (25p) and 7s 6d (37 $\frac{1}{2}$p) per week, but of forty-one weavers' families surveyed in the *Manchester Guardian* on 30 January 1830 the average weekly income was as little as 2s 11d (15p). A power-loom weaver in the late 1820s could earn 12s (60p) a week, though even this wage compared badly with that of an experienced spinner.

Manchester's top mule spinners, usually men, could earn between 25s (£1·25) and £2 per week, although they were left with less than that after paying their piecers, the children who crawled under the spinning machines to join or piece the threads, who earned between 3s and 8s (15p–40p) depending on age and experience. Women spinners and carders, mostly women, earned between 8s and 9s (40p–45p) a week. These sums were paid for an average sixty-nine-hour week. In comparison, a constable in the police force earned £1 for a seventy-hour week, a bricklayer's wages were around 27s (£1·40) per week, his labourer's around 18s (90p). A street labourer or carter could earn up to 16s (80p), but it was casual work and his income was insecure.[17]

But if factory wages were poor, the work, argued Andrew Ure, was beneficial. In his tour of the manufacturing districts Ure had seen operatives, many
of them too frail to have earned an income by any other means,

> earning abundant food, raiment, and domestic accommodation, without
> perspiring at a single pore, screened meanwhile from the summer's sun and
> the winter's frost, in apartments more airy and salubrious than those of the
> metropolis, in which our legislative and fashionable aristocracies assemble. In
> those spacious halls the benignant power of steam summons around him his
> myriads of willing menials, and assigns to each the regulated task, substitut-
> ing for painful muscular effort on their part, the energies of his own gigantic
> arm, and demanding in return only attention and dexterity to correct such
> little aberrations as casually occur in his workmanship.[18]

Ure's idyllic factories were portrayed by Dr Kay, who had a closer knowledge of factory conditions, in a more realistic light:

> The operatives are congregated in rooms and workshops during twelve hours
> of the day, in an enervating, heated atmosphere, which is frequently loaded
> with dust or filaments of cotton, or impure from constant respiration, or from
> other causes. They are engaged in an employment which absorbs their atten-
> tion, and unremittingly employs their physical energies. They are drudges
> who watch the movements, and assist the operations, of a mighty material
> force, which toils with an energy ever unconscious of fatigue. The persevering
> labour of the operative must rival the mathematical precision, the incessant
> motion, and the exhaustless power of the machine.[19]

Ure's most romantic vision was of the piecers, the 'lively elves' whose work
'seemed to resemble a sport, in which habit gave them a pleasing dexterity'
and who were continually 'taking pleasure in the light play of their muscles. It
was delightful to observe the nimbleness with which they pieced the broken
ends, as the mule-carriage began to recede from the fixed roller beam.'[20] Henry
Morley, writing in Dickens's *Household Words* in 1854, took a somewhat more
jaundiced view:

> There are many ways of dying. Perhaps it is not good when a factory girl,
> who has not the whole spirit of play spun out of her for want of meadows,
> gambols upon bags of wool, a little too near the exposed machinery that is
> to work it up, and is immediately seized, and punished by the merciless
> machine that digs its shaft into her pinafore and hoists her up, tears out
> her left arm at the shoulder joint, breaks her right arm, and beats her on the
> head. No, that is not good; but it is not a case in point, the girl lives . . . She
> had her chance of dying, and she lost it. Possibly it was better for the boy
> whom his stern master, the machine, caught as he stood on a stool wickedly
> looking out of the window at the sunlight and the flying clouds. These were
> no business of his, and he was fully punished when the machine he served
> caught him by one arm and whirled him round and round till he was thrown
> down dead.[21]

Morley was discussing the recent (1853) legislation which demanded the fencing of dangerous machinery, though only to a height of 7 ft. He points out that in the previous three years 106 lives were lost, 142 hands or arms were severed, 1,287 fingers were removed, 1,340 bones were broken, 559 heads were injured and 8,282 operators suffered miscellaneous injuries. But, of course, humans were replaceable, as Cooke Taylor had noted: 'derangements of machinery are very expensive accidents to remedy . . . I have had some opportunities of estimating the cost of accidents, and I know that the engineer's bill is considerably heavier than the surgeon's.'[22]

Whatever went on behind those towering walls of brick, the mills of Manchester were making an impact, changing for ever the scale and grain of the town. Schinkel, one of the great German architects of the nineteenth century, wrote of Ancoats in 1826, 'Here are buildings seven to eight storeys, as high and as big as the Royal Palace in Berlin.' But 'set up by a contractor alone without any architect and made from red brick for the barest necessity only, make a rather gloomy impression'. His companion Beuth had written in a similar vein to Schinkel in 1823, 'the miracles of the new age are the machine and the buildings for it called factories'.[23]

Important though factories were to Manchester, of even greater significance was the growth of warehousing. By 1815, although about a quarter of the country's spinning was carried out in Manchester, the number of warehouses was six times that of mills. The economic significance of warehouses outweighed all other assets. 'A town where capitalists directed a larger proportion, albeit marginal, of their capital into the building of public houses than cotton mills, is stretching to almost breaking point the notion of a 'factory town' . . . Cotton factories were swamped in Manchester's property asset structure by warehouses, who [sic] provided 48 per cent of the total valuation, excluding housing . . . Manchester in 1815 was a warehouse town.'[24]

Between 1807 and 1825 the number of warehouse units increased by over 50 per cent, to 1,800, even though many were small, often only a few rooms in a house.[25] To set up a mill meant expertise and money. To set up a warehouse merely meant taking a commercial risk, and there were many willing enough to take one, as Richard Cobden recalled:

> I began business in partnership with two other young men and we only mustered a thousand pounds amongst us, and more than half of it was borrowed . . . We introduced ourselves to Fort Bros. and Company [calico printers who had a warehouse in Cannon Street], a rich house, and we told our tale, honestly concealing nothing. In less than two years from 1830 we owed them forty thousand pounds for goods they had sent us . . . upon no other security than our characters and knowledge of our business.[26]

The warehouses performed two functions, one of which was the specialised storage, handling, packaging, sorting and stock control of a range of products from raw to spun cotton, grey (unbleached) cloth and finished or printed cloths. They were also places of display, and goods were sold either by public auction on the premises or by private sale. Drapers and dealers would arrive in

Manchester by stagecoach, and would put up at one of the inns. Clerks from the various warehouses would be despatched to visit new arrivals, and it is recorded by Swindells that one such gentleman, newly arrived from London, was visited by no fewer than forty clerks before breakfast.[27] Freelance 'hookers-in' also scouted the arrivals and tried to persuade them to visit their clients' warehouses, for payment of a commission. One hooker-in, a Mr Lewis, was known, from an earlier attempt at suicide, as 'Sudden Death'.

The second function of the warehouse was as part of the 'putting out' system. Yarn was put out from the warehouse to be woven into cloth and then brought back for finishing and sale. Nathaniel and George Gould, who operated a large warehouse in Peel Street, put out to weavers around seven to ten miles from Manchester. The woven cloth was fetched back to the warehouse, from where it was sent out to cutters and finishers. Some warehousemen would directly employ their own weavers, often on their own premises. Massey & Sons, who operated from Marsden Square, sold yarn and cloth in Manchester on a commission basis and also employed 1,200 to 1,400 hand-loom weavers. The firm moved into calico printing and in 1824 purchased a large spinning mill.

Cannon Street, High Street and the area behind Piccadilly became the prime centre of cotton warehousing. Cromford Court, Hodson Square and Pool Fold had been covered by cottages, barns, gardens and pigsties but 'building after building arose and dwelling after dwelling were metamorphosed into warehouses'.[28] Swindells suggests that it was Robert Peel's initiative which started the rush to Cannon Street.[29] Peel (the first baronet, MP and father of the famous statesman) with Messrs Yates Tipping & Haliwell started with a warehouse in Cannon Street in the 1780s, and Robert Peel, with various partners, went on to import his own cotton, and carried out spinning, weaving, bleaching and printing. Thomas Bell had developed the technique of printing by rotating copper rollers in 1783, and Peel immediately adopted his invention for printing calico. His first design was based on the parsley leaf, and became famous as 'Parsley Peel'. Eventually Peel's firm had factories in Bury, Radcliffe, Heywood, Bolton, Warrington, Blackburn, Burnley, Padiham, Stockport, Bradford, Lichfield, Tamworth and elsewhere. Sir Robert Peel died on 3 May 1830, leaving property valued at £2 million. By 1815 there were 129 calico printers in Manchester, among them Thomas Hoyle, who built his printing and dyeworks at Mayfield in Ardwick – then among the largest in the world.

Henry Tootal & Co. also had warehouses on Cannon Street and Fountain Street, and on Cannon Street were the warehouses of Benjamin Binyon and Francis Marris Son & Co., though these early warehouses were still on a small scale. In 1831, according to Slugg,

> The large warehouses in Parker Street, behind the Infirmary, had then no existence, whilst George Street and Faulkner Street contained principally private residences . . . I cannot remember that there was a single warehouse in either of these streets, Mosley Street, Portland Street, Peter Street, Oxford Road or Dickinson Street, except that in the latter street was Pickford's canal warehouse . . . where the boats were loaded with goods for London . . . The

streets in which the principal Manchester warehouses were to be found, were High Street, Cannon Street, Marsden Square, Church Street, and the smaller streets running out of these . . . There was not then, or for some years after, a single warehouse in Manchester making any pretensions to architectural effect . . . Not only were the buildings . . . very plain structures, but they were to be found mostly in retired situations, such as Back George Street, Mulberry Street, Queen Street and Back [now West] Mosley Street.[30]

Until 1827 Mosley Street itself had been residential, and included such notable personalities as Hugh Birley, S. L. Behrens, founder of the shipping firm, and Samuel Brooks the banker. Nathan Meyer Rothschild, of the banking dynasty, lived at the corner of York Street in 1808–09 and carried on business at 3 Back Mosley Street, purchasing goods for his father's firm in Frankfurt, until he left for London in 1812 on his father's death. His business intelligence contacts were such that he heard of Bonaparte's escape from Elba twenty-five hours before the British government did. Daniel Grant, a calico printer, lived in Mosley Street and with his partner and brother William bought Robert Peel's warehouse in Cannon Street in 1806. At dinner with Gilbert Winter, a Manchester solicitor, in November 1838, they met Charles Dickens on his first visit to the city. Dickens was so impressed by their personalities that he metamorphosed them into the Cheeryble brothers in *Nicholas Nickleby*.

The residential calm of Mosley Street was to change in 1827 when Henry Charles Lacy converted a house on the corner of Market Street and Mosley Street into the 'Royal Hotel and New Bridgewater Arms' and built a coach house at the corner of Back Mosley Street over which he allowed David Bannerman (whose nephew Henry Campbell-Bannerman became the leader of the Liberal party) to use the rooms as a warehouse. By the beginning of the 1830s there was a rash of warehouse building, a speculative boom in converting what had been houses of the 'gentry' into warehouses.

John Macfarlane, who had established himself as a commission agent in Back Piccadilly, purchased some buildings at the corner of Mosley Street and York Street and converted them into warehouses with the stipulation that the windows should resemble those in private residences. On the other corner of York Street was a silk mill belonging to Cardell Longsworth & Co. The mill was pulled down in the 1830s and a warehouse for E. & J. Jackson erected, the premises later being sold to the Manchester & Salford Bank.

Richard Cobden, who had recently purchased a house in Mosley Street in order to convert it into a warehouse, wrote to his brother Frederick in September 1832,

My next-door neighbour Brooks, of the firm Cunliffe and Brooks, bankers, has sold his house to be converted into a warehouse. The owner of the house on the other side has given his tenant notice for the same purpose. The house immediately opposite me has been announced for sale, and my architect is commissioned by George Hole, the calico printer, to bid six thousand guineas for it; but they want eight thousand for what they paid only four thousand five hundred for only five years ago.[31]

In August 1834 the old Club House in Mosley Street was sold to John Dugdale for £7,500, double the sum it was worth a few years before. Within a decade most of the private residences had been converted into warehouses, and the gentry were moving out of the city centre.

> Within the last few years Mosley Street contained only private dwelling-houses: it is now converted almost entirely into warehouses; and the increasing business of the town is rapidly converting all the principal dwelling-houses which exist in that neighbourhood into mercantile establishments, and is driving most of the respectable inhabitants into the suburbs. So great, about the year 1836, was the demand for such conversions, that some of the land in Mosley St, intended for warehouse erections, sold for a rental of 14s. per square yard per annum. On land purchased at so high a rate new buildings have generally been erected; and, to make the most of it, a more than usual number of warehouses are raised on a limited space, the towering height of which makes up for their contracted width.[32]

By 1838, as Henry Noel Humphreys observed in Loudon's *Architectural Magazine*, 'On entering Manchester by the suburb called the London Road, it becomes at once evident that you are approaching a manufacturing town of the first rank. It is at a glance observable that it infinitely surpasses Birmingham in the general style and more lofty proportion of the houses, and in its noble range of warehouses, which are much more imposing from the superior height, than any buildings of the same description in Birmingham.'[33]

What Humphreys ignored, or failed to notice, was what was going on in the streets and courts behind the noble warehouses he so admired.

3

HOUSING

IN THE
NINETEENTH CENTURY

But who could describe the interiors of these quarters set apart, home of vice and poverty, which surround the huge palaces of industry and clasp them in their hideous folds? [Alexis de Tocqueville, *Journeys to England and Ireland*, 1835]

MANCHESTER was rapidly becoming covered by houses, factories, mills, warehouses, workshops and markets. Little legislation existed for the regulation of either buildings or streets, and as a consequence, outside the fashionable streets and squares, there was a jumble of narrow lanes, alleyways and courts, covered with a profusion of small buildings. The scale of the buildings can, with some imagination, still be sensed in some of the smaller streets around the Northern Quarter. Harder to imagine is the noisome smell emanating from distilleries, abattoirs, hide and skin yards, tanneries, bone yards and glue works, dyeworks and excrement both animal and human.

It is difficult, too, to picture the rate at which people were entering the town and the close herding together especially of the poorer sections of society. The increase in the number of buildings was nothing compared with the increase in population: while Manchester's built-up area trebled in size between 1750 and 1850, its population quadrupled. In the mid-1770s some 24,000 people were estimated to live in the town, and by the time of the first census in 1801 the figure had risen to 75,000. In 1811 London, the largest city in the Western world, had a population of over 1 million; Manchester was the next largest town in the country, with a population of 137,000, followed closely by Edinburgh and Glasgow each with a population of over 100,000.

In common with every other town and city in the country, Manchester's housing conditions at the beginning of the nineteenth century were intolerable, but the growth of the town had been so fast that little effectively had, or perhaps could have, been done. Immigration into the town of Manchester was taking place at an incredible rate, and as people flocked into the town speculators bought up small parcels of land and erected cheap 'jerry-built' terraces of houses on them [8].

These dwellings, usually of two rooms, one above the other, and with walls often only one brick thick, might be inhabited by a family of seven people or more, the upstairs room being used for sleeping in, the lower for cooking, eating, living and sleeping and sometimes work. Overcrowding was rife: in the three-storey weavers' houses at 46 and 48 Back Irk Street, Irk Town, for example, lived twenty-two people. The cellars of dwellings, where they existed (and there were many in Manchester), were usually let out to other families or lodgers; at 4 John Street, a cellar dwelling, there were the eight members of the Reilly family and eleven lodgers.[1] In 1835 the Manchester Statistical Society was formed and published probably the first social survey undertaken in the country. They found that there were about 3,500 cellar dwellings housing nearly 15,000 people, or about 12 per cent of the population.

In order to earn maximum rent, the houses were packed as densely as possible, and no legislation existed before 1830 to forbid the building of back-to-backs (where two rows of buildings shared the same rear wall), or courts (where dwellings were inserted into the open spaces between buildings or streets, and often with access only through a narrow 'tunnel' entrance at ground-floor level). Friedrich Engels noted the courts on the bank of the river Irk:

> Right and left a multitude of covered passages lead from the main street into numerous courts, and he who turns thither gets into a filth and disgusting grime, the equal of which is not to be found – especially in the courts which lead down to the Irk, and which contain unqualifiedly the most horrible

8] Nineteenth-century housing

dwellings which I have yet beheld. In one of these courts there stands directly at the entrance, at the end of the covered passage, a privy without a door, so dirty that the inhabitants can pass into and out of the court only by passing through foul pools of stagnant urine and excrement.[2]

These speculators' houses were built without any form of water supply or means of removing sewage, and at best an open drain from an ashpit privy might run down the middle of the street or court. Unsurprisingly, disease was rife, and in 1832, following one of the worst outbreaks of cholera (which began in Somerset Street, Dolefield, and for the next two years ravaged Angel Meadow, Deansgate, Portland Street, Little Ireland and Bank Top), Dr James Phillips Kay carried out the first investigation into the conditions of Manchester cotton workers. 'The population . . . is crowded into one dense mass, in cottages separated by narrow, unpaved, and almost pestilential streets; in an atmosphere loaded with smoke and the exhalations of a large manufacturing city.'[3]

Kay noted 'Little Ireland', which lay in a curve of the Medlock, south of the site of the present Oxford Road Station between Gloucester Street and Great Marlborough Street. 'This unhealthy spot lies so low that the chimneys of its houses, some of them three storeys high, are little above the level of the road.'[4] More evocative is Engels's harrowing word picture of the area:

> In a rather deep hole, in a curve of the Medlock and surrounded on all four sides by tall factories and high embankments, covered with buildings, stand two groups of about 200 cottages, built chiefly back to back, in which live about 4,000 human beings, most of them Irish. The cottages are old, dirty and of the smallest sort, the streets uneven, fallen into ruts and in part without drains or pavements; masses of refuse, offal and sickening filth lie among standing pools in all directions; the atmosphere is poisoned by the effluvia from these, and laden and darkened by the smoke of a dozen tall factory chimneys . . . The race that lives in these ruinous cottages, behind broken windows, mended with oilskin, sprung doors and rotten doorposts, or in dark, wet cellars, in measureless filth and stench, in this atmosphere penned in as if with a purpose, this race must really have reached the lowest stage of humanity . . . But what must one think when he hears that in each of these pens, containing at most two rooms, a garret and perhaps a cellar, on the average twenty human beings live; that in the whole region, for each 120 persons, one usually inaccessible privy is provided.[5]

Little Ireland was only one of Manchester's Irish communities: a third of Manchester's population increase between 1841 and 1851 was due to Irish immigration, and by 1851 a seventh of the population of Manchester was Irish. The migration from Ireland had been forced on the populace by famine brought about by successive failures of the potato crop in the years 1846–51, and these desperate immigrants were the poorest of people and forced to accept the worst housing conditions, often taking on the jobs that the English would not or could not do. 'These were men, women and children in extreme poverty and desperation, described as "bringing pestilence on their backs, famine in their stomachs", and not uncommonly dying on the streets on their arrival.'[6]

Little Ireland was neither unique nor the worst in Manchester, for as Kay had already noted, 'In Parliament Street there is only one privy for three hundred and eighty inhabitants, which is placed in a narrow passage, whence its effluvia infest the adjacent houses, and must prove a most fertile source of disease. In this street also, cess pools with open grids have been made close to the doors of the houses, in which disgusting refuse accumulates, and whence its noxious effluvia exhale.'[7] *The Cotton Metropolis* described housing in Ancoats in 1849:

> The oldest and the worst working district of Manchester, is the region known as Ancoats . . . Many of its streets, particularly the great thoroughfare called the Oldham Road, are magnificent in their vast proportions, but the thousands of by-lanes and squalid courts, the stacked-up piles of undrained and unventilated dwellings, swarm with the coarsest and most dangerous portions of the population. Here the old and inferior mills abound; here the gin-palaces are the most magnificent, and the pawn-shops the most flourishing; here, too, the curse of Lancashire – the 'low Irish' – congregate by thousands; and here principally abound the cellar dwellings, and the pestilential lodging houses where thieves and vagrants of all kinds find shares of beds in underground recesses for a penny and twopence a night.[8]

The 1843 *Manchester Directory* lists, in Oldham Road alone, eight pawnbrokers, twenty public houses and twenty-one beer retailers (the 1830 Beerhouse Act permitted virtually anyone who had paid a small fee to sell beer on his premises – these were known as Tom and Jerry shops). In the whole of Manchester there were 920 beer shops, 624 taverns and pubs, 31 inns and hotels, a total of 1,575 establishments, or one to every 154 inhabitants. It was estimated too that Manchester had illicit stills which produced over 156,000 gallons of spirit per year. Yet, when the poor attempted to drown their sorrows, they brought moral opprobrium on their heads.* Dr Kay complained, 'Amongst the poor, the most destitute are too frequently the most demoralised – virtue is the surest economy – vice is haunted by profligacy and want. Where there are most paupers, the gin shops, taverns and beer houses are most numerous.'[9] Though, as Cooke-Taylor acceded, 'The plain fact is, that in too many instances the only resource which the mechanic has for the excitement and emotions necessary to his existence is the public house . . . Music, singing and dancing are prohibited in the majority of public houses, under the pretence that they might prove too attractive . . . I heard with my own ears a music licence magisterially refused, on the ground that it was advisable to render vice repulsive.'[10]

Engels described the dwellings of the poor as stretching like a girdle a mile and a half in breadth around the commercial district. Outside the girdle, the middle bourgeoisie lived in areas like Chorlton and Cheetham Hill, the upper bourgeoisie in Ardwick, Broughton and Pendleton, 'in free, wholesome country air, in fine comfortable homes, passed once every half or quarter of an hour by omnibuses going into the city. And the finest part of this arrangement is this,

---

* On 12 May 1830 the first temperance meeting was held in Manchester. The moderation pledge was abandoned on 26 February 1835 and a new society was formed.

that members of this money aristocracy can take the shortest road through the middle of all the labouring districts to their places of business, without ever seeing that they are in the midst of the grimy misery that lurks to the right and the left.'[11]

Plymouth Grove, Ardwick and Greenheys (which was to become the centre of the German community) were starting to be built on from the 1820s for the houses and villas of merchants and manufacturers. The dormitory village of Withington was created by Lord Egerton, Mr Fielden and Mr Bury (a banker), who all gave land for the construction of middle-class housing. The total cost of the construction, including the laying of sewers, was £12,000, and when it was finished it was handed over to the Trustees of the Wilmslow Road for £8,000. The villages of Didsbury and Withington were served by omnibus by the 1820s.

Whalley Range was purchased by Samuel Brooks, the banker, in 1836 and named after his birthplace. He built Whalley House in 1834, and developed an estate on what had been little more than moorland. The houses, because the land was low-lying, were built on terraced basements, and the estate was laid out with the assistance of John Shaw, a landscape gardener. The land was drained by a new water drain laid to the river at Ashton, three miles away, at a cost of £12,000. Chorlton Road was built to give access to the site, and, to maintain privacy, gates were erected at the Brook's Bar end of Chorlton Road and on Upper Chorlton Road. In 1831 Whalley Range had a population of 208, and by 1871 the population had risen to 5,403. Brooks carried out other schemes at Baguley, Sale, Timperley, Partington and Carrington Moss (purchased from the Earl of Stamford). An astute man, he would observe and note at dinner those who ordered extravagant dishes which they could ill afford in case he had to deal financially with them later. On his death, in 1864, he left £2 million.

Victoria Park was opened on 31 July 1837 (in Queen Victoria's coronation year), formed by a company of gentlemen, to build villa houses at rents varying from £100 to £250 a year, on a plot of 140 acres.[12] Five miles of roads in crescents and terraces with trees, shrubs and flowers were fenced around and provided with toll gates. It combined, in the words of a contemporary commentator, 'the advantage of close proximity to the town with the privacy and advantage of a country residence which, in the rapid conversion of all the former private residences of the town into warehouses, has long been deemed to be a desideratum.'[13]

Richard Lane was commissioned to draw up a plan for the estate, and he laid out the roads and sewers, and designed the gate lodges, though these were later demolished. Lane's only extant building is Addison Terrace at 84–106 Daisy Bank Road, a terrace of Regency style houses but with Gothic arches over their doors and some of their windows, and with drip mouldings and sculpture. At No. 102 lived Charles Hallé in 1848 and Ford Madox Brown between 1883 and 1887.

By December 1838 only nine houses had been built, the company was declared bankrupt, and it was not until 1845 that a new group, the Victoria Park Trust, was founded to develop the site. By 1850 sixty-five properties had been erected in the Park. The Gables, behind the Rampant Lion public house on Upper

Brook Street, was built by Edward Salomons and he resided there between 1885 and 1891. The building is, unfortunately, being allowed to rot – it is a pity that it could not have been incorporated into the new student residences which were built in 1998 on the city's last piece of woodland.

Even by the turn of the century the houses had started to be converted into hotels, college buildings and nursing homes. As Simon pointed out in 1936, 'the type of house which, with its garden, maintains the character of places like Victoria Park is not suitable for family life conceived in terms of today. The large mansion, built for a large family, served by a large staff, can only be conserved as a hostel, or for some purpose of a similar character, and is very often not particularly suitable for that use.'[14] Nonetheless, the Park still provides good examples of the Victorian villa. (Manchester has only one remaining mansion and that is 'The Towers' at Didsbury.)

By the 1850s strips of cottages (two-up, two-down terraces) had been built on the eastern and southern side of the Park, and in the 1870s and 1880s large-scale terraces were being built to the north of Plymouth Grove. In 1850 the township of Rusholme, of which Victoria Park was part, had 431 houses and 2,000 inhabitants in an area of 973 acres, but outside the Park there were was no lighting, and the streets were for the most part unpaved and undrained. Rusholme was incorporated into Manchester in 1885.

If the merchants were able to retreat to their 'country' houses, the poor were left behind in the town. Faucher wrote in 1844,

> And thus at the very moment when the engines are stopped, and the counting houses closed, everything which was the thought – the authority – the impulsive force – the moral order of this immense industrial combination, flies from the town, and disappears in an instant. The rich man spreads his couch amidst the beauties of the surrounding country, and abandons the town to the operatives, publicans, mendicants, thieves, and prostitutes, merely taking the precaution to leave behind him a police force, whose duty it is to preserve some little of material order in this pellmell of society.[15]

Even in the year Faucher was writing, some steps, if faltering ones, were being taken to ameliorate the conditions of the poor. The 1844 Manchester Borough Police Act required that no new house could be built without running water and a toilet in the house or the yard [9]. This was the first such Act in the country, and meant, effectively, that no back-to-back houses or courts were built in Manchester after that date, though they were still being built in Bradford and Openshaw, which were incorporated into Manchester in 1885 and 1890.* By 1900 there were only 5,000 back-to-backs left in Manchester and these had been removed or converted to 'through' houses by 1939. *The Cotton Metropolis* noted that houses in Hulme were of better quality than those in Ancoats, because they were built after the Act. They had a street door opening into a passage, and not into a room, and many had four rooms with bay

---

* Nottingham nominally banned back-to-backs in 1845, but effectively in 1874. Bradford banned them in 1860, Liverpool in 1861. Leeds continued to build back-to-backs until the 1930s.

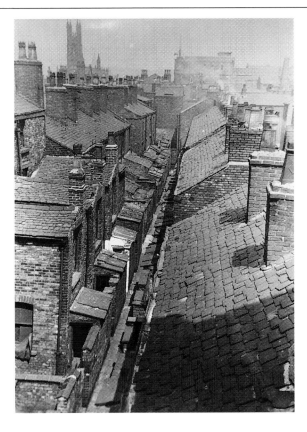

9] Nineteenth-century houses
with privies

windows and water closets in their yards, 'and the provisions of the Building
Act, against tenements being raised back to back, have been strictly observed'.[16]

Water had been a constant concern to the growing town. Before the nineteenth century, water had been supplied from a conduit in the Market Place,
fed by springs in what are now Fountain Street and Spring Gardens (for the
coronation of Charles II claret ran from the conduit until after sunset). Towards
the end of the eighteenth century Sir Oswald Mosley installed a pumping
engine which raised water from the Medlock which was then stored in the
Shudehill pits and the Infirmary Pool. The Manchester & Salford Waterworks
Company was established in 1808 and built small reservoirs at Gorton, Beswick,
Bradford and Audenshaw, which supplied 2 million gallons of water per day to
the town, first in stone pipes, which, being liable to burst, were replaced by
iron pipes in 1817. In 1831 water from standpipes was also supplied for three
or four hours per day in Market Street, where the water was received into a
large stone cistern at the bottom of which was a porous stone filter. Even so,
less than half the population had access to clean water.

The 1847 Manchester Corporation Waterworks Act authorised the Borough
Council to levy a water rate on all its citizens and to build a series of reservoirs
in the Longendale valley.[17] The Longendale water scheme cost £650,000 and
was intended to supply 30 million gallons of water per day, though even by
1851 it provided only 8 million gallons per day. Eventually Manchester was

supplied by water from the Lake District, first from Thirlmere in 1879 and then from Haweswater in 1919. Taking the supply from Thirlmere was itself a major piece of engineering. Thirlmere is 210 ft above the level of the service reservoirs at Audenshaw, some 106 miles distant. This allows an average fall of nearly 2 ft per mile which enables the water to flow by gravitation along fourteen and a quarter miles of tunnel, thirty-six and three-quarter miles of covered channels and fifty-five miles of pipes ranging from 40 in. to 54 in. in diameter. The fountain in Albert Square, designed by Thomas Worthington, was erected in 1879 in celebration of the Thirlmere scheme.

It was not just the lack of clean water but the spread of diseases like cholera and typhoid through sewage-contaminated water that took its toll of the population. Rivers would periodically flood,* and from early in the nineteenth century they were heavily polluted by sewage from innumerable privies and, of course, by chemicals. Diarrhoea came from infected water or food and was a major cause of death among the youngest children. As a report of the Poor Law Commissioners said in 1842, 'Of all who are born of the labouring classes in Manchester, more than 57 per cent die before they attain five years.'

The Public Health Act of 1848 (which laid the foundations of all subsequent housing legislation) gave local authorities powers to supply water, to pave and clean streets, to arrange the collection of refuse and the whitewashing and purifying of houses. The General Board of Health was set up at same time to enforce the Act if the death rate rose above twenty-three per thousand, and Edwin Chadwick, first Secretary to the Poor Law Commissioners, was one of three members. Local Boards of Health now had laws sanctioned by the General Board of Health rather than by Parliament. Between 1832 and 1861 (increasingly after the 1848 Act) the municipality of Manchester paved, drained and flagged the footpaths of 1,578 streets, measuring upwards of sixty miles in length, and covering about 205 statute acres; ninety miles of main sewers and forty-nine miles of cross-sewers were laid, and 12,948 siphon traps were laid in connection with them. By 1866 there were ninety-five miles of main sewers and nearly 148 miles of cross-sewers. These were, of course, rain sewers, and there remained the major problem of the safe disposal of 'night soil'. In the 1870s 'Dolly Varden' pail closets were introduced, but it was not until the building of the Davyhulme sewage works in 1894 that a waterborne sewage system was introduced. In 1894 there were 24,300 water closets, 78,486 pail closets and 35,700 midden privies, though even by 1927 there were 230,046 water closets, and still 1,108 pail closets and thirty-five midden privies.[18]

---

* 13 July 1872 saw the most disastrous flood to hit Manchester. An ordinary month's rain fell on the 12th and 13th. The Irwell flooded parts of Peel Park. On the Medlock at Clayton Bridge the river was 12 ft above normal level. By noon the flood had breached one of the walls of the cemetery near Phillips Park; coffins were washed out of the ground, dashed to pieces against an adjoining weir and over fifty cadavers swept downstream. In Ancoats, in a heavily populated district near Palmerston Street, the water rose to the height of the bedrooms, and rafts had to be used to rescue the victims. Similar scenes took place in Ardwick. In some of the manufacturing areas the water rose to 15 ft above normal. Surprisingly, only one life was lost.

Manchester prohibited cellar dwellings by a local Act of 1853, and 454 cellar dwellings were closed as unfit for human habitation between 1854 and 1861, though no provision was made for rehousing the occupants. In 1867 the Man-
~ster Improvement Act allowed the appointment of a Medical Officer of Health
᠁. The Act was the first in the country to grant powers to close,
᠁ion, any houses unfit for habitation, and although it did not
᠁placements in practice the Corporation paid £15 com-
᠁ed, and £2 10s towards the cost of converting
᠁e grant remained in force until 1906.
᠁bout room sizes, window areas and for
᠁yard at the rear. The Act also required
᠁rlier Manchester Act of 1830 had set a
᠁lings were two storeys, a street width of
᠁ore storeys the minimum width was 45 ft.
᠁inimum area of 70 ft^2 at its rear. It took
᠁l legislation applied the same conditions in
᠁Subsequent histories have tended to ignore
᠁improvement of working-class housing, even
᠁Smethwick admitted in 1934, 'The civic fathers
᠁the Parliament of the Derby–Disraeli administra-
᠁er of closure of unfit property ever embodied in a
᠁liability to compensate. The principle was reflected
᠁e of the following year. It has been maintained with-
᠁out the whole course of housing legislation.'[19]
᠁to by the Town Clerk was W. M. Torrens's Artisans'
᠁gs Act of 1868. The Act dealt only with single houses,
᠁n for compensation. It provided for the 'gradual improve-
᠁of the dwellings of the working classes, and for the build-
᠁e of improved dwellings.' It also obliged owners of dwellings
᠁property. In 1875 (Cross's) Artisans' and Labourers' Dwellings
᠁ was introduced to provide the mechanism of slum clearance.
᠁israeli's Home Secretary.) However,

᠁ry was clumsy and, in a well-intentioned attempt to safeguard the
᠁e property owners, when a whole area was designated an Improve-
᠁eme, it had inadvertently opened the way for unscrupulous owners
of slum property to claim compensation as though their buildings were in a perfect condition. In addition, the valuation was for a house on land usually ripe for commercial redevelopment . . . the local authority was obliged to acquire all the land, to lay out the streets, and sell off plots to anyone willing to build working-class housing . . . with the caveat that they must provide accommodation for the same numbers as had been displaced.[20]

The Act was amended in 1879, as was Torrens's 1868 Act, and again in the 1890 Housing of the Working Classes Act, but like most of the legislation of the nineteenth century these were adoptive Acts, leaving the local authority the power to enforce or not.

The closing of unfit dwellings and the commercial pressures on the centre were displacing the working classes, who were increasingly being driven to the outskirts of the city, and, as the richer members of society were leaving their large homes in Cheetham Hill or Ardwick's Polygon or Grosvenor Square for houses in the outer suburbs, so the poor were moving into them in more and more crowded conditions. The Bishop of Manchester noted in 1879,

Within a radius of five miles . . . there must be aggregated a population of probably 750,000 persons . . . Fifty years ago the wealthier merchants of Manchester lived in the heart of the town, in streets in which today there is not a single gentleman's residence. Tradesmen lived over their shops; manufacturers found existence tolerable under the smoke of their tall chimneys, surrounded by the cottages of their people. Now all these conditions are changed. You will hardly find one of our wealthiest men living within two miles of his place of business or of the Exchange . . . The centre of the city at night is a mass of unoccupied tenements. The working class and the poor still cluster thickly together in some of the murkiest and dismalest quarters of the town . . . The houses in the centre have been removed to meet the exigencies of commerce, and the remainder of the city up to its boundary is now nearly covered.[21]

By 1879, in Manchester, the housing and sanitary regulations were being enforced. A report by Dr Leigh, the city's first Medical Officer of Health, summarised the work of the Health Committee in that year:

All underground dwellings, such as inhabited cellars, which were very numerous in the city ten years ago, are closed . . . The committee have diverted from the sewers all excretal matters, except such as drain into them from the few water closets in the city. They have constructed, within about 1,000, the whole of the old midden closets in the city, amounting to nearly 60,000. All such closets are emptied bi-weekly, and their contents converted into valuable manure and mortar, with great reduction of the volume of effete material . . . The importance of this may be estimated from the fact that the amount of matter which, under the old system . . . would annually fill an area equal to St Ann's Square . . . to a height of eighty ft, is now satisfactorily disposed of without the production of any nuisance. The city is divided into sanitary districts, over which inspectors are appointed, and which are visited also by the officer of health, and the chief officers of his staff. All houses are being closed as rapidly as possible which are deemed unsuitable for human habitation.[22]

But there was no major slum clearance until the 1880s, and even by 1889 Robert Blatchford noted in an article in the *Sunday Chronicle* (5 May 1889) that there were slums of courts, back-to-backs and alleys everywhere that had not changed in the previous fifty years.[23]

The architect Thomas Worthington commented,

It is absolutely certain that the present condition of things cannot continue. This heaping up and crowding must have limit. The available area in the centres of towns is gradually diminishing. It must not be allowed to continue that the landlord shall be able to extort double the rent for dens unfit for human habitation, or that where one family has lived two must live in the future . . . The poor and working class population ought to be discouraged from living in the central quarters of large towns, and attractive and well constructed dwellings should be built for them in the outlying districts.[24]

Worthington should be remembered as perhaps the most socially committed architect in Manchester, for, apart from his commercial work, he lectured on the problems of social housing, designed a housing scheme in Salford and public baths in Salford, Ardwick and Hulme. His was the Chorlton Union Workhouse, of 1865, now part of Withington Hospital, and his designs for Prestwich Infirmary of 1866 so impressed Florence Nightingale that she copied the plans and had them distributed at home and in the colonies. Worthington set the standard for Victorian infirmaries.[25]

For the Salford Improved Industrial Dwellings Company Worthington designed a tenement building in 1868–71, between Caygill Street and Bond Street in Salford, near his Greengate Baths. The tenement, tucked into a small 80 ft wide site between the Irwell and the railway line, was of two parallel blocks of four storeys, built in common brick with Staffordshire blue bricks at the window heads and sills. The blocks were separated by a 26 ft wide courtyard into which the bedrooms and clothes-drying balconies looked. Within the blocks were thirty-six two-room, twenty three-room and six four-room flats, each with its own kitchen and lavatory.

Other, small-scale housing schemes were also being undertaken. In 1881 the Bishop of Manchester and others formed the Manchester & Salford Working Men's Dwellings Company and in 1883 commissioned Lawrence Booth to design a three-storey 'semi-detached' tenement block on Cyrus Street, Holt Town. It was followed by the acquisition of a mill in Jersey Street in 1892 which was converted into a building of 149 dwellings (architect, C. J. Maycock). In 1885 the Corporation created 'The Unhealthy Dwellings Committee', which dealt especially with courts. Back-to-back houses were demolished or made into through houses and some houses in congested groups were demolished to provide more space and air for the remainder. In 1889 the City Council applied the provisions of the Artisans' and Labourers' Dwellings Act to substitute new homes for old. Public complaints about the conditions on Oldham Road galvanised the Corporation into action, and one area in Oldham Road and another in Pollard Street, Ancoats, were declared unfit and a rearrangement was made of the streets and houses in the area.

A competition was set up for the design of tenements on Oldham Road which was won by Henry Spalding of London, an architect who had been employed to design tenements by the London County Council.[26] The flats presented (and still present) a forbidding impression [10]. There are five floors of red brick and only the front façade has any pretensions to style – Queen Anne – primarily by the use of terracotta detailing, oriel windows and gables. There was no front entrance, the entries being through the back and sides of the site. Externally, the ground floor was given over to shops and, internally, the dwellings were arranged round a central courtyard with communal walk-ways approached by stone steps in the corners of the building. Laundry and drying rooms were provided in each of the corner towers. The dwellings were in pairs, each generally of two rooms, and every two dwellings shared a sink and water closet. Spalding's experience in London suggested to him the use of cement skirting boards, for the working classes would remove wooden ones for their fires, and iron pipes, not lead, or they would sell them. Spalding had particular views on providing homes for the poor, and these were expressed in 1900:

> We seem to have taken it for granted that if we design tenements on the most approved methods of hygiene, the working classes will adapt themselves to their new surroundings. I do not wish to under-rate the importance of hygiene, but hygiene is not valued by the working man and so for its advantages he does not care to pay. For example, if we provide a system of fresh-air inlets and outlets to his rooms, we shall find that in a very short time they will all be blocked up. I fear it is not much good to argue with the working man about sanitation or ventilation. He does not appreciate them . . . Some years ago it was the custom to provide baths in many of the dwellings; now it is seldom done, and considering that public baths are accessible in most neighbourhoods, I think it is an open question whether they should be provided in these buildings. Also, it is no great hardship for people for this class to share a scullery with another family; they have for the most part been used to it for most of their lives, living as they do in houses with sanitary accommodation for one family and with rooms let to three or four. The first thing, then, is to find out the mode of living and habits of the working people, for unless we give them what they are accustomed to we shall find the class of people for whom we intend to provide will not live in our buildings.[27]

10] Tenement, Oldham Road, Henry Spalding, 1889

The only other major tenement block undertaken by the Corporation was the 135 room, five-storey Pollard Street Dwellings of 1894. This was designed by Spalding & Cross, but with even less architectural detailing than the Oldham Road scheme. Neither this nor the Oldham Road block was fully tenanted in its first twenty years. As a result, apart from a four-storey tenement built on the Rochdale Road in 1904, no such similar schemes were built by the city before World War I. Instead, between 1897 and 1904 various small-scale schemes were undertaken, generally two and three-storey blocks known as 'tenement houses'.

The Manchester Reconstruction Scheme, presented to the City Council in 1891, proposed the clearance of some of the worst parts of Ancoats. But little was carried out, as the 1890 Housing of the Working Classes Act required local authorities to build adequate housing to replace demolished buildings. It also, in effect, required building to a high (and too expensive) standard which matched that of the London County Council.[28] Manchester's Medical Officer of Health pointed out in a report of 1891–92 that back-to-back properties were still causing mortality from diarrhoea twice as heavy as well ventilated houses. But T. R. Marr's report, *The Housing Conditions of Manchester and Salford*, of 1904, recommended the continuance of further demolition of such back-to-backs, or their conversion to through houses as had been done.[29]

Rusholme, Bradford and Harpurhey were amalgamated with Manchester in 1888; Newton Heath, Blackley, Moston, Clayton, Openshaw, Kirkmanshulme and part of Gorton in 1890; Withington, Chorlton-cum-Hardy, Didsbury, Moss Side and Levenshulme between 1904 and 1913. The city took on responsibility for their housing, and their overcrowding. In 1901 the Corporation bought 238 acres at Blackley for a suburban Cottage Dwelling Scheme, but from then on until after World War I Manchester concentrated on refurbishing the buildings within its new boundaries, rather than rebuilding.

Most housing built before World War I was private and speculative, there was no planning as such, and as the population grew more houses were built in straight 'bye-law' rows by speculative builders on the fringe of existing housing areas. The working classes were still leaving the central part of the city: in 1851 about 90,000 people lived in the central part of the town, by 1900 the number was down to about 30,000.[30] But, behind many of its fancier façades, squalor still existed. As Swindells pointed out in 1908, 'To the Manchester man of today Oldham Road is a wide thoroughfare bounded through its entire length by rows of shops and houses, behind which are situated narrow streets, squalid courts, jerry-built cottages, mills and workshops, with scarcely a trace of brightness to relieve the dull monotony of the prevailing grey and gloom.'[31]

Ancoats, of course, had always been the most impoverished part of the city. In 1877 Thomas Coghlan Horsfall, Chairman of the Manchester Citizens' Association, and acknowledged as one of the leaders in the early stages of the Garden City movement, had opened a museum of art treasures in Ancoats Hall, Great Ancoats Street, to bring a little joy to the most deprived citizens. In 1904 he published *The Improvement of the Dwellings and Surroundings of the People – the Example of Germany*, and, as Professor Tarn wrote of him, 'He was an influential figure in the pressure group which prepared the way for the 1909 Act.'[32] The Act referred to was the 1909 Housing, Town Planning, etc. Act, the first to mention town planning. In introducing the legislation its proposer, John Burns, President of the Local Government Board, said, 'The object of the bill is to provide a domestic condition for the people in which their physical health, their morals, their character and their whole social condition can be improved by what we hope to secure in this bill. The bill aims in broad outline at, and hopes to secure, the home healthy, the house beautiful, the town pleasant, the city dignified and the suburb salubrious.'[33]

In 1909 Manchester appointed a Town Planning Committee to help create the town pleasant; the home healthy and the suburb salubrious had to wait until after World War I.

PLATE 1] View of Manchester

PLATE 2] Cathedral

PLATE 3] St Ann's Church

PLATE 4] St Ann's Square

PLATE 5] Mills, Redhill Street,
Ancoats

PLATE 6] City Art Gallery, Mosle
Street, Charles Barry, 1829–35

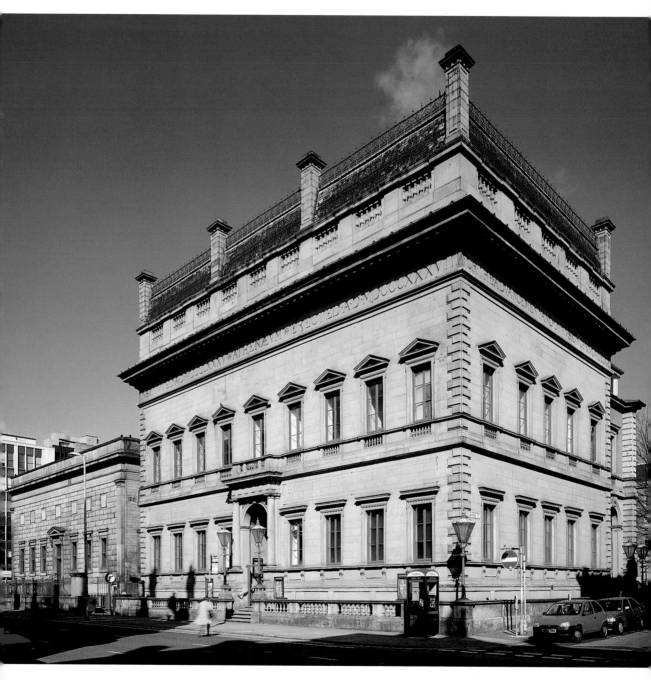

PLATE 7] Athenaeum, Princess
Street, Charles Barry, 1836–39

PLATE 8] Free Trade Hall, Peter Street, Edward Walters, 1853

PLATE 9] Britannia Hotel (Watts Warehouse), Mosley Street, Trav & Mangnall, 1855–58

PLATE 10] Royal Bank of Scotland (Manchester & Salford Bank), Mosley Street, Edward Walters, 1861–62

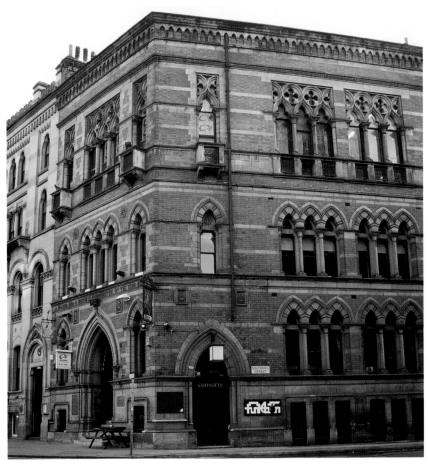

PLATE 11] Memorial Hall, Southmill Street, Thomas Worthington, 1863–66

PLATE 12] Town Hall, Albert Square, Alfred Waterhouse, 1867–77

PLATE 13] Crown Courts, Aytour Street, Thomas Worthington, 1867–73 and Hurd Rolland Partnership, 1996

4

THE COMING
OF THE RAILWAYS

No speed with this, can fleetest Horse compare
No weight like this, canal or Vessel bear.
As this will Commerce every way promote
To this let Sons of Commerce grant their vote.

[Thomas Gray, *Observations on a General Iron Way*, 1822]

IN 1830 the railway came to Manchester, and its consequences were to be profound. The Liverpool & Manchester Railway had its origins in 1821 when the Liverpool & Manchester Railway Company was set up, following a meeting between Joseph Cowlishaw, a Manchester corn merchant, Joseph Sanders, a Liverpool corn merchant, and William James, a wealthy estate agent and surveyor.[1] James completed a survey of the intended route in 1822, but opposition from both landowners and canal owners forced a rethink. James was made bankrupt in 1823, and the railway company engaged George Stephenson to survey the route prior to an application being made to Parliament.

Stephenson's survey was completed by 1825, and was submitted to Parliament in the spring of that year. On the second reading, the Liverpool and Manchester Railroad Bill went to committee, where it met strong opposition, not least from Miss Byrom and her sister Mrs Atherton, who had inherited considerable land on the site of the proposed Manchester terminus, and from the Old Quay Company, which owned the Mersey & Irwell Navigation. The opponents of the scheme were able to show that the survey, carried out, with scant supervision, by Hugh Steel and Elijah Galloway, Stephenson's inexperienced and junior assistants, was remarkably inept. The survey was inaccurate, the intended levels were badly calculated, and the large number of errors cumulated at the Manchester end of the line: the survey placed the river Irwell 30 ft above Vauxhall Road, whereas it lay 5 ft below it. The position of the Manchester terminus was, perhaps purposely, ill defined. Stephenson, under examination by eminent engineers, was shown to be an incompetent civil engineer, and its supporters withdrew the Bill.

For the following session of Parliament the company engaged the services of the leading engineers George and John Rennie,[2] with Charles Blacker Vignoles as surveyor. A Bill was presented to Parliament in 1826, and this time it was successful, not least because the Marquess of Stafford, heir to the Bridgewater estates, had been persuaded to buy 1,000 shares in the company. The terminus, in the new submission, was to be situated not in Manchester but under the walls of the New Bailey Prison in Salford, thus avoiding conflict with Miss Byrom and Mrs Atherton. On May 1826 the Manchester and Liverpool Railway Bill passed through the House of Lords.

Stephenson, in spite of the earlier fiasco, still carried much support from the board of the railway company, and he rather than Rennie was appointed principal engineer.[3] Under his supervision the draining of Chat Moss commenced in June 1826, the first shaft of the Liverpool Grand Tunnel opened in September, and earthworks began in January 1827. A terminus in Salford, on the wrong side of the Irwell, was obviously unsatisfactory, and it may be questioned whether it was ever the intention to build one there. In 1827 6,000 square yards of land partly occupied by the dyeworks of Rothwell & Harrison were purchased, and later 35,500 square yards of land belonging to Gilbert Winter, and the company now owned land bounded by Liverpool Road, Water Street and Charles (now Grape) Street. The Irwell was crossed by a new bridge, after the Old Quay Company had agreed to sell some of its land on the west side of the Irwell, on the proviso that the new bridge should have provision for a cart track not less than 18 ft wide at the side of the railway. An Act of 14 May 1829 allowed the diversion and the bridge, and the first locomotive crossed the bridge in August 1830.

The railway line continued by a brick viaduct to the station, but in crossing over Water Street had to span a distance of 24 ft at a height of 17 ft. An iron bridge was obviously called for, but the span was too long for the sort of beams in normal use. Fortunately, Stephenson had a local expert in William Fairbairn, who for some time had been carrying out tests on a new form of cast-iron beam developed by Eaton Hodgkinson, a physicist and ex-pupil of John Dalton. 'Hodgkinson' beams were the ideal solution for the Water Street bridge, and it was the first time that such beams were used. It was not until Fairbairn built Orrell's Mill in Stockport, in 1834, that the Hodgkinson beam was used in a building. The five major beams of the bridge were cast by Fairbairn & Lillie, the largest two each weighing four tons. The bridge superstructure was carried on two rows of nine cast-iron columns, and a parapet 6 ft high was built to conceal the railway from the road. In 1905 the Water Street bridge was demolished and replaced, following the failure of similar bridges in 1882 and 1891. The London & North Western Railway Company, of which the Liverpool & Manchester had become part, realising the historical importance of the bridge, suggested it should be re-erected in one of Manchester's parks, but the Council declined, considering the cost – a few hundred pounds – too much.

Liverpool Road Passenger Station opened on 15 September 1830, the oldest extant railway building in the world.[4] The booking hall for first and second-class passengers was on Liverpool Road, with separate stairs leading to the waiting rooms above, level with the railway line (only the first-class stairs remain). On the corner of Water Street was the Agent's House, and on the right-hand side of the 1830s building was an extension (rebuilt in 1837) for the booking hall of the Grand Junction Railway [11]. There was originally a sundial over the entrance to the first-class booking hall, since local time was set by the sun: it was not until 1847 that Manchester Corporation adopted 'railway time'.

Opposite the station is the 1830 Goods Warehouse, which stored goods, primarily corn and general groceries, brought in from Liverpool. The 320 ft long and 70 ft deep building was proposed in March 1830 and completed by 15 September that year. David Bellhouse Jnr was appointed contractor, and built the warehouse in four months from receipt of tender.[5] The building was curved to meet the line of the railway, and six spur tracks ran into the building through loading bays.

In 1831 the 200 ft long, three-storey No. 1 Cotton Store was built parallel to the 1830 warehouse, and this was followed by the No. 2 Cotton Store of a similar size. A Shipping Shed, 225 ft long and 42 ft wide, followed, built along the Liverpool Road, and in 1837, the Goods Shed for the Grand Junction Railway opened. All these were demolished in the 1860s when the station was extended by the London & North Western Railway. By 1837 warehouses and stores covered five acres with a storage capacity of 4 million ft³. In 1855 a Freight Shed was added to allow perishables such as fruit and vegetables to be off-loaded quickly.

In 1867–69 the Bonded Warehouse on Grape Street was built for the London & North Western Railway, and reached by a separate viaduct across Water Street. This building is 200 ft long and 100 ft wide, of five storeys and a basement, with arched doorways on the viaduct side. The Lower Byrom Street warehouse of the Great Western Railway was added in 1880, and is of four storeys with huge square openings at rail level.

On the other side of Manchester in 1842, Store Street Station (renamed London Road Station, and later Piccadilly) was built, for the Manchester & Birmingham Railway, over an enormous brick undercroft. Little is left of the original surface buildings since the rebuilding of the station in 1969, but the cast-iron and glass train shed of the 1880s remains, and has been restored. The huge seven-storey goods warehouse, of 1867, behind the station on Ducie Street is all that is left of the expanse of goods sidings and buildings which once characterised the site.

In January 1844 passenger services to Liverpool were withdrawn from Liverpool Road Station to the newly opened Hunt's Bank (later Victoria) Station, then the largest in Britain. The Liverpool & Manchester line was extended to Hunt's Bank by means of a viaduct which ran across Salford from Liverpool Road Station, and which has marred that part of Salford ever since, forming a denser barrier between the cities than the river Irwell ever has. The original station and the 700 ft long cast-iron and glass train shed were designed by George Stephenson, and parts of his original station can still be seen on the extreme left-hand side, though most of the present façade was built by William Dawes in 1909. The station was once approached by a wooden footbridge over the river Irk, but subsequent enlargements meant building over the river. Todd Street was widened in the 1880s to provide easier access to the station, and at the same time the buildings between Cathedral Gate and Cateaton Street were rebuilt. Richard Lane's Corn Exchange, a trapezoidal building behind a Classical portico, was demolished to make room for the road widening and was replaced by the present building, by Ball & Elce and by Potts Son & Pickup, in a staged building programme between 1890 and 1914. Exchange Station in Salford was built in 1884 by the London & North Western Railway Company. Its frontage was destroyed by bombs during the war, and the station closed in 1969, but it was once linked to Victoria Station by the longest platform in the world at 2,194 ft.

By 1844 there were six railway lines connecting the city with London, Liverpool, Birmingham, Leeds, Sheffield and Bolton.[6] Faucher recorded:

> The Leeds railway connects Manchester with Oldham, which contains 60,000 inhabitants; also with Bury, Rochdale and Halifax, each of which numbers from 24,000 to 26,000 souls; the Bolton railway connects it with Bolton, Preston and Chorley, which together have more than a hundred factories and 114,000 inhabitants. On the Sheffield line a few minutes suffice to reach the establishments of Stalybridge, Ashton, Dukinfield and Hyde, peopled by more than 80,000 inhabitants; the Birmingham line incorporates it with, so to speak, the 50,000 inhabitants of Stockport; that of Liverpool connects it with Wigan and Warrington. Thus we have 15 or 16 seats of industry forming this great constellation.[7]

In 1846 the newly formed London & North Western Railway took over the Liverpool & Manchester, the Manchester & Birmingham, the London & Birmingham and the Grand Junction Railways, and now owned both Liverpool Road and London Road Stations. The Manchester Sheffield & Lincolnshire Railway shared London Road Station and had a separate booking hall and offices, but operations were carried out under increasingly acrimonious conditions: signs were painted out or removed, the public were misdirected or arrested for using the wrong tickets, and clerks were thrown through booking-office windows. The more recent privatisation of the railway system has, fortunately, led to fewer disputes.

The MS&L company also had a goods yard on the north-east side of the station, backing on to the Manchester terminus of the Ashton Canal, which primarily carried limestone from the Peak District. The canals had large basins and storage areas, which by 1846 had been acquired by the railway companies. The Ashton Canal was leased in perpetuity to the MS&L, and on the Rochdale Canal the MS&L shared a twenty-one-year lease with the L&NW. The railways did not immediately replace canals for carrying bulk goods, but their impact on the subsequent appearance of Manchester's buildings was soon evident:

> The railways have brought excellent stone from the immediate neighbourhood of the quarries, at so low a rate of carriage, that its cost is often exceeded by brick work, and consequently it is much used for the whole fronts of buildings . . . The stone most used is known as 'Yorkshire pierpoints'; it is a sandstone of good yellow colour, and according to one architect, is nearly as cheap as the best red facing bricks, and quite as cheap as what are called in Manchester 'seconds'.[8]

The railways produced two of the great names in locomotive manufacturing, Beyer and Peacock. Charles Beyer (1813–76) moved from Saxony to the Manchester drawing office of Sharp Roberts & Co. and eventually became their chief engineer before setting up on his own in 1853. Richard Peacock (1820–89) became locomotive superintendent of the Leeds & Selby Railway at the age of eighteen and, after working in Swindon for Sir Daniel Gooch, came to Manchester in 1841 as head of the locomotive division of the Manchester & Sheffield Railway, and set out its works in Gorton. In 1854 he entered into partnership with Charles Beyer and then Henry Robertson and they established their works opposite the Manchester–Sheffield line workshops. By the late 1860s over forty acres were covered with sidings and works, with another forty acres and thirteen miles of sidings in Newton Heath.[9] One of their great locomotives, built for the South African Railways, can be seen in the Museum of Science and Industry.

Peacock lived at Gorton Hall, a brick building of the early nineteenth century, which was extended and improved by Thomas Worthington. When he decided to replace the Old Chapel in Gorton he naturally approached Worthington, who designed for him the Brookfield Unitarian Church on Hyde Road, in 1869–71. At same time Peacock's partner, Beyer, was endowing St James, Gorton, for his Anglican workers.

Possibly the first hotel in the country for railway travellers was the Queen's Hotel, on the corner of Piccadilly and Portland Street, of 1845. Originally the town residence of William Houldsworth, a cotton magnate, the painted stucco house was built on the site of a bowling green. The house was left to his nephew, Thomas Houldsworth, racehorse owner and owner of Houldsworth's factory on Little Lever Street, who transformed it into the hotel. The hotel was later extended to include two more large brick-built houses, one belonging to Robert Ogden, cotton spinner, and the other to two partners in Hargreaves & Dugdale, calico printers, whose warehouse was in Marsden's Square.[10] The Queen's Hotel was replaced in the 1970s by an office block.

Journey times were considerably reduced for people as well as goods, and journeys now took hours rather than days; Manchester to London by train took nine and a half hours. The railways were sounding the death knell of the stagecoach, and Cooke-Taylor in 1841 noted that the number of people arriving weekly by train was 35,700 but by coach only 3,661.[11] Sport became more accessible; the cricket ground station at Old Trafford in the 1860s was the first such in the country. And there was a less well known, but even more important, spin-off: the urinals and water closets installed in stations soon commended themselves for public parks; 'the requisite conveniences for persons frequenting the parks, which have been so judiciously provided by the railway companies'.[12]

There were, of course, disadvantages, not least to the men building the railways. 'A navvy was expected to shovel about twenty tons of earth and rock a day on the basic jobs of cutting, banking and tunnelling.'[13] Injury and death were always present: in the Woodhouse tunnel between Manchester and Sheffield, between 1839 and 1845, 400 men were injured, 140 seriously injured and thirty-two were killed out of a total work force of about 1,000.

The impact of the railways on towns and their inhabitants was tremendous, and the blight of railway lines, especially their viaducts, impacted mostly on the poor. The Manchester South Junction & Altrincham Railway Company built Oxford Road Station in 1849 on top of the long viaduct which divides Oxford Road from Oxford Street, partly on the site of Little Ireland. The seven-year-long negotiations were with several landowners; with Sir Thomas de Trafford, who did not object, with Lord Francis Egerton, whose objections were overcome by the offer of shareholdings in the scheme, and with Sir Booth Gore, who owned land south of Grosvenor Square and who objected to views of the viaduct from his 'estate', even though his view, by 1849, had already been obscured by a chemical works, a calico printing works, factories and speculative housing.[14]

Much of the land through which the railways ran was owned by a few, usually absent, landlords. Hunt's Bank ground was owned by the Lords Derby and Ducie, Oldham Road's by Ducie and Taylor. London Road Station was less problematical: the line cut through land on which little building existed in 1836 when the Bill was authorised, though subsequently Thomas Tipping built a number of speculative small properties. Extensions of the Oldham Road Station in 1845 meant dealing with two proprietors, Mary and Sarah Taylor, who directly owned 100 cottages, houses, rag shops, smiths', coopers' and wheelwrights' workshops, a public house and a police lock-up. The Mosleys sold their land adjacent to Mosley Hall to the Midland Railway Company in the 1860s, and left Manchester shortly after. The large landowners often sold off plots to smaller owners. In 1861, when the extensions to Victoria Station were planned, the land which only a few years earlier had been owned by Lord Ducie was now in multiple ownership, with an unusual number of solicitors and trustees owning blocks of ten or twenty dwellings. Even in 1861 it seems that speculators were buying up property in the hope of realising increased land values. By 1900 the railways owned over 7 per cent of land in the central zone of the city, much of it for goods yards and the viaducts which cross the city.[15]

Manchester's stations lie outside the central zone and the major displacement of people was around the fringes, where the lines ran and where the goods yards were, particularly in areas like Ancoats where the poor lived. The number of people displaced by railway building is difficult to estimate, and the railway companies' figures grossly underestimated the numbers. Kellett[16] has calculated for Glasgow that 20,000 people were actually displaced rather than the 8,230 estimated by the railway companies. A similar figure may well be appropriate for Manchester. Some 600 houses were demolished between 1861 and 1871 for the new goods station at London Road, and when Central Station was built in the 1870s 255 houses, home to 1,200 people, were demolished for it. The Central Station and Great Northern Railway Company's Goods Warehouse site cover an area of nineteen acres and for their building a total residential population of 5,500 was lost.

A series of maps drawn up in the 1850s by Richard Bastow show that no attempt was made to renew the housing through which the railway lines ran. Railways, on viaducts or embankments, crossed streets where they would. If the railways created urban blight, then that blight remained. As the Town Clerk of Manchester observed, 'You see it in all towns if you go along a railway with a viaduct; the very character of the property you look down upon shows that it is not the place where improvements may be looked for – the viaduct puts a stop absolutely to any improvement from the time it is constructed.'[17] Oldham Road Station was built in 1839 for the Manchester & Leeds Railway Company, and terminated in a huge area of goods sidings bounded by (now) Oldham Road, Thompson Street and Sudell Street. There is little evidence of the railway except a huge tract of derelict land which houses only the city fire station; the viaduct, though, is still visible along the length of New Allen Street. But, of course, in Ancoats the blight already existed.

Neither did the early railways allow the working classes to live in the outer suburbs – the fares were beyond their means – and not until the advent of cheap workmen's fares[18] and Corporation-run electric trams did the suburbs become available to them. (By 1905 Manchester had four times more trams *per capita* than London.) It is later in the century, when more people were being employed in better-paid jobs in warehousing and shipping, that the suburbs of Rusholme, Levenshulme and Longsight were developed. A new line by the Midland Railway to Central Station opened up Didsbury and Chorlton-cum-Hardy to commuters in the late nineteenth century. The trains which ran to the outer regions of Marple and Disley and Alderley Edge, places hitherto known only to the traveller, were for the new housing developments for the middle classes. In 1847 Thomas Worthington designed 'Broomfields' for John Swanwick, a friend and fellow member of the Cross Street Chapel. This was one of the earliest Victorian houses in Alderley Edge, and as a lure the newly formed Manchester & Birmingham Railway offered gold medal passes to new residents, entitling the head of the household to twenty-five years of free travel.

Liverpool Road, Oldham Road and London Road Stations all preceded the creation of the Borough Council. Hunt's Bank Station was authorised in the borough's first year, 1839, but not until 1863 did the Corporation set up a parliamentary sub-committee to scrutinise Bills affecting the town. Many councillors were shareholders in the railway companies and not a few were also directors. The Manchester Sheffield & Lincolnshire Railway, in 1865, intended to break the monopoly of the existing companies by making a new connection between Manchester and Liverpool. The line would have been raised on a huge viaduct, three miles long, spanning Deansgate, Oxford Street and Piccadilly, with a new station in the centre of the city. The scope of this scheme was concealed not only from the Corporation but even from Parliament. Only eventual pressure from the Corporation stopped a development which would effectively have cut the town in two.

The Central Station scheme re-emerged in 1873 and was to create Manchester's fourth railway terminus. It is significant that Manchester had four great railway terminuses – a generator of railway lines rather than an inheritor of them. The Cheshire Lines Committee which built it was formed by agreement between three companies, the Midland, the Great Northern and the MS&L. Work on Central Station commenced in October 1875. The original train shed design is in some part attributed to Sir John Fowler, engineer to the very similar St Pancras Station in London. The main difference between the two structures was the use of a substantial brick undercroft at Manchester, which supported the wrought-iron arches forming the main volume of the hall and rendering unnecessary the horizontal tie beams utilised at St Pancras. The train shed's 210 ft span is only 30 ft less than that of St Pancras (see [131]) Detailed responsibility for the design lay with the chief engineers of the railway companies involved, Sacré, Johnson and Johnson. Central Station opened on 1 July 1880, and both the *Manchester Guardian* and the *Evening News* commented on the unfinished appearance and on the large number of workmen being engaged on completing the building. In fact the station was never properly completed; the frontage, which comprised the booking hall, stationmaster's office and waiting rooms, was made of wood, the plan being to build an hotel as at St Pancras. The project, however, was shelved and the temporary wooden structures were left intact. The money was spent on more pressing requirements, such as additional platforms provided by building extensions at the side and rear.[19] In the end the Midland Railway built a grand hotel across the road.

Between 1893 and 1895 the Knott Mill and Deansgate Station was built for the Manchester South Junction & Altrincham Railway, replacing an earlier station on Hewitt Street. Its battlemented corner reflects the style of the nearby railway viaducts which acknowledge the presence of the Roman fort at Castlefield. The Corporation took the opportunity of the railway line proposals to widen Gaythorn Street and to build Whitworth Street West as a route from Deansgate to Oxford Road.

The last major piece of railway architecture was the Great Northern Railway Goods Warehouse, 1896–98, an enormous building 267 ft long, 217 ft wide and 75 ft high (see [**169**]). 'Over 800 men were employed on site. 25 million bricks, 50,000 tons of concrete, 12,000 tons of mild steel and 65 miles of rivets were used in its construction.'[20] The ground and first floors were loading platforms, the first floor being reached by a ramp from Watson Street. The warehouse had a capacity of sixty railway wagons at high level and ninety at low level, and the sidings outside could accommodate a total of 500 wagons. The Manchester & Salford Junction Canal is in a tunnel 35–40 ft below ground level, reached by shafts, creating a unique interchange of three transport systems; road, rail and canal. The buildings on Deansgate which mask the site make up the longest Victorian frontage in the country. The construction of the warehouse and its ancillary buildings and roads removed virtually all trace of Alport Town, a community of over 300 homes. The story of the warehouse continues in Chapter eleven.

5

1840–60

THE ARCHITECTURE
OF COMMERCE

Our Market Street was so narrow,
There was hardly room to wheel a barrow.
But now 'tis made so large and wide, sirs,
Six carriages may go side by side, sirs.
Sing heigh, sing ho, sing hey down gaily,
Manchester's improving daily.

[Song by Ben Oldfield, a ballad singer, 1820s]

A
T THE BEGINNING of the nineteenth century Manchester was still a
small town of some 600 streets, bordered by fields and meadows. At one
end of the town lay Chetham's College and the Collegiate Church, at the other
end St Peter's Church, completed only in 1794. The windmill near St Peter's
was still standing in 1811, and even by 1819 St Peter's Fields was a space large
enough to accommodate the 60,000 people of Peterloo. Deansgate was a narrow
road leading to the countryside and the market gardens of Knott Mill (Castlefield),
and was extended past Yate Street only in 1812. The Red Bank Highway was
the only notable route out of Manchester to the north. To the south, Granby
Row Fields was notable for its partridges, and Oxford Road was a merely a way
across meadows. Broughton, Hulme and Chorlton-on-Medlock were simply pas-
tures, and as late as 1829 there was still a view across the fields from Chorlton-
on-Medlock town hall to St George's, Hulme.

Market Street was the main thoroughfare, and was undoubtedly the most
hazardous street in the town. Records of injury and death are legion. Although
twenty-one yards wide at High Street [12], the street narrowed to only five
yards at St Mary's Gate, and this included a mere 2 ft of pavement on either
side. There was considerable traffic on the street, not least that of stagecoaches

12] Market Stead in 1835

and loaded waggons. Such were the congestion and peril that, in 1821, Manchester obtained an Act of Parliament to widen the street. The Market Street Commissioners had no power to raise money for widening but had to rely on profits from the gasworks and any additional rate levied for the purpose. Consequently, the widening was done in sections as money would allow, and the Act allowed twelve years for the task. The average setback was ten yards, in parts sixteen, and the width after the improvements was twenty-one yards.

The widening commenced in June 1822 with the demolition of Messrs Schofield & Mawn's shops, and was completed in 1834, the last old building to disappear being the Palace Inn, which had been built in 1745. It was replaced by the Palace Buildings, completed in August 1839 (and subsequently demolished). Swindells notes[1] that the first plate-glass window installed in Manchester in the 1820s was at No. 21 Market Street, where William Mountcastle, a hatter, installed two panes of glass each 2 ft long and 18 in. wide, held in by brass frames; the cost of the two was £30. The tallest building in the new street was Mr Zanetti's picture-dealing shop at No. 94, where the young Thomas Agnew worked.[2]

The 1820s also saw the widening of Todd Street (then Toad Lane, improved again in 1831–32), the opening of King Street to Deansgate and the widening of Toll (now St Ann's) Street. Pool Fold, Cross Street and Red Cross Street were widened and straightened in 1828 to create the new Cross Street. New Brown Street was opened in 1831, giving an approach from Market Street to Shudehill. On 19 October 1831 Bury New Road was opened, extending from Broughton Lane to Kersal, and the same year the Ducie Bridge across the river Irk was erected. On 10 September 1832, Stretford New Road was opened from Cavendish Street to Old Trafford.

The demolition of the old lanes and houses which lay between the Collegiate Church and the river Irwell (to create Victoria Street) was begun in 1833, and five years later Victoria Bridge Street opened to give access to the proposed Victoria Bridge. After floods had washed away the first stones in October 1838 and January 1839, the bridge was finally opened on 20 June 1839, on the second anniversary of the young Queen's coronation. The total cost of £20,800 was raised by the inhabitants of Salford.

In the decade 1811 to 1821 Manchester's population grew from 137,000 to 187,000 inhabitants, and to meet its spiritual needs new churches were being built. Alarmed at the growth of Nonconformity in the expanding industrial towns, Parliament in 1818 enacted 'An Act for Promoting the Building of Additional Churches in Populous Parishes' and voted for a fund of £1 million to ensure the building of new Anglican churches. The Act was administered by the Commissioners for Building New Churches, and their buildings are consequently referred to as 'commissioners' churches' or 'million churches'. The churches were intended to seat as many people as possible, and because the commissioners usually only made a contribution toward the cost – to a maximum of £20,000 for a church to seat 2,000 – the churches tended to be simple and undecorated.[3]

Altogether 214 churches were built under the Act, of which 174 were built in the establishment Gothic style. In the Manchester area St Matthew, Campfield[4] (demolished), St George, Tyldesley, St Thomas, Pendleton, St George, Chester Road, St Andrew, Ancoats, St Luke, Cheetham Hill, and All Saints, Stand, Prestwich, were built in the Gothic style; St Thomas, Stockport, and St Philip, Chapel Street, Salford, were Classical.

Manchester's earthly needs were still being ministered to by the Boroughreeve and the Court Leet, and although even small villages like Newton-le-Willows returned a Member of Parliament, Manchester had none. Manchester, exceptionally of the nineteenth-century towns, also had little influence from aristocratic society and was 'innocent . . . of all forms of inherited influence . . . it lacked even a resident gentry'[5] and, unlike the established towns, had no guild system to regulate trade or manufacturing. It was undoubtedly the lack of an ordered power structure which fostered the unprecedented upsurge of entrepreneurial activity, unmatched by any other city, as Gary Messinger has pointed out:

Manchester was an extraordinarily open town which took full advantage of its position between a geographic frontier to the north and an economic frontier to the south. It became a kind of Eldorado. From the farms, villages and towns of neighbouring areas, successive waves of English labourers migrated towards it. From across the sea came the poor of Ireland. From the north came Scotsmen fleeing the harsh life of the highlands and the slums of Edinburgh and Glasgow. And from the Continent more settlers arrived; some fleeing religious persecutions, others fleeing civil strife, such as the Greeks during the revolution of 1821 and Italians during the wars leading up to national unification in the 1840s; others, under clandestine conditions, either offering to sell or hoping to steal the secrets of new industrial techniques; still others, particularly the large number of Germans from Hanseatic cities, attracted by the chance of high monetary returns for their business skills.[6]

Manchester.
King Street.

13] Old Town Hall, King Street,
George Goodwin, 1819–34

The rapid influx of population and the increasing administrative burden meant that a town hall with offices for the growing band of permanent officials was becoming urgently needed.* In King Street, then fashionably residential, but soon to become the banking heart of Manchester, the house and grounds belonging to Dr White (who had founded the Lying-in Hospital) were purchased for the not inconsiderable sum of £6,500. The style of the new building, of course, had to be Classical, for the Greek Revival was reaching its zenith in the 1820s, and even as the new town hall was being considered in 1821 the Greek wars of independence were capturing the public imagination – the birthplace of modern civilisation throwing off the shackles of an oppressor.

The architect, Francis Goodwin (1784–1835), had been in independent practice in the Midlands from 1819, and was as capable of building in the Gothic style as in the Classical – *vide* St George's, Hulme, of 1826–28, altered 1884. Architects for commissioners' churches were chosen by local committees, and Goodwin inundated them with schemes. By 1819 he had received so many commissions that the Church Commissioners introduced a ruling to limit the number built by any one architect to six.[7] In the end, he built nine churches for the commissioners and another five otherwise financed. Goodwin entered every major architectural competition going, and, perhaps unsurprisingly, died of apoplexy on 30 August 1835 whilst working on designs for the Houses of Parliament. His major work, though, was Manchester's Town Hall.

Work started on the Town Hall on 19 August 1822, and the building work was finished in 1825 [13]. The building itself was full of symbolism. The architectural style of the entrance portico was like the Erectheion at Athens, the dome in the centre of the building was similar to the octagon tower of

* The first town hall was recorded in the fifteenth century – the Boothes in St Mary's Gate, consisting of a building with a courthouse and town hall on its upper floor.

Andronicus, also known as the Tower of the Winds, and both were illustrated in Stuart and Revett's second volume of *The Antiquities of Athens* of 1789. This publication was undoubtedly Goodwin's source, since he, like Harrison, had never travelled to Greece. And where better to copy a modern democratic town hall from than Athens, the *fons et origo* of democracy? The symbolism of the sculpture on the façade of the building suggests that links with democracy were in Goodwin's mind, for in niches on the front were the figures of Solon and King Alfred, and in the attic were medallion portraits of John Locke, Solon and Matthew Hale.[8]

The building measured 134 ft wide and 76 ft deep. On the ground floor, symmetrically arranged around the entrance lobby and staircase, were (by 1849) committee rooms, rooms for the Chief Constable and the police, for the Land Surveyor and his assistants, for the Inspectors of Weights and Nuisances, the Treasurer, clerks and a Gas Office. The first-floor central assembly rooms – a series of three interlocked rooms, measuring 130 ft by 38 ft – took up almost half the floor and were decorated in the Ionic style. The central dome, which was raised on a drum, was supported by segmental arches and a barrel vault. The vault was painted by Augustine Aglio, and showed more recent events from England's history – Britannia overthrowing Napoleon, Lord McCartney meeting the Emperor of China, an Egyptian offering the Nile to England. And the building was not cheap; the cost of building (to June 1825) was £28,035, and finishing the large assembly room alone cost £5,012. The total outlay, including the land, was £39,547. The building was demolished in 1912, but after pressure from local architects, including Edgar Wood, the central façade was removed to Heaton Park, where it can still be seen. Heathcote's Lloyd's Bank now occupies the site.

The Town Hall was finished well in time for the important constitutional changes which were to affect Manchester. In 1829 an Act remodelled the town's constitution and provided for separate police commissioners from Salford. The Reform Act of 1832 gave Manchester its first two MPs (and Salford one).* On 12 December 1832 the first parliamentary candidates appeared at the hustings in St Ann's Square. Mark Philips (2,932 votes) and Charles Poulett Thomson (2,068 votes) were elected by the 9,688 voters.

The most significant change came with the Municipal Reform Act of 1835 which provided for the election of borough councillors and borough magistrates if sufficient local support could be shown. Following a campaign by Richard Cobden, a petition signed by 15,000 people was submitted to the Privy Council in March 1838, and on 1 November 1838 a charter was received constituting Manchester as a municipal borough of just over 4,300 acres, including Chorlton-on-Medlock, Hulme, Ardwick, Beswick and Cheetham. The borough

---

* Actually, the first MPs were returned in the seventeenth century, when Oliver Cromwell required the burgesses of Manchester to return a member to Parliament; Charles Worsley was returned on 19 July 1654 and Richard Ratcliffe on 12 August 1656. With the Restoration of the monarchy the franchise was withdrawn from Manchester.

was to be run by a mayor, sixteen aldermen, forty-eight councillors and thirty-one borough magistrates. The election of councillors, by a constituency of 11,995 voters, took place on 14 December and the first meeting of the Council took place the following day. Thomas Potter was appointed mayor and Joseph Heron, attorney, was appointed town clerk.

Strong opposition came from three existing bodies: the Police Commissioners, who collected the Police Rate; the Overseers and Churchwardens, who collected the Poor Rate; and the Surveyor of Highways, who collected the Road and Bridge Rates. Because the Act did not refer to the transfer of power, the old collectors of rates continued to collect them and ignored the new administration. The county magistrates (generally from the older landowning classes) also objected to the new borough magistrates (who were generally merchants). The New Bailey prison refused to accept prisoners committed by the borough magistrates unless they were also county magistrates. The new Council was even barred from using the new Town Hall, and conducted its meetings in the York Hotel, next door, on King Street. It was not until 1842 that the Borough Charters Incorporation Act confirmed the powers of the new mayor and council. In 1845 the Corporation purchased the lordship of the manor and the Court Leet from Sir Oswald Mosley,* and the power of the burgesses came to an end. On 29 March 1853 Queen Victoria conferred the title of city on Manchester by royal charter, and fifty years later, in 1893, the title of Lord Mayor was created by charter.

In 1825 Salford commenced building its own Town Hall and Assembly Rooms (its incorporation did not take place until 1844), designed in the Classical style by Richard Lane, a local architect. Of Lane's early life or training little is known, though he was admitted to the Ecole des Beaux Arts at Paris in 1817 as a pupil of the French architect A. Leclerè,[9] and was in practice in Manchester from 1821, when he was made Land Surveyor to the Police Commissioners. He was one of only nine architects in Manchester and Salford listed in Baines's *Lancashire* of 1825, and of the other eight little is known.[10]

In 1830 the Police Commissioners of the township of Chorlton Row, who were responsible for the administration of the area, asked Lane to design a town hall for them, for they too needed a more appropriate base for their duties. Industry was flourishing on the banks of the Medlock and workers were flocking to live in the area. Chorlton was typical of the tremendous growth of population around the edges of Manchester in the early years of the nineteenth century, but the scale of the increase in population is hard to conceive: in 1801, according to the census returns, Chorlton's population was only 675, but by 1831 it had grown to 20,569, and by 1851 to 35,558.

Lane's building, which commenced on 13 October 1830, and was finished precisely one year and one day later [14], housed not only the Police Commissioners

---

* In 1808 Oswald Mosley had proposed to sell the manor of Manchester to its inhabitants for £90,000 but failed when only £70,000 was offered. On 24 March 1845 the Town Council resolved to purchase the manorial rights from Sir Oswald Mosley for the sum of £200,000, of which £50,000 was to be paid as a deposit, with repayments at between £4,000 and 6,000 per year.

but also the Poor Law Guardians. Also included was a large meeting room, and on the right-hand side of the building were rooms for the Chorlton Row Dispensary, which had been established in 1825 during an outbreak of fever in the township. Only the façade is left: nine bays of ashlar stone separated by plain Doric pilasters and a portico of four fluted Doric columns supporting a pediment, with triumphal wreaths on the entablature as its only decoration.

On 23 June 1832 an Act was passed, for 'improving and regulating' the township of Chorlton Row, the new township hereafter to be known as Chorlton-on-Medlock. Chorlton was lighted by gas on 27 July 1833. In 1838 the township was transferred to Manchester Borough Council. The dispensary part of the building was eventually sold to the city for use by the School of Art, and in the 1970s the building behind the façade was demolished. Behind the façade are new buildings belonging to the Metropolitan University.

Richard Lane was one of Manchester's most prolific architects in the 1820s and 1830s. His is the Friends' Meeting House, Mount Street, of 1828–30 [15]. Externally there is an elegant Ionic portico and internally a gallery is supported by cast-iron Doric columns. Before the alterations of 1923 the room could be divided by sliding partitions which were raised by machinery, half the partition sliding up into the ceiling, the other half down into the floor. Among the congregation were Dr John Dalton, John Edward Taylor, founder of the *Manchester Guardian*, Thomas Hoyle, calico printer, the architect Alfred Waterhouse and George Bradshaw, originator of the railway guide and uncle of the architect Alfred Darbyshire.

14] Chorlton-on-Medlock Town Hall, All Saints, Richard Lane, 1830–31

The Gentlemen's Concert Hall on Lower Mosley Street was also by Richard Lane, 1831: a brick building with a stone front of six giant-order Corinthian columns carrying an entablature and pediment. Membership was limited to 600, and an annual subscription of £5. It was here that Mendelssohn visited as guest conductor in 1847 for a performance of *Elijah*, and Chopin gave one of his last performances in 1848. In 1897 the site was sold for building the Midland Hotel, which was obliged to include a theatre to replace the demolished Concert Hall.

In 1835 the Infirmary was refaced by Lane, thanks to a piece of posthumous philanthropy. At the top of King Street, occupying the space now partially bounded by Brown Street and Chancery Lane, was a handsome private house with a large garden containing six or eight tall trees in which rooks built their nests. Among the last residents was the Hall family, strong supporters of the Stuarts, whom Prince Charles Edward visited on his southward march in November 1745. The youngest daughter, Frances Hall, died on 4 June 1828 aged eighty-four, and in her will she bequeathed £44,000 to local charities, part of which went to the Infirmary to defray the whole cost of casing the structure in stone and adding a portico of four fluted Ionic columns. The portico, erected in 1832 and subsequently enlarged, was similar to that of the Friends' Meeting House. At the same time the Asylum was given a Doric portico, similar to the one on Stockport Infirmary, which had also been designed by Lane in 1832.

By the 1830s Lane had become Manchester's leading architect, and became the first President of the Manchester Architectural Society in 1837. He designed

15] Friends' Meeting House, Mount Street, Richard Lane, 1828–30

the Corn Exchange on Hanging Ditch (1835–37, demolished and replaced), and the Union Club, Mosley Street (1836, demolished). These were in the Classical style, and although Lane designed some buildings, especially churches, in the Gothic style (for example, St George, Chester Road, 1826, and St Thomas, Pendleton, 1829–31, both designed in partnership with Francis Goodwin), his one secular Gothic building in Manchester, the Deaf and Dumb School and Blind Asylum (Henshaw's Institute), Old Trafford, of 1836–37, was something of a curiosity, with tall turrets marking the corners – picturesque but with little sense of historical accuracy.[11]

However, Lane will be best remembered for his restrained and not inelegant Classical buildings. Alfred Darbyshire said of him, 'His practice was almost exclusively devoted to an attempt to force upon a commercial nineteenth-century town, with a sunless and humid climate, the refinement and perfect beauty of the art of the Greeks in the golden age of Pericles.'[12] Lane, himself, however, in his first presidential address to the Manchester Society of Architects in 1837, said that Manchester 'afforded little scope or encouragement for architectural display'.[13]

Yet, in that very year, the sculptural decorations of the Royal Manchester Institution (the RMI) were being completed, and as the *Builder* was later to remark, perhaps with Lane's buildings in mind, 'Mr Barry's Royal Institution was at this time a building calculated to set the architects of Manchester thinking for themselves. Scarcely any of its details were to be found in "Stuart's Athens", and yet the building is more completely Greek than many others claiming to be so.'[14] But, of course, Barry had actually been to Greece in 1817 with Charles Locke Eastlake, and had seen the buildings first-hand – his was no mere copybook architecture.

The Manchester Institution had been founded on 1 October 1823 following an initiative by the Associated Society of Artists of Manchester to form an institution to promote the fine arts and to establish an annual exhibition of the works of living artists. The artists' concept had been hi-jacked by local businessmen, who purchased for the purposes of the institution, at £5,750, properties at the junctions of King Street, Brown Street and Spring Gardens (where the Reform Club was later built). Shares in the properties were offered at £50 each, hereditary governorships of the institution were offered at forty guineas, life governorships at twenty-five guineas and annual governorships at two guineas. By December £11,000 had been raised. When King George IV graciously conferred the title 'Royal' on the institution over £20,000 had been raised and the committee resolved to erect a more worthy building. Dr William Henry, a chemist and friend of John Dalton, was persuaded to sell his property and substantial grounds on the corner of Mosley Street and Bond (now Princess) Street for £3,225. The original premises on King Street were sold to defray some of the cost.[15]

On 26 April 1824 six architects were invited to submit designs for a building 'combining ample interior accommodation and chaste Architectural design'. Only four designs were submitted, including one from Francis Goodwin, the architect of the Town Hall. Two of the invited architects, Robert Smirke (the

6] Royal Manchester Institution
(City Art Gallery), Mosley Street,
Charles Barry, 1829–35

architect of St Philip, Salford) and Thomas Harrison (who had built the Portico Library), declined on the grounds that the cost for such a building was too low at £15,000. Although all the entrants to the competition submitted their schemes under mottoes to ensure anonymity, there is some evidence that the London architect Charles Barry, already known to Manchester for his building of All Saints, Stand, Prestwich (1822–25), and St Matthew's, Campfield (1823, demolished 1951), had an early hand in the deliberations of the committee. A letter in the RMI collection, dated 15 April 1824, says, 'I should recommend them [the committee] to apply to about 4 or 5 architects of talent and reputation but whose occupations are not of such an extensive nature as to make them indifferent to success, which will be the case with most of the persons named.'[16]

Barry's own scheme, submitted under the motto 'Nihil pulchrum nisi utile' (Beauty is nothing without utility), was chosen and the foundations of the building were started on 27 April 1827. Here is a building rather different from Harrison's or Goodwin's or Lane's [16]. In Barry's building the deep portico is carried on six plain Ionic columns, and, as if to emphasise its depth, the three bays on either side are set back and fronted by a pair of Ionic columns in antis. The end three bays break forward and their corners are visually strengthened by Doric pilasters. (In Barry's original drawing, and in the model, the windows of these bays are also each flanked by pilasters.) The beautiful wooden model made by George Strutt in 1825 shows some variations from the executed building: fewer pilasters on the front wings, lowering of the height of the hall, a 12 in. increase in the height of the parapet to conceal the roof lights, steps added in front of the portico and the columns consequently raised on bases.

The shell of the building was completed by October 1829, from which time annual art exhibitions were held, and the building was virtually finished inside and out by 1835, although the sculptural decoration on the front, by John Henning Jnr, was not completed until 1837. Sandstone from Catlow, near Colne, was used first, but it ran out and was followed by a slightly inferior stone from Saltersford, which also ran out. Finally the building was completed with a sandstone from Leeds. Subsequent variable decay has meant much patching.

Not only had almost all the Institution's funds been expended on the land, the building and its decoration – in all, about £32,000 – but its annual income equalled its expenditure, and little was left to carry out the original intention of enriching the interior with works of art. But what the building did was 'reflect on the public spirit and good taste of the founders, and be considered more accordant with the wealth and consequence of the town of Manchester'.[17]

Gifts were presented to the Institution: a mummy from Peru; a mammoth's tooth from Bognor Regis; casts of classical figures by various artists and, most important, Westmacott's casts of the Elgin marbles, presented by George IV in 1830. These casts are mounted high on the walls of the entrance hall. Internally, arranged around the central staircase, there were exhibition and meeting rooms, and a semicircular lecture room with tiered seats which ran through two floors. This room was subsequently converted into display galleries; only its doorway is left, and can be seen behind the clock at the top of the staircase.

The Institution needed to raise rent, so space was let out to the Choral, Madrigal, Medical and Geological Societies, and, until their own building was erected some nine years later, to the Athenaeum Society. By 1838 a School of Design had been founded in Manchester and was using the library, the secretary's room and some basement rooms. On 24 June 1881 the School of Art, as it had become, moved to Redmayne's purpose-built structure in All Saints.[18]

In the autumn of 1882 the RMI was transferred to Manchester Corporation on the condition that the sum of £4,000 per annum was spent over the next twenty years to acquire works of art. In 1892 the Corporation decided to convert the two magnificent colonnaded sculpture galleries into rooms suitable for hanging paintings, in spite of strong objections. With the sort of objective, aesthetic sense so often displayed by some Manchester councillors over the years, Alderman Hopkinson described the galleries as 'only a sort of tunnel'. The *Manchester Guardian* wrote on 14 April 1892, 'We have every respect for individual judgement, but if Mr. Alderman Hopkinson were to rise in Council and say conscientiously that the large Turner now in the permanent collection "was in his view a sort of daub" could he reasonably expect us all to be glad of its removal? He calls Sir Charles Barry's work a tunnel and proposes that the City Surveyor shall make us something better.'

The building continued to be overcrowded, and, until the Corporation purchased the Athenaeum in the 1930s as an extension of the gallery, it was long intended to create a new gallery in Piccadilly Gardens on the site of the old Infirmary.

In 1836 Barry was back in Manchester, designing the Unitarian chapel in Upper Brook Street (1836–39)[19] and the Athenaeum in Bond (now Princess) Street for 'an institution for literary, political and scientific uses, by a number of gentlemen who felt a desire to bring together in such a Club the class of superior mercantile servants and young men. The subscription of 30s per annum, which admits to the news-room, the library, lectures, etc.'[20] Its cost of £18,000 had been raised by a public sale of shares of £15,000 (£10,000 was raised in three weeks), and by a mortgage for the remainder.

The Athenaeum took a similar form to the Travellers' Club in London, which had been designed by Barry in 1829. The style of both buildings was based not on ancient Greece but, influenced perhaps by Sir William Chambers's *A Treatise on Civil Architecture* of 1791, on the palaces of Rome and Florence of the late fifteenth and sixteenth centuries. These '*palazzi*' were large buildings, built throughout in stone, generally around a central colonnaded courtyard, and, with few exceptions, such as the Palazzo Rucellai in Florence and the Cancelleria in Rome, without reference to the Classical orders. The ground floor was used for entrances and storage, and the more decorated first floor, the *piano nobile*, was where the major members of the family lived and carried out their business. The upper floors were for lesser members of the family, and tucked beneath the overhanging cornices – necessary to shade the walls from the noonday sun – were rooms for the servants.[21]

The foundation stone of the Athenaeum was laid in May 1837, and the building was opened on 28 October 1839. Internally the building was quite unlike its Renaissance predecessors, and much closer in its construction to the mills of the time, with load-bearing brick walls and cast-iron columns supporting floor beams. Inside was a large reading room taking up the width of the ground floor and enclosing a smaller library. Above were the lecture theatre, accessed by stairs from George Street, and smaller meeting and dining rooms. It is only in its external appearance that the building pays heed to its antecedents [17]. Here is a stone-clad brick building of nine bays, with tall, square-headed windows on the ground floor, and pedimented windows with low stone balconies on the *piano nobile*. (In an early design there are small rectangular windows under the cornice.) The entrance has a Doric portico reminiscent of Domenico Fontana's porch to the Palazzo della Cancelleria in Rome, and the cornice and the inscribed frieze are like that on Raphael's Palazzo Pandolfini, Florence. In its scale, elevation and use of pedimented first-storey windows it is like Biagio Rossetti's Palazzo dei Diamante, Ferrara, but without that building's faceted stone-cutting.[22]

The ugly balustrade and raised roof over the cornice were added following a fire on 24 September 1873 which nearly burnt the building to the ground and caused damage to the tune of £12,000. Barry's Reform Club, in Pall Mall, London, of 1837–40, shows what the Athenaeum would have looked like before the later roof was added. The membership was 2,000, which, significantly, included Richard Cobden and Robert Owen; Nathaniel Heywood was the first president, Hugh Birley, the cotton spinner, one of the vice-presidents, and J. S. Grafton, calico printer, was chairman. Dickens presided over the first annual *soirée* in 1843, at which Disraeli was one of the speakers.[23]

Manchester was now possessed of a building with which its merchant princes could feel proud to be associated – the equal of anything similar in the metropolis, and designed by the architect of the new Houses of Parliament, for Barry had received that most prestigious commission in the same year the

Athenaeum was commenced. But the real importance of the Athenaeum was as the prototype of a new architectural style which was to form the basis of virtually all commercial buildings in Manchester for the rest of the century. And it was a fortuitous meeting in, of all places, Constantinople, between a member of the Athenaeum and a young London architect, that paved the way.

Richard Cobden, merchant, MP for Stockport, Anti-Corn Law campaigner and the 'Apostle of Free Trade', had gone east ostensibly for the sake of his health, but also to learn the secrets of producing a colour called 'Turkish red'. Whilst staying in Constantinople in 1835 he met, probably in the Ottoman Club, the architect Edward Walters, who was supervising the construction of a small-arms factory for Sir John Rennie.[24] By 1839 Walters had arrived in Manchester, probably at the behest of Cobden, and was designing a warehouse for him – Harvest House at 16 Mosley Street, near the corner of Marble Street.

17] Athenaeum, Princess Street, Charles Barry, 1836–39

Walters stayed for the rest of his working life in Manchester, working from 20 Cooper Street until his retirement in the mid-1860s.[25] He died of pleurisy on 22 January 1872 in Brighton, age sixty-four.

In Cobden's Harvest House can be seen the beginnings of the Italian or *palazzo* style, a version of Barry's club house modified for commercial purposes [18]. This is a brick building, the severe functionality of which is relieved by the stone detailing, on the quoins which mark out, and visually strengthen, the end bays, in the window arches and keystones of the ground and second floors, in the cornice and in the string courses which disguise the height of the ground floor. The floor above the cornice is a later addition. The interior was completely demolished and rebuilt in the early 1990s, and the ground floor, which had been converted to shops in the 1950s, has been restored.

In 1845 Walters designed a warehouse for S. Schwabe at 46–54 Mosley Street, in red brick, of fifteen bays with five portals, (subsequently replaced by the large sandstone Williams Deacon's bank building in the 1970s). These buildings were arguably the first town-based warehouses designed by an architect.[26] Structurally they follow the form of earlier warehouses, with cast-iron columns supporting iron or wooden beams on which wooden floors were laid [19, 20]. The walls were still load-bearing, and the windows were made as large as the load-bearing walls could take, for it was important to get as much light into the warehouse as possible. Basements, or more usually semi-basements, contained machinery for compressing bales of cloth; the other floors were given over to inspection, sorting and packing. The offices of the owner, clerical workers and counting houses were almost invariably set on the first or second floor, never on the ground floor,[27] and there is logic in this, for the owner would want to be away from the din of the cobbled streets. But it was also an aesthetic consideration – for if the Italian merchant owners of the *palazzi* had their *piano nobile* on an upper storey, then their imitators, the 'merchant princes' of the nineteenth century, would do the same. In Harvest House the *piano nobile*, for the offices of Richard Cobden, is marked by the embellished second storey.

The *Builder* occasionally carried descriptions of Manchester warehouses, and it is worth examining two of these, Collie & Co.'s and Sam Mendel's, in a little more detail, for they are revealing of the way the warehouse worked. On Aytoun Street in 1867 Alexander W. Mills (1812–1905) and James Murgatroyd (1830–94) built a warehouse for A. Collie & Co., on the site of the old House of Recovery. Mills had been a pupil of Bunning in London and moved to Manchester to work for Richard Tattersall. Bunning in 1838 suggested they become partners, and Mills stayed to look after the Manchester office. When Bunning retired in 1853, Mills took his pupil Murgatroyd into partnership. Edgar Wood was their pupil from 1880 to 1885.

The warehouse is faced with Darley Dale stone, and the principal doorway cased with red granite. At the rear elevation was a loophole the whole height of the building, with loading doors on to it on each floor and covered at the top with glass. The centre of the warehouse was lit by a light well 30 ft long and 20 ft wide pierced through at each floor. The lower cellar contained steam machinery and boilers. The upper cellar had hydraulic presses arranged round

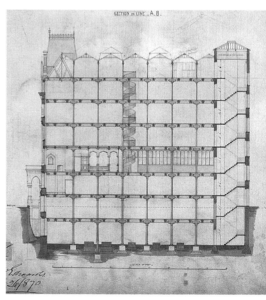

18] Harvest House, Mosley Street
Edward Walters, 1839

19] Worthington's elevation
drawing for the Reiss Bros
Warehouse, Quay Street,
dated 1870

20] Section through the
Reiss Bros warehouse

the sides of the packing room. On each floor were arranged the counting houses of the different departments. The principal floor was about 17 ft above street level and contained, in addition to the warerooms, the chief counting house and private offices. '5,000,000 pieces, equal to 100,000 bales, weighing 16,000 tons, can easily be prepared and disposed of to different parts of the world in one year. The length of this number of pieces would be upwards of 200,000,000 yards, or equal to more than four times the circumference of the globe. The floors of necessity have to be constructed with great strength, being weighted frequently up to about 2½ cwt. to the square foot of flooring.'[28] This building was converted into the Grand Hotel in 1880 and subsequently, in 1998, into apartments.

Samuel Mendel's Warehouse, Chepstow Street, 1874, was designed and partially built by Speakman & Charlesworth, and completed by their successors, Speakman Son & Hickson.[29] John Charlesworth (1832–71) had been a pupil of Isaac Holden, and then entered the office of Speakman from 1852, becoming his partner in 1862. After the death of Charlesworth in 1871, Speakman went into partnership with his son and Hickson. This brick building with stone dressings has three storeys above a semi-basement, on a frontage of 304 ft. In the roof space were a further floor, lit by dormer windows, and gabled windows at the corners [21]. On each floor, cast-iron columns, 7 ft apart, carried the floor beams and on them were laid the flooring of 11 in. by 3 in. planks, tongued and grooved with hoop iron.

The semi-basement floor was chiefly for packing and making up goods, the packing being done by fourteen hydraulic presses, and under this floor ran a portion of the river Tib which had to be diverted. The engine and boilerhouse were under the loading way at the Chepstow Street end, the chimney rising from the back of the building. The engines, boilers and presses were supplied by Nasmyth Wilson & Co. of Patricroft. The ground floor was for general warehousing, and above it was the principal floor of the building. Here a 7 ft wide corridor, which ran the whole length of the rear of the building, served the offices and the sample room. A further corridor ran along the right-hand side of the building serving the long pattern room and the Entering Clerk's office. Stone stairs at each end of the corridor gave access to all floors. Bounded by the corridors was a warehouse space, with a counter which ran under the windows along the Chepstow Street length of the building. On the left-hand side of the wide corridor, taking up the Great Bridgewater Street end of the first floor, was a general office containing a huge safe. The upper floors were used for warehousing, and on the top floor were a kitchen and dining room for the use of the clerks, though not, presumably, for the other, more menial, workers. Three large hoists ran from the basement to the top floor. Each floor had lavatory and w.c. provision, and heating was by large coils on each floor, heated by boiler in the basement. The total warehousing space was 2,400 square yards, and the cost, excuding site and machinery, was £40,000.

Exceptionally in this building a grand 10 ft wide principal staircase, handsomely arcaded on either side in stone, led from the front entrance to the first floor. At the top of the stairs, on the first floor, was a waiting room and a 14 ft wide corridor leading to a suite of offices at the back of the building and directly to Sam Mendel's large, public office – he had a separate smaller, private office with a w.c. and wash basin farther along the floor. The flooring of the corridor, as of the stairs, was covered with 6 lb lead with french-polished margins of pitch pine. On either side were moulded and panelled pitch pine screens, filled in with chequered and plain plate glass. A hundred and fifteen years later the warehouse was converted by Beazer Homes into Chepstow House, and its interior transformed into seventy-six one or two-bedroom flats.

These later warehouses were variants of the style introduced by Walters, and the originality of his work cannot be overestimated. It may well have been Cobden, who, knowing the Athenaeum, saw the potential of a new building type. Nevertheless, in Walters he had just the architect to develop this novel built form. Walters's early training was in the Classical style, he having been a pupil of Isaac Clarke and an assistant of Lewis Vulliamy, but he had also worked for Thomas Cubitt, perhaps the greatest property developer of the nineteenth century,[30] and that may well have sharpened his commercial acumen.

21] Chepstow House (Mendel's Warehouse), Chepstow Street, Speakman & Charlesworth, 1874

The *Builder*, even by 1847, was singing the praises of Manchester buildings: 'For the proof that warehouses may be designed of a character in accordance with their purpose, and yet without any absence of the graces of art, we need not now point exclusively to the commercial cities of Italy. It has been manifested in Manchester, that a town where large warehouses are constantly being commenced, is indeed in a favourable position for acquiring an appearance of elegance in its "street architecture".'[31]

By 1849 the *Builder* was illustrating parts of Italian palaces as 'Hints for Street Architecture', giving examples of cornices and the windows of the Palazzo della Consultà, Rome, and of the palace on the Lungo l'Aroro, Pisa.[32] Whether this influenced Walters or was picking up what was going on in Manchester is arguable. Walters had seen Italian buildings at first hand when he returned from Constantinople in August 1837, in the company of the engineer W. H. Barlow.[33] They returned to England via Malta, Rome, Florence, Pisa, Leghorn and France, arriving in England in January 1838.

Walters designed more than fifteen warehouses as well as a number of villas for his merchant clients, and the *Builder* noted in his obituary in 1872 that he was 'An architect who during a professional practice of about thirty years in the City of Manchester and its neighbourhood produced a series of important and most original works, which have imparted a marked character of dignity and picturesque effect to what was before an uninteresting, although an important, provincial city.'[34]

The *Manchester Critic* carried an obituary of Walters on 16 December 1871 and wrote, 'we well remember the surprise and wonder excited by, we think, his first great warehouse, the one built for Messrs Brown & Co., at the corner of Aytoun-street and Portland-street: the style was new; there was a freshness and purity about it which quickly took hold of men's minds, and the building of Italian warehouses became almost a rage.'

This was not his first warehouse, of course, for the style had already been rehearsed in Mosley Street, Charlotte Street [22, 23] and elsewhere, but it certainly was his first great one, for the Portland Street warehouses have a scale and quality which mark them out. It was undoubtedly the proximity of Portland Street to London Road Station which provided the impetus for such lavish buildings, for it was the line from Euston that brought important clients up from London, and in the 1850s Portland Street was being extended to Oxford Street, the David Street cotton mill, the huge Globe Iron Works and the Oxford Street Saw Mills being removed to make way for the new street.

Towards 1835 Messrs A. & S. Henry had erected warehouses at 32 Portland Street, but the rest of the road at that time, apart from a couple of silk mills, comprised only small buildings for grocers, plumbers, upholsterers, fishmongers and beer retailers. The building of Brown's warehouse at No. 9 changed not only the scale of the street but also the scale of the city, and undoubtedly demonstrated that Manchester merchants were now making enough profit to erect such profusely decorated buildings. Here were pride and wealth displayed; Manchester merchants were, in the main, self-made men with no gentlemanly forebears, no handed-down country estates, and they were gentrified through their homes and, most important, from Walters's time, through their 'palaces' of commerce.

The warehouse for James Brown & Son, built between 1851 and 1852, on the corner of Aytoun Street, is a handsome building of York stone [24]. It has only four storeys, and above the tall rusticated ground-floor arches which enclose the semi-basement the three upper storeys are each 11 ft high, providing a good scalar relationship in the 62 ft high building. The *piano nobile* is on the second floor, and is marked by segmental-pedimented windows. There is great richness in the deep sculptural decoration, and it has been argued that this is because the Portland Street façade faces north-west and would receive very little light in dimly lit Victorian Manchester. However, the south-facing Aytoun Street elevation is as ornately carved, and even for a Walters building this one is extravagantly decorated, so we must assume that here, more importantly, is a visible demonstration of the patron's wealth – a building to outdo all others being built in the city.

Next to Brown's warehouse, at No. 7 Portland Street, Walters built the Kershaw Leese & Sidebottom warehouse in 1852. Taller than No. 9, the building was of stone and of five (now six) storeys rising over a semi-basement with a minor cornice acting as a window sill for the fourth-storey windows, and with a deeper cornice over the fifth storey. The *piano nobile* is marked out at first-floor level by pedimented windows. The sixth storey and dormered roof, both later additions, make the building loom over its neighbours far more than originally intended. At Nos 3–5 Portland Street is the last of Walters's warehouses in this group, the E. & J. Jackson warehouse of 1858, like Brown's warehouse, of four storeys and stone-clad.[35] There is a much greater sense of assurance in this building; the ratio of window to wall, the heights of windows

22] William Scott Warehouse, 34 Charlotte Street, Edward Walters, 1855

] Charlotte House, 12 Charlotte
Street, Edward Walters, 1860

24] Warehouses by Walters,
Portland Street

in relation to the height of the building, the elegance of the ground-floor
'arcaded' openings all give a sense of quiet majesty and suggest that Walters
had learned much from building the Free Trade Hall, the building which symbolised so much of Manchester's political aspirations.

Free trade was a cry against the Corn Law which, in 1815, was enacted to
protect British farmers and landowners by prohibiting the import of grain until
domestic prices had risen above 80 s per quarter, thus ensuring artificially high
prices. The Manchester Anti-Corn Law League was formed in 1838, becoming
the Anti-Corn Law League in 1839, and the league was long associated with
Manchester in spite of moving its headquarters to London. '"The League is
Manchester," Cobden once wrote, and both his Tory opponents and his radical
rivals agreed with his judgement.'[36] By 1846 'the Anti-Corn Law League was
the most powerful national pressure group England had known, and upon their
techniques of mass meetings, travelling orators, hymns and catechisms a good
deal of later Victorian revivalist and temperance – and even trade union –
oratory was based.'[37] The Corn Laws were finally repealed in 1846 by Robert
Peel's government.

The first Free Trade Hall was a wooden structure on St Peter's Field on a
plot given by Richard Cobden to supporters of the Anti-Corn Law League,
and about 4,000 people attended a banquet on its opening on 13 January 1840.
In 1843 a brick building, 136 ft by 103 ft, replaced the wooden one. On
31 January 1849 a great banquet was held to mark the final repeal of the Corn
Laws (the implementation of the Act of 1846 had been delayed for three years
for financial reasons), and in 1853 Walters was commissioned by Richard
Cobden, one of the leaders of the league, to commemorate the victory with a
stone-clad building [25].

The building was based not, as has been so often suggested, on Palladio's
Basilica at Vicenza but more likely, as Stewart suggests in his *Stones of*

Manchester, on the Gran Guardia Vecchia at Verona, which has a similar ground-storey arcade, though rusticated rather than ashlar, and tall coupled columns at the first floor carrying round-headed arches with pedimented windows between. Stewart says (*Stones*, p. 40) that Walters sketched this building on his return to England in 1837, though, according to his obituary, he did not visit north-east Italy, and very few of his drawings exist, since in later years he was in the habit of destroying his early work whenever he stumbled across it. The deeply articulated sandstone façade has sculptural decoration by John Thomas: the lower reliefs, in the spandrels of the ground-floor arcade, are the badges of the towns associated with the free-trade movement. In the tympani of the upper arches are figures representing Free Trade, flanked by Arts, Commerce, Manufactures, Agriculture and the four Continents. Here is a solemn, but not sombre, building whose deep reveals and rich decoration give it great visual strength, and it is the most Italianate building in the city. The Free Trade Hall is probably the only assembly hall in the country to be named after a concept. It was, of course, expensive (at £40,000) and sumptuous, as befitted its function, and unarguably was Walters's finest building. Appropriately adding to its symbolism, the hall was built on the site of the 1819 massacre of Peterloo.[38]

Dickens, Disraeli, Gladstone, Lloyd George, Winston Churchill and Christabel Pankhurst have all spoken from its stage, but it was for its association with the Hallé Orchestra that the Free Trade Hall became most famous. In 1848 the twenty-nine-year-old pianist Charles Hallé was invited to Manchester by Hermann Leo, a calico printer and a director of the Gentlemen's Concert Orchestra, but Hallé, after hearing the orchestra, seriously considered leaving: 'The orchestra, oh, the orchestra! I was fresh from the Concerts du Conservatoire, from Hector Berlioz's orchestra, and I seriously thought of packing up and leaving Manchester so I might not have to endure a second of these wretched performances. But when I hinted at this, my friends gave me to understand that I was expected to change all this – to accomplish

25] Free Trade Hall, Peter Street
Edward Walters, 1853

a revolution, in fact.'[39] And he did accomplish the revolution, continuing as a soloist, and then conductor, bringing in new talent and more disciplined rehearsals.

For the Art Treasures Exhibition in 1857 Hallé was invited to form a fifty-piece orchestra to perform daily in the building at Old Trafford. When the exhibition closed, Hallé engaged the orchestra at his own risk to provide a weekly series of concerts. From January 1858 the Hallé Orchestra performed at the Free Trade Hall, and here the first English performances of Elgar's First Symphony and Berlioz's *Damnation of Faust* and *Symphonie fantastique* were performed. Hallé also helped to establish the Manchester College of Music, which eventually became the Royal Northern College of Music.[40] In 1888 he was knighted for his services to music, and his orchestra was to be conducted by, among others, Sir Thomas Beecham during the 1914–18 war and Sir John Barbirolli for over twenty-five years, from 1943 to 1970. The Hallé is Britain's oldest orchestra and the fourth oldest in the world.[41]

It may seem remarkable that it was Manchester and not London which staged the Art Treasures Exhibition of 1857, the first ever national exhibition of works of art. But north-western patrons had for some time been buying the works of living artists from Agnew and other dealers, and, as Sir Austen Layard pointed out, 'As enlightened and liberal patrons of art they had long been honourably known . . . In their dwellings . . . many of the finest pictures which annually adorn the walls of the Royal Academy find a resting place.'[42] Thomas Fairbairn,[43] son of William Fairbairn, had been a commissioner of the Great Exhibition of 1851, and to him it was suggested that a collection of the art treasures of Great Britain could be brought to view under one roof. Under his guidance a committee of influential Manchester businessmen was formed, the Queen was successfully solicited for her patronage, the Earl of Ellesmere, Lord Lieutenant of Lancashire, was appointed president of the council, the mayor, James Watts, was elected chairman, and J. C. Deane, whose original idea the exhibition was, was appointed general commissioner.

Thomas Fairbairn was given the job of finding a suitable architect, and designs were invited for a building of 15,000 square yards which could be erected in six months at a cost less than £25,000. Twenty-five designs were received, five were shortlisted, and the four unsuccessful designers were each given the princely sum of twenty guineas for their trouble. C. D. Young & Co., ironfounders, of Edinburgh, were awarded the contract for a cast-iron and glass building. The building was 656 ft long and 200 ft wide and comprised a central barrel-vaulted nave supported on cast-iron columns, with a 104 ft span, flanked with lower barrel-vaulted aisles, and crossed at 500 ft from the entrance by a vaulted transept. There were corrugated iron sides and only the upper three panels of the vaults were glazed. The interior had a lining of wood, covered with canvas and painted. The building was remarkably like Young's 'Brompton boilers', the early buildings of the new Museum of Science and Art in South Kensington,[44] but the Manchester scheme was fronted by an ornamental white and red brick building designed by Edward Salomon, architect to the committee.

The exhibition building was erected next to the gardens of the Botanical Society at Old Trafford, and on the other side of the building a new railway station with a covered platform 800 ft long was created for its visitors. Works of art, of old masters, Italian and Flemish 'primitives', as well as of notable living painters, were collected from all over the country – even the Queen and Prince Albert loaned part of their collection, twenty-two from Buckingham Palace and seventeen from Windsor – and it was estimated that the exhibition housed at least a third of the country's art treasures. Prince Albert opened the exhibition on 5 May 1857, and stayed overnight at James Watts's residence, Abney Hall, near Cheadle, then furnished with some of the finest Pugin furniture north of London. On 29 June 1857 Queen Victoria attended the exhibition – her second visit to Manchester – dined with the nobility and knighted the mayor, James Watts. Over 1,300,000 visitors attended the exhibition before it closed on 17 October. It had been open 142 days, of which two, the opening day and the day of the Queen's visit, were reserved for two-guinea ticket holders. The total number of paying visitors was 1,053,538, and of ticket holders, 282,377, a total of 1,335,915. Receipts amounted to £98,500, expenditure £99,500, the deficit of £1,000 being offset by the sale of the building materials. Of the building and the event no trace, outside the literature, remains.[45] Manchester, it seems, simply went back to work, for, as John Cassell pointed out in 1858:

> The Art Treasures Palace . . . was, from the very nature of the undertaking, of an ephemeral character. The masterpieces of the great chiefs of the various schools . . . will, in all human probability, never again be united under the same roof. The risk of injury was too great, the expense of conveyance, and the anxiety which even the temporary removal of artistic treasures . . . occasioned their possessors, to whom nothing could compensate for their loss, were too serious to be again lightly incurred.[46]

Sir James Watts, together with his brother Samuel, was in process of building a warehouse on Portland Street, and if Walters's warehouses on Portland Street were lavish, then the S. & J. Watts Warehouse, by Henry Travis and William Mangnall (the architects of Abney Hall), 1855–58, outdid them in sheer scale.

William Mangnall (fl. 1855–82) was in partnership with Henry Travis in 1855, when they built the Watts Warehouse in Portland Street. In 1865 Mangnall was joined by John Littlewood (1829–1901) and in 1875 by his brother William Henry Littlewood (1838–1921), after which the firm practised as Mangnall & Littlewoods, and they were responsible for the Upper and Lower Campfield Markets as well as the Wholesale Fish Market on Shudehill, which opened on 3 June 1879, on an area of 2,000 square yards. (Only the trading hall remains as the Craft Centre.)

The Watts Warehouse is 100 ft high, 300 ft long and 90 ft deep [26]. There are eleven bays on Portland Street and seven bays on the Minshull and Chorlton Street façades. Each of its five storeys is in a different architectural style: above the rusticated, Italianate ground floor is a first floor in the Elizabethan style, the second floor is Italianate, the third floor French Renaissance and the fourth floor Italianate again. The building is topped, not by a cornice, but by a deep

26] Watts Warehouse, Portland Street, Travis & Mangnall, 1855–58. Just visible on the left, GMC County Hall, Fitzroy Robinson, 1974

frieze with strap-work decoration, once adorned with huge urns. Above the end bays, and above the entrance bays, are towers containing rose windows with thick bar tracery, reminiscent of French Gothic cathedrals.

The major façades are faced in Derbyshire stone, though the rear elevation is left in unadorned brick; but then, no clients, arriving in a Hansom cab from the station and setting down on Portland Street, would ever see the back of the building – Manchester's patrons were pragmatic people. The visitor would have been impressed by the decorated wrought-iron staircase which runs majestically through all the floors, a feature still worth visiting the building for. The statistics are staggering: 73,000 ft^3 (5,600 tons) of stone, 700 tons of iron, 40,000 ft^3 of timber, 27,000 ft^2 of glass, three acres of floors. The cost of the land was £29,000 and of the building and its materials £880,000. When finished it was by far the largest building in Manchester – a veritable cathedral of commerce. The S. & J. Watts company lasted until 1960, when it merged to become Cook & Watts, and in 1969 it was taken over by the Courtaulds Group.

Inside the original warehouse, 600 staff looked after finished goods: on the ground floor, hosiery, linens, carpets, flannels, whites, greys, fustians; on the first floor, merinos, dresses, woollens, ready-mades, dyed goods, Scotch and muslin and worsteds; on the second floor, umbrellas, trimmings, fancy haberdashery, bags, satchels, portmanteaus, small wares, stays and corsets, waterproof goods, table oil baizes, boots and shoes, gloves; on the third floor, ribbons, bandannas, silks, skirts and underclothing, mantles and costumes, prints and fancy flannels; on the fourth floor, flowers, millinery, lace, sewn muslins, furs and straws. In one room alone there was a stock of £40,000 worth of ribbons. The firm's trade list was 384 pages long.[47]

If the contents of the warehouse read like the contents of a department store it is hardly surprising, for John Watts of Didsbury had opened a draper's shop, 'The Bazaar', on Deansgate in 1796, as an outlet for ginghams hand-woven by his wife and six sons, and this has been identified as the rightful 'first department store' in the world.[48] John Watts was joined by his brothers James and Samuel and they removed to better premises in Brown Street, building up the largest wholesale drapery business in Manchester, before constructing their warehouse in Portland Street.

Three employees of the original Watts shop, Thomas Kendal from Westmorland and James Milne and Adam Faulkner, both of Manchester, bought the premises in 1836, and in 1862, on the death of Faulkner, the shop became Kendal Milne & Co. The original five-bay building was of two storeys over a double-fronted shop, with a central door flanked by display windows, typically for the time, of small panes set in glazing bars. Deansgate in those days was lined with drapers' shops, hosiers, corsetiers, hat and bonnet makers, shoe makers, spectacle makers, tailors and, of course, pubs, all of two or three storeys. To the left of Kendal Milne's was the shop and warehouse of Mr Gatenby, silk mercer; to the right after Hatters' Lane (now built over) were Lamb & Lea's shop and Royle & Co., hat makers.

27] Kendal Milne's, Deansgate, E. J. Thomson, 1873

28] Portland Buildings (Louis
Behrens & Sons Warehouse),
Oxford Street/Portland Street,
Phillip Nunn, 1860

The store was rebuilt in 1873 by E. J. Thomson in a thin Italianate style, but above the later shop fronts are some finely detailed Venetian openings [27]. Waterstone's, Manchester's largest bookshop, now occupy most of the building. Across the road were cabinet showrooms and workshops, replaced by Beaumont's building in 1938. By the end of the century Kendal Milne & Co. had a seven-storey cabinet factory behind the Deansgate store, an upholstery works in Back Bridge Street, a timber yard in Wood Street and a four-storey *palazzo*-style drapery and fashion house on the corner of St Ann's and Police Streets (demolished in the 1960s). Of particular interest is that the store stocked William Morris wallpapers and fabrics.

When the Watts Warehouse commenced building in 1855, Portland Street had only seven warehouses on the south-west side of the street, but by the time the Watts Warehouse was finished, in 1858, four more had been opened. The very end warehouse, at the junction with Oxford Street, is the plain and functional brick building of Louis Behrens & Sons, by P. Nunn, 1860 [28]. The building has only four storeys but is twenty-three bays long on Portland Street. The ground floor is stone-clad with a number of entry bays and office doorways. The upper storeys are of common red brick with stone detailing, and the first and second storeys are connected by brick piers with round-headed arches in stone. The corner with Oxford Street is turned with two similar bays, and the first four bays on Oxford Street repeat the motif. The last five bays on Oxford Street are framed in cast iron, possibly for Behrens's own offices, and behind this façade, in 1938, was the Koh-i-Nor restaurant, probably the first Indian restaurant in Manchester.

From the mid-1850s architect-designed warehouses were springing up all over the city centre, and by 1868 the *Builder* was moved to write: 'A new school of architects has sprung up, many of them young men; and it is greatly to the credit of the merchants of the town that they have had the judgement to use the services of architects, in buildings in which they are seldom applied to, and it is greatly to the credit of the architects that these appeals have been replied to by them almost universally in the best manner.'[49]

On the corner of Spring Gardens and Fountain Street was a brick and stone-dressed warehouse, built for Daniel Lee & Co. in 1856 by the young Edward Salomon (1828–1909). It had a most remarkable stone entrance, cut so hard and crisp as to make it look almost like cast iron, with columns literally immured in the frame of the entrance and carrying a 'monstrous curved pediment' without which, said the *Builder*, 'this would have been the handsomest warehouse in Manchester – and that is saying much for any structure'.[50] Salomon had been a pupil of J. E. Gregan, and then worked in the office of Bowman & Crowther, where he made drawings for their *Churches of the Middle Ages* (1845–53, in two volumes). By 1852 he was in practice on his own (from 1870 he worked in partnership at different times with John Philpot-Jones, Ralph Wornum, John Ely, Alfred Steinthal and Nathan Solomon Joseph), and the Lee warehouse was his first major commission. The building has been demolished, but on the

29] Manchester & Salford Trustee Savings Bank, Booth Street, Edward Salomons, 1872

30] Warehouse, 109 Princess Street, Clegg & Knowles, 1863

corner of Fountain Street and Booth Street is another warehouse dated 1868, probably by Salomons (the s had been added to his name by 1867[51]), this time in the Venetian Gothic style, with polychromatic arches in stone and brick, and grouped windows. A pretty building, but nowhere near as good in its details as his Prince's Chambers, 16 John Dalton Street, of 1865, the showrooms for Lamb's furniture manufactory.

Farther along Booth Street are two more Salomons buildings, the Manchester & Salford Bank of 1872 at No. 8 [29] and Massey Chambers of 1879 at No. 6. The bank has a curved pediment over its doorway, and the first storey has two-light windows contained within round-headed arches on which are carved heads. Massey Chambers, built for a solicitor, Jepson Thomas, also has carved heads in the spandrels of the first-storey windows and includes an unusual veiled head above the entrance.

Two more of the younger breed of architects were Charles Clegg and John Knowles. Charles Clegg was born in the same year as Salomons, and was articled to Edwin Hugh Shellard for five years. By 1851 Clegg was in independent practice, and in 1858 he was in partnership with John Knowles, about whom little else is known. In 1868 Clegg & Knowles had offices in Manchester and Blackpool, and from 1882 Clegg's son Charles Theodore Clegg was in partnership. Clegg & Knowles's warehouse of 1863 at 109 Princess Street [30] is a delightful little building of eight bays and four storeys over a semi-basement, and there is another of theirs at 101 Princess Street. In contrast, their earlier warehouse, the Pickles Building, for Hugh Balfour & Co. of 1858–63, on the corner of Princess Street and Portland Street (now the Princess Hotel, [31]) is another Italianate building but the details are in a debased Gothic, particularly evident in the quatrefoils and the stiff-leaf foliage of the window colonettes.

The *Builder* was not always complimentary to young Manchester architects, and there is evidence that by the late 1860s the *palazzo* style was already becoming *passé*. Having lavished praise on Commercial Chambers in Cross Street (Walters Barker & Ellis, 1867–68), the writer goes on to describe a warehouse in Peter Street:

> Opposite the Free Trade Hall is a large square block of Classicality just completed, with a ground storey of rusticated masonry, forming a series of circular-headed openings . . . Above the first-floor string there is nothing to praise. There are three storeys of windows of the most common and conventional classic type . . . If Messrs. Grey & Knowles, to whom persons wishing to rent these offices are referred, were the architects thereof, we cannot congratulate them.[52]

People have taken this article to refer to Clegg & Knowles, and to Harvester House, 37 Peter Street [32], built by them for the Ralli brothers in 1868 (a clue to its Clegg & Knowles origin can be seen in the right-hand ground-floor bay on Peter Street, where, anomalously in a classicising building, there are thin colonettes and pilasters with Gothic foliage). But the article in the *Builder* prompted a speedy and somewhat curt reply from Messrs Walters Barker & Ellis: 'We beg to inform you that we were the architects of the Commercial

Chambers and Stock Exchange, mentioned in your Art-Notes in Manchester; also of the warehouse in Peter Street.'[53] This warehouse, at 35 Peter Street, was built earlier that year, and was subsequently demolished and replaced by the extension of Petersfield House (Howitt & Tucker, 1965). The Grey & Knowles referred to by the *Builder* were indeed letting agents, not the architects.[54]

Hundreds of warehouse *palazzi* were built in Manchester, and dozens remain, despite the ravages of rebuilding in the twentieth century. Above the doors, as well as names like Hollins, Watts, Henry and Richardson, there were Hadji al Akbar, Kostoris, Phethean, Abramovitch, Piczenic, Rosenzweig, a Babel of nationalities. By the 1850s there were over 150 Greek merchants, living mostly in Kersal and Higher Broughton, and by 1860 a Greek Orthodox church had opened on Bury New Road. By 1880 there were thirty Armenian business-men in Manchester, and their little Gothic Revival church is still on Upper Brook Street. In the 1851 census 1,000 persons of German birth were recorded, and by 1870 there were about 150 German business houses in Manchester. The Schiller Anstalt (founded in 1859 to mark the anniversary of the death of the poet) had among its members Charles Hallé, Friedrich Engels, the manufac-turers Henry Gaddum and Salis Schwabe and the Behrens banking family. Salomons renovated the Anstalt building in 1885.

Louis Behrens was the Anstalt's second chairman, and he was also a member of the Reform Congregation which included Edward Salomon's father, H. M. Salomon, a cotton merchant of Plymouth Grove. The large Jewish community[55] was mostly concentrated around Red Bank, Strangeways and Lower Broughton,

31] Pickles Building, Portland Street, Clegg & Knowles, 1858–6

32] Harvester House (for Ralli Bros), Peter Street, Clegg & Knowles, 1868

and, in 1857, the Reform Congregation and the orthodox Old Congregation vied with each other to erect new synagogues. The Reformists, naturally enough, chose Edward Salomon to design the 'Manchester Synagogue of British Jews' in March 1857, in the 'Lombardic, or even Saracenic version, of the Byzantine. It has lofty aisles with three storeys of windows, a very low clerestory, and a polygonal apse, and makes much display of coloured pattern-work in the bricks moulded and plain.'[56] The synagogue is now demolished. The Old Congregation purchased land opposite Cheetham Town Hall from the Earl of Derby, and in the same year commissioned Thomas Bird, the architect of Cheetham Town Hall (1856), to build their synagogue. The 'Great Synagogue' was built in the Italian manner, with giant-order Corinthian columns and pilasters, and with two domed corner towers. The building was consecrated on 11 March 1858, fourteen days before Salomon's building, but was abandoned in 1986 when its congregation moved to Salford.[57]

Salomons built a later synagogue of 1873–74, at 190 Cheetham Hill Road, for the Sephardic community of Spanish and Portuguese Jews, also in the Moorish

33] Spanish and Portuguese Synagogue, Cheetham Hill Road, Edward Salomons, 1873

style [33]. Smaller than the two earlier synagogues, it was built for a congregation of only thirty families, and was designed to hold 200 men and 100 women, with space for possible future extensions and a school. It is now the Manchester Jewish Museum. Salomons was never active in the Jewish community, and his obituary in the *Jewish Chronicle* merited only a brief paragraph beneath the results of a golfing competition. His son, Gerald, changed his surname to Sanville and was baptised into the Church of England.

At the side of Cheetham Town Hall, in the same year that the Reform and Great Synagogues started, Mills & Murgatroyd were erecting the Assembly Rooms, a building with a double cube ballroom, 80 ft long by 40 ft wide and 40 ft high, divided into three domed compartments, all with gilded cornices and mouldings and relief decoration. It had crystal chandeliers and huge mirrors on each of the walls, and the floor parquetry was lavishly inlaid with marquetry work. It was all in the style of Louis XV, the decorations being by John Gregory Crace, one of the best interior decorators in the country. The building was demolished in 1966, and a petrol station now graces the site.

The young Thomas Worthington had entered the competition for the Assembly Rooms, and submitted two schemes, both in the Italian manner, but his first and only extant essay in the style was the Overseers' and Churchwardens' Office (1851–53) at 46 Fountain Street [34]. It was a modest two-storey building in brick and York stone, with a cornice over. In 1858 the original roof and cornice were replaced by the present upper two storeys – the second floor containing a board room extending the width of the building. The upper floor windows are incorporated into a stone frieze with 'more than a passing resemblance to Tite's interior court of the Royal Exchange in London'.[58]

It is the warehouse which provides the enduring image of Manchester, yet the Italian style was not limited to warehouses; offices, banks and shops all shared the ubiquitous style, for as a built form it could transmogrify itself with appropriate ease into many uses. In 1854, in Princess Street, John Edgar Gregan (1813–55) was building the new Mechanics' Institute. The 'Mechanics' Institute for the diffusion of useful knowledge and the encouragement of the educable working class' had opened on 30 March 1825 in Cooper Street, the first such institute outside London. The original intention was the private education of its 'operative members' who by attending evening classes could be instructed in English grammar, writing, arithmetic, Latin, French and German, algebra, geometry, mechanical drawing, figure, landscape and flower drawing, gymnasia and vocal music. Subscribers ranged from principals of businesses and professional men to clerks and shopkeepers. In 1834 a day school was established for the education of 210 boys, followed by a girls' school for 100 pupils. Benjamin Heywood was the chairman of the board from the beginning, with William Fairbairn first as secretary and then as president from 1840.

The new building, in the *palazzo* style [35], was needed to cope with increasing numbers, and provided a more fashionable, club-like, building. In red brick, with stone detailing, the institutional role of the building is given away by its tall windows, especially the triplet of windows on the Major Street façade which mark out the lecture hall. The Mechanics' Institute was one of Gregan's

34] Overseers' and
Churchwardens' Office,
Fountain Street, Thomas
Worthington, 1851–53

5] Mechanics' Institute, Princess
Street, John Gregan, 1854

last buildings. He died on 29 April 1855, aged forty-two, of an effusion of water on the brain, and his practice was taken over by William Reid Corson, a fellow Scot and, like Gregan, a former pupil of Walter Newall. Corson came to Manchester to join Gregan in 1854, and together they designed the church of St John, Miles Platting, in 1855. After Gregan's death[59] Corson was joined by Robert W. Aitken, another Scot, and they designed, in 1880, Central House on the corner of Princess Street and Whitworth Street, appropriately enough, in the Scottish baronial style [36].

Gregan may have been chosen as the architect of the Mechanics' Institute since he had already designed a bank in 1848 for Sir Benjamin Heywood, MP, successor to the banking firm which started in Liverpool in 1773 and which was established in King Street by 1784.* For Heywood's new bank, on St Ann Street, Gregan designed a three-storey stone-clad building in the Italian style, with a deeply rusticated ground floor and two upper floors in ashlar [37]. The ground-floor windows, large to light the banking hall, have arched openings,

---

* Manchester's first bank, the 'Manchester Bank' of Byrom, Allen, Sedgwick and Place, was established on 2 December 1771 at Bank Street, St Ann's Square (subsequently demolished).

inside which the arched windows are flanked by Classical columns. Next to it is a similar building in brick with stone detailing which was the home of the bank manager. On the bank, the voussoirs of the ground-floor arches, like the quoins on the corners of the building, are deeply stressed, and there are three distinct planes back to the windows themselves. The bank, therefore, gives an appearance of solidity and strength – necessarily so, for banks had to give an impression of safety and security. The success of a business relied on dealings with men of integrity – trust was everything.

When Arthur Heywood's bank commenced trading in Manchester, banking had less to do with hard cash than with paper transactions, promises to pay or discounting. Moneylending was often done by merchants: for example, John Jones & Co. are listed in 1772 as 'Bankers and Tea Dealers' at 104 Market Stead Lane. After the death of their father in 1775 the four sons appear to have given up the tea business and, moving to premises at 36 King Street, concentrated on banking. By 1797 the Manchester firm had become Jones Fox & Co, predecessors of Slater Heelis & Co.

Anyone who could persuade people to trust in his probity could issue paper 'promissory' notes which were tansferred from one person to another, with the signatures of the current and previous owners on the back. Coins were often issued against promissory notes by publicans and other small traders, but specie was always in short supply. In order to obtain larger amounts of cash, provincial bankers had agents of the Bank of England in London who would exchange promissory notes for coin of the realm.* There was no national paper

36] Central House (Dominion), Princess Street, Corson & Aitken, 1880

37] Benjamin Heywood's Bank, St Ann Street, John Gregan, 1848

---

* Before the introduction of the penny post on 10 January 1840 it was expensive to 'post' to London. Ways were found of getting local drafts carried by a third person. Two Manchester banks would send theirs in bulk via Pickford's vans, with a guard seated in the rear with a blunderbuss.

money until 1793, when the Bank of England issued the first £5 notes (the first £10 notes were not issued until 1795), and it was not until 1844 that the Bank Act saw the end of locally issued banknotes and prepared the way for the Bank of England to be the only issuer.

The importance of specie was demonstrated in December 1825 when there was a run on money, and the bullion in the Bank of England sank to £1,261,000. Of paper money there was plenty, but little coinage. In Manchester the corn market's business was suspended, cotton mills were closed, and merchants failed right and left because they were unable to pay their manufacturers; Manchester banks were fast running out of cash. Mr Brooks of Cunliffe & Brooks bought bags of grain, opened them and placed a thick layer of coins on top of the grain. The bulging 'sacks of gold' were left untied where all customers could see them: the ruse succeeded and gained the bank a few days' much needed respite. At another bank, coins were heated over the back parlour fire and handed out as 'new', the clerk in charge calling out every half hour, 'Now, Jim, do be getting on with them sovereigns; folks is waitin' for their money.' The folks naively thought the production of coins boundless, and the run ended.[60]

In 1708 the Bank of England had obtained an Act which forbade more than six persons to associate together as bankers. Joint-stock holding, outside London, was permitted after 26 May 1826, and in the provinces there was a rapid increase in the number of banks now that they had both shareholders and money, and the first joint-stock bank in Manchester was the Bank of Manchester, established on 10 January 1829. Trading started in March 1829 in Market Street, on the corner of Brown Street, behind the Post Office and Borough Court House. By August 1831 there were 600 shareholders and 700 accounts. Following a fraud by Mr Burdekin, the manager, in October 1842, the bank was wound up; the premises were sold and converted into shops.

In 1834 the Manchester & Liverpool District Bank, on the corner of Spring Gardens and Marble Street, was built by Thomas Witlam Atkinson (1799–1861), and the *Builder* later wrote, 'The building of the District Bank was as important an event in the architectural history of Manchester, as that of the Travellers' Club was in London; since it showed the local public that effect was not dependent on mere "orders", that there was something more than these in the matter of architecture.'[61] The bank was demolished for the tall, pebbledashed NatWest building which now occupies the site.

The Manchester & Salford Bank was founded in the spring of 1836 with a capital of £1 million in 50,000 shares of £20. It had branches in Manchester and throughout Lancashire, and its head office, on the corner of Mosley Street and Marble Street, was designed by Richard Tattersall [38]. Three tall bays in stone contain the banking hall windows, high and rectangular on Mosley Street and high and arched on Marble Street. On the major façade on Mosley Street the upper two floors are overlaid with attached giant-order Corinthian columns carrying a deep entablature and pediment – a temple front standing on a rusticated base, restrained and handsome, more Roman than Greek. The present owners, the Bradford & Bingley Building Society, have restored and cleaned the building well.

Richard Tattersall (1803–44) was one of first architects to take on commercial work. He was articled to William Hayley of Manchester, in whose office he stayed until setting up in 1830. He became deaf in 1835. Tattersall was the architect of Dukinfield Unitaran Chapel, 1840–45, St Barnabas, Rodney Street, Oldham Road, 1842–44, and restored the Derby Chapel in Manchester Cathedral. J. S. Crowther was a pupil until 1843, and he went on to become the diocesan architect. Tattersall died, in 1844, in course of building the Moral and Industrial Training School, Swinton, 1842–45, the building being completed by T. Dickon and W. H. Brakspear.

By 1845 the *Builder* was moved to say,

After a long period of depression, art in Manchester has sprung into vigorous existence. The tide of prosperity in trade has influenced architecture, and the town is now a striking example of prevailing good taste. The speculative mania has infected Manchester, probably in a greater degree than in any other place in the kingdom; and it would be easy to name several most remarkable instances of good fortune. Tradesmen, attorneys, surgeons, dentists and many more needy adventurers of one time, we now find metamorphosed, every man of them, into share-brokers.[62]

38] Manchester & Salford Bank Mosley Street, Richard Tattersall, 1836

In that year the new* Manchester and Salford branch of the Bank of England was completed. For its new branch the bank had chosen its own architect, Charles Robert Cockerell (1788–1863), who, in 1833, had taken over from John Soane.[63] Cockerell had a reputation as an archaeologist (he had discovered a number of major works on his Grand Tour of Italy and Greece), but his Bank of England at 82 King Street is no mere slavish copy of Classical styles [39]. The giant-order Tuscan columns, the huge blocks of stone with deeply channelled rustication, give an impression of great strength and weight – appropriate to a bank. But the overall appearance is more Baroque than Classical, and the way in which the rusticated walls become the voussoirs of the door arches is reminiscent of Hawksmoor, whose St Mary Woolnoth, London, opposite the Bank of England, must have been well known to Cockerell.[64]

Work started in 1861 on a new headquarters for the Manchester & Salford Bank on Mosley Street at the corner of York Street, and the bank moved from Tattersall's building on 15 August 1862. The new bank was Edward Walters's last great work, and the last great *palazzo*-style building in Manchester [40]. Clad in a yellow-grey York stone, the building has tall and elegant windows

---

* The Bank's first provincial branch was set up in Gloucester on 19 July 1826, followed by Manchester on 26 September, and by Swansea on 23 October, and in 1827, by Birmingham, Liverpool, Bristol, Leeds and Exeter.

lighting the banking hall over which there are two storeys of restrained Italianate windows. Adjoining the building on Mosley Street, and linked to it by a Doric entrance, is a four-bay extension of the 1880s, by Barker & Ellis, the young partners and successors of Walters, whom, according to the *Builder*, he entirely reared and educated.[65] The managing director of the bank, from 1854 to 1876, was William Langton, who was on the board of the Mechanics' Institute, and had helped to set up the Athenaeum, the Manchester Statistical Society in 1833 and the Chetham Society in 1843. Randolph Caldecott was a clerk in the bank.

41] Lombard Chambers and Brooks's Bank, Brown Street, George Truefitt, 1868, dwarfed by Ship Canal House and the Midland Bank

In 1874 the Manchester & Salford Bank took over the business of Heywood Bros & Co.[66]

In 1868 Lombard Chambers and Brooks's Bank, Brown Street, on the corner of Chancery Place (George Truefitt, 1824–1902),* was being built for William Cunliffe Brooks (his initials are carved on the façade). Roger Cunliffe and William Brooks were manufacturers who had carried on a banking business as early as 1793 but did not assume a position as bankers until 1815. Their first bank, in Market Street, was designed by Thomas Royle and Robert Unwin in 1827 in the Greek Revival style, but was subsequently destroyed by fire.[67] Their second bank, in King Street, lies under Ship Canal House. Their third bank, Lombard Chambers [41], is a confection of Gothic and Italian forms, but in this building the *palazzo* style has become wayward, and is evidently losing out to the more fashionable Gothic.

There were a number of banks erected in the King Street area in the 1870s, all of which were demolished for later buildings. The Lancashire & Yorkshire Bank was at 73–5 King Street, an early building by Heathcote & Rawle.[68] Adjacent to it was the Manchester Trust building, red stone, red brick, picturesque and good Queen Anne Revival. Both were demolished for the Norwich Union building. The Manchester & County Bank of 1877, on the site of the old York Hotel, King Street (next to the Old Town Hall), was by Mills & Murgatroyd, and this was replaced by the NatWest building in 1966.

The growth of banking reflected the increasing importance of Manchester as a commercial town, and trade in cotton was driving the engines of commerce. Still at the centre of trade was the Cotton Exchange, and here could be seen more of Mills & Murgatroyd's work. The old Exchange had been extended in 1836 and 1845, and in 1851, on the occasion of her first visit to the borough, Her Majesty granted the title of 'Royal' to the Manchester Exchange. In 1874 Mills & Murgatroyd were commissioned to design a new large building, and in order to make room for it Newall's Buildings (where the Manchester Anti-Corn Law league once had its headquarters) were demolished.

The building is an Italianate design with four upper storeys raised over a rusticated ground floor, all in sandstone [42]. The first and second-storey windows are coupled within decorative arched openings, the imposts of the arches set on simple Doric pilasters. Above the arches are the smaller rectangular third-storey windows. All three floors are set within a peristyle of round and square attached Corinthian half-columns carrying a deep entablature, above which are the windows of the fourth storey. The mouldings are deep, as are the reveals to the openings, and the modelling of the surfaces by the play of light and shadow must have been noticeable even in nineteenth-century Manchester sunlight. The most notable feature was the huge octastyle portico of Corinthian columns raised over the ground floor on Cross Street, though this was removed in 1914. At the rear, marking the corner of St Mary's Gate and Exchange Street, a dome and lantern are raised on a tall drum.

---

* It was Truefitt who introduced Cheshire 'black and white' architecture, in imitation of the mediaeval, by nailing blackened boards to white plasterwork walls.

Internally the Royal Exchange trading room was lit by three domes of blue glass, and the ceiling was carried on enormous piers and columns of brick clad in red Cork marble, with metal bases cast in Berlin. The Royal Exchange was only for overseas trade, and half past two on a Tuesday and Friday was High 'Change, when 8,000 traders met on the floor and carried out business under the blue domes. The Manchester building was different from most exchanges in that it was merely a place of assembly for spinners, manufacturers, merchants and agents, and they met on a simple plan, based on the columns. These were labelled alphabetically and numerically, so that a member's position was indicated where two imaginary lines would meet. Transactions were arranged quietly between buyers and sellers, there being no calling out of prices as on other exchanges.

In one corner were traders in iron and steel, but these were not 'Manchester merchants' for that name was reserved for those who shipped cotton goods to Lancashire's foreign markets.

> The Manchester merchant is the link between the Lancashire cotton industry and the foreign consumer of cloth. He buys grey, unfinished cloth from the manufacturer or his agent, and ships it abroad, after having it bleached or dyed or printed, and finished or packed, and he finances the cloth until it has been sold to a foreign importer or dealer . . . some merchants import cotton and other produce from the countries to which they ship cotton goods; some own or control cotton mills in Bombay or Shanghai as well as shipping goods to those places.[69]

Painted beneath the larger dome of the Exchange were figures of Commerce, Science and the Arts, and beneath the smaller domes were foliate decoration and figures representing the seasons. The *Builder* noted, 'The base of the [largest]

42] Royal Exchange, Cross Street Mills & Murgatroyd, 1874

dome bears the inscription, from the Book of Proverbs, "A good name is more to be chosen than great riches, and loving favour rather than silver and gold" or to that effect. One gets rather tired of this cant of painting up such texts in places of business. Everyone on the floor of the room will be occupied in the pursuit of riches, and what is the point of denying it on the ceiling?'[70]

If the riches of the merchants were shown in their houses of commerce, then the wealth of the city was shown in its later civic buildings, and for these picturesque Gothic rather than staid Classical was to be the style.

6

1860–90

CONFIDENCE
AND CIVIC PRIDE

Once on a time this good old town was nothing but a village.
Of husbandry, and farmers too, whose time was spent in tillage,
But things are altered very much, such building now allotted is,
It rivals far and soon will leave behind the great Metropolis.
O dear O, Manchester's an altered town, O dear O.

[A song sold on Manchester's streets in 1842]

MANCHESTER'S early leaders after incorporation in 1838 were a liberal elite, but they quickly gave up power to 'hard-headed shopkeepers', creating a 'shopocracy' of manufacturers and merchants, shopkeepers and small proprietors. As Asa Briggs has pointed out, Manchester, in the early nineteenth century, witnessed the creation out of a new order of businessmen an 'urban aristocracy – men who were beginning to seek political as well as economic power, power not only in Manchester but in the country as a whole.'[1] But by the middle of the century, things were changing. The Queen's visit in 1851 had provided the impetus for other national figures to visit the town, and had given it respectability. By the time Manchester was granted its city charter in 1853 it was no longer the talked-about 'shock city' of the nineteenth century. Manchester even had a bishop, the collegiate church of St Mary, St Denys and St George having been designated a cathedral in 1847.

All the local instruments of authority and power (the municipal council, the magistracy, boards of the Poor Law Guardians, police, voluntary societies, etc.) were distinctively bourgeois in tone and composition and under middle-class control. Manchester's leaders, by the middle of the century, formed a complex group with establishment Church of England Tories, the Quakers based in the Friends' Meeting House and the Unitarians based on the Cross Street and Mosley

Street chapels. Ten of the first twenty mayors of Manchester and fifteen Lancashire MPs were members of the Cross Street or related chapels. Nathaniel Gaskell had been an original member of the congregation, and his grandson became Lord Clive of India. Another descendant was William Gaskell, whose wife, Elizabeth, enriched English literature with her novels. Among the congregation of the Mosley Street Chapel were G. W. Wood, E. Potter and R. H. Greg, who all became MPs, and John Kennedy, Henry McConnel, Peter Ewart, Leopold Reiss and Leo Schuster, all manufacturers.

In the elections of 1857 John Bright, the free-trade reformer, was defeated by John Potter of Salford, a member of the Potter dynasty, whose Potter & Norris Warehouse was one of the largest in Manchester. The other victorious candidate in the election was James Aspinall Turner, a cotton spinner and chairman of the Manchester Commercial Association, which had split from the Chamber of Commerce in 1845 in opposition to the chamber's free-trade fanaticism (though the two bodies were reconciled in 1858). Both Potter and Turner were worshippers at the Cross Street Chapel, and they had the backing of the *Manchester Guardian*, whose editor, John Taylor, was in the congregation of the Friends' Meeting House. In 1868 Hugh Birley, a descendant of the Hugh Birley of Peterloo infamy, was elected to Parliament as a Conservative candidate. In 1874 two of the three successful parliamentary candidates were Conservatives.

The new borough administration was already effecting changes in the town. Albert Bridge was thrown across the Irwell in September 1844, and Albert Street, Bridge Street and John Dalton Street (John Dalton died in July 1844) were created from a tangle of old streets and alleys. Lower King Street and St Mary's Gate had been widened and straightened. In the 1850s Spring Gardens was opened to Fountain Street and Corporation Street was being extended from Market Street to Withy Grove.

On 22 August 1846, in the year the Queen gave her assent to the repeal of the Corn Laws, three parks were opened, the first public parks in a provincial city. On 29 March 1845 the Committee for the Formation of Public Parks in Manchester had purchased the Lark Hill estate, Salford, from William Garnett, for the sum of £5,000 (to become Peel Park, named after Sir Robert Peel). In May 1845 the committee purchased the Hendam Hall estate, Harpurhey, the property of Jonathan Andrew, for £7,250 (named Queen's Park), and in the same month the Bradford estate, from Lady Houghton, for £6,200 (called Phillips's Park in honour of Mark Phillips, MP, who financed it).*

Parliament, in August 1851, allowed the enactment of 1/2d rates for the creation of public libraries and museums, and in 1852 the Manchester Public Free Library, Tonman Street, Campfield, opened. The building was originally

---

* The sixty-two-acre Alexandra Park was opened in August 1870. Its greenhouses contained over 150,000 bedding-out plants. On 21 May 1874 the Aquarium in Alexandra Road opened, facing the centre of the lawn of Alexandra Park. The building was divided into one grand central saloon and two side wings or corridors. On display in cases alongside the walls of the main saloon were cod, whiting, sole, skate, lobster and crab, pike, roach, dace, tench and carp and a large collection of anemones.

the Hall of Science, built for £5,000, but purchased by the borough, with freehold, for £2,147 plus £4,816 for repairs, alterations and furnishings. It was partly financed by the rates but with voluntary subscriptions for the purchase of books. E. Edwards of the British Museum was appointed librarian, and in its first year over 138,000 books were issued. The building was found to be unsafe in 1877, and it was decided to install the library in the old Town Hall on King Street, where it remained until 1912, when the old Town Hall was demolished.

Manchester in the 1850s had become prosperous, was by now firmly established as the provincial capital, and public buildings were to be erected which reflected Manchester's civic pride. But if Manchester had led the country in introducing the palazzo style, for its new civic buildings only the fashionable Gothic would do. The Classical Revival of its earlier civic buildings was virtually spent as a national style, as James Elmes, the father of Harvey Elmes of Liverpool's St George's Hall, pointed out: 'We had converted Greek architecture into the most humdrum sort of design. Nay, it seems to have paralysed our powers of design and composition altogether, so that the only alternative left was to escape from it by plunging *headlong* into the Gothic and Italian styles.'[2]

The Gothic style had never entirely died out, of course. Wren and Hawksmoor had built 'Gothick' in the universities, and in the eighteenth and early nineteenth centuries Walpole, Wyatt, Smirke and others were building picturesque Gothic fantasies, though their Gothic was decorative rather than structural. Antiquarian source books were published, like John Carter's *Views of Ancient Buildings in England*, 1786–95, and *Ancient Architecture of England*, 1795–1807, and it was Carter who coined the phrases 'first and second period', and 'pointed' architecture, hence recognising, perhaps for the first time, the principles of mediaeval architecture. In *The Gentleman's Magazine*, from 1798 until his death in 1817, he wrote 212 articles attacking the neglect and fake restoration of Gothic cathedrals and churches.

Thomas Rickman (1776–1841) took up Carter's ideas and, in 1812, started writing *An Attempt to Discriminate the Styles of English Architecture, from the Conquest to the Reformation*, based on lectures he had given to the Chester Lit & Phil. (Thomas Harrison had invited him after Rickman had sent him sketches of buildings.) The work was published in 1817, and by 1881 had been through seven editions. It was Rickman who devised the nomenclature still applied to periods of mediaeval architecture: the first period or Norman style; the second period, or Early English; the third period, or Decorated; the fourth period, or Perpendicular style, and 'these distinctions which, being once laid down with precision, will enable persons of common observation to distinguish the difference of age and style in these buildings as easily as the distinctions of the Grecian and Roman orders'.[3]

Rickman, who had trained in pharmacy and surgery, went to Liverpool in 1806, where he was employed as an accountant. His architectural practice started in 1812 with the church of St George, Everton. St George, Chorley, 1820, is also by him, but his design for St Thomas, Pendleton, was rejected in favour of

Goodwin & Lane's. A pupil of Thomas Rickman was Edmund Sharpe, who, in 1851, produced *The Seven Periods of Church Architecture*, and provided the term 'Geometrical' as a classification of the Decorated style. He was the architect of the Church of the Holy Trinity, Platt Lane, 1845, built of terracotta blocks.

If Rickman and Sharpe had categorised mediaeval architecture, it was Pugin who rationalised the relationship between structure and decoration. For Augustus Welby Northmore Pugin, co-architect with Charles Barry of the Houses of Parliament, and a notable architect and designer in his own right, the only correct architecture was that of the thirteenth and fourteenth centuries, a view he proselytised in a series of publications between 1836 and 1844.[4] Pugin extolled the value of Gothic or 'pointed' architecture, not only for spiritual reasons but also for good practical ones.[5] As he wrote in *The True Principles of Pointed or Christian Architecture*, 'In pure architecture the smallest details should have a meaning or serve a purpose . . . Construction should vary with the material employed . . . The external and internal appearance of an edifice should be illustrative of, and in accordance with, the purpose for which it is destined.'[6]

Pugin, through writing and example, did more than anyone to make architects consider the structural as well as the decorative principles of Gothic architecture.[7] G. G. Scott, who said he was awakened from his slumber by the thundering of Pugin's writings, published his *Remarks on Secular and Domestic Architecture, Present and Future* in 1857, and presented the case that Gothic was an adaptable architectural form suited to the building techniques of the nineteenth century, fit for secular as well as ecclesiastical buildings.

Their views were shared by John Ruskin, one of the most effective and persuasive of writers, and the doyen of art and design criticism. His lectures were listened to and his books read with considerable respect, not just by architects and their patrons but by the public at large. In the *Seven Lamps of Architecture* of 1849 he reiterated the need for honesty in structure and decoration, but even more persuasively in his *Stones of Venice*, published in three volumes between 1851 and 1853, he extolled the virtues of Venetian Gothic architecture, a style which had developed from an admixture of Gothic and Classical elements. Venetian architecture was colourful, varied and dynamic and, importantly, was picturesque. Ruskin provided the ethical sanction for fine craftsmanship, for truth to materials, for the therapeutic power of creativity, and he provided, if one were needed, the authorisation for the Gothic Revival.

Gothic, whether rooted in England or Venice, was also a useful style: buildings could be more easily generated from the inside out; plan and elevation could come together, and for many of the modern buildings being erected, with a complexity of use unknown to previous generations, Gothic was an ideal solution. The Classical style had been borrowed from abroad; the Gothic style evoked England's past, important in a period in which nationalism was sweeping across Europe.[8] Architects were in any case turning away from the rigours of the Classical, for the style was already becoming too sterile, as the *Surveyor, Engineer and Architect* journal had noted: 'Though we admire Grecian architecture as far as it goes, we must confess that it goes but a very little way.'[9]

In 1858 a competition was announced for the design of the new Assize Courts to be built in Great Ducie Street, Manchester. The building, also to be used for sittings of the Court of Chancery of the County Palatine of Lancaster and the Salford Hundred Court of Record, was to be erected on the site of Strangeways Hall. This was a major commission, for it was the first civic building to be erected in Manchester since Goodwin's Town Hall of 1819, and the first for the new Corporation. The *Builder* reckoned its importance second only to the new government offices in Whitehall. It attracted the interest of the cream of the architectural profession, and architects from across the country submitted 107 schemes. Altogether 940 drawings were submitted for the competition, and when these were exhibited in the upper galleries of the RMI they covered 8,410 ft^2, and attracted 1,000 viewers on the first day. No style was specified in the brief, which led one candidate, perhaps to cover all eventualities, to submit six different designs all based on the same plan, ranging from Greek to Gothic.

Thomas Allom, an ex-pupil of Goodwin, gained the second premium with one of the two designs he had submitted, both Classical but with Gothic details and with central domes; John Robinson won the third prize with a Greek design. Norman Shaw, William Nesfield, Cuthbert Brodrick (already the architect of the Classical Leeds Town Hall) and George Truefitt of Manchester all submitted Gothic schemes. Thomas Worthington's design was based on the richly decorated town halls of the Netherlands and France (especially the Hôtel de Ville in Louvain). Edward Walters, as might be expected, submitted a Renaissance design.

The commission of JPs, however, awarded the first prize to a relatively unknown twenty-nine-year-old architect, Alfred Waterhouse (1830–1905), who had only been in practice for four years. Waterhouse may have benefited from his acquaintance with Edmund Ashworth, the Quaker chairman of the commission, for whom he had already done some work, and to whom he had been introduced by his master, P. B. Alley (another Quaker), but he had designed little apart from a domestic house in Neston, Cheshire, the Ragged and Industrial School, 1857 (demolished), and a warehouse and sugar refinery in Chester Street, Chorlton-on-Medlock (1855–56), for Messrs Binyon & Fryer. This building, now demolished, had a polychromatic brick upper wall copied from the Doge's Palace in Venice.

As an ex-pupil of Richard Lane and P. B. Alley, it might have been expected that Waterhouse would have submitted a Classical scheme, for, as Alfred Darbyshire later wrote, 'In spite of the unpoetic title of the firm, it was the local centre of classic thought; and the office at the corner of Chapel Walks and Cross Street was regarded in my young days with veneration and a certain amount of awe by the aspirants to architectural fame.'[10] But Waterhouse evidently had an eye for current fashion and national taste, for his submission was in the Gothic style, and to some effect, for Ruskin later said, 'A very beautiful and noble building indeed and much beyond anything yet done in England on my principles.'[11] Perhaps Ruskin was influenced by the irresistible fact that 'the clerk of the works, when he was a youth, copied out the whole three volumes of the *Stones of Venice*, and traced every illustration.'[12]

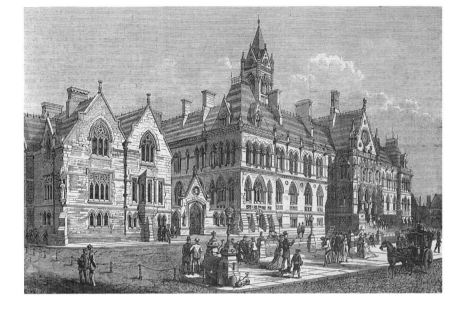

43] Assize Courts, Great Ducie
Street, Alfred Waterhouse, 1858

Waterhouse had made a trip to Belgium as recently as September 1858, and
had been impressed by the civic buildings of Antwerp and Bruges. The high-
pitched roofs of the Assize Courts (and his later Town Hall and Owens College)
certainly reflect this interest. Waterhouse wrote in his submission for the courts,
'The designer has not endeavoured slavishly to copy the Gothic of any particular period or country, though the noble civic buildings of the Low Countries
and Italy may have given him suggestions.'[13]

One competitor complained that Waterhouse's scheme was deficient on a
number of counts, not least because he had forgotten to provide a jury room
for the criminal court and had placed the female witnesses' rooms next to the
gentlemen's lavatory – something entirely at odds with nineteenth-century
notions of prudery. But this was a complex building, the first of its kind, and
it was a remarkable achievement for an inexperienced architect. The Assize
Courts made Waterhouse's reputation as 'the recognised master of planning
large public buildings'.[14] Significantly, although G. E. Street, in 1866, won the
competition for the better-known Law Courts in the Strand, London, his floor
plans were flawed to such an extent that he had to utilise the plans of one of his
major competitors, those of Alfred Waterhouse.

The Assize Courts commenced building in 1859, a huge rectangular building
of two floors over a semi-basement [43]. Five bays on each side of the central
entrance porch, and pavilions at each corner of the main façade. The entrance
was originally designed with a strange little turret with a clock, but in the final
execution had a rose window inserted into the main gable. The walls were
faced in Darley Dale stone with banding, string courses and alternate arch
voussoirs in greenish-blue Forest of Dean stone. The shafts of the windows and
entrance portal were in polished Dalbeattie granite. Internally, there were plain
walls pierced with deep arched openings; the floors were laid with glazed tiles

in chocolate and cream. The entrance hall, which spanned the two bays either side of the central entrance pavilion, led to the two courts, civil and criminal, and ranged around them were rooms for the judiciary, barristers, witnesses, a sheriff's court and a library. The judges' lodgings ran off via a wing from the left-hand side of the building. The first hearings took place in July 1864 before the Lord Chief Justice, Sir A. J. E. Cockburn.[15]

The whole of the courts was demolished when the blitzes of 1940 and 1941 destroyed everything but the judges' lodgings and the Ducie Street façade. All that is left are fragments of Thomas Woolner's sculptures, now in the museum in the Crown Court, Crown Square, and difficult to access.

Even before the Assize Courts were finished, Waterhouse was asked to design the adjoining Strangeways Gaol on the site of Strangeways garden and park. This was to be a large prison for a thousand inmates; a practical building – mostly brick, with some stone detailing, primarily for structural strength around the cell windows – and little chance of architectural display. Waterhouse was first approached in December 1861 and early the next year he visited the gaols at Reading, Winchester, Holloway and Wandsworth. Waterhouse showed his design to Joshua Jebb, the Surveyor General of Prisons, who had designed a radial plan for Pentonville in the 1840s.

Like Jebb's design (and like the New Bailey in Salford), Strangeways has wings radiating out from a central hall which provided ease of observation of the individual wings. Much of the detail is Romanesque in style (visibly in the upper windows of the central hall) though the interior arches were pointed in the Gothic manner. The huge campanile which towers over the site was part of the heating system. The gaol was completed in 1869, and the cost of £170,000 was £50,000 more than the Assize Courts.[16]

Also in 1861, Waterhouse carried out renovations to the Royal Infirmary and built the Royal Insurance building (later the Vulcan Boiler & General Insurance) in King Street. This compact little Venetian building had striped gable ends and chimneys, clustered Gothic windows with red and yellow voussoirs, miniature balconies and, idiosyncratically, storks perched on dormer windows. The building still existed at the time Cecil Stewart wrote his *Stones of Manchester*, and as he pointed out, it was 'as though Waterhouse had tried to concentrate in one little building everything he knew of Venice, and, by adding the dormers and storks, a little of Bavaria as well'.[17] The building was demolished in the 1960s. In 1861 Waterhouse also built Barcombe Cottage, Wilmslow Road (now demolished), for himself and his wife, although within four years the prospect of a commission for the Law Courts in London had enticed him to the capital, and most of Waterhouse's future work was to be away from Manchester.

The year 1861 marked the beginnings of one of the greatest cotton famines of the nineteenth century, and by October that year cotton mills were beginning to run on short time. By January 1862 the lack of trade was causing enormous hardship among the workers of Manchester and Lancashire. In March, at its peak, 240,466 persons were out of work, and 420,243 on relief. Such was the hardship that even Parliament had to take note; in July £17,000 was subscribed in five days by the noblemen and Members of Parliament for the Lancashire distress, and the Palace of Westminster eventually raised a total of £52,000. In September £30,000 was received from Australia for the relief of poverty, and on 19 December the Mansion House committee gave a grant of £55,000 (the Lancashire Memorial Window was later placed at the east end of Guildhall, London, paid for by penny subscriptions in Lancashire, in thanks for the efforts of the Lord Mayor's committee). By 8 February 1864 the total funds contributed were £1,485,883. The hardship was noted even in the United States, and on 9 February 1863 the SS *George Griswald* from New York arrived in the Mersey with provisions for the distressed operatives of Lancashire, and was greeted with a royal salute. On 30 April 1863 1,000 operatives emigrated to New Zealand. The distress lasted until early 1865, but by June 1865 unemployment had fallen and relief was virtually discontinued. The cotton famine had lasted nearly four years.

The *Building News* noted in 1861, 'Manchester is a more interesting city to walk over than London. One can scarcely walk about Manchester without coming across examples of the *grand* in architecture. There has been nothing to equal it since the building of Venice.'[18] Somewhat extravagant praise, and had the article been written just two years later it might have been written with some degree of accuracy, for it was at this time that the City of Manchester was commencing the layout of its new civic square.

The creation of the new space arose from the most momentous news of 1861, the death from typhoid of Albert, Prince Consort to Queen Victoria. The nation was shocked, even the hard-headed businessmen of Manchester, for typhoid, a disease associated with the poor, had hit one of the highest in the land. But how was a suitable memorial to be created for such a man? The city's Memorial Committee considered, among other proposals, new botanical gardens, a museum for the arts and sciences, a lending library, model housing and new public baths. Eventually they settled on a single monument which would incorporate the statue of Albert, by the sculptor Matthew Noble, which had already been commissioned by the mayor, Thomas Goadsby.

The design of the statue was submitted for approval to Her Majesty, who expressed her satisfaction with it, and with the design, by Thomas Worthington, of the canopy to house it. It was appropriate that Worthington was to make the canopy, for it was Prince Albert himself who, in 1844, had presented the eighteen-year-old Thomas with the Royal Society of Arts' Isis Gold Medal for a design for a chancel in the Gothic style.

Thomas Worthington (1826–1909), the son of a wealthy merchant and member of the Cross Street Chapel, had been articled to Henry Bowman (another of the Cross Street congregation and a Gothicist) and Joseph Stretch Crowther at the age of fifteen. He measured buildings for Bowman's *Specimens of the Ecclesiastical Architecture of Great Britain*, published in 1846, and, like his fellow pupil Edward Salomon, provided several of the illustrations for Bowman and Crowther's *Churches of the Middle Ages*. Worthington left Bowman & Crowther's office in 1847 to work in the office of William Tite, but left in 1848 for his first study tour of Italy. By February 1849 he had returned to Manchester at Tite's suggestion, and commenced his practice.

Worthington's design for the Albert Memorial was to place the statue of the Prince Consort under a ciborium in the mediaeval manner [44]. This was an original idea, though its origins may well have come from George Kemp's statue of Sir Walter Scott in Prince's Street, Edinburgh, built some twenty years earlier. But Worthington's elegant design was based on the church of Santa Maria della Spina in Pisa, which he had sketched in some detail on his first tour of Italy. The spire of the monument, faced on each side by a crocketed gable and flanked by canopied pinnacles standing on colonnettes, is very much like a single bay of that church.[19] The canopies contain the figures of Art, Commerce, Science and Agriculture. Below Art are minor figures representing Painting, Architecture, Music and Sculpture; below Commerce are the Four Continents; below Science are Chemistry, Astronomy, Mechanics and Mathematics; below Agriculture are the figures of the Four Seasons.

The design was published in the *Builder* on 27 September 1862, fifteen months before G. G. Scott's similar, though much more grand and lavish, design in Kensington. Scott believed his design to be totally original, and wrote later in his *Recollections*, 'I well remember how long and painful was the effort before I struck out on an idea which satisfied my mind . . . My idea was to erect a type of ciborium to protect the statue of the Prince . . . This was an idea so new as to

44] Albert Memorial, Albert Square, Thomas Worthington, 1862–67

45] Memorial Hall, Albert Square, Thomas Worthington, 1863–66

provoke much opposition.'[20] Is it really conceivable that Scott did not know of Worthington's monument?

Having determined upon the memorial, the committee's problems were not over, for there was a long delay in finding a suitable location. Piccadilly was the obvious site, and a full-size wooden model of the memorial was erected in front of the Infirmary, where Onslow Ford's statue of Queen Victoria now stands, but it was realised that its Tuscan Gothic style would clash with Lane's Classical building. Eventually, in 1863, the Corporation offered some derelict land on Bancroft Street, adjacent to the Town Yard. The area was, to say the least, seedy, and the only 'gentrified' buildings were the Friends' Meeting House and St Andrew's Chapel and School in Mount Street (the latter now underneath the Town Hall extension).

The committee accepted the site with the proviso that the land near Town Yard would eventually be cleared to make a public square. When the foundations of the memorial were being laid, it was found that the site was riddled with culverts and drains, and the building of the foundations took up all the initial allocation of 50,000 bricks – a gift from the Manchester Brickmakers' Protection Society 'as an expression of sympathy towards our beloved Queen'. Notwithstanding a further appeal for money being made in the last phases of the great cotton famine of 1865, the cost of £6,249, excluding the statue, was raised. The memorial was presented to the city in 1867, and it is appropriate that the monument which was erected by public subscription was restored in 1977 again by public subscription.[21] Fittingly, too, Arthur Little of Thomas Worthington & Sons was appointed honorary consultant architect to the restoration, which in 1979 won a Civic Award for outstanding contribution to the quality and appearance of the environment.

It has been written that the visit by the Prince and Princess of Wales to the Albert Memorial in 1869 set the seal on the development of Albert Square, but long before the visit developments were taking place. At some point before 1863, South (now Southmill) Street was driven through to meet Pool Street (now the road traffic part of Albert Square), and the first architect-designed building on the site was erected on the new corner of South Street and Lloyd Street – the Memorial Hall (1863–66), designed by Worthington for the Unitarians. The memorial in this case was not for Albert but a commemoration of 1663, when 2,000 Puritan ministers were ejected from their livings by the Act of Conformity of 1662.

The Memorial Hall is the most complete evocation of a Venetian *palazzo* in Manchester, if not in the whole country [45]. The building rests on a semi-basement of cream gritstone above which are carried three floors of orange Knutsford brickwork, with the string courses, the surrounds of doors and windows and the cornice all in buff Hollington stone. The windows, like fourteenth-century Venetian palaces, are grouped as singles and threes, and the voussoirs of the ground and first-floor window arches are structurally polychromatic bricks in red and blue. But it is the top-floor windows, tall because they screen the meeting hall, which are so reminiscent of the Doge's Palace or the Palazzo Franchetti or the Ca' d'Oro in Venice.

Whilst in Venice in 1858, on his second tour of Italy, and guided by Ruskin's *Stones*, Worthington had studied Venetian buildings at first hand, and he had lodged in the Ca' Loredano. The Memorial Hall, however, is no mere copy, being well adapted to the difficult site, on the angles of the new street lines and restricted by existing buildings in Century Street. As the *Manchester Guardian* was later to say, 'He was never a mere copyist, and from whatever source his inspiration was drawn, his work was always that of a refined and educated English architect who possessed a wide and catholic grasp and appreciation of different styles and periods.'[22] The main entrance is on Albert Square and a staircase rises cleverly in the corner to the third-storey public hall which took up the whole of the floor. Because of the high value of land in what was going to become an important civic site, the Unitarians sensibly decided that the lower parts of the building should be rented out for warehousing or other purposes.

The hall became home to the Hallé Choir, the Photographic, Statistical, Horticultural and Elocutionist Societies and the Manchester Unitarian Sunday School Union. The original internal iron structure was replaced in the 1970s by an internal steel frame. A mock Victorian pub now graces its basement, its upper floor looks bleakly unoccupied and it is sad to see so unique a building in such a state of neglect.

The area to the west of the Town Yard had started to be cleared of its old building stock in 1864, ready for the creation of Albert Square. This required the demolition of the Engraver's Arms public house, the Manchester Coffee Roasting Works, a coal yard, a smithy, a number of warehouses and workshops and a warren of back-to-back houses and courts; on what is now the open space of Albert Square were crammed about 100 buildings. By 1867 the area was cleared, and Manchester's new town hall was in process of being built.

The Corporation had decided that the old Town Hall, now fifty years old, and far too small to house the various departments of a modern civic administration, needed to be replaced. Town Yard would make an ideal site for the new town hall; the Corporation owned the land, and the yard was a relatively open space bounded by the town fire engine house, the town weighing machine, factories, mills, workshops and housing. It would, therefore, be cheap to develop – that it provided a difficult, triangular shape on which to build the seat of local government seemed not to matter. There were attempts by Alderman King to get the town hall built on a rectangular site, but the Building Sub-committee estimated that it would add an extra £300,000 on top of the estimated cost of £500,000.[23] Even after the competition had been decided, there were still abortive attempts by the Manchester Architectural Association to secure a better site, though, surprisingly, the young Manchester Society of Architects had not become involved, although all the principal Manchester architects were members.[24]

In March 1867 a two-stage, open competition was announced.[25] However, unlike the Assize Courts competition, the commission, composed of city councillors, would be assisted by professional assessors. No style was preferred, but details of site and function were defined. There were to be four floors and a basement, and a Grand Front would face on to Albert Square and the new memorial. The main rooms were to be behind this façade on the first floor, and there was to be independent access to the mayoral suite of rooms and private accommodation. Ashlar stone was to be used for internal surfaces and York or Darley Dale stone for the exterior walls. Each entrant had to submit a maximum of five drawings. There were to be no coloured drawings and no perspectives – it was not unknown for a cleverly tricked-up perspective to fool a would-be client. Such was its national importance, the competition attracted 137 entries from 123 competitors.

The committee, between August and September 1867, selected eleven schemes, and another four were added at the request of individual councillors. These were then assessed down to a shortlist of nine by George Godwin, editor of the *Builder*, though one was later rejected for failing to comply with the competition rules. Pseudonyms were adopted to preserve the anonymity of the entrants, although the *Builder* objected to the motto system, especially given that the shortlisted competitors had to provide a different pseudonym for their second submission – after all, wouldn't the committee members recognise a resubmitted scheme?[26] Nonetheless, as reported by the *Builder*,

> It was resolved by the Council that the following mottoes/devices be invited to submit drawings for the second stage: St Michael; 'Ring out the old, ring in the new'; A circle within a ring; 'Time tryeth Truth'; 'Polyanthus'; 'Municipal'; Three Hebrew Characters; and 'Au bon droit'. These were the works, though not in order, of: Mr Cuthbert Brodrick, London; Mr William Lee, London; Edward Salomons, Manchester; John O. Scott, London; Speakman & Charlesworth, Manchester; Alfred Waterhouse, London; Thomas Worthington, Manchester; T. H. Wyatt, London. We have given the names alphabetically, not in the order of mottoes.[27]

The second stage of the competition was judged by Professor T. Donaldson, the first President of the RIBA, and a classicist, and G. E. Street, the gothicist. For the second stage each competitor received £300 for the provision of more detailed drawings, which could include coloured and perspective drawings. This stage was assessed under six headings: external and contextual; internal arrangements; natural light provision; heating and ventilation; acoustics of the hall and council chamber; reliable accuracy of estimates. The finalists were, with their mottoes or devices:

1. 'Arnolfo di Lapo', Cuthbert Brodrick, a Gothic design.
2. 'Faire sans dire', Thomas Henry Wyatt (who was assisted by his more eminent brother Sir Digby Wyatt), in the Renaissance style.
3. 'Fides', William Lee, Gothic.
4. 'Sperandum', John Oldrid Scott (son of George Gilbert Scott), Gothic.
5. 'St Valentine', Alfred Waterhouse, Gothic. ('St Valentine' because drawings were submitted on 14 February 1868.)
6. The Masons' symbol of crossed triangles, Speakman & Charlesworth, Gothic.
7. 'True to the Line', Thomas Worthington, Gothic.
8. 'Valentine', Edward Salomons, Renaissance.

Donaldson and Street considered 'Numbers 6, 4, 7 and 5 are the works of the finest design and may be considered to stand in the order in which we have placed them.'[28] However, in terms of general arrangements Waterhouse came first (the next two being Speakman & Charlesworth and Salomons); for lighting, ventilation and warming there were no runners-up – only Waterhouse's name appears – and Waterhouse, Salomons and Worthington were deemed the least costly.

Waterhouse gained the contract on the grounds of architectural merit, construction, excellence of plan and arrangement, light, cost and provision of spare room, 'the last named . . . much superior to the others in respect to the supply of light, the facility of ventilation, the ease of access, and the general excellence of the plan'.[29] though some consideration had to be given to the externals and to the meagre (economical) courtyards (which were a failure in all the schemes). The assessors reported, 'The architectural character of this design is, as we have said, not so good as some of the others, but the plan has such great merits, is so admirably and simply disposed, and so well lighted, that we cannot but feel that it is thoroughly entitled to the first place.'[30]

The choice of Waterhouse did not meet with universal favour, however. Worthington's design was preferred by many and was described by the *Manchester Examiner* as 'like a Rhineland vision'[31] [46]. There was, perhaps, a sense

46] Town Hall, Albert Square, Thomas Worthington's perspective drawing, 1868

47] Town Hall, Albert Square, Alfred Waterhouse, 1867–77

of unfairness in giving the job to the man who came only fourth in terms of quality of design. A letter to the *Builder*, signed merely 'F.', complained that, given the excellence of their designs, Nos 6, 4 and 7 weren't chosen. After all, 'we know from experience, of at least one of these, that he is not infallible in making estimates, *vide* the new Assize Courts.' 'F.' goes on to suggest that Waterhouse's design needed more work on the great entrance, the clock tower and the angles of the principal front, and argues reasonably, 'If the other architects would be allowed to make alterations of equal importance in their plans and designs . . . I think that the few advantages in Mr. Waterhouse's designs . . . would soon disappear.'[32]

Donaldson and Street were asked to expand on their comments, and provided a lengthy confidential report to the committee, after which they retired from the debate. But an examination of Speakman & Charlesworth's plans shows how much better Waterhouse's planning was for the disposition of rooms and for circulation patterns.[33] This was, after all, a complex series of rooms to fit on a difficult site, and he had already made his mark as a spatial planner in the Assize Courts, and had already built in Ancoats on a triangular site – the Congregational Chapel and School (1861–65, subsequently demolished).

Waterhouse was duly appointed by the committee and the foundation stone was laid on 26 October 1868. The last great Gothic building in the country (328 ft long on Albert Square, 388 ft long on Princess Street and 350 ft long on Lloyd Street) was under way, thirteenth-century in spirit but, in the words of its architect, 'essentially of the nineteenth century, and adapted to the wants of the present day.' The building, Gothic in appearance with its lancet windows, quatrefoil tracery and crocketing and internal piers supporting what look to be groin vaults, is actually a 'modern' building constructed of brick, and clad externally in Spinkwell stone, a hard, resistant sandstone from a quarry near Bradford [47]. The exposed elements internally are in stone or terracotta. Wrought-iron beams provide the internal support, and the building contains the latest Dennett 'fireproof' system – the vaults and office ceilings are lined in concrete and filled to floor level.

During the early part of 1869 Waterhouse was revising the angles of the Albert Street façade and, importantly, modifying the design of the clock and bell tower, which in his first submission had been a rather unsatisfactory pointed dome set on a drum. Eventually he designed a tower, more than twice the height of the Town Hall, and rather more like the tower of Worthington's submission. This still did not satisfy the architect, for in July 1875, even as the tower was being built, Waterhouse returned to the council to ask for another 16 ft to be added to its height, at a cost of £500. In the end the tower presents a rather more elegant and pleasing shape than the somewhat squat earlier versions, and the spire, it may be noted, reflects not a little the appearance of the Albert Memorial. The original bell of 6 tons 9 wt was replaced in 1882 by a bell of 8 tons 2 wt, 6 ft high and 7 ft 7 $\frac{1}{2}$ in. in diameter – the largest perfect bell in the UK.

That Waterhouse was able to make major changes to his design shows the advantages of the Gothic style. As Ruskin had put it so well in *The Stones of Venice*,

Gothic is not only the best, but the only *rational* architecture, as being that which can fit itself most easily to all services, vulgar or noble. Undefined in its slope of roof, height of shaft, breadth of arch or disposition of ground plan, it can shrink into a turret, expand into a hall, coil into a staircase, or spring into a spire with undegraded grace and unexhausted energy: and whenever it finds occasion for change in its form or purpose, it submits to it without the slightest sense of loss either to its unity or majesty . . . And it is one of the chief virtues of the Gothic builders that they never suffered ideas of outside symmetries and consistencies to interfere with the real use and value of what they did. If they wanted a window, they opened one; a room, they added one; a buttress, they built one; utterly regardless of any established conventionalities of external appearance, knowing (as indeed it always happened) that such daring interruptions of the formal plan would rather give additional interest to its symmetry than injure it.[34]

On Waterhouse's building the major first-storey 'state' rooms on the Albert Square façade have large windows, reflecting the status and size of the rooms; the windows on the second floor are smaller, for the smaller offices; dormer windows pop out of the roof space for the minor offices; the corner pavilions have an additional floor. A look inside the Lord Mayor's banqueting room will show just how well Waterhouse was able to disguise the difficult angle on Albert Square and Princess Street. Waterhouse's façade on Albert Square is far from symmetrical, and this adds to its interest, although away from Albert Square on the Princess Street and Lloyd Street elevations the beat of the fenestration is far more regular, and consequently looks far less picturesque. 'Waterhouse's buildings, however, are not only monuments of the Gothic Revival; they are also examples of his power to organise diverse and complicated plans on a modern scale, if not in a modern style. That was something new in architecture

48] Town Hall, the banqueting room, Alfred Waterhouse, 1867–77

— something that had not been needed since the Romans had had to handle the crowds of the Colosseum and the Thermae. It was the organisation of space as opposed to mere façade.'[35]

The entrance on Albert Square, like a small version of the portal of a French cathedral, climbs over granite steps from Newry in Armagh, and through a lobby whose walls are 7 ft thick to support the weight of the tower above. This opens out into the vaulted ground-floor antechamber which extends left and right the full extent of the building. On the right, the sculpture hall is furnished with Bath limestone panels and dark grey sandstone from the Forest of Dean supported on granite piers – red granite from Inverness, pink and grey granite from the Ross of Mull, dark grey and white from Newry. The ceremonial route progresses up stately staircases to the right and left of the ground floor which lead to the first-storey antechamber, top-lit and the glass emblazoned with the names of mayors and aldermen: to one side is the great hall and to the other the open, arcaded corridor off which are the 'state' rooms; the Lord Mayor's reception rooms, the banqueting room [48], and the council chamber and its lobby. All these rooms have elaborately decorated panelled ceilings, high dados in polished oak, and remarkable alabaster and oak fireplaces. The walls above the dados are now wallpapered but were intended to be covered with murals.

There are three circular staircases at each corner of the building, named from their granite steps and piers: English, from Shap in Cumbria at the Albert Square/Princess Street corner; Irish, from Newry in Armagh at the Albert Square/Lloyd Street corner; Scottish, from Dalbeattie in Kirkcudbrightshire at the Princess Street/Lloyd Street corner. Throughout, in the floor and vault mosaics and the diaper pattern on the walls, is the cotton flower, symbol of Manchester's wealth. Also on the floor is the bee, symbolic of Manchester's industriousness.

49] Town Hall, the great hall, Alfred Waterhouse, 1867–77

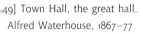

Corridors run back along the Princess Street and Lloyd Street fronts to the offices of the Corporation officials and the departments of water and gas, and cross-passages and minor staircases run from these corridors. In the bays are seats for consultations with the officials.[36]

The great hall, set within the internal triangular courtyard, is magnificent [49], with its mock hammerbeam timbered ceiling, the panels of which are decorated with the arms of the countries with which Manchester traded, and at the far end an organ by Cavaillé Coll of Paris, then the world's greatest organ maker. The murals under the huge side windows are by Ford Madox Brown and depict, not always accurately, Manchester's history.[37]

As well as a telegraphic communication system between the major offices, Waterhouse also provided an up-to-date heating system throughout building by heating coils in the basement (three large and one subsidiary boilers provided the heat). The English staircase, 21 ft in diameter, contained a central cylinder flue 6 ft 6 in. in diameter. Heating was also by hot water pipes in floors.

Some 1,373 drawings were produced, many in Waterhouse's hand or with his annotations; sometimes the contractor had to produce three-dimensional models for Waterhouse to approve. From 1875 Waterhouse was designing furniture and fittings, curtains for the banqueting room (made by the Royal School of Needlework), lettering for the departments, china for the dinner service, and even lamp standards for the surrounding streets. The statistics are memorable: 14 million bricks, 500,000 ft^3 of stone, 1,700 ft of granite shafting, 30,000 ft^2 of glass and 14,000 ft^2 of ornamental glazing, 68,000 ft of polished oak. There are 350 rooms, over 700 external windows, and eighty water closets.

For all the stone cutting a huge number of stonemasons were employed: there were upwards of 1,000 men on site, and for the last twelve months over 700 masons. Ten tool sharpeners were employed, each man turning out about 600 tools, a remarkable total average of 6,000 per day. The builders were George Smith & Co. of London, and their account with the Corporation was £230,000. The builder's plant alone cost £20,000, and included three steam engines, thirteen steam and hand cranes, eight steam saw frames (which operated day and night for two years), eight steam polishing tables, two lathes for turning and polishing stone shafts, a sand washer and a circular saw.[38]

The building was topped out on 4 December 1875 and opened on 13 September 1877, attended by the Lord Mayor and Council, the Lord Chief Justice of England, seventeen present or former MPs and the mayors of twenty-six other towns and cities. Four hundred people attended the banquet, though Her Majesty, apparently still in mourning for Albert, declined to attend. On the Saturday a three-mile procession of 44,000 working men, with banners, bands and the tools of their trade, paraded through the city to the Town Hall, watched by a crowd of 66,000.

The Times, perhaps a little unfairly, claimed that the Town Hall had been constructed 'to provide . . . a suite of civic state apartments such as might relieve the local rulers from too painful a sense of contrast when they thought of the Guildhall or Mansion House in London'. Though it did go on to say, 'All the world has heard of the scale on which Manchester has organised a local

50] Cobden Building,
Quay Street, 1700s

administration with many departments – Police, Water Supply, Gas Works, Paving, Sewering, and everything requisite for keeping so great a city in tolerable order.'[39] And as Joseph Chamberlain pointed out in his inaugural speech as Mayor of Birmingham on 13 January 1874, 'In Manchester the Corporation possessed the gas and water works, and they secured from the profits of these undertakings an enormous capital. He was told that at present the amount was something like a million sterling, with which they were able to erect those corporate buildings which were the glory of the town.'[40]

While the work on the Town Hall was proceeding, Waterhouse was building another great Manchester institution, Owens College on Oxford Road, later to become the Victoria University of Manchester. The college was named after John Owens, a wealthy merchant, who, in 1846, bequeathed £96,000 for the foundation of a college for the instruction of young men 'in such branches of learning and science as are now and may hereafter be taught in the English universities'.[41] Richard Cobden's old house in Quay Street (on the corner of Byrom Street) was purchased [50], and Travis & Mangnall were contracted to build a two-storey laboratory and lecture hall in place of the stables behind the house. Professors of classics, mathematics and natural philosophy, mental and moral philosophy and English language and literature were appointed, sixty-two students were enrolled, and the college opened on 13 March 1851. By 1856 the number of day students had fallen to thirty-three, and during this lean time Henry (later Sir Henry) Roscoe, Professor of Chemistry, was standing at the college entrance one evening when a man approached him. 'Maister, is this th' neet asylum?' With a doleful shake of the head Roscoe replied, 'Not yet, my man, but if you come in six months' time I fear it will be.'[42]

When examinations of the University of London were introduced to Owens College from 1859 student numbers soared, and it was quickly realised that a new campus was required. By October 1868 a site on Oxford Road had been found, and almost £77,000 had been subscribed to the general fund. Waterhouse was appointed architect, and the first stone was laid in September 1870, by the Duke of Devonshire, president of the college. Behind Waterhouse's soaring Gothic Revival façade [51] was a basement, with a chemical theatre, museum and lecture laboratory, rooms for natural philosophy and engineering, examination rooms and a geological museum. The ground floor contained the boardroom, secretary and clerks' rooms, lecture rooms and apparatus rooms for natural philosophy, a large arts classroom, engineering rooms and drawing office. On the first floor were arts classrooms, natural history classrooms and museum, staff rooms, students' reading room, the library, and a freehand drawing room. The spacious attics were used as a temporary museum. Behind the main building was a quadrangle, with a chemical laboratory block which was said to be the most complete in Britain. In, and fronting, Coupland Street was the medical school (amalgamation with the Manchester Royal School of Medicine had taken place in 1872). On 7 October 1873 the new Owens College opened to students. The college was to all intents a university, and any degree which London University could bestow could be obtained at the college. On the payment of a fee of 10s 6d a student could go through the full course of lectures.[43] The college itself cost nearly £180,000.

Even before an architect was appointed to the Town Hall, it was realised that the inclusion within the Town Hall of the intended police courts would not be

51] University, Owens Building, Oxford Road, Alfred Waterhous 1870–98

52] Police and Sessions Court, Minshull Street, presentation drawing, Thomas Worthington, 1867–73

possible, so in the summer of 1867 six Manchester practices were invited to compete in a closed competition for the new Police and Sessions Courts. The firms were Clegg & Knowles, Speakman & Charlesworth, Edward Salomons, Alfred Waterhouse, Mangnall & Littlewood and Thomas Worthington. Mangnall & Littlewood declined, as did Waterhouse, perhaps in anticipation of winning the Town Hall competition. The remainder submitted their schemes on 7 September 1867. The Stipendiary Magistrate and the Clerk to the Justices recommended Worthington's designs and the General Purposes Committee accepted their view. Work commenced in March 1869 and, in spite of many difficulties, including a builders' strike of thirteen months, was completed by 1873. Worthington's estimate was £35,700; the final cost was £81,000.

The site was a cramped one amid the warehouses of Aytoun and Minshull Streets. Only oblique views of the courts were possible, but Worthington handled the site restrictions well [52]. A tall bell and clock tower on the import-ant Minshull Street/Bloom Street corner, a high central gable over the magistrates' entrance opposite Richmond Street and a tower on the Canal Street corner provide a strong visual marker on each of the streets.

Finances precluded the use of stone cladding. On a semi-basement of mill-stone grit, the building is in an orange-red brick, and the plane walls are given interest by white stone dressings, constructively as the door and window arches, and decoratively as string courses, on the quoins, as a band at the top of the tower and for the tourelles of the bell tower and central gable. The use of red brick with white stone detailing is characteristic of a number of Gothic buildings in the Veneto, and a watercolour by Worthington titled 'S. Fermo Maggiore [sic], Verona', undoubtedly provided a source for the building. The tall roof structures of the courts, however, are much more reminiscent of the roofs of southern Germany. The windows are grouped in the Venetian manner in pairs and threes, their lights separated by granite-shafted columns, the larger openings having stone spandrels with multifoiled openings. The beautifully carved capitals and mythical creatures at the side of the doorways are well worth viewing.

For reasons of security, and to minimise the noise from the surrounding streets, the four law courts were situated in the centre of the complex and lit by clerestory and gable windows. Surrounding the courts were rooms and corridors, the only exception being on the Aytoun Street side, where the goods roadway of an existing building came right up to the walls.[44] Access for the public, jurors and magistracy was through separate entrances on Bloom and Minshull Streets, and cleverly designed circulation routes kept them separate throughout the whole building. Prisoners were fetched to cells in the semi-

53] Reform Club, King Street, Edward Salomons, 1870–71

basement via an open courtyard, and each cell had its own w.c. and wash basin. Across the open courtyard ran a glazed bridge. Heating was by boilers in the basement, and a heat-exchange plant directed warmed air through brick ducts to the courts – the tall campanile in the centre of the courts was the boiler chimney. The courts were drastically 'modernised' in the 1960s, but more recent building work has restored them – the refurbishment will be dealt with in a later chapter.

The last major Venetian Gothic building to be erected in Manchester was the Reform Club of 1870–71 on King Street, by Edward Salomons and John Philpot-Jones [53]. In this building of York sandstone it is the *piano nobile* that takes the attention. Soaring windows of two lights separated by thin stone colonnettes are contained within polychrome arches of a distinctly Venetian shape, and are tall to illuminate the meeting room. The arches are carried on polished Shap granite columns. Little balconies cover the bases of the windows, and a larger balcony is supported by the columns flanking the major entrance on King Street. On the second storey, pairs of smaller windows with pointed arches are also flanked by columns. On the corners of the building what can only be described as oriel towers rise through the upper floors, culminating in gazebos and (originally) in domed roofs. Above the body of the building was a steeply pitched roof which had dormer windows and a flèche spire. The roof of the main building and the towers have been modified, and consequently the building has lost some of its *élan*. The Reform Club opened its doors on 19 October 1871. Internally a grand staircase, lined with linenfold panelling, ran to the two-storey-high dining room on the *piano nobile* and then up to the billiard room in the roof, running the whole width of the building. In the 1890s the remarkable marble-lined lavatories were installed, together with a card room with painted panels on the top floor.

Land in the city centre was now too expensive for domestic residences, and Albert Square, like Deansgate, King Street and Cross Street, fast became a favoured location for offices. The demand for buildings was, of course, pushing up land prices in the business sector. In 1873 land at Chancery Lane was selling at £33 per square yard, in Fountain Street at over £41 and on the corner of St Ann Street and Cross Street at almost £65 per square yard. This is comparable with prices in Paris, where land at the Place de l'Opéra sold in 1869 at £68–£72 per square metre for corner plots, and even similar to prices in London outside the centre of the 'Square Mile'. Near London's Royal Exchange the highest prices were a considerable £40 per superficial foot, though £30 was probably average for the City. But at the end of Cornhill land was only 10s per superficial foot, and across Bishopsgate 5s per foot.[45]

From the early 1870s the new Town Hall was beginning to make its influence felt, and the impact of its style can be seen in the new buildings erected in Albert Square. On the corner of Southmill Street and Lloyd Street is Lloyd's House, by Speakman (*fl.* 1867–74) & Charlesworth (1832–71), built by 1868. This is a brick and stone-dressed building with windows in the Venetian manner, undoubtedly in recognition of the Memorial Hall opposite. Next door to the Memorial Hall, on Albert Square, is Albert Chambers (Clegg & Knowles, 1868),

54] Buildings on Albert Square
(Lloyd Street)

55] Lawrence Buildings,
Mount Street, Pennington
& Bridgen, 1874

built as offices for the Manchester Corporation Gas Works.* Here is a debased form of Venetian Gothic, and the details of the building show a strong debt to the Memorial Hall, though the building is entirely clad in Darley Dale stone and there is no sign of the structural polychromy of Worthington's building [54].

At the far end of the block, on the corner of Albert Square and Mount Street, is St Andrew's Chambers, by George Tunstall Redmayne (1840–1912), and dated 1872, by which time the Albert Square elevation of the Town Hall was well under way. This building, also in Darley Dale stone, reflects the style of the Town Hall, with tall lancet windows and quatrefoil tracery, perhaps because it faced the Town Hall, or as likely because Redmayne had been a pupil of, and then assistant to, Waterhouse. The elevation, like the Town Hall, is enlivened by spiky little turrets, and was described by the *Builder* as 'one of the best examples of street architecture in the city'.[46] The middle building in the block is the Bridgewater Buildings by Clegg & Knowles, dated 1873, again in Darley Dale stone, and also in a thirteenth-century Gothic style reminiscent of the Town Hall. Just around the corner, on Mount Street, between County Street and Central Street (once Chapel and Dickinson Streets) are the Lawrence Buildings of 1874, by Nathan Glossop Pennington (*fl.* 1849–1900) and Thomas Edward Bridgen (1832–1895) [55]. This building too is stone-clad, and the style is a florid fourteenth-century Gothic. This was a building for the Inland Revenue and Government Excise Inspectors.[47]

Two years later, on the newly widened Deansgate,[†] on the corner of John Dalton Street, Pennington & Bridgen built another government office, Queen's Chambers [56]. Unlike their Lawrence Buildings, this building is Gothic but no longer High Gothic, except for the corner entrance with its triplet of pointed arches. What distinguishes the building is the variety of window openings, almost all with mullions and transoms. Also by Pennington & Bridgen is the Glasgow Assurance Building on Albert Square, on the corner of Cross Street, of 1877, a frothy confection of red brick and white stone, prominent gables and chimneys [58]. Here can be seen the first stirrings of the Queen Anne Revival in Manchester, but the building has too much Gothic detail to be properly Queen Anne, and it is not until the comparatively late date of 1888, at Elliot House on Deansgate, by Royle (1839–1904) & Bennett (1841–1901), that the Queen Anne Revival arrived in the city – red brick, gables and chimney stacks, and now with long sash windows [59].[48]

---

* The first gasworks were in Water Street in 1817, and the first Gas Act for the supply of gas to the town was obtained in 1824. By 1826 the town was lit by 3,000 lamps, of which 1,120 were gas, the remainder being oil lamps. By 1831 there were four gasworks in the town. They were made a municipal undertaking in 1843 – the only large town in the country to have its own municipal supply. Gas fires and stoves were 'rented' by the Gas Committee in 1884, and in 1890 the committee provided the first coin-in-the-slot gas meters.

† The Corporation started the widening of Deansgate in 1869, under the terms of the *Manchester Corporation Street Improvement Act*. Prior to its widening and straightening, Deansgate had been only 30 ft wide; the line of the west side of the street was retained, but all the buildings on the east side of Deansgate were demolished.

In the last two decades of the nineteenth century, architects, nationally, were borrowing freely from Elizabethan and Jacobean sources as well as from Continental sources, often lavishing a profusion of styles on the same building. As Professor Simpson told the Liverpool Architectural Association,

> It is no unusual thing to find men designing in Gothic one day, in Classic the next, or indulging in their odd moments in the delectable compound called 'Queen Anne'. They were like children, who, with several sweetmeats before them, nibbled a bit first from one and then from the other. This architectural jumble was due as much as anything to the changed conditions of the time.

56] Queen's Chambers, Deansgate, Pennington & Bridgen, 1876

57] Barton Arcade, Deansgate, Corbett Raby & Sawyer, 1871

58] Glasgow Assurance Building, Cross Street, Pennington & Bridgen, 1877

59] Elliot House, Deansgate, Royle & Bennett, 1888

60] Prudential Assurance Company Building, 76–80 King Street, Alfred Waterhouse, 1881

] Lancashire & Yorkshire Bank, Spring Gardens, Charles Heathcote, 1890

Sketch-book architecture became the rage. Flemish gables, German doorways, French windows and Spanish ironwork crossed the Channel to form original architectural designs . . . It tickled the palate, but it did not fill the stomach.[49]

In Manchester, too, architects were developing freer architectural forms, and a look at the buildings on King Street and Spring Gardens reveals the move away from the restraint, and constraint, of the Italianate style.

At 76–80 King Street is the Prudential Assurance Building of 1881 by Alfred Waterhouse [60]. It is in red terracotta,[50] red sandstone and vibrant red brick, characteristic of a number of Prudential Assurance buildings by the architect, and giving rise to the epithet 'Slaughterhouse Gothic'. Gothic here is in the mind rather than in the eye – there are no pointed arches, no crocketing, no tracery. The round-headed arches are positively Romanesque and it may be significant that Waterhouse's Romanesque Natural History Museum in London had just opened. A year later he built the Commercial Buildings at 60 Spring Gardens (now Gan House) as an office block in a restrained *palazzo* style. On the opposite corner at 47 Spring Gardens, rounding the corner of Concert Lane, is the Commercial Union Buildings (later Martin's Bank), by Charles Heathcote, 1881–82.* Under its skin this is a *palazzo*-style building, but the pilasters which decorate the façade are Jacobean, not Classical, and all the decoration is thin, complex and fanciful. Next at 43–5 Spring Gardens, and acting as a termination to King Street, is the Lancashire & Yorkshire Bank, by Heathcote & Rawle, 1890 [61]. This has cross-windows, deeply rusticated, square 'Doric' piers and paired Corinthian columns supporting a gable like an Italian Baroque church.

* Charles H. Heathcote (1850–1938) was one of Manchester's most prolific, yet little-known, architects. Heathcote had been articled to Charles Hansom from January 1865 to January 1869, then after a brief time in the offices of Hirst, Lockwood and Mawson, he joined Edward Salomons, before setting up on his own in Manchester in 1873.

As if trying to outdo its neighbours in magnificence is the National Provincial Bank at 41 Spring Gardens, on the York Street corner, by Waterhouse, 1888–90. Giant-order Doric and Ionic pilasters and broken-headed arched pediments vie with gables and balconies carried on Elizabethan consoles – Classical as it rounds the corner but Mannerist on King Street. On the opposite corner of Spring Gardens and York Street is Parr's Bank by Heathcote, 1902, which in contrast to the other earlier buildings is in red sandstone [62]. Here, set on huge bases, are columns which support nothing but escutcheons, and a corner dome supported on two sets of paired Ionic columns which are themselves supported by giant attached 'columns' running the whole height of the building. This is as Mannerist as buildings get in Manchester, and the whole thing looks as if Heathcote is trying to outdo Waterhouse on the opposite corner.

Among this conflict of styles arose the last Gothic Revival building in Manchester, the John Rylands Library on Deansgate [63]. The main façade is covered in a delicate filigree of tracery in the Perpendicular style, and there are towers on each corner, like ornate versions of the lantern of Ely Cathedral. Inside, it is just like a small vaulted cathedral. The stone is a dark red St Bee's sandstone from Langwathby near Penrith, Cumbria. The extension at the rear is in sandstone from Rainhill.

The building, which commenced in 1890, was a remarkable memorial to one of Manchester's greatest and probably least known cotton magnates. John Rylands became the sole owner of the family business in 1847 after the death

62] Parr's Bank, Spring Gardens
Charles Heathcote, 1902

63] Rylands Library, Deansgate
Basil Champneys, 1890–99

of his father, and considerably expanded the concern over the next forty years. He produced textiles, cabinets and printing machines, and had four large warehouses in Market Street and Tib Street. Before his death at Stretford, on 11 December 1888, aged eighty-seven, Rylands had been the country's largest cotton manufacturer and the largest textile distributor in the UK, as well as becoming Manchester's first ever multi-millionaire. His seventeen mills and factories employed 15,000 people and contained 200,000 spindles and 5,000 looms, and his finishing works at Heapey, which was half a mile in circumference, was turning out cloth at thirty-five tons a day.[51]

Rylands's widow, Mrs Enriqueta Augusta Rylands, met the architect Basil Champneys (1842–1935) in the library of Mansfield College, Oxford, designed earlier by Champneys. She was after a suitable memorial for her late husband, and found in the library something sympathetic to her ideas – Rylands had himself built up a huge collection of books in his lifetime, particularly of religious works – and Mrs. Rylands commissioned Champneys to design a suitable library in her husband's memory.

The building was to be lavish, using the best stonemasons, woodcarvers and metalworkers, and every detail had to be submitted to Mrs. Rylands for her agreement. To make the building fire-resistant, the stone vaulting was topped with six inches of concrete, instead of the customary timber roof. Since the architect did not know what the final building was to be like, he provided the whole site with a foundation layer of concrete 4 ft 6 in. deep. To equip the library, Mrs Rylands spent nearly a quarter of a million pounds on the finest collection of books she could find: the library of Earl Spencer at Althorp cost her £210,000, and later the Crawford manuscript collection cost £155,000. Altogether £1 million was spent on the building and its collection, which contains a copy of the 'Wicked Bible' in which the printer has omitted the word 'not' in the Seventh Commandment. The library was opened on 6 October 1899, and Mrs Rylands was given the freedom of the city. In 1972 it merged with the University of Manchester library to form the John Rylands University Library of Manchester, the third largest academic library in the country. Beresford Pite said of the building, 'Mr Champneys has given us a building which has at last removed the reproach that the Law Courts were the last word on the subject of English Gothic . . . Rylands is a monument to a great benefactor, a monument to a great idea, carried out by an architect with a great ideal.'[52]

As the chapter started with one pupil of Lane & Alley, so it cannot end without a reference to another, the architect of the Comedy Theatre of 1884, which stood on the corner of Mount Street and Peter Street; in brick and stone, and vaguely Venetian Gothic, but now demolished.* The architect was Alfred Darbyshire (1839–1908), the son of a cloth dyer, and a nephew of George

---

* It later became the Gaiety Theatre, and Miss Horniman moved there from the Midland Hotel, put on plays by Shaw, Galsworthy and Drinkwater, and encouraged the 'Manchester school' of contemporary realism. It became the Gaiety Cinema in 1930s and was pulled down in the 1950s to make room for offices.

Bradshaw of railway timetable fame. He was articled on 31 October 1855 to Lane & Alley, though he never was, contrary to popular belief, a fellow pupil of Alfred Waterhouse, who had already set up his own practice. From 1862 Darbyshire was in practice in his own right, taking premises in St James's Square. He soon turned from Alley's classicism, for in 1864 the young architect made his first study tour to the Continent, through Belgium, Germany and Holland, and 'returned convinced there was no art equal in beauty and poetry to that of the Middle Ages'.[53] In that year he was both elected ARIBA (and eventually was made vice-president) and appeared on stage in the Theatre Royal as Jacques in *As You Like It* – and was offered, but refused, a professional acting contract.

In 1865, at Bury, he played Polonius to Henry Irving's Hamlet. Irving had spent five years in Manchester at the Theatre Royal, and this performance was to be his last before leaving for London and eventual knighthood. In 1878 Irving asked Darbyshire to redecorate the Lyceum Theatre in London, and when Darbyshire's autobiography, *An Architect's Experiences: Professional, Artistic and Theatrical*, was published in 1897, it was dedicated 'to my old friend Sir Henry Irving . . . with love and greeting'. Through his amateur dramatics Darbyshire knew Charles Calvert, actor-manager of the Prince's Theatre, who employed him in 1869 to redecorate the theatre. From then on he spent much of his practice designing and staging plays, and in redecorating and designing theatres as well as Pendleton Town Hall, Heaton Moor Reform Club, Salford Police Station, a mill in St Petersburg and various schools, clubs, libraries and factories.

In 1884 Irving and Darbyshire came up with the idea of the Irving–Darbyshire Safety Theatre, which called for an asbestos safety curtain which, in the event of fire, would instantly segregate the audience from the stage, and a glazed and louvred lantern so that smoke and fire would make for the shaft. Theatres would be physically isolated from other buildings, with plenty of emergency exits with easy access to the streets, and 'every space upon which the human foot is planted in the auditorium and escape staircases must be absolutely fireproof and unburnable'.[54] Some of these measures were put into effect in 1884 in the Comedy Theatre, but it was not until a disastrous fire at the Theatre Royal, Exeter, on 5 September 1887, when nearly 200 people were killed, that the need for fire safety was broadly recognised. In 1889 the people of Exeter asked Darbyshire to design their New Theatre Royal. The ensuing publicity spread the creed of the Irving–Darbyshire Safety Plan, and all subsequent theatres have been based on their ideas. For that, if for nothing else, Darbyshire should be better remembered.[55]

The Palace Theatre of Varieties on Oxford Street was designed by Darbyshire in 1889–91, where again he was able to incorporate many of his safety concepts. The Palace was originally stone-clad in a free Renaissance style, with paired columns and pilasters on each of three floors, topped, on the Oxford Street façade, by a large, decorated gable. In the centre of the first floor on Oxford Street was an open loggia in the manner of Palladio or Sansovino. All rather clumsy, but now all gone; the exterior was altered in 1913, and in 1956 clad in tiles like a public lavatory. The interior, however, was beautifully restored in the 1980s, thanks to the efforts of Sir Robert Scott.

Alfred Darbyshire died on 5 July 1908, and one of the last jobs of his declining years was the design of the triumphal arches for the Queen's opening of the Manchester Ship Canal in 1894, an event as important to Manchester as had been the arrival of the railways.

7

1890–1940

AMBITION – FROM THE SHIP CANAL TO WORLD WAR II

Far more than Lancashire realises is growing up another Greater London, as it were – a City Region of which Liverpool is the seaport and Manchester the market, now with its canal port also; while Oldham and many other factory towns, more accurately called 'factory districts' are the workshops. [Patrick Geddes, *Cities in Evolution*, 1915]

WHEN, in June 1882, a canal to the sea was first promoted by Daniel Adamson[1] and other businessmen, Manchester was in a state of decline, 'with whole streets of empty houses, derelict warehouses, falling population. Since the canal was opened almost the whole of the centre of Manchester has been rebuilt, the major industrial area of Trafford Park has been created, and the flow of trade so stimulated that Manchester is now [1948] the fourth port in the kingdom.'[2]

The Ship Canal was not intended to replace Liverpool as a port but to reduce the price of transport into Manchester; because of the high rates charged by Liverpool, it was said to be cheaper to bring goods into Manchester by rail from Hull. To get the Ship Canal built took a considerable battle in Parliament, with opposition from Liverpool, the railway companies and some Manchester men with interests in Liverpool shipping lines. It took three years, three Bills and £172,500 (plus a similar sum from its opponents) to get through Parliament. At one committee stage the Lords called 151 witnesses, some 25,367 questions were asked and the answers filled a book of 1,861 pages. The third Bill passed through both Houses in 1885, and work on cutting the canal started in 1887. The total cost was some £15 million, including £5 million invested by Manchester

Corporation in 1893 when the money ran out. There was also an investment by 39,000 shareholders, the largest number of investors in a private company to that date.

The canal is thirty-five and a half miles long, connecting Manchester with the Mersey at Eastham, six miles above Liverpool. It took six years to build and was officially opened by Queen Victoria on 21 May 1894. A CWS ship, the *Pioneer*, landed the first inward shipment on New Year's Day 1894, and was the first vessel registered in the new port. On the same day Manchester was created a customs port. The Ship Canal is often dismissed as merely another river navigation, yet, at the time of its completion, there were only five ships in the world which were too large for the canal. In its first year the Ship Canal handled 925,659 tons of cargo, and in the following year 1,358,875 tons (and by 1963, 15,112,884 tons, by when Manchester had become the country's third largest port).

Firm opposition in its early days from established shipping lines and railway companies, as well as the Ports of London and Liverpool, debarred Manchester from direct trade with Australia and the United States. The Mersey Docks & Harbour Board dredged away the Mersey Bar and 'extended its accommodation for the trades in cattle, wool and timber threatened by the competition of Manchester. Liverpool merchants opened branches in Manchester in order to retain control over the import of timber, grain and cotton.'[3] Liverpool jealously tried to retain its pre-eminence in imports of raw cotton, having had links with New Orleans since 1820, but to little avail, for the Manchester Cotton Association[4] was established on 1 October 1895, and direct links were set up between Manchester and Galveston, New Orleans and Florida. About one-fifth of the American cotton, and more than half the Egyptian cotton, for manufacture in Lancashire came into Manchester, Egypt having succeeded India as the second largest supplier of raw cotton in 1891. Manchester rose from the fourth largest importer of cotton in 1894 to the second largest in 1896, and by 1908 Manchester imported more Egyptian cotton than Liverpool. After the opening of the Ship Canal, Manchester became the foremost banking, commercial and transport centre outside London. By the end of the nineteenth century it had the largest number of provincial clearing houses in the country, and by 1902 Manchester clearings were six times higher than Bristol, four times higher than Birmingham and 48 per cent higher than Liverpool. Manchester had become important enough as a trading centre that, by 1900, thirty-six governments had established consular or other diplomatic offices in the city.

Adjoining the Ship Canal was the Trafford Park estate of 1,183 acres of parkland with deer and a notable hall (destroyed in the blitz of 1940) belonging to Sir Humphrey de Trafford. Manchester Corporation had considered buying the park for Manchester's equivalent of Hyde Park but temporised too long over purchase of the land, and it was left to a private developer, Ernest Terah Hooley, who bought the land for £360,000 and floated Trafford Park Estates on 17 August 1896. Marshall Stevens, who had been Adamson's deputy, and general manager of the Ship Canal Company, became general manger and persuaded Hooley to develop the park as the world's first 'industrial estate'.

Within five years of the establishment of Trafford Park Estates, forty firms had established themselves there, and Trafford Park, Europe's largest industrial estate, was becoming the workshop of Manchester.

Among the earliest structures were grain silos, for grain was a useful import, as it provided ballast for ships carrying raw cotton (and even as late as 1970 Manchester ranked as the sixth largest grain port in the UK). A wooden silo with Europe's largest grain elevator was built opposite the entrance to the Ship Canal's No. 9 dock in 1898 (destroyed by fire in the air raids of 1940), and in 1906 the Hovis flour mill was linked to the elevator by an underground conveyor belt. The mill was the nucleus of Rank Hovis McDougall, and four more mills were established in 1911–13. In 1912–15 the No. 2 grain elevator to the south of No. 9 dock was built in reinforced concrete.

The Co-operative Wholesale Society bought land at Trafford Wharf in 1903, where it opened a bacon factory and flour mill, and in 1905 opened its first building in Manchester, the CWS Building, Corporation Street (F. E. L. Harris). In 1906 the CWS purchased the Sun Mill, and ended inland milling in Rochdale and Oldham. Doubling the Sun Mill in 1913 made it the UK's largest mill, with its own wharf, elevator and silos.

The British Westinghouse Electric Company bought 11 per cent of the estate in 1899, and erected the country's largest engineering works, manufacturing steam turbines and turbo-generators. It also created the 'Village', a fifty-five-acre site of 600 homes, built for Westinghouse employees and laid out on an American grid system with names like 'Second Street' and 'Third Avenue'. By the end of 1903 Westinghouse employed 6,000 of the 12,000 workers in the Park. It was reorganised as Metropolitan Vickers Electrical Company in 1919, the year when John Alcock met A. W. Brown in the Metro-Vick factory and persuaded the management that it was possible to fly the Atlantic. Their epoch-making flight in a Vickers Vimy aircraft took place on 14 June 1919.

Westinghouse's American architects were assisted in the planning and construction of their factory by Charles Heathcote. His connections with the Ship Canal and Trafford Park were considerable: by 1899 he had built fifteen warehouses for the Manchester Ship Canal Company, together with others for the Liverpool Warehousing Company, and refrigerated stores for the Colonial Company in Manchester; half the factories in the Trafford area were by his firm.[5]

The Ford Motor Company arrived in 1910, and by 1913 had become the country's largest car manufacturer. Its factory, too, was designed by Heathcote. Ford left Trafford for Dagenham in 1931 in order to be closer to its European markets (and Heathcote with his sons designed the Ford factory at Dagenham in 1928–31 and Ford's offices and showrooms in Regent Street, London), but returned in World War II, employing 17,000 workers to build Rolls-Royce Merlin engines. Henry Royce had already set up an early factory there, building cranes. Brooke Bond erected a large warehouse for blending and packing tea in 1922, and Guinness sunk artesian wells for their brewery. Kellogg's, in 1938, opened its £1 million headquarters for European manufacturing. ICI built the first UK plant there for the bulk production of penicillin. By 1937 industry

64] Northern Rock Insurance Building, Cross Street, Charles Heathcote, 1895

65] Lloyds Bank, King Street, Charles Heathcote, 1915

had grown so much that the petty township of Trafford was granted the status of a borough, and its mayor was given a knighthood. The development eventually spilt over on to the Ship Canal Company's land – the Barton Dock estate. At its peak, during World War II, the Park employed 75,000 workers.

In contrast to his severely functional buildings in Trafford Park, Heathcote continued to produce ebullient office buildings in the city centre in a restless range of styles. At the junction of King Street and Cross Street are three Heathcote buildings: at 64 Cross Street the Northern Rock Insurance building, of 1895, Flemish Renaissance [64]; at 37 Cross Street, the Eagle Insurance building, of 1911, a mixture of Classical, Gothic and Flemish; and at 35 Cross Street (on the site of the Old Town Hall), Lloyds Bank of 1915 [65]. The bank is an extravagantly Baroque building in Portland stone, and is strongly reminiscent of A. Brumwell Thomas's Stockport Town Hall of 1904–08, or T. E. Collcutt's Lloyd's Registry of Shipping, Fenchurch Street, London of 1900–01, but 1915 is very late for such an excessively ornate building. Reilly contrasted it with Cockerell's Bank of England, and wrote: 'Although they [bankers] do not come down to their business in fancy dress they have, apparently, no similar code for their buildings. But this is a serious matter. What is it that is really wrong with Lloyds' Bank building? It is simply or very largely a matter of dress. If one shaved off all the ornaments and columns . . . it might be a satisfying building.'[6] The fourth building on the junction is the red-brick building for the Ottoman Bank (Mills & Murgatroyd, 1889), notable for its corkscrew chimneys.

66] Prince's Building, Oxford
Street, I. R. E. Birkett, 1903

At 107 Piccadilly, Heathcote built the sombre Baroque mass of Sparrow Hardwick & Co.'s building in banded red sandstone and brick (1898), and at the other end of Piccadilly, at Nos 7–9, is perhaps one of his most bizarre works, the Moorish Kardomah Coffee Company building of 1910. The upper storey has, unfortunately, lost its Moorish domes, but here was a miniature Alhambra in grey-white glazed faience. Heathcote was not alone in adopting unusual sources: at 22 Brown Street is an imitation Norman castle, by Briggs Wolstenholme & Thornley, of 1909; on the Prince's Building, Oxford Street (I. R. E. Birkett, 1903), is the city's one Art Nouveau façade (only the front wall remains), with biomorphic shapes in the terracotta panels which surround the windows [66].

In contrast, the YMCA building, Peter Street (Woodhouse Corbett* & Dean, 1909), is the first structural use of reinforced concrete in the city, and among

* Alfred Edward Corbett was probably the son of E. A. Corbett of Corbett, Raby & Sawyer who built the Barton Exchange.

67] YMCA, Peter Street,
Woodhouse, Corbett &
Dean, 1909

the first in the country [**67**]. This is a steel and concrete-framed building, with
lateral stability being given by the reinforced concrete stair shafts. There were
concrete barrel vaults, concrete floors and partitions, concrete hangers and
purlins; internally it was very complex, no two rooms being the same size or
height. Externally, it is clad in terracotta, banded and henna-colour at ground
floor level and straw-coloured above, and with details in a formalised Art
Nouveau style.

It had a 60 ft by 21 ft swimming pool on its fourth floor, a gymnasium
on the fifth, with a seventy-three yard oval running track as a 'gallery' on the
sixth floor, as well as a fives courts, all built, in ferro-concrete, over the void
of the large lecture hall. There was a large lecture hall for 1,000 people, a
'cinematograph', lounges, shops, a billiard room, a smoking room, a dining room
and even a photographic dark room. A public entrance in Mount Street gave
on to a separate staircase – surprisingly, perhaps, for a YMCA, there were
women's changing rooms on the seventh floor, with stairs down to the running
track and gym, though not to the baths.

Increasingly, larger buildings were being erected for the headquarters or
regional headquarters of companies, replacing the textile warehouse as the most
important built form, and for these clients a more imposing style of architecture
was needed which would draw together the elements of the façade in a way
that the Classical had done. From the 1890s a number of prominent London
architects had been extolling the virtues of the architecture of the seventeenth
and early eighteenth centuries. J. A. Gotch published *The Architecture of the
Renaissance in England* in 1894, and Birch published his *London Churches of the
seventeenth and eighteenth Centuries* in 1896. Between 1898 and 1901 John Belcher
and Mervyn Macartney produced *Later Renaissance Architecture in England*,
and in 1907 Belcher published his *Essentials in Architecture*, and it was these

volumes which helped to revive interest in the buildings of the William and Mary, Queen Anne and early Georgian periods.[7] Belcher's (and Beresford Pite's) hall of the Institute of Chartered Accountants building in London of 1889–92 was influential throughout the country. Nearer to Manchester is his Ashton Memorial, in Lancaster, of 1906.[8]

In 1896 the *Architectural Review* was founded, with an editorial board consisting of Reginald Blomfield, Mervyn Macartney and Ernest Newton.[9] Reginald (later Sir Reginald) Blomfield, who published *A History of Renaissance Architecture in England 1500–1800* in 1897, was probably the most influential architect of the period, and C. H. Reilly, Roscoe Professor of Architecture at Liverpool University, acknowledged the debt to him: 'its teaching at the beginning of the new century was largely based on Sir Reginald's. His books became textbooks for professors and students alike. It was due to his influence, more than to anyone else's, that the Orders, and all they implied in big scale and simple shapes, were once again thoroughly studied.'[10]

The Baroque of Sir Christopher Wren and his contemporaries was well suited to modern large buildings: it used the Classical orders to compose the elements of a façade without the orthodoxy of the Greek Revivalists and, importantly, it had its roots in Britain. As Robert Macleod put it, 'In Wren, Hawksmoor, and Vanbrugh could be found a combination of regularity, order, a well-assimilated

68] Refuge Building, Oxford Street, Alfred and Paul Waterhouse, 1891 and 1910

native tradition, the pomp and circumstance which the Edwardian age found so necessary, with the individuality and pictorial effects which the Victorian age had made imperative.'[11]

One of the largest Baroque Revival buildings in the city is Alfred and Paul Waterhouse's Refuge Building, 1891–1910, on the corner of Oxford Street and Whitworth Street [68], an imposing structure of specially made bricks (small and crisp and red but not 'Slaughterhouse' red, they are too dark for that) and brown terracotta. Alfred Waterhouse did the first block on the corner with Whitworth Street in 1891, three floors of tall mullioned and transomed windows, with a shorter fourth storey with 'buttresses' between the windows on which are the prows of small arks – symbols of security. The Whitworth Street corner is marked by a tower and two tall gables, and a similar gable next to the clock tower marks what was the other end of the building. Internally, there are remarkable glazed terracotta panels all over, and, like the exterior, the interior is listed Grade II*.

The second block, of 1910, next to the railway viaduct, is by Waterhouse's son Paul, similar to the first block, but there are subtle changes, and on the corner a drum and dome that are remarkably Hawksmoor-like. Between the two blocks, and pulling them together, is the 220 ft high clock tower, under which is the *porte cochère*, though no longer used as such. The tower has a base of Dalbeattie granite and bands of lighter bricks. Above the clock is a dome carried on four banded columns bearing concave entablatures. The Oxford Road façade was described by Reilly as looking rather like 'a tall young man in flannel trousers escorting two charming, but somewhat delicate old ladies dressed in lace'.[12] On Whitworth Street is the third block, by Stanley Birkett, superficially a copy of the earlier blocks, but of the 1930s.

Almost opposite the Refuge Building is the Tootal Broadhurst Lee & Co. Building, by Joseph Gibbons Sankey (1860–98), designed in the last year of his life [69]. Over a ground floor and semi-basement, rusticated by raised bands of terracotta, rise four storeys banded in red brick and fawn terracotta. The seven central bays on Oxford Road are united by an arcade of attached giant-order Corinthian columns, and on the Rochdale Canal side the same motif is repeated using pilasters. Above the deep cornice is another floor. Angular towers mark the corners, and the entrance is stressed by banded columns carrying an open-headed pediment. Two sculpted figures support the Great Bridgewater Street corner, and the loading bay on this street is a granite-surrounded twin arch. Here is a building very much in the spirit of the Wrenaissance.

Between 1898 and 1903 the Midland Hotel, St Peter's Square [70], was built by Charles Trubshaw (1841–1917), architect of the Midland Railway Company. The hotel was designed as a northern counterpart of Gilbert Scott's great Gothic St Pancras Hotel. The Midland, which covers two acres, has lower floors of granite – pink from Peterhead and bands of dark Shap – and its upper floors are of brick and brown glazed terracotta from Burmantofts.[13] A profusion of ornamental details covers all four façades, but because they are all in glazed terracotta they are consequently soft. The site is triangular, and the narrowest façade, on Windmill Street, was connected to Central Station by a covered

walkway. The hotel, which had 400 bedrooms, boasted a palm court, winter gardens, a roof garden, its own post office and a two-storey theatre to replace Lane's Gentlemen's Concert Hall, which had been pulled down for the hotel. Miss Horniman established the first repertory theatre company in England here. And it was in the Midland that Henry Rolls first met Frederick Royce.

Opposite Piccadilly Station, on London Road, is the Police and Fire Station of 1904–06, replacing the outdated one in Jackson's Row. A design competition was organised (with a brief from George Parker, Chief Fire Officer), with premiums of £300, £200 and £100 for the best schemes. Twenty-five entries were received, and the winning design was by John Henry Woodhouse, George Harry Willoughby and John Langham, who came together especially for the job.* The triangular site had accommodation for firemen and their families (thirty-eight flats on three floors with galleries on to the courtyard), horses and appliances and workshops around a central yard, and there was also a police station, an ambulance station, a bank, a gas testing station and the coroner's court. The Fire Station was completed by September 1906, at a total cost of £142,000. The exterior façades are of Accrington brick and brown glazed terracotta from Burmantofts [71]. It is difficult to see beneath the grime which has been allowed to settle on this much-neglected building, but the profusion of architectural forms is almost overwhelming – here the influence is Hawksmoor, Gibbs and, almost certainly, Belcher's hall of the Institute of Chartered Accountants. However, the details are all in glazed terracotta which does not mould crisply, and it lacks detail. Had it been in stone, it would have been a remarkable building.[14]

69] Tootal Building, Oxford Street, J. Gibbons Sankey, 1898

70] Midland Hotel, St Peter's Square, Charles Trubshaw, 1898–03

---

* The partnership had earlier existed between 1886 until 1893, though Woodhouse joined Corbett and Dean for the YMCA job in 1909. Woodhouse and Willoughby had both been assistants to Royle & Bennett.

71] Police and Fire Station,
London Road, Woodhouse
illoughby & Langham, 1904–06

Given the excess of terracotta – good, of course, at resisting the acid rain
and black smoke of early twentieth-century Manchester – it is refreshing
to find a Baroque Revival building in crisp Portland stone and red brick, the
Hospital for Skin Diseases, Quay Street, of 1903–06, by T. Worthington & Son
[72]. This was actually by the eldest son, Percy Worthington (1864–1939), for
Thomas was in semi-retirement from 1895, and the partnership was formally
dissolved in 1906. The Portland stone is used for detailing around the windows
and for the quoins and entablature, and the whole of the central bay on Quay
Street reads like a giant Venetian opening. The hospital cost £39,043. In 1901

72] Hospital for Skin Diseases,
ay Street, Thomas Worthington
Son, 1903–06. The building was
demolished late 1999

73] Opera House, Quay Street, Richardson & Gill and Farquharson, 1912

it was equipped with Finsen light machines* and X-ray equipment, the first institution after the London Hospital to be so appointed. There is a later three-bay extension on Quay Street, and there are additions on Byrom Street in an Arts and Crafts style, even though of 1927.

Reginald Blomfield was still on the board of the *Architectural Review* in 1906, and Macartney was its editor, when it started publishing a series of plates called 'The Practical Exemplar of Architecture', illustrated mainly with examples of English eighteenth-century architecture. The plates, with examples of proportions and details, could be bought separately in folders for use in the architect's office, and 'in the schools, Richardson & Reilly set their students making measured drawings of buildings by Adam, Chambers, Elmes, and above all Cockerell, the great master whose intellectual scholarship had for long been unappreciated.'[15]

A. E. Richardson, as a young man, had gone into the office of Frank Verity, an enthusiastic francophile who adopted Continental Beaux Arts classicism rather than classicism based on English Baroque. Lovett Gill was also an assistant in Verity's office, and set up in partnership with Richardson in 1908. Their first major commission, in 1912, was the New Theatre (Opera House) in Quay Street [73] for Irene Vanbrugh – a stripped Classical and Cockerell-inspired façade. Reilly described it as being in First Empire manner, the details scholarly 'yet . . . in essence dignified and simple. All the various functions of a theatre are indicated but without a trace of vulgarity.'[16] Richardson said, 'It was 70 ft high and cost £40,000, but they never paid us our fees. At the first performance in 1912, sewer rats came out of the river among the audience.'[17]

* Niels Ryberg Finsen, a Danish physician, originated the treatment of skin diseases by focusing the light either from electric lamps or from sunlight passed through an ammoniacal solution of copper sulphate. He won the Nobel Prize for Medicine in 1903.

74] St James's Building,
Oxford Street, Clegg Fryer
& Penman, 1912

However, Beaux Arts classicism had little impact upon Manchester's architects, and in the same year that the New Theatre opened, St James's Building, Oxford Street (Clegg Fryer & Penman, 1912) was completed and still in the Baroque style [74]. It is a large building, of seven storeys and twenty-seven bays on Oxford Street, and the Portland stone-clad façade uses three huge aedicules which rise through four storeys to disguise its bulk. (These and the central tower are strongly reminiscent of Nicholas Hawksmoor's work at Greenwich and Blenheim.) Behind the façade 1,000 rooms run back along corridors in a plain, undecorated office block.

St James's Building was built for the Calico Printers' Association, and was erected at a time when the cotton industry was making huge profits. Vast amounts of money were to be made in the first decades of the century, and very ordinary mill owners were able to pay themselves as much as £20,000 to £60,000 per year, considerable sums in those days. During each of the boom years of 1910–12 the UK exported 6,651 million linear yards of cloth, compared with 156 million from Japan (the next highest).[18] By 1913 exports of cotton cloth had risen to 7,000 million yards, and of every five pieces of cloth shipped in international trade, three pieces had been made in Lancashire. Some 620,000 people were working in more than 2,000 mills in the north-west, supplying about a quarter of Britain's visible exports. Manchester remained, until World War II, the most important cotton goods market in the world.

To meet the needs of the export market, and to take advantage of the opening of the Ship Canal, Lloyd's Packing Warehouses came into being in 1896, when three firms who packed cloth for the export trade joined forces. 'At that time many of the larger Manchester shipping merchants had their own staffs, presses and equipment for the packing and despatch of consignments to overseas customers. Fluctuations in trade, however, could leave gaps in the functioning of supply and demand; presses and labour for individual firms would then suffer from periods of suspended animation; they stood idle when their services were unrequired.'[19] Lloyd's Packing Warehouses provided a service whereby in one building a number of shippers had accommodation for their office staff, and the landlord packers provided the labour and machinery for packing and despatch of the goods. Their first acquisition was Lloyd's House, Lloyd Street, which was already owned by the Manchester Shipping Offices & Packing Company. On the opening of Whitworth Street in 1899, Whitworth House was built for them on the corner with Sackville Street, followed by buildings at the Oxford Street end.

It is here that the architect Harry Smith Fairhurst (1868–1945) enters the picture, an architect who was to become as important to the image of Manchester in the twentieth century as Walters had been in the nineteenth. Harry S.

75] India House, Whitworth Street, H. S. Fairhurst, 1905

Fairhurst was born in Blackburn in 1868, and was articled to Maxwell & Tuke of Manchester in 1888. After several visits to Italy, he joined the Cardiff office of William France, architect to Lord Bute. He commenced independent practice in Blackburn from 1895 until 1901, when he moved to Manchester. Apart from the large commercial buildings in Manchester, Fairhurst helped Richard Harding Watt to design the Watt's Building in Knutsford.[20] The firm he founded is still in successful practice in Manchester.

Fairhurst married into the Lloyd family, so it is hardly surprising that his first major commission in 1905–06 was India House, a Lloyd's Packing warehouse [75]. The building shows Fairhurst's ability to give his clients just what they wanted: as much light as possible for checking finished and printed cloths, flexible internal spaces to allow for a variety of client firms, good basement areas for storage and pressing bales of cloth, sensible provision for loading and unloading goods, all contained behind an imposing but not extravagant facade. India House has seven storeys over a semi-basement, and twelve bays interrupted by two tower bays, with gables concealing the main chimney stacks. There is Aberdeen Correnie granite at the base, and above it red Accrington brick and glazed sienna tiles and mouldings. At the rear the building is plain brick.

Internally there is a framework of steel beams encased in concrete, allowing large windows for the 'warerooms' for checking finished and printed cloths on long tables in front of the windows. Necessary, too, were the labelling and stamping of cloth with trade marks. Because cotton was sold in pieces rather than rolls, since 1842 the Design Copyright Act had required the marking of the front of each piece, and this was done by hand with a wood and copper trade stamp. In 1913, at the peak of the export trade, 7,000 million yards of cloth were exported, requiring the stamping by hand of about 250 million pieces.[21] The basement at the rear of the building runs right to the edge of the river and is lit by windows in the retaining wall of the river Medlock. At each end of the basement was a bale hole, or well, with a crane for loading and unloading lorries. The internal partitions were constructed in sections and jointed so that they would create flexible and changeable spaces. In the basement were hydraulic presses for baling cloths; compression helped against theft and made the bulk smaller. It was possible for 2,500 pieces of cloth to be folded, stamped, packed and baled, and on the dockside in three and a half hours. The building has been converted to a low-rent residential property for the Northern Counties Housing Association, and it is a pity that, as a consequence of inserting small apartments into tall floors, the upper halves of the windows, which are now in the voids between ceilings and floors, are painted black.

Next door to India House is another Lloyd's Packing warehouse, Lancaster House, also by Fairhurst, 1909. Like India House, this steel-framed building has Aberdeen Correnie granite at the base, above which is Accrington brick and sienna terracotta dressings [76]. And, like India house, the rear is plain brick. The two buildings are linked by a wonderful gateway, the slender semicircular arch of which carries an elegant lamp.

On the opposite side of the road is Bridgewater House (H. S. Fairhurst, 1912). This, the most impressive of the packing warehouses on Whitworth Street, looks

at first sight like Portland stone [77], but it is all covered in white matt-glazed faience tiles – cheaper than stone and self-cleaning.* The entrance on Whitworth Street is clad in granite, and there is a sandstone bust of the Duke of Bridgewater over the door. There are nineteen bays, and the bulk of the building is broken up by breaking forward alternative bays as oriels. In this building, Fairhurst revolutionised the internal movement of goods. Behind the Whitworth Street façade were three large ground-floor warerooms and behind them a loading bank, running the width of the building, with five hoists to the upper floors. Lorries entered at the rear of the building from Atwood Street, unloaded or loaded on to the ground-floor loading bank, and left from the Palace Theatre end of the building. Half the ground floor was given over to goods movement, and there was space for twenty-six lorries to be dealt with simultaneously. The lifts and stairways were grouped in hallways behind the entrance doors.

76] Lancaster House, Whitworth Street, H. S. Fairhurst, 1909

77] Bridgewater House, Whitworth Street, H. S. Fairhurst 1912

* Doulton produced 'Carrara Ware', a whitish or cream faience in imitation of Portland stone, resistant to weather and pollution, but because of the plasticity of the clays was unable to be moulded in high relief.

What these buildings, and their imitators, provided for Whitworth Street was a sense of majesty and scale, brought about, not by the use of the orders (the Baroque style was too lavish for such workaday buildings), but by the regularity of cornices, heights and masses. Bridgewater House was built up to the maximum height restriction of 108 ft, India House is 95 ft high to its eaves, with its two towers rising to 120 ft, Lancaster House is 106 ft high to its eaves, and its tower on Princess Street rises to 150 ft.

In the year that Bridgewater House was completed, the foundation stone was laid of the new Lewis's store on Market Street. The original store had been built, in 1877, in a French Renaissance style (Horton & Bridgford), at Nos 110–12 Market Street (the firm having been established in Liverpool for twenty-five years). When opened, it was intended to be a retail shop for men and boys only, but women's clothing as well as food was eventually sold. As well as 400 shop assistants, there were 300 working tailors and 200–300 employed in making shoes; Lewis's was as much a factory as shop. American-style marketing methods included such attractions as distorting mirrors along the Market Street frontage, a magic lantern show in one of the windows, a model of the clock from Strasbourg Cathedral and, on one occasion, flooding the sub-basement and floating gondolas in a replica of Venice.

The new store opened in the autumn of 1915 (J. W. Beaumont & Sons), and was two and a half times larger than old store.[22] In return for surrendering 7 ft of pavement along the 210 foot frontage [78], Lewis's were able to enclose the narrow back street of Mosley Buildings and extend the store to Meal Street. Toward Piccadilly, the Royal Buildings were acquired. There was a great dome, over 100 ft above ground-floor level, 36 ft in diameter. Additionally there was a glass-roofed arcade, the only arcade in Market Street. The first escalators outside London, the largest soda fountain outside the United States and a sprung marble dance floor were also installed. Two hundred radiators provided heat throughout the store, and each was equipped with a thermostat (the first such to be installed in Manchester). A further extension was added in 1929, in steel and concrete, faced with Portland stone. The shop fronts and doors were of bronze set within polished black marble, the window casements of steel.

After the building of the Ship Canal, such had been the increase in the number of traders using the Royal Exchange that there had long been talk of removing to a larger building in Piccadilly Gardens, or of extending into St Ann's Square. Instead, the building was extended to Old Bank Street, still in the Italianate style of the original building [79]. The portico, which was no longer centrally placed, was removed and replaced by a far less grand entrance. The enlargement by Bradshaw Gass & Hope,* which started in 1914, occupied 1·7 acres, and the exchange hall, lit by six domes and twice its present size,

---

* Jonas James Bradshaw (1837–1912) and John Bradshaw Gass (1855–1939), his nephew, had a flourishing partnership, designing mills in Bolton, Leigh and Atherton from the 1890s to the 1920s. From 1913 they developed a broader-based architectural practice. Arthur John Hope became a partner in the firm in 1902, having earlier been a pupil. Bradshaw & Gass also designed thirteen cottages for Port Sunlight.

was the largest trading room in the country. The building, delayed by World War I, was reopened by King George V in October 1921, just in time for the start of the contraction of the cotton industry.

Lancashire men had ignored to their peril the growth of cotton production in Russia, Germany, France and Italy, and especially in Japan and India (Lancashire's largest overseas market). Between 1900 and 1914 some £6·5 million worth of textile machinery had been exported annually, enabling other countries to increase their production capacity enormously.[23] World War I had affected Britain's exports of cotton and allowed other countries to consolidate their position. By 1921 'falling prices and wholesale cancellations of orders by overseas buyers rapidly led to stagnation in trade, short-time working, and the blight of heavy unemployment. This was the dark cloud of contraction which was to hang like a damp fog on the cotton towns, with scarcely a break to let in a shaft of sunshine, for the next eighteen years.'[24] By 1926 India's trade with Lancashire was less than half, and China's less than a third, of the 1913 average. Undercutting of prices, in the hope of an end to the recession, drove more and more companies to the wall, and even the short-lived (1926–27) Yarn Association, which attempted to set minimum prices, failed to stop undercutting and the collapse of the industry. By the end of 1927 at least 200 mills in Lancashire were in the hands of their banks.

78] Lewis's, Market Street, J. W. Beaumont & Son, 1929

79] Royal Exchange, St Ann's Square, Bradshaw Gass & Hope 1914–21

PLATE 14] Barton Arcade,
Deansgate, Corbett, Raby &
Sawyer, 1871

PLATE 15] Palace Hotel (Refuge Building), Oxford Street, Alfred and Paul Waterhouse, 1891–1910

PLATE 16] Midland Hotel from G–Mex, Charles Trubshaw, 1898–1903

PLATE 17] Rylands Library,
Deansgate, interior, Basil
Champneys, 1890–99

PLATE 18] Bridgewater House,
Whitworth Street, H. S. Fairhurst,
1912

PLATE 19] Ship Canal House, King
Street, H. S. Fairhurst, 1924–26,
and the Atlas Assurance Company
Building, Michael Waterhouse,
1929

PLATE 22] Central Reference Library, St Peter's Square, interior, E. Vincent Harris, 1930–34

PLATE 23] Aerial view Town Hall, extension and Central Reference Library

PLATE 24] HSBC (Midland) Ba[
King Street, Edwin Lutyens,
1933–35

ATE 25] Daily Express Building,
eat Ancoats Street, Sir William
Owens, 1935–39

PLATE 26] CIS Building, Miller
treet, G. S. Hay and Sir John
Burnet, Tait & Partners, 1962

PLATE 27] Piccadilly Plaza, Cove
Matthews & Partners, 1959–6

PLATE 28] Highland House,
Victoria Bridge Street, Leach
Rhodes Walker, 1966

o] Blackfriars House, St Mary's
Parsonage, H. S. Fairhurst, 1923

In spite of the contraction of the industry, the figures for cotton production were still spectacular. In 1928 membership of the Royal Exchange was 11,000, including spinners and cloth manufacturers controlling some 60 million spindles (of a world total of 164 million) and 750,000 looms (of a world total of 3 million). There were also approximately 500 brokers, 1,800 yarn agents, 120 yarn dyers, 300 waste dealers, 1,800 cloth merchants, 200 bleachers, 120 calico printers, 250 dyers of piece goods, 150 finishers and over 1,000 shippers.[25] Cotton goods comprised nearly one-third of all exports of manufactured goods, the largest export of any commodity in the world. It was estimated that 10 million of the population owed their livelihood directly or indirectly to the cotton industry, and Sir William Himbury warned in 1929, 'If the cotton trade ceased to exist tomorrow Great Britain would become a third-rate power, from a commercial point of view, and probably at least one-fourth of the population would have to emigrate, as it would no longer be possible for them to earn a living in this country.'[26] Notwithstanding the continuing collapse of the cotton industry, there was still considerable wealth in the city, and in the period between the two World Wars, Manchester erected some of its most notable, and expensive, buildings. Portland stone, rather than brick and terracotta, characterises the city in the 1920s and 1930s.

Harry S. Fairhurst, after World War I, was still designing buildings for the cotton industry. Blackfriars House, St Mary's Parsonage, of 1923, was for the Bleachers' Association [80]. A tall but shallow building tucked in between the Parsonage and the Irwell, it has too many layers: banded rustication on a two-storey ground floor, then four floors of ashlar, a deep string course, another floor of ashlar topped by a deep cornice, and another floor tucked away above that. Baroque, but the orders are inferred rather than shown. It is in Portland stone and still soot-blackened. Near by, at Arkwright House, Parsonage Gardens, Fairhurst designed a new headquarters for the English Sewing Cotton Company in 1927 [82]. On the gardens façade the central nine bays are flanked by giant-order Corinthian pilasters rising through three storeys to support an entablature and cornice which continue round the building. On the college land façade the right-hand bays are flanked by two giant-order Corinthian columns; the left-hand half is three storeys of plain wall. Above all this is another storey with its own cornice, and above that a further stepped-back storey over the central bays only.

One year earlier, at Ship Canal House (1924–26) on King Street, Harry Fairhurst had completed the headquarters building of the Manchester Ship Canal Company – a building intended to be the focal point of a comprehensive development of the area [83]. Like Arkwright House, it has a rusticated ground floor followed by an ashlar first floor with a deep string course, above which are three more storeys of ashlar. Then on the sixth storey is a colonnade of paired Corinthian columns, which runs through two floors and is surmounted by a cornice and parapet. On the centre of the parapet is a sculptural group representing Neptune. Ship Canal House was much taller than any contemporary building in Manchester, and an Act of Parliament was required to set aside the existing regulations regarding building heights, and perhaps for that reason the top three storeys, above the cornice, are set back 15 ft. The building is steel-framed, with reinforced concrete

81] National Boiler & Generator Insurance Company (later the National Vulcan), St Mary's Parsonage, H. S. Fairhurst, 1908

82] Arkwright House, St Mary's Parsonage, H. S. Fairhurst, 1927

83] Ship Canal House,
King Street, H. S. Fairhurst,
1924–26, and the Atlas
Assurance Company Building,
Michael Waterhouse, 1929

Lee House, Great Bridgewater
Street, H. S. Fairhurst
& Son, 1928–31

floors. The main façades on King Street are clad in Portland stone, but the T-shaped extension at the rear is clad in white glazed tiles.

The symmetry of Ship Canal House was spoilt by the erection, in 1929, of the Atlas Assurance Company building next door, on the corner of Brown Street (Michael Waterhouse, grandson of Alfred). The Atlas Assurance building is tall and narrow, and its proportions relate directly to Ship Canal House, giving the latter a decidedly lopsided look. Professor Reilly suggested, 'Perhaps that was the revenge of fate on the Canal Building for lifting high above the town not only its comely front but a Mary Ann back made of a cheaper material.'[27] In fact the Mary Ann back of glazed tiles was built in the expectation of taller buildings being erected behind Ship Canal House, and the tiles were there to reflect light into the rear of the building.

The Fairhursts' architectural style was changing, and it may have been due to the influence of Harry's son, P. Garland Fairhurst, who had joined the firm in 1925. Lee House, on Great Bridgewater Street [84], was designed by H. S. Fairhurst & Son in 1928–31 as an extension of the Tootal Building, and here was intended to be a remarkable building, an English equivalent of the American skyscraper. Harry Fairhurst had visited the United States in 1926, as had his son, P. Garland Fairhurst, in 1928, perhaps at the behest of Kenneth Lee, the chairman of Tootal Broadhurst Lee, who had an American wife and was himself a frequent visitor to the United States. Only the lower portion was built, but the building was originally designed to rise in three stages to seventeen storeys, and would then have been the tallest building in Europe, at 217 ft. The building looks more austere than originally intended; the stone cladding

85] Rylands Building, Market Street, H. S. Fairhurst & Son 1929–32

of the ground floor was meant to extend all the way up,[28] and the omission of the cladding, and the reduced height, were perhaps due to the stringencies of the depression of 1929.

On Market Street is the Rylands Building, now Debenham's department store [85], of 1929–32, ostensibly by P. Garland Fairhurst, though the project architect was Ted Adams, who perhaps deserves more credit for the building.[29] The site created some difficulties: neither the High Street nor the Tib Street front

86] Masonic Temple, Bridge Street, Percy Worthington, 192

runs back at right angles (they are about 95° and 120° respectively), and building-high octagonal corner bays, canted at 45° (like Lewis's corner towers on the opposite side of the street), mask the corner angles, and terminate the 230 ft length of the Market Street façade. They also provide a vertical mass to offset the horizontal mass of the six-storey front, and provide a marker from Market Street and Piccadilly. This is a steel-framed building with a Portland stone cladding, but the classical vocabulary of earlier days has been abandoned.

The building was designed as a warehouse, but with provision around the edges of the ground and first storeys for shops. Marks & Spencer took up most of the corner on High Street, the Midland Bank was on Bridgewater Place, and on Market Street were the shops of H. Samuel, Weaver to Wearer, Wallis, and on the Tib Street corner, Dolcis Shoes. On Tib Street was the Piccadilly Restaurant. Placed on top of the building, after World War II, was a beacon with a revolving searchlight, visible for sixty miles, as a guide to aviators flying into Ringway. Great Universal Stores bought out 97 per cent of Rylands ordinary shares in 1953, and the Rylands Building became a department store, first for Paulden's, and then for Debenham's.

The modern movement had come to Manchester, and, on Quay Street, Sunlight House was being built as Manchester's first speculative development by, and to the designs of, the expatriate Russian Joseph Sunlight. The building was completed in 1932, and was then the tallest commercial building in Manchester, and the first higher than the Town Hall [87]. Several floors were leased to Inland Revenue inspectors, who undoubtedly used the swimming pool in the basement which was opened by Douglas Fairbanks. Notable is the polygonal lift tower. The lifts, in Sunlight's day, were manually operated, and it is said that when the lift operator went off duty for his lunch, Joseph Sunlight, to avoid paying for a relief operator, would work the lifts himself. The building was totally refurbished in 1997 (by Holford Associates), when it was found that the steel bolts holding on the Portland stone cladding were rusted through. A separate internal wall was built, the stone cladding was removed and replaced, this time with stainless steel fixings.

On an island site on King Street, between 1933 and 1935, was erected one of the most significant buildings in Manchester, and one to equal the mass of Ship Canal House, the Midland Bank by Sir Edwin Lutyens (in collaboration with Whinney Son & Austen Hall, the bank's principal architects) [88]. Under the Portland stone cladding is a steel frame, but the deep reveals of the openings suggest a building of some weight and solidity, appropriate for a bank building. The corners of the building are cut back, and the upper storeys are cut back further still, giving an effect of great monumentality and *gravitas*. And there are more subtle effects: each course of stone is about 0·27 in. less in height than the one below, and the windows diminish in proportion; each face has a batter (an inward slope) of one foot in every eleven.

In his original design, Lutyens provided an open roof and a deep light well, but the upper stages of the building were substantially redesigned at the suggestion of Reginald McKenna, chairman of the bank, and these add an over-decorative touch to an otherwise wonderfully austere and crisp building.

Frederick Hyde, of the Midland, persuaded Lutyens to add the polished marble plinth at the base of the building, and exhorted the architect to omit the intended marble border to the banking hall, 'in view of the fact that a considerable number of people in Manchester wear nails in their boots, [and] the risk of slipping is even greater than it is in London'.[30] The Midland Bank is one of Lutyens's last commercial buildings in Britain, and his northernmost one.[31]

Apparently retrospective are the two contrasting buildings erected on St Peter's Square in the 1930s, the Central Reference Library and the Extension of the Town Hall, but both had been designed in 1925 by the London architect E. Vincent Harris (1876–1971).

The foundation stone of the library was laid by the Prime Minister, Ramsay MacDonald, in 1930, and was opened by King George V (accompanied by Queen Mary) on 17 July 1934. The cost of the building and equipment was £410,000 and that of the site was £187,797. The architect stated that in general design the exterior followed the tradition of the early English Renaissance. Over a steel frame, the circular Portland stone wall rises to total height of 90 ft [89]. There are two rusticated lower storeys to give a broad effect of strength, and above them are two storeys behind giant Doric columns. Above these is a recessed blank wall behind which is spare storage accommodation. The dome

89] Central Reference Library, St Peter's Square. E. Vincent Harris, 1930–34

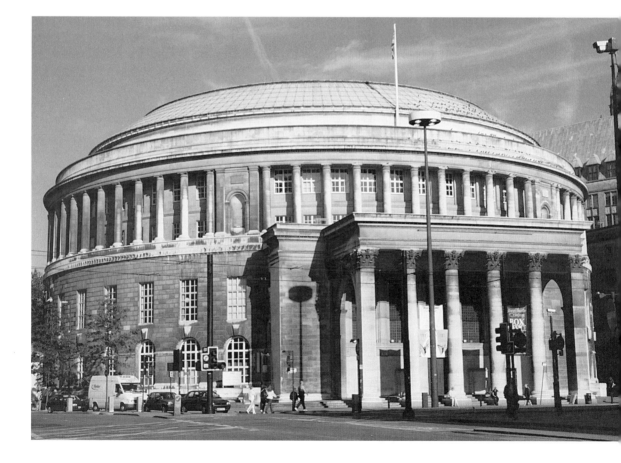

of the great hall is hidden by a higher lead-covered roof. On St Peter's Square the entrance portico is supported by four giant-order Corinthian columns. The core of the building is the four-tier book stack with accommodation for over 1 million volumes, with a lower tier at basement level. Above the book stack is the great hall, seating over 300 readers, the largest in Britain outside the (old) British Library reading room.

The *Architect and Building News* wrote, 'The Manchester library is of international importance. In arrangement it resembles no other building of its kind; the way in which the "bones" of the plan are put together contributes something new to the theory of planning.'[32] The only precedents were the New York Public Library (1911) and a library in Philadelphia (1927), 'but in neither of these examples has the theory been allowed to dominate the whole conception of the building'. The journal went on to say, 'If Sir William Chambers were to return suddenly and demand to be shown some new civil architecture, Mr Harris's are almost the only buildings one could show him without complete embarrassment.'[33]

Following the completion of the library in 1934, it was intended to extend St Peter's Square to Albert Square to create a new Civic Centre, but the site on the corner of Mosley Street and Dickinson Street (for Century House) had already

90] Town Hall Extension, St Peter's Square, E. Vincent Harris, 1934–38

been sold to the Friends' Provident Century Life Office and the decision to purchase the site compulsorily, for £46,000, was rejected by just one vote.

In that year the foundation stone of the Town Hall Extension was laid [90]. The nine-storey building was designed for the municipal trading departments as well as for the council chamber, and the Gas and Electricity Departments occupied the Mount Street and St Peter's Square ground floors, with a cinema and demonstration rooms beneath them. The arcade at Mount Street provided access to the gas showrooms and the arcade on St Peter's Square gave access to the electricity showrooms. The great curved 'Rates Hall' is 200 ft long, and accessed from a wide public corridor which runs the whole length of the building. The interior walls are clad in pale creamy-grey Hopton Wood carboniferous limestone from Derbyshire and dark Ashburton limestone 'marble' from near Torquay.

The Extension includes a new 62 ft square council chamber occupying the Mount Street end at first-floor level, and this is lit on the street side by three huge mullioned windows and on the opposite side by two similar windows looking into a deep well at the centre of the extension. The council chamber, which has seats for 145 councillors, has a gallery, an ante-room and committee rooms. The seating is English oak with hogskin upholstery. The walls of the chamber, and of its ante-room, are lined with polished Portland stone. The committee rooms, members' rooms, library and consultation rooms are all panelled in limed oak, mahogany, chestnut or pearwood. The walls and floor of the corridor to the suite are lined in Hopton Wood limestone. The exterior is clad in Stancliffe sandstone from the Darley Dale quarries in Derbyshire, and the roof covered in cast lead sheets. Connecting to Waterhouse's Town Hall are two bronze bridges. Unsurprisingly, given the quality of its materials, the total cost was £750,000. King George VI opened the Extension in 1938, Manchester's municipal centenary year.

If the Town Hall was built in the spirit of the thirteenth century, then it was in the spirit of a cathedral; the Extension is much closer in spirit to a thirteenth-century Cloth Hall, but writ much larger. Ian Nairn perceptively wrote of the three buildings after one of his visits to Manchester, 'A view down Mount Street [91] catches the eye as though it were part of a vast course in solid geometry, spinning out a theorem as elemental (though less nobly detailed) as the famous sequence of St Mary's and the Radcliffe Camera in Oxford: spire, gable end, cylinder. The spire is Waterhouse, both gable end and cylinder are due to Vincent Harris, no small achievement of relationship.'[34]

In the summer of 1939 J. M. Richards wrote *An Introduction to Modern Architecture*, in which he appealed for buildings to express the spirit of the modern industrial age. For Richards, clothing steel-framed buildings in masonry, in imitation of the solid stone of earlier ages, was false.[35] Modern architecture had learnt from engineers the use of new materials, simplicity of line and honesty of expression, and the fundamental architectural qualities of rhythm and scale. The use of ferro-concrete and steel girders increased floor spans and window openings, and removed the need for a load-bearing wall; the building could be supported on fewer points of support, and be more closely connected to site.

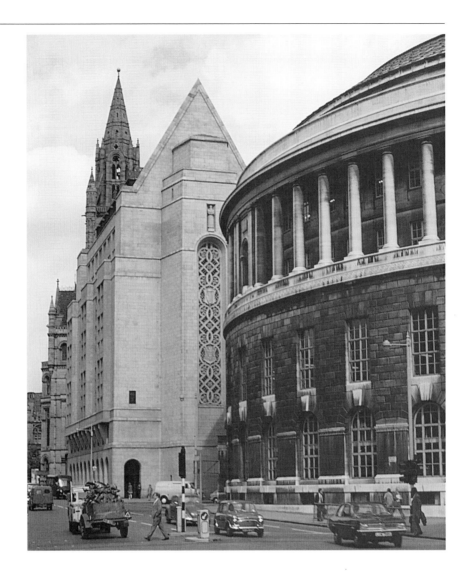

91] 'Spire, gable end
and cylinder'

The ultimate expression of the wall-less building came in the shape of the *Daily Express* Building on Great Ancoats Street in 1936–39 [92]. This great glass and black 'Vitrolite' building was designed by the engineer/architect Sir Owen Williams in the manner of his more famous one in Fleet Street in London. Once huge printing presses could be seen on the ground floor, but newspaper printing has almost entirely removed from the city. The building has since been rescued from an uncertain fate by Express Printers.

Kendal Milne's new store on Deansgate (J. S. Beaumont, 1938), was Manchester's other pre-war 'modern' building [93]. Unlike earlier steel-framed, stone-clad buildings, there is no pretence here; the structure of the building, a steel framework with reinforced concrete floors providing over 1,060 ft^2 of clear span between stanchions, is clearly expressed by the piers and the continuous windows which run the whole height of the building.

Kendal Milne's was not opened as a store until after World War II, and in the immediate pre-war period the cotton trade was declining at an alarming rate. By 1938 exports of cotton pieces had fallen to 1,449 million square yards. The numbers involved in spinning, doubling and weaving fell from 621,500 to 393,000. By the end of the 1930s the number of firms was reduced to less than 1,200, the number of spindles went down by one-third, and that of looms by almost half. The nation's share of the world's cotton trade, which had been 82 per cent in 1882–84, was reduced to 28 per cent by 1939. Yet, although Lancashire became a depressed region in the 1920s and 1930s, it was successful in attracting the growth industries of vehicles, chemicals, paper and printing, food, drink and tobacco and metal manufacturing,[36] and Manchester remained the region's commercial centre as well as its port. By 1937 the Bankers' Clearing House returns for Manchester, at £566 million, exceeded the aggregates for Newcastle, Birmingham and Liverpool. Through the Ship Canal the city handled imports to the value of £45 million and exports amounting to £12·75 million in the year before World War II.

92] *Daily Express* Building, Grea Ancoats Street, Sir William Owens, 1935–39

93] Kendal Milne's, Deansgate, J. S. Beaumont, 1938

8

HOUSING

BETWEEN THE WARS

The mad building of suburbs must be stopped – before it strangles the towns themselves. If half the energy and money poured into the suburbs in the last 17 years had been spent on the towns inside them, the country would be a better place, and the towns more fit to live in. [Geoffrey Boumphrey, *Town and Country Tomorrow*, 1940]

THE TUDOR WALTERS REPORT in October 1918 recommended that houses should be built on cheap undeveloped land on the outskirts of cities, carefully phased with the development of tramways; that houses should be built not more than twelve to the acre, and that each house should have its own garden. Every house should have a large living room with a sunny aspect, and should be fitted with a bath in a separate room, a water closet under cover, a larder and a coal store. Plans for such houses were to be drawn up by architects.

Tudor Walters was a Liberal MP who was also director of the Hampstead Garden Suburb Trust, and, significantly, one of the members of the Tudor Walters Committee on Housing was Raymond Unwin, the co-designer of Hampstead Garden Suburb and Letchworth. Unwin had produced a pamphlet in 1912, *Nothing Gained by Overcrowding*,[1] which recommended a minimum distance between houses of 70 ft, the use of short rows of terraces (in place of the long 'bye-law streets' which had been built since the 1875 Act), a garden for each house, spare land at the rear of houses to be used for recreational spaces, and the use of culs-de-sac for children to play safely. The Tudor Walters Report included much of Unwin's pamphlet. The government accepted the report in its Housing and Town Planning Act of 1919 (known as the Addison Act, after Dr Christopher Addison, Minister of Reconstruction), and in the same year produced a *Housing Manual* which carried forward all the Tudor Walters recommendations, and these new standards were to last, in effect, until the Dudley Report of 1944.

The 1919 Act also made local authorities responsible for meeting the housing needs of their area, and gave them (but not private builders) a subsidy to enable houses to be let at reasonable rent. House building costs had risen enormously by 1920. As Sir Ernest Simon had stated when Chairman of the Manchester Housing Committee,

> Materials were scarce and kept rising in price; contractors formed rings and, genuinely scared by the instability of markets, demanded and obtained high profits as a safeguard against great risks; labour worked shorter hours than in pre-war days and produced less for increased wages. Houses that had cost £250 in pre-war days could not now be built for less than £1,250. The economic rent of such houses . . . was over 30/- a week, and we could not let them for more than 12/6.[2]

Though the subsidy, as Simon pointed out, removed the financial responsibility for good management from the local authorities. In Manchester, working-class housing was being built in accordance with the *Housing Manual* at twelve houses per acre (compared with densities pre-war of thirty to forty per acre). The Housing Committee intended to build 17,000 houses within four years, although in practice only 21,000 houses were built between 1919 and 1935. Estates were also planned (the Act made the preparation of town planning schemes obligatory for towns of over 20,000 population), and council housing was now being built around squares or circles in blocks, generally of two, sometimes of four houses, and private housing was following these schemes as well. 'At these new standards, development could generally only take place on virgin land on the periphery of towns, and municipal estates grew alongside the private suburbs.'[3]

The provision of high-standard houses in garden city-like estates, however, was proving too expensive for the government, and lower subsidies were introduced by the Housing, etc., Act of 1923, introduced by the Conservative Minister of Health, Neville Chamberlain. The Chamberlain Act extended subsidies to private enterprise building (though this was discontinued in 1927), and between 1923 and 1933 12,000 private houses were built in the suburbs of Manchester, and because agricultural land was cheap, affordable housing was built in outlying areas like Cheadle Hulme, Sale and Timperley. Families with modest incomes could buy a three-bedroom house for £1 a week in the 1930s. Someone with an income of £300–£500 per year – the professional classes – could buy a detached house in the suburbs. Companies like Costain, Laing, Taylor Woodrow, Wates and Wimpey put up speculative housing. In 1920 the RIBA had banned speculative architectural design, so many houses between the wars were designed by non-professionals, often from pattern books, and this gave rise to what Osbert Lancaster called 'Mock Tudor or By-pass Variegated'.[4] Only in the 1930s did speculative building firms start to use architects.

Suburbs of new civic estates were built close to the new private ones: based on Kingsway and Princess Parkway, huge housing estates were built in Withington; in Chorlton-cum-Hardy, originally part of Withington Urban District Council, the wide open spaces early on attracted attention for civic housing, and large estates were built on land owned by Lord Egerton of Tatton; in Longsight, in an area of middle-class housing, the Anson estate was one of Manchester's first civic ventures and one of the most pleasant. 'One can go into almost any of the 20,000 municipal houses in Manchester and find that the tenant spends many pleasant hours in his garden, produces beautiful flowers, and has real pride and happiness in his work. Large numbers of back gardens are devoted to vegetables and produce crops which are of substantial value.'[5]

This period marked a further movement out of the city, by blue-collar as well as white-collar workers, leaving the poorer sections of society in the city, as Alfred Simon pointed out:

> The main stream of Manchester's social life as it exists today flows away from the centre. Even places of amusement, chiefly in the shape of picture theatres, follow the trend of sectionalised suburban life. The City, for the present, serves only our workaday needs; it is a desert in the evenings and at weekends. It would seem practical, therefore, to take the line of least resistance and begin our planning where there is already some evidence of community life, and where we may hope to find some expression of cumulative human needs and activities.[6]

The Wheatley Act of 1924, introduced by John Wheatley, the Minister of Health in the first Labour government, restored some of the lost subsidies, but at a lower level than the 1919 Act. Worse, the Wheatley Act failed to provide for the lower-paid, who generally had the least income and the largest families. Simon contrasted a family of four, all earning wages, living in a subsidised 'Wheatley' house, with the wife of a railway worker with eight children living in poverty in a condemned area of the city. Moving families from low-rent properties into higher-rent Corporation properties left them worse off: paying higher rents meant less money was spent on food; the death rate and tendency to become ill among these families was much higher than before removal, and the difference was ascribed to undernourishment.[7]

But something needed to be done to rehouse the people living in the slums of Manchester. The slum area formed a semicircle around the commercial centre about a mile and a half to two miles wide, but extending farther in the east along the lines of old canals. This belt, of over 3,000 acres, over half of which was occupied by dwellings, contained nearly all the slum dwellings in the city, most of them built before the bye-laws of 1868, and practically all before 1890. And in the slum area there was hardly any green land. Thus it contained the oldest housing, built when there was little or no control or planning, and where the worst housing conditions and the worst health problems were met. In Ancoats, 'the thickly populated districts served by the hospital have at the present day a death rate of 20·9 per 1,000 as compared with that of 13·77 for the whole city.'[8]

Greenwood's (Minister of Health in the second Labour government) Housing and Slum Clearance Act of 1930 was a turning point in slum clearance. It inaugurated a national slum clearance campaign, and introduced the 'improvement area' where unfit houses could be brought up to a reasonable standard. Procedures for compulsory purchase were simplified, 'unfitness for human habitation' was defined, and the emphasis was shifted from unhealthiness to bad housing conditions *per se*. The Act was designed expressly to build houses for rent at prices affordable by the poorer classes. The Wheatley Act was repealed in 1932 by Sir Hilton Young (Minister of Health in the National Government), and local authority building was confined to slum clearance and rebuilding. The effect of the Act was to remove any subsidy on local authority housing, and to leave private enterprise free to build cheap public housing.

In 1932 Manchester had 180,000 houses, nearly half of which were in the slum belt, mostly two-up, two-down in bye-law rows. Few of the slum dwellings had baths, though most had separate back yards, water closets and water laid to the house. These houses were packed at fifty to sixty per acre and mixed with industrial premises. Manchester had fewer than forty back-to-back houses, no cellar dwellings and no courts. 'In comparison, Birmingham still had tens of thousands of back-to-back houses and many courts of a kind which have been abolished in Manchester for over a generation, and yet Birmingham, which seems to have a gift of municipal publicity denied to Manchester, is generally quoted as the city which shown the way in the reconditioning of slum dwellings!'[9] Manchester had 'none of the really bad courts which are still found in Birmingham, Liverpool, and elsewhere. But even so, the worst of these houses are dilapidated, verminous and damp.'[10]

Under the Greenwood Act, Hulme in 1934 was declared a clearance area, the largest in Britain, at over 300 acres. Hulme had an average population density of 134 persons per acre, and in its northern parts 196 per acre, compared with Manchester's average of thirty-four persons per acre. The housing stock was mostly of terraces of two-up, two-down houses, and had been condemned by the Medical Officer of Health. Yet an architect writing in the *Manchester Guardian* said, 'I do not consider the houses unhealthy. I consider them well lighted. I do not like the arrangement at the back; it is too confined, and the yard space is too small. But I do consider they are in a reasonable state of repair and fit for habitation, and I also think they supply a want for poor people.'[11] The architect had a point – they were affordable properties. Earlier, in 1925, some 200 houses in the Medlock Street area had been demolished, but only one third of the former tenants had been re-housed in Corporation property; the rest were added to the already overcrowded slums near by. The land from which the 200 houses had been cleared had been valued at £12,000 per acre – and no one wanted to buy it at that price. It was still lying fallow in 1933, even though the price had been reduced to £7,250 per acre – the price was still to high to be affordable for working-class housing.

In the 1930s a number of surveys were undertaken, primarily by the Manchester and Salford Better Housing Council, which provide much information about these dwellings. In Chorlton-on-Medlock, for example:

No. 4, F Street. The general appearance and condition of this house inside are very miserable. It is a dark house and the plaster on the passage walls, in particular, was in bad condition. There is no tap or sink in the house; they are in the small yard, consequently in frosty weather the family is without water. In this house live a man and his wife, and seven children, ranging from 15 to 1, and a large, if varying, number of rats.

No. 9, B Street. In this house the rain had come through so often that the plaster in one bedroom was bulging dangerously and might have fallen at any time. There were no doors on the bedrooms. Under the window in the front room downstairs mortar had fallen out from between the bricks so that one could see daylight coming through the street.[12]

In Chorlton-on-Medlock some 23 per cent of houses were overcrowded; in Ancoats, 31 per cent; in Hulme, 44 per cent. Here 'overcrowding' meant more than two and a half persons per bedroom, and where there was no separate sleeping accommodation for persons of the opposite sex over ten years of age.

No. 6, U Street, Ancoats, is a one-up and one-down house; it is damp and very verminous, though the tenants do their best to keep it clean. The family consists of husband, wife, sons aged 19, 14, 7, and 1, and daughters aged 17, 11, and 5 – nine people in all. Of these only the son of 19 sleeps in the living room. No. 3, T Street, Ancoats, has two small bedrooms and one living-room; it is in a very poor state of repair. It is occupied by husband, wife, sons aged 10, 8, and 7, and daughters aged 14, 6, 4, 3, and 1 – ten people in all. The living room is not used for sleeping purposes.[13]

The worst crowding, however, was not in the two-up, two-downs, but in the larger, once middle-class, houses which were let as lodgings; there were 1,600 such houses – the 'super-slums' as Simon called them. The worst slums were in lodgings in old middle-class housing with, say, eight to ten rooms. In most cases there had been no attempt at reconditioning, and, unlike controlled rent on unfurnished properties, if the landlord let the rooms furnished he could charge whatever rent he liked. In a survey of Chorlton-on-Medlock there is mention of a five-room house in which two rooms contained a man, his wife and two children; the remaining three rooms were occupied by a single man and four couples with eleven children – twenty-four persons living in a house which had never been altered since it was built for a single family. It was estimated that some 7,000 families in the city lived in single-room tenancies.[14]

The 1935 Housing Act made overcrowding a statutory offence, and this created problems for Manchester, since, especially from 1929, there was little land available to build on. The Medical Officer of Health, in 1935, condemned 30,000 of the 80,000 houses in the slum belt as unfit for human habitation. The remaining 50,000, he suggested, could not be brought up to modern living standards by reconditioning. The only option left was to demolish them. The City Council undertook a slum clearance programme to clear 15,000 of the worst slum houses in the following five years, rebuilding enough houses and flats to rehouse the displaced families.

Manchester, in the 1930s, was fortunate in having land available in the southern suburb of Wythenshawe. Wythenshawe was a gift from the industrialist Sir Ernest Simon[15] and his educationalist wife Shena, a former Lord Mayor and Lady Mayoress of Manchester. They purchased Wythenshawe Hall and 250 acres of land and gave them unconditionally to the city. Abercrombie[16] was brought in as a consultant, and recommended that the city should buy a 4,500 acre estate, and the city purchased half of this in 1926. In 1927 Barry Parker,

Unwin's partner at New Earswick, Letchworth and Hampstead Garden Suburb, was commissioned to design the estate, and after protracted parliamentary battles to incorporate the land into the city's boundaries, Parker was given complete control in 1931 over the design of 5,500 acres of ground, for an intended population of over 100,000.

Parker designed 'parkways' for access to the residential areas, thus avoiding ribbon development. He explained that 'such roads . . . will lie in strips of parkland and they will not be development roads. They have been planned to skirt existing parks, future recreation grounds, school playing fields, existing woodlands, coppices and spinnies, the proposed golf course, the banks of streams and everything which will enhance their charm and will widen them out into great expanses of unbuilt upon country.'[17] The major north–south road, Princess Parkway, was originally planned with junctions to the local street system, but was upgraded to motorway status in the 1960s. The other parkway remained unfinished.

Within Wythenshawe, Parker introduced 1,000 semi-detached, neo-Georgian vernacular houses, based on 'neighbourhood' units, set around small, green spaces, with tree-lined roads, parks and Wythenshawe Park in the centre.[18] By 1938 there were over 7,000 Corporation and 700 private houses: Wythenshawe was then larger than Letchworth or Welwyn, and still only one-third of the way to its target of 107,000 souls. There was a fast intake of population, and by 1939 there were nearly 40,000 inhabitants in 8,145 homes. But with rents ranging from 9s (45p) to 15s 9d (78p) per week, these were not for the ex-slum dwellers. 'Not everyone could get a house in Wythenshawe. Before we got one an official from the Town Hall wanted to know all about us . . . We had to prove we would be good tenants. We . . . heard that some people were from the slums but we never met any of them.'[19]

The second and third generation of incomers treated the place less well, perhaps because although the houses and trees were fine, few amenities were provided.[20] As Kennedy has pointed out, 'neighbourhood planning' looks good to the planner and visitor, but can create a sense of isolation, and loneliness, and of a place with no soul. 'People who moved there said it took them two years to find their way about, there were long walks to bus stops, and long journeys to work unless you were one of the 60 per cent employed at factories on the estate, chief among them Ferranti, AEI and Timpson's Shoes.'[21] The three industrial zones, at Sharston, Roundthorn and Moss Nook, were not completed until the 1950s, the shopping centre was not built until the 1960s, and it was not until 1969 that the foundation stone was laid for the civic centre.

Wythenshawe is separated from Manchester by a half-mile-wide 1,000 acre green belt along the river Mersey, and until the industrial zones were built, subsidised buses took people into Manchester for work. It was not until after World War II that attitudes toward the role of the Wythenshawe estate changed: 'A significant feature of the post-1945 period has been the revised concept of Wythenshawe as a new and substantially self-contained satellite rather than a dormitory housing estate. The undeveloped lands at Wythenshawe have been developed in accordance with the revised proposals included in the Development

Plan, which envisage a series of residential neighbourhoods adequately supplied with shops, schools, etc., focusing on a main civic centre.'[22] By 1970, 102,000 people lived in Wythenshawe in 23,000 council houses and 4,400 private houses, and as Peter Hall has written, 'For all its latter-day shabbiness, it fully deserves the appellation of third garden city.'[23]

Although Wythenshawe eventually took a considerable overspill population, there still remained the question of the slum dwellers, and it was quickly realised that it would be impossible to replace slum housing with suburban cottages – there was insufficient room, and many people objected to the higher fares to and from work which would be entailed. Elizabeth Denby, who had toured European capitals in 1933, wrote in *Europe Re-housed*,

> Vienna with 1,800,000 citizens has 14 square miles of built-up area and 93 square miles of woodland, while Manchester with only 759,000 inhabitants covers 43 square miles, under 4 square miles of which is open space. How absurd for questions of existing city density to be disregarded. How lazy to advocate decentralisation and the creation of new satellite towns! Is there not a good case . . . for examining the structure of each town and relating new areas to the best traditions of the past?[24]

The City of Birmingham, too, had sent a deputation to look at Continental practices, and its report was influential on Manchester's thinking. 'This report . . . is undoubtedly the most authoritative report which has yet been published in this country on the question of cottages *versus* flats, and we believe their conclusions to be sound.'[25] The report said, 'Our investigations have satisfied us that both adults and young children can be housed quite satisfactorily, comfortably, and happily in flat or tenement dwellings . . . provided that the necessary amenities are included within the scope of the scheme . . . these amenities can only be justified when the colony of flats is sufficiently large. In our opinion, this must be within the figure of from 500 to 1,000 dwellings.'[26]

Simon and Inman also pointed out that 'housing directors are themselves frequently architects and are certainly influenced by the architects in their office. A great tenement block, including a few hundred flats, is a fine opportunity for an architect . . . A suburban housing estate gives much less opportunity.'[27] It is worth remembering too the influence from the Modern Movement architects – the heroes of the tutors and their students in the schools of architecture – Le Corbusier, and his seminal writings *Towards a New Architecture* and *La Ville radieuse*, Mies van der Rohe, Walter Gropius, the CIAM (Congrès internationaux d'architecture moderne) exhibitions and conferences which extolled social mass housing and the Weissenhof (Stuttgart) housing exhibition of 1927.

By 1935 high-rise housing was coming to be seen as important in the context of slum clearance following the publication of the government White Paper *Houses: the Next Step*, and in later Ministry of Housing manuals and design guides. The Council for Research on Housing Construction considered prefabricated methods in the light of the lack of skilled labour and materials. The French MOPIN system was the most completely prefabricated method then devised – a steel frame with reinforced concrete panels – and it was used at

Quarry Hill flats, Leeds, in 1936. But the system was organisationally difficult, and Quarry Hill was demolished in the 1970s because of the deterioration of fabric; the steel was corroding and the concrete crumbling. The Council turned to Dyke's 'clothed concrete' system, which used prefabricated panels mounted on a reinforced concrete frame.

In Manchester, R. A. H. Livett (who later, as City Architect for Leeds, built the Quarry Hill flats), designed the city's first great block of post-1918 civic flats, Kennet House, Smedley Road, Cheetham, 1933–35. Here, though, the structure was traditional, and concrete was simulated by cement rendering over brick. The storeys ranged from two to five because of the slope of the ground, and the structural effect was like a monstrous steamship. The 181 flats were set in an elliptical shape around a central garden, and each flat had a balcony which opened from its scullery. Stairwells gave access to two flats on each floor, and a washhouse was built on the top floor. The community hall, four shops and areas for children proposed by the architect were not adopted by the Council. The total cost was £83,000.[28]

Kennet House (since demolished) was designed for a housing density of forty dwellings per acre, and this was the density adopted for all other buildings by the Corporation. All over the slum belt, blocks of flats were being erected, and between 1933 and 1939 Manchester built the astonishing number of 9,000 flats, far more than any other provincial city.[29] The major slum clearances, however, had to wait until after World War II.

9

1940s–60s

POST-WAR PLANNING
AND ITS IMPACT
ON THE CITY

Mainly in two 'blitz' raids, at Christmas 1940, hundreds of factories and thousands of houses were damaged and destroyed. The Free Trade Hall, classic home of music and oratory, was destroyed; the Royal Exchange, largest of its kind in the country, was partly gutted; the massive Assize Courts were demolished; the Cathedral was hit; frightful gaps were torn in Portland Street and Mosley Street, the finest commercial thoroughfares in Britain; the quaint historic survival known as the Shambles was burned out. [S. Reece, *Guide to Manchester and Salford*, 1948]

WITHIN A MILE of Albert Square 165 warehouses, 150 offices and 200 other business premises were destroyed or badly damaged. An area from Cateaton Street to St Mary's Gate was razed to the ground. So too was the area between the Irwell and the railway. Victoria Street had been one of the Corporation's most lucrative markets but was totally destroyed by the bombs. The Cross Street Chapel and the Methodist Central Hall were obliterated. Air raids continued until December 1944, but it was the raids of 22 and 23 December 1940, in which 600 people in Manchester, Salford and Stockport died, that inflicted the heaviest damage. The devastation of Manchester had not been as great as in London or Portsmouth or Coventry, but nonetheless the heart of the city had been taken out.

In the immediate post-war period there was a chance to rebuild something new, to create not only homes fit for heroes but a city fit for them too. In May 1945 the *City of Manchester Plan* was published, not as an official plan, but presented 'to the citizens of Manchester' as a discussion document. The plan was produced by Roland Nicholas, City Surveyor, with assistance from the City Architect, G. Noel Hill, and his department, the Director of Housing, John Hughes, and Roy Hughes of the LMS Railway Company. The plan envisaged a city in which all the old grimy, out-of-date, irrational buildings of the Victorian era would be swept away to be replaced with bold, new buildings of the twentieth century, for:

> We have come to accept the background of our daily business without questioning the fitness of its too familiar features – the numerous traffic blocks during rush hours, wasteful of time, energy and substance; the lack of architectural form in the drab buildings fronting our main streets, each of a different style, width, height and ornamentation; and behind this motley façade a huddle of buildings where thousands spend their working days in cramped, dark and badly ventilated offices.[1]

Out of the chaos of the nineteenth century a new city would arise – healthy, practical and zoned. No longer would people have to live cheek-by-jowl next to their place of work, now they would live in comfortable houses and flats, surrounded by grass and trees, travel to work in new offices in the city centre, to new warehouses and factories on the outskirts, be entertained in new palaces of amusement, and be administered from new civic buildings – all reminiscent of a modern version of Ebenezer Howard's garden city.

The plan was based on detailed physical and sociological surveys, and looked at both housing and working conditions, for 'it would be little use to remedy shortcomings in the home if conditions in the office, shop or factory, where a major part of the day is spent, were to remain unsatisfactory',[2] and at civic amenities, recreation and cultural pursuits, smoke abatement* and transport. The plan recommended the re-zoning of industry, provision of decent housing and open spaces, improving the rivers, creating an entertainment zone, making a cultural, educational and medical centre, based on the Victoria University and the hospitals, and reorganising the road and rail connections to improve communications. The few industrial buildings which still existed in the city centre, mostly around Withy Grove and alongside the Rochdale Canal, would be resited when possible. Warehouses, which occupied the largest area, had to go. Most of them had been erected before 1890, and:

> Apart from such exceptional examples as India House, Bridgewater House and Rylands [Debenham's], most of them are outdated and interlaced at close intervals with narrow streets affording poor facilities for loading and unloading. The number of separate ownerships is large and sites have been developed with little regard for order, logic or economy . . . Many are insufficiently lit and inadequately ventilated as a result of gross overcrowding on the site; these can only be called commercial slums.[3]

---

* On 1 May 1952 a 105 acre area of central Manchester was declared a smokeless zone. By 1970 smokeless zones covered 13,000 acres. The Clean Air Act of 1956 introduced smokeless zones nationally.

94] The 1945 plan. The proposed
Cathedral quarter

These buildings needed to be demolished, but here was the problem. 'Many of our present difficulties are complicated by the fact that in the last century commercial and other buildings were designed to last too long; they have remained structurally sound long after they have been rendered obsolete by changes of function and progress in building technique.'[4]

Most of the city's shops fronted on to major traffic roads, whose pavements were too narrow for the number of shoppers who used them. Few of the shops, said the plan, had any architectural merit, with the notable exception of the new Kendal Milne building on Deansgate, but even the newer stores lacked provision for the loading of goods or car parks. The plan envisaged replacing most of the out-of-date city centre with new buildings, phased in over a period of time – it would all take some fifty years – uniform pavilion blocks, with wide streets between, and green spaces [94].

And there would be exciting new buildings too. There was the creation of a new Education Precinct to a plan prepared by the City Architect in collaboration with Hubert Worthington, architect to the university. Between Cambridge Street and Brook Street a community was to be built as a counterpart to London's Chelsea or Bloomsbury or New York's Greenwich Village.

> Here Manchester's artists, writers, dons, students, Continentals, journalists, architects, actors, musicians, engineers, and others whose jobs or leisure interests link them with the cultural centre and the activities it fosters, should find dwellings designed to cater for their personal and professional needs . . . In such an environment cultural societies would flourish as never before, the arts of conversation and of civilised living would be restored to their proper status.[5]

There were to be new entertainment and sports facilities. Large (*sic*) 14,000–20,000 seat stadia would be built for athletics and cycling and boxing demonstrations, and further buildings would provide for squash, badminton, ice skating and gymnastics. An amusement centre was proposed in the People's Piccadilly Gardens, in an enlarged area contained by Portland Street, Charlotte Street, Mosley Street and Parker Street. Here might be a cinema, theatre, dance halls, skating rink, boxing stadium, restaurants and buffets, all within gardens with a fountain, floodlit at night, and trees festooned with lights. The amusement centre would not only add to the city's attractions, but would also ensure the prosperity of the shopping area around. This, the plan noted, would all require a larger space than presently allotted, and 'it will be some years before . . . the Portico Library and the adjoining office buildings can be removed'.[6]

The plan proposed a new Exhibition Hall, to rival London's Earl's Court or Olympia, on the site of Exchange Station. The river Irwell would be covered over to make room for a large roundabout and approach to the station [95]. This, together with new Law Courts, would all help to revitalise the long-neglected border between Manchester and Salford. The new Law Courts were to be rebuilt as a major piece of civic endeavour. The Assize Courts had been demolished by bombing, but the council had already determined that a new site would be used to bring all the court facilities of Manchester and Salford together; an area of nearly nine acres, bordered by Gartside Street, Quay Street and Bridge Street was in process of being purchased. The accommodation of all the courts of law in one new building would be both economical and 'would be the largest of its kind in the country, worthy of a prominent position in the centre of the city and adding greatly to its dignity and prestige'.[7]

In the pre-war period, the idea of a ceremonial processional route from the Town Hall to the Law Courts had been envisaged. And the plan, although modifying this scheme, still saw the ceremonial route as necessary. Brazennose Street and Queen's Street would be turned into one wide avenue, and the houses between simply demolished. Albert Square was to be relieved of all its traffic, and was to be extended southwards to meet Peter Street. New buildings

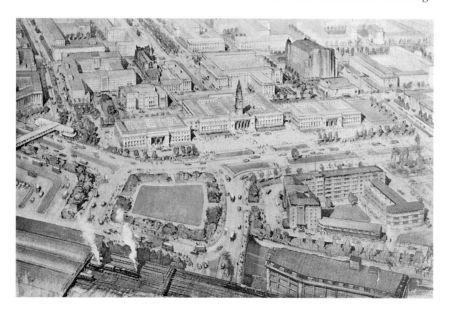

95] The 1945 plan. The proposed Law Courts area

5] The 1945 plan. The proposed
new Town Hall and
processional route

on the Peter Street side would create an appropriate sense of civic space. South Street (Southmill Street) Police Station would face the Library across an open grassed square – never mind the destruction of the Memorial Hall and the other buildings on that side of Albert Square; existing properties were unsatisfactory by modern standards. A new extension of the Town Hall was needed, and for this purpose the old properties on Princess Street facing the Town Hall could be demolished.

As far as the Town Hall itself was concerned there were two options. The Town Hall Extension could be removed in due course – perhaps in eighty years – leaving the old Town Hall and Library standing in formal gardens. The proposed building on Princess Street could be the new civic centre, leaving the old Town Hall only for ceremonial and council purposes. The alternative suggestion – and only a suggestion – was to remove the old Town Hall entirely and replace it with a smaller building [96], thus leaving valuable room for car parking on ceremonial occasions.

The concluding paragraph of the plan noted, 'We are entering upon a new age: it is for us to choose whether it shall be an age of self-indulgent drift along the pre-war road towards depopulation, economic decline, cultural apathy and social dissolution, or whether we shall make it a nobler, braver age in which the human race will be master of its fate.'[8]

For Manchester, however, the new age was a long time coming. Manchester, not alone among the towns and cities of the north of England, suffered badly from the economic and political events of the post-war period. The problem of inner-city blight was not unique to Manchester, it was a problem shared by most of the cities which had sprung up in the nineteenth century. But Manchester was particularly disadvantaged by two major factors which affected its growth: the continuing collapse of the cotton industry, on which the economic wealth of the city had been built, and, as important, central government assistance being directed to other areas of the country. 'For most of the post-war period the Greater Manchester area has found itself stranded between the two growth zones of the country; the south and midlands where there was spontaneous economic growth, and the north and west where growth was stimulated through incentives.'[9]

The war had, of course, considerably reduced the opportunities for the export of cloth but the home market was also changing. In 1958, for the first time in its history, Britain imported more cotton cloth than it exported. In spite of attempts to modernise the industry, decline was inevitable, for, as other countries with cheaper labour costs developed their own industries, Britain's market share had to fall, and as Singleton has pointed out, 'Britain possessed no unique advantages as a cotton textile producer.'[10] During the 1960s much of the cotton industry was absorbed by the man-made fibres industry, and huge mergers of firms took place from this period. By 1966 cotton production was effectively in the hands of four firms: Courtaulds, Viyella International, English Sewing Cotton and Carrington & Dewhurst. By 1968 Courtaulds alone owned 30 per cent of the Lancashire spinning industry, and by now Manchester had only fifteen active mills.[11] Hardly surprisingly, the Cotton Exchange ceased trading in 1968. As Bowker had written prophetically forty years earlier, 'The men are spent. The machine is broken. The glory is for ever departed.'[12]

The government reinforced the collapse of the Lancashire industry by providing subsidies to Development Areas – areas of high unemployment designated under the terms of the Distribution of Industry Act of 1945 – at the expense of the traditional textile areas.[13] 'Unhappily, most of the major investments (especially by the Courtauld Group) were attracted away from east Lancashire by the offer of regional incentives within the Development Areas: thus modern, capital-intensive factories were built, for example, in North East England, Northern Ireland and at Skelmersdale.'[14]

New industrial buildings over 5,000 ft^2 required specific consent from the Board of Trade, which was also empowered to offer loans and grants and build new 'Advance Factories' to attract industry to the right region: of the 124 announced between 1964 and 1968, only eight were in the north-west. Additionally, by withholding an Industrial Development Certificate (IDC), the Board of Trade could prevent new building projects considered inconsistent with the 'proper distribution of industry'. Manchester, like London and Birmingham, had many IDCs refused. Even Winsford, which was taking part of Manchester's overspill population in the early 1960s, was refused IDCs.

The reuse of old buildings did not require an IDC, so many old mills were converted to new uses. Ferranti, for example, in 1967 employed 10,000 people in electronics, aerospace and communications in and around Manchester, and four of their factories were in converted textile mills. But for most firms the lure of the Development Area was irresistible. By 1968 the financial benefits were grants of up to 35 per cent toward the cost of new factories or extensions, and 45 per cent toward the cost of new plant and machinery, as well as subsidies for workers.

Between 1945 and 1967 metropolitan Manchester gained only 9,000 jobs (of a total regional inflow of 108,000) and lost 32,000 as a result of industrial policy guidance. It was hard for Manchester to compete with the Development Areas, especially Merseyside, which had enormous unemployment problems.[15] Manchester was able to attract some new industries because of a strong engineering tradition, but 'there can be little doubt that Merseyside has attracted industry which would have gone to Greater Manchester had it not been for the action of the Board of Trade.'[16]

Fortunately, in the Greater Manchester area there was still much industrial activity unrelated to cotton. Twenty thousand people were employed in Wythenshawe, particularly in the manufacture of electrical apparatus, clothing, plastics, food and drugs. Mather & Platt, with 6,000 workers in the Manchester area, once makers of textile machinery, diversified into other areas such as food processing. ICI was investing heavily in chemicals; there was the huge Shell petrochemical plant at Carrington. Developments around the docks and the eastern end of the Ship Canal in the first half of the 1960s amounted to 1·75 million ft^2. The Port of Manchester still ranked fifth in the country in terms of the value of dry goods handled, and eighth in terms of total tonnage, and remained so until 1976. The port had been the second most important oil port since the early twentieth century, but increasingly oil operations were concentrated at Barton and then (especially when Shell built their enormous refinery in 1949–51) at Stanlow,[17] and the importance of the docks declined. The growth of containerisation from the mid-1960s meant the death of the port, which was not large enough for the huge container ships.

Trafford Park Estates started a process of diversification, converting itself into a holding company in 1958, and beginning to acquire land in other parts of the country, in Hereford, Wakefield, Sunderland and Wigan. Trafford Park, though, was still the industrial heart of Greater Manchester. Metro-Vick employed 20,000 workers, and AEI/GEC over 16,000. Ciba-Geigy expanded their capacity in the 1960s. Trafford Park in 1967 employed over 50,000 people in 200 factories. But the merger of AEI, English Electric and GEC cost Trafford Park nearly 10,000 jobs overnight, and that loss of jobs typified huge underlying problems. No other major industrial city in the country, apart from Glasgow, came close to Manchester's loss of employment in the 1960s and 1970s. Census reports show that between 1961 and 1971, in the inner city of Manchester, manufacturing lost 33 per cent of its jobs, construction and public utilities 14·7 per cent, other services 25·0 per cent, a total fall in employment of 26·2 per cent.[18] And the loss continued: the inner area of Manchester–Salford–Trafford had 90,000 jobs in 1966; by 1975 almost 40,000 of them had been lost.

Yet, in spite of the tremendous loss of jobs, development incentives were still being withheld from Manchester during the 1960s and most of the 1970s, Merseyside and North Wales being the major beneficiaries of industrial development policies in the north-west. What help was given to Manchester was at a very low level. 'During the 1960s, no part of the area received assistance, and tight IDC controls were placed on industrial development in an attempt to persuade firms to move to the assisted areas . . . From 1972 to 1982 all parts of

Greater Manchester had Intermediate Area status, with grants for buildings. This was at the lowest level of assistance.'[19] In 1982 even this Intermediate Area status was withdrawn. 'More seriously the area has suffered from regional economic policy because nearby areas like Merseyside, North East Wales and also Northern England have had higher and longer assisted area status.'[20] The only major assistance from central government was in the building of motorways, and it could be argued that these merely hastened the dispersal of firms out of the centre.

Part of the reason why assistance was withheld was that as employment in the city was falling the population was declining at about the same rate, and consequently Manchester suffered unemployment only at about the national average. Between 1951 and 1971 there was a 23 per cent loss of population, and as Paul Lawless has suggested, 'The cities have tended also to be penalised because of their declining populations. Such reductions in support, however, all too readily assume that a socio-economic cross-section of the population leaves when in fact it tends to be the more affluent who move out, and also that services can be reduced *pro rata* when facilities may be indivisible.'[21] Manchester has a relatively small rateable area, yet its rate-subsidised facilities are used by lots of others in the Greater Manchester conurbation. Those people left in the city centre were predominantly lower-income groups.

Nonetheless, Manchester was still the regional capital and retained its national importance; in the mid-1960s the major provincial cities in rank order were: Manchester, Liverpool, Birmingham, Leeds, Newcastle, Sheffield, Bristol, Nottingham, Leicester, Hull, Southampton, Plymouth, Coventry and Norwich.[22] Fortunately, in spite of its ranking, it could ill afford the measures of the 1945 plan or the comprehensive post-war reconstruction undertaken by other cities – and this protected the city's architectural heritage in the immediate post-war period.

The need for the comprehensive redevelopment of war-damaged towns and cities had been recognised even before the war had ended, and provision was made in the Town and Country Planning Act of 1944 to confer considerable powers on local authorities. These powers were extended by the provisions of the 1947 Town and Country Planning Act, which set up county councils and county borough councils as planning authorities, with powers to prepare 'development plans' for their areas showing land use: residential, commercial, industrial, educational and open spaces. They had to show principal roads, areas designated for mineral workings, sewage works and 'green belts'. The Act also gave powers to preserve trees and to list and preserve historic buildings. For the first time, these plans required the permission of the responsible Minister, who was entitled to hold planning inquiries, and provided that all future development should require planning permission from the planning authority. Co-ordination of the plans was to be by the new Ministry of Town and Country Planning. Enormous powers were given both to local authorities and to central government.

The 1947 Act created Comprehensive Development Areas (CDAs) which allowed planning authorities to go beyond the standard planning procedures and to acquire through compulsory purchase any properties that they needed to for developing outworn areas – often old city centres – and these powers were

97] Granada Television Centre,
Quay Street, Ralph Tubbs,
1956–66

considerable. Future land development was, basically, nationalised. What was novel under the Act was that landowners owned only the existing rights and value of their land: any foreseen future increase in value due to 'development' was to be paid for by a one-off compensation payment. But developers were to pay a 100 per cent surcharge on the increase in value of the land resulting from development, and not surprisingly, therefore, there was little private interest in development in the immediate post-war period. Symbolically, perhaps, the first buildings to be restored after the war were those which had typified Manchester's dominance in the nineteenth century.

The Free Trade Hall had been gutted during the blitz, leaving only the damaged Peter Street façade and the return into Southmill Street. It was rebuilt in 1951 by Leonard C. Howitt, the City Architect, who restored the front elevation and provided a brand-new interior, which became well known to Hallé concertgoers. The new brick rear elevation has tall brick pilasters carrying small sculptures depicting past activities in the hall.[23]

That other symbol of Manchester, the Royal Exchange, had also suffered serious bomb damage, and was restored and reopened by 1953. The collapse of the cotton industry meant that membership was less than half its pre-war figures, and in the rebuilding half the interior was partitioned off and divided horizontally for office space, leaving a smaller trading hall of 52 m by 40 m under the three glazed domes at the Old Bank Street end of the building. The original three domes of the 1870s building were replaced by a flat roof.

The third rebuilding of symbolic importance was the Cross Street Chapel. The chapel had been destroyed in the war, and was rebuilt in 1958–59 by F. Leslie Halliday, though in a style closer to the 1920s than the 1950s. It was preceded by the brick Synagogue tucked away in Jackson's Row (P. Cummings and E. Levey, 1952), the first new building put up in post-war Manchester. It was not until 1956 that the first new commercial post-war building was erected in the city, the Granada Television Centre on Quay Street [97], and it was significant that Sidney Bernstein chose Manchester as the centre of his new operations. The building, or rather buildings, were designed by Ralph Tubbs, the architect of the 'Dome of Discovery' for the 1951 Festival of Britain. The first building was of two storeys, on New Quay Street, followed by the second-phase building, the long, eight-storey Granada House. This is one of the first examples of curtain walling in the city; a thin, non-structural skin set in front of the structural shell of the building – light grey granite, sills of highly polished black gabbro, the supports between windows in white marble and dark grey limestone. The façade on Byrom Street was a later phase of 1966. Soon after, in 1959–60, Granada's rivals ABC Television built their curtain-walled offices (J. E. Beardshaw & Partners) on the corner of Mount Street and Peter Street, on the site of the old Gaiety Theatre [98].

In 1953 the Conservative government had repealed the development charge of the 1947 Act, leading to a free-for-all in market values, but the real take-off in building came from 1959, when it denationalised development values and restored market prices as the basis of compensation in the Town and Country Planning Act of that year. Land now had to be purchased at current market values, and, as a result, high land values, high rents and high interest rates meant that local authorities were unable to compete with developers for desirable city

98] ABC Television House, Mount Street, J. E. Beardshaw & Partners, 1959–60

99] Telephone House, Portland Street, E. Norman Bailey & Partners, 1959–61

land. There was growing pressure on local authorities from developers, many of whom had made their money by buying up derelict sites cheaply during and after the blitz. Land was becoming increasingly expensive as commercial interest grew, so, in order to maximise profits, new building techniques had to be developed – fast-track and economical. Telephone House, Portland Street (E. Norman Bailey & Partners, 1959), is typical of the type of building erected in the 1950s and early 1960s; a tall tower rising from a ground-floor podium filling the site boundary [99], and with more floor space than any other building in Manchester. This reflected government policy toward building densities, and concern to respect the right to light of adjoining buildings, for, although their footprint was smaller, these buildings were considerably taller than most of the existing buildings around them.

Steel and concrete construction was a way to build quickly and economically, and without dependence on the traditional craft skills so conspicuously lacking in the aftermath of the war. Reinforced concrete was a cheaper alternative to steel framing, and in the early 1960s a number of building firms were starting to import new ferro-concrete building technologies from the United States and particularly from France and Denmark, where the techniques had been developed for mass social housing.

At St Andrew's House, Portland Street (1962) [100], and at Highland House, Victoria Bridge Street (1966) [101], Leach Rhodes Walker were experimenting with the new techniques. In both buildings the core was made by means of a continuously climbing shutter (sliding shutters which rise at about 15–38 cm, 6–15 in. per hour, while concrete is poured and reinforcements are put in place), and the pre-cast concrete cladding panels, made off-site, were lifted into position by a tower crane. The use of tower cranes (which had been introduced to Britain in 1950) and the absence of scaffolding meant that not only was the procedure fast and cost-effective, but tenants were able to move into the lower floors while the upper ones were still being constructed.

At Scottish Life House, Bridge Street (now Manchester House), in 1965, Leach Rhodes Walker introduced another innovative technique. The building is only eight storeys over a two-storey podium, but the novel approach was first to erect the central core of steel columns and then cast the eight floor slabs individually on the ground, one on top of the other, each floor separated by a layer of resin to stop them sticking together – all rather like a large liquorice allsort. When all the floors had been cast, they were individually hoisted into position by pulleys and then pegged into place. People flocked to see the building being erected, but although the technique was designed to be time and cost-saving, it was never repeated.

At Quay House, Quay Street (1964–65), H. S. Fairhurst & Son erected a monumental block of eight floors and thirty-eight bays [102], but gave the building scale by the use of cut-back stair towers and floor-height sandstone-textured concrete panels. These new buildings were changing the face of Manchester. 'As soon as it was possible to span large areas with reinforced concrete the nature of building in town changed. It was no longer possible to fit in alongside your neighbour because the modern style was such a complete break with the past.'[24]

While these buildings were being erected, Arthur Gibbons of Cruickshank & Seward was introducing the city to pure white concrete architecture – buildings which won him awards from the Concrete Association. Gibbons had been to Brasilia and was inspired by Oscar Niemeier's white and functional concrete buildings, and on Styal Road, near the airport, Renold House (1954) and in Manchester, at the UMIST Halls of Residence (1964) and the Students' Union Building (1966), large, white in-situ blocks of concrete were cast. Arthur House (Cruickshank & Seward, 1963) is a smaller, seven-storey building [103] whose scale matched the nineteenth-century warehouses then present in Chorlton Street.

Cruickshank & Seward, incidentally, were also responsible for the National Computing Centre on Oxford Road, a white-tiled building of two storeys cantilevered out over a ground-floor podium. The building was put up in 1964 during Harold Wilson's 'white heat of technology' era, and one evening John

100] St Andrew's House, Portla
Street, Leach Rhodes Walker, 19

101] Highland House, Victoria
Bridge Street, Leach Rhodes
Walker, 1966

Seward was telephoned by one of Wilson's aides who said, 'The Prime Minister is announcing the opening of the NCC, can you do us a model for tomorrow?' Seward telephoned Peter Sainsbury, an architect and draughtsman who could translate designs into beautiful perspectives, and between them the architectural concept was conceived virtually overnight. Harold Wilson made the announcement with Sainsbury's picture behind him, and the building was erected to match the illustration.[25]

For concrete to look well, and last well, the careful selection of materials is required, together with highly specified concrete and close control over the aggregates.

> Concrete caught on, in part, because it seemed to be a cheap and very plastic material. But in fact, to produce high quality and durable concrete finishes has proved to be both difficult and costly, and it called for a practical design skill and knowledge of the material that most architects lacked. The innumerable buildings with drab, grey, begrimed, streaky, cracked concrete finishes, designed with little understanding of drips and weathering, or designed to be covered with paint that the client cannot afford are silent witnesses to the technological inadequacy of the architectural profession, which was carried away by images that could not be realised within the limits of its skill, the resources of industry, and the cash available. The use and abuse of concrete, perhaps more than anything else, account for the hostility to many recent buildings and to the architects who are rightly held largely responsible for them.[26]

Many utilitarian buildings were being erected in the 1960s; they were generally public buildings, and it is evident that cost took priority over materials. The College of Commerce, Aytoun Street (S. G. Besant Roberts, City Architect, 1962), and the Sorting Office, Lever Street (1965–68) and Parcel Post Office, St Andrew's Street and Fairfield Street (1966–68, both by H. G. Swann, Ministry of Public Building and Works), for example, are all concrete and glass and rather grim.

The very nature of modern buildings created difficulties: cornices and sills no longer existed to throw water off the surfaces of walls; joints between the cladding allowed water to run down façades and create staining. Water staining could be minimised by the use of a rough aggregate or by ribbing, as at Aldine House, New Bailey Street (Leach Rhodes Walker, 1967), or by the use of decorative panels as on the end of Sunley House, Piccadilly Plaza, but too many of the buildings of the 1960s were built without enough regard to the effects of weathering. The Rodwell Tower, Piccadilly (Douglas Stephen & Partners, 1965–66), is a notable building of eighteen floors carried on four huge piers, back and front, which support the building over the Rochdale Canal [104]. It was praised by Pevsner as belonging to the 'Louis Kahn succession'.[27] But the in-situ concrete has not worn well, and has had to have a number of repaints.

Some older buildings were even failing structurally: calcium chloride, a rapid setting agent, corroded reinforcing bars if too much had been thrown into the cement; high-alumina cement, if made too wet, became crumbly. All too often, though, it was not the concrete framing which created the eyesore, but the cheaper infills. Lance Wright in a special edition of the *Architectural*

104] Rodwell Tower, Piccadilly, Douglas Stephen & Partners, 1963–66

105] Peter House, St Peter's Square, Amsell & Bailey, 1958

Review wrote of 'badly fitting buildings, grotty concrete steps, cheap twisting aluminium trim, rough precast concrete panels, like giants' breakfast food, thin broken plastic infill panels – the whole unclean and uncleanable, unloved and unlovable, the architecture of greed and carelessness'.[28]

Rod Hackney, who was an architecture student at Manchester University in the early 1960s, recalls that they were not taught traditional building methods – concrete, metal and plastics were the materials of the age.[29] Brick was hardly to be seen and stone was restricted to occasional use as a cladding material for prestigious buildings, or where offices needed to fit in with their neighbours, as at the Portland stone-clad Peter House, St Peter Square (Amsell & Bailey, 1958) [105], or where money seems to have been of little consequence, as at Albert Bridge House, Bridge Street (E. H. Banks of the Ministry of Works, 1958) [106]. The steel-framed Courts of Justice, Crown Square (Leonard C. Howitt, City Architect, 1960–62), have a 'polite' cladding of shelly Portland roach, befitting a law court (see [114]). The Commercial Union Building, Mosley Street (Watney Eiloart Inman & Nunn, 1964–66) also has a shelly Portland roach cladding, but over a concrete frame, and its boxed-out windows in fair-face concrete demonstrate its modernity [107].

The development of electric saws after World War II allowed the cheaper cutting of expensive and harder stones into ashlar sheets 30–40 mm thick. Traditional cladding like Portland stone was now in competition from native granites and marbles from abroad, especially Italy and south Germany. By 1969 the chairman of the Bath and Portland Group was moved to report,

> Stone masonry continues to suffer from extreme shortage of business and, although returning a profit, succeeded only at a level totally unrewarding for the volume of capital employed, in spite of severe cuts in costs and considerable efforts on the part of its management. Only seven years ago stone masonry provided a major part of our profits and from deep into history commanded a high capital investment which restrictions and changes in architectural fashion have left largely idle.[30]

The Royal London Insurance offices, St Ann's Square (H. S. Fairhurst & Son, 1959), were clad in polished granite and Westmorland slate, though were overclad in 1986 by David Backhouse to create 'The Gardens'. Polished granites can be seen at Williams Deacon's Bank headquarters, Mosley Street (H. S. Fairhurst & Son, 1965) [108], and at Petersfield House, Peter Street (Howitt & Tucker, 1965) [109], where the white Derbyshire stone of the window mullions and transoms, and the white Sicilian marble sill panels, are difficult to differentiate from the concrete structure. Woolwich House, Mosley Street (H. S. Fairhurst & Son, 1965) [110], shows how the finer-grained Whitbed Portland stone, when not rainwashed, can blacken badly and look as unprepossessing as concrete.*

---

* Sulphur dioxide formed by the burning of sulphur compounds in coal dissolves in water to become sulphurous acid, which reacts with the carbonates in limestone. This eventually forms calcium sulphate as a hard, glassy skin on the surface of the stone, particularly where the stone is not frequently washed by rain. The sulphate skin can lead to blistering and scaling of the surfaces.

106] Albert Bridge House, Bridg
Street, E. H. Banks, Ministry o
Works, 1958–59

107] Commercial Union
Assurance, Mosley Street, Watn
Eiloart Inman & Nunn, 1964–6

The *Architectural Review* in August 1960 complained that Manchester buildings were being designed by London firms with less care than if they were building in the capital, though the writer failed to mention that ground rents in London allowed better-quality material to be used. In Manchester £5 per square foot was the ceiling, so buildings tended to be built up to that figure. It is the architect's job to provide a conceptual strategy which lifts the building above the developer's vision, but property developers are naturally very demanding, and the architect works under considerable complexities and pressures of time, legislation and, especially, money. So, often, in the end, the built form reflects the amount of money expended on it. Elizabeth House, a concrete-framed building on St Peter's Square (Cruickshank & Seward, 1959–60), for example, was intended to be a handsome stone-clad building to reflect the quality of the surrounding buildings. The developer, however, ran out of money and the building became a shadow of what the architects had intended [111].

Where money was available, Manchester would occasionally attract very expensive buildings such as the £12 million National Westminster Bank (Casson Conder & Partners, 1966–69). An important building, it was the bank's northern headquarters, controlling over 700 branches, and the design competition was won by an important architect, Hugh (later Sir Hugh) Casson, the man who had laid out the Festival of Britain and was later to become President of the Royal Academy. Constructed of in-situ concrete, the building is basically a concrete shell with transfer beams and holes punched out for the windows. There are three basement floors, including vaults below the rock table. Sun Alliance had a rectangular building next door, so the bank was dumb-bell-shaped to preserve ancient lights. The building looms darkly nowadays [112], but the cladding of hand-tooled, vertically-ribbed dark Swedish granite was consciously designed to match the soot-covered Manchester buildings of the time.

In 1969 Sun Alliance replaced their older building with Pall Mall Court, designed by Brett & Pollen, the Brett of the partnership being Lionel Brett, Lord Esher, President of the Royal Institute of British Architects in the 1960s. The building was designed like a reversed figure 2, wrapping around the back of the existing Norwich Union building. The windows, of bronze glass, are boxed-out in discrete rows and columns from the wall, and reflect the surrounding buildings (see [112]). On some of the Court walls, and on the tall service tower, there is deep blue-bronze mosaic cladding. The raised piazza between the two buildings was a result of co-operation between the two firms, and provided useful access to Marsden Street. Underneath are garages for the office blocks. Both buildings won RIBA awards, and both form a marked contrast to the Norwich Union Building, next door, a typical curtain-walled building of the 1960s. Here two separate towers rise above a ground-floor podium; eight storeys for the offices, and an even taller service tower, all in concrete and glass, apart from the brick wall on the west side of the service tower, which had been hidden by the old Sun Alliance building next door.

King Street is an ideal example of the way in which the city changes piece by piece, building by building. The Bank of England, the Reform Club, Ship Canal House, the NatWest building and Pall Mall Court all introduced variety and organic growth on to the urban landscape. In this street is a splendid juxtaposition of buildings of different ages and different styles. The *Architectural Review* in 1960 recognised that variety was necessary. 'Every big scheme must contain a mixture of uses unless the city is to become a strictly zoned collection of mausolea: the zoning should occur organically, by character or pattern, rather than literally, by exact interpretation or categories of use . . . clutter is bad

111] Elizabeth House, St Peter' Square, Cruickshank & Sewarc 1959–60

2] National Westminster Bank,
Casson Conder & Partners,
966–69, and Pall Mall Court,
Brett & Pollen, 1969

when it obscures a deliberate architectural effect . . . but in other places and particularly in some city streets it may be essential.'[31]

In *The Englishness of English Art*, published in 1956, Nikolaus Pevsner had called for an examination of the character of a site: not only its geographical but also its aesthetic, social and historical character – the *genius loci*. He asked for a change from wearisome uniformity, quoting Sir Joshua Reynolds, 'It may not be amiss for the Architect to take advantage some times of . . . accidents, to follow where they lead, and to improve them, rather than always to trust to a regular plan . . . The forms and turnings of the streets of London and other old towns are produced by accident, without any original plan or design, but they are not always the less pleasant to the walker or spectator on that account.'[32]

What makes the character of a city is its mixture of buildings of different styles, old and new – variety is important to the urban landscape. Relationships grow and change as the city destroys and rebuilds; uniformity is the death of the accidental relationship. But the old, the casual, accidental grouping of buildings was much disliked by the planners of the 1960s. Franklin Medhurst of the Town and Country Planning Department of Manchester University dismissed his city in 1960: 'Today the centre of Manchester is in essence as the Victorians built it and consequently it is largely obsolete.'[33] And his view was confirmed in 1962 by Roland Nicholas, author of the 1945 plan, who wrote,

> Manchester has become crystallised in its Victorian setting and stabilised, so that it is still essentially as the Victorians built it. A new look for the City has long been overdue . . . Its unsightly areas of mixed industrial, commercial and residential development need to be systematically unravelled and redeveloped on comprehensive lines. Only in this way can a City assume its proper place as a regional centre. One thing that should be obvious to all property owners at the outset . . . is the impossibility of achieving any satisfactory rearrangement of the highway pattern, pedestrian access, re-allocation of space and improvement of buildings, daylighting and car parking, by the piecemeal development of small sites.[34]

What the author of the 1945 plan would have given Manchester was block after block of uniform, pavilion-like buildings, all of an age, all of a style. Moreover, as Simon perceptively put it, 'We talk of "planning for fifty years" but in practice we are only too ready to consider immediate interests, to plan for results that we ourselves may hope to see.'[35]

Although the 1945 plan was over fifteen years old, it was still the basis of the Development Plan submitted in draft in 1951 and intended to cover a ten-year period. But the Development Plan was approved by the Minister of Housing and Local Government only in 1961, after ten years of delay, and consequently it fell into disuse quickly. The 1961 Development Plan covered fourteen major subject areas: housing, shopping, education, open space, industry, the city centre, minerals, roads, communications, tree planting, public utilities, university, cultural areas and health, and still harked back to the ideas of 1945: 'But not until it has been completely cleared of its slums, has had its entire major road system remodelled and its central area redeveloped on modern lines, with many new office blocks, wider streets, adequate parking space, and improved daylighting conditions, will the Manchester of the future become the City which is portrayed in its Development Plan.'[36]

Yet, by its insistence on planning and zoning and clearing the city centre for new buildings, the City of Manchester was itself guilty of compounding the unemployment problem. An analysis of plant closures, between 1966 and 1972, showed that 13 per cent of the closures in inner Manchester were due to Compulsory Purchase Orders.[37] Much of the closure was of small firms employing fewer than ten workers, and these small companies were closing at about twice the rate of larger firms. 'A thousand (mostly small) industrial enterprises died in the six years 1966–72 in the inner areas. Many were affected, directly or indirectly, by planning actions: most occupied small, perhaps converted premises and were non-conforming uses . . . The crisis of the Inner City, to a significant degree, springs partly from the failure and insensitivity of the planning process.'[38]

Within the central area of the city the large-scale development was to continue, concentrating primarily on the war-ravaged areas of Strangeways, Market Place, Water Street, Swan Street, Shudehill, Piccadilly, Portland Street,

[113] CIS Building, Miller Street,
G. S. Hay and Sir John Burnet
Tait & Partners, 1962

Oxford Street and Faulkner Street. By 1960 Manchester had bought up a number
of sites – 90 per cent of them at 1939 prices – either through Purchase Notices
or by negotiation. On this land, and on other land the authority was obliged to
buy under Purchase Notices, a number of redevelopment schemes were being
undertaken, in the Comprehensive Development Areas of Miller Street, the Old
Shambles, Gartside Street to Albert Square and Piccadilly/Portland Street, and
it was these large-scale, city-led schemes which radically changed the face of
Manchester in the 1960s.

On Miller Street (named after Arkwright's Mill, the first cotton mill in
Manchester) the CIS building (1962) rose twenty-five storeys over a five-storey
podium, and at 400 ft was then the tallest office block in Europe [113]. The
mosaic-covered concrete service core (five men, in twelve months, stuck on
14 million inch-square mosaic pieces) braces the steel frame of the office block,
curtain-walled in glass, aluminium and black vitreous-enamelled panels. The
building held 2,500 workers in thirteen acres of floor space, and the offices
(by Sir Mischa Black and the Design Research Unit) were an early example
of *Bürolandschaft* in the UK. Black elements of the CIS building were taken up
in the adjacent Conference Hall and the fourteen-storey CWS building in Corporation Street. The whole group was by G. S. Hay of the CWS and Sir John
Burnett Tait & Partners.

The Old Shambles had been blitzed in the war, and the fish and oyster stalls and underground skittle alleys had been destroyed. On part of this derelict site Cruickshank & Seward built Queen's House, in the early 1960s, for Unicorn Property: six storeys of exposed concrete, mosaics and Portland stone slabs. The office windows were an early example of double-glazing, unusual in a speculative development. From 1969 Cruickshank & Seward developed the Old Shambles for Central & District Properties, and created the new Market Square with the refurbished Sinclair's Oyster Bar and the Old Wellington Inn (both raised 4 ft 9$^1/_2$ in. to meet the height of the new square) as counterpoints in the stark white concrete. In 1973 Marks & Spencer moved their store from the ground floor of the Rylands building (now Debenham's) into the new building on Cross Street, now extended back along St Mary's Gate, and Queen's House became St Michael House. The wavy external canopy of the store, cantilevered and with an internal membrane, familiar to all shoppers, amazingly survived almost intact the direct blast of the IRA bomb in 1996. Fairburn House (Cruickshank & Seward, 1974–75), the office block on the other side of Deansgate, was built as the final stage of scheme, and was subsequently converted into the Renaissance Ramada Hotel.

In 1962 the grand 'processional way' from the Town Hall to the new Law Courts proposed in the 1945 plan was dropped in favour of a more relaxed scheme. In an unusually close collaboration, Rowland Nicholas, the City Surveyor, and S. G. Besant Roberts, the City Architect, and their staff drew up a scheme which was published in the *Architectural Review* in August 1962. The route from Crown Square via Spinning Fields and Brazennose Street to Albert Square was redefined as a major piece of town planning, and was seen as only the first stage in the provision of a pedestrian network for the whole of the city centre. 'The Albert Square/Deansgate section will contain a large pedestrian square, a meeting place where people can stroll, shop or just sit; this is something Manchester badly needs. Here the emphasis will be on gaiety and life. By contrast the Deansgate/Courts of Justice section will aim at a quiet collegiate atmosphere.'[39]

114] Courts of Justice, Crown Square, Leonard C. Howitt, City Architect, 1960–62

Crown Square, in which only the Courts of Justice (Leonard C. Howitt, 1960–62) were yet built [114], was visualised as an Italian *piazza* from which a ramp would lead first to a dignified, tree-shaded square and then to a secluded courtyard behind the proposed law library. The square and courtyard were to be hemmed in by almost domestic-scale buildings, home to barristers' chambers in the manner of one of the London Inns of Court. From Spinning Fields a footbridge would take pedestrians over Deansgate, and lead to a large square where there would be trees, cafés, restaurants, pubs, kiosks, seats, flowers and water. The upper end of Brazennose Street would be enclosed by a long office block, raised on columns so that the activity of Albert Square could be seen, and with a central glass link to reveal the Town Hall's tower. The west side of Albert Square would be pedestrianised, leaving traffic to the east, Town Hall, side. A high-level walkway would connect the scheme from the side of the Church of the Hidden Gem to St James's House, St James's Square (Leach Rhodes Walker, 1965, demolished and replaced by a Fairhurst's building, 1997).

However, as Kenneth Browne pointed out in his critique of the scheme in the very same issue of the *Architectural Review*, 'As it is, T squares being what they are, you can look right through it from end to end like a gun barrel for there is a dead, repeat dead, alignment of the pedestrian route ... it needs more to bite on, more mystery, more variety of experience, and the route needs to feel its way along the plan rather than being a slot cut through it.'[40] And Browne thought great care was needed to ensure that the area did not become dead at night.

Opposite the Courts building, Dean's Court was built in 1965–67 as chambers for counsel. The ramp of the original scheme was replaced by steps which lead to a square enclosed by the opposing façade of Dean's Court and by Cumberland House [115], home to Manchester Education Committee (all by Leach Rhodes Walker). The concrete square has concrete planters bare of any foliage and some broken wooden seats. The Register Office is now in Cumberland House, having moved from Elliott House, and a bleaker location in which to register

115] Education Offices, Crown Square/Spinning Fields, Leach Rhodes Walker, 1965–67

births and marriages cannot be imagined. Fortunately, the whole of the area is due for redevelopment.

In 1971 the City Magistrates' Court (Yorke Rosenberg & Mardall) [116] was built, flanking the Courts of Justice and terminating the square. It is in concrete with a tiled cladding but, typical of the work of the architects, with a Miesian attention to detailing and to bold expression of the formal structure; the windows set back deeply behind the structural frame. Crown Square was closed to traffic in 1971, paved over and planted with trees, and in the same year Leach Rhodes Walker started the pedestrianisation of Spinning Fields, the book extension to the rear of the Rylands Library, and the extension of the *Daily Mail* offices (completed without disrupting the printing presses). Lincoln Square in Brazennose Street was built more or less as the original scheme suggested, and is wide enough to bear the seven storeys and forty-eight bays of Brazennose House which flanks it, and there *is* a water feature, and outside office hours the area is still dead.

If Crown Square was the largest civic development, then the Piccadilly Plaza complex (Covell Matthews & Partners, 1959–65, for the Colman Group) was one of the most visible pieces of private development. The buildings (mostly nineteenth-century warehouses) on the Parker Street side of Piccadilly Gardens were destroyed in the war, and on this site were placed three buildings [117]: a nine-storey hotel, carried on a huge concrete cradle supported by piloti; Sunley Tower, a twenty-four-storey office block (made to look even taller by the three plant floors on top); and the separate idiosyncratically roofed seven-storey Bernard House. This assembly of buildings (group is not the word to use, since they have no visual relationship to each other) sits on top of a two-level shopping complex.

Whether or not any or all of the buildings have any architectural merit, their placement took no account of the grain of the area, and the whole block forms a barrier across the city in a way that no other set of buildings do – it sits

116] Magistrates' Courts, Crown Square, Yorke Rosenberg & Mardall, 1971

7] Piccadilly Plaza Buildings,
Piccadilly, Covell Matthews
& Partners, 1959–65

across the ends of Faulkner, George and Back George Streets and entirely cuts off that sector of the city from Piccadilly. The blight is made worse by having a large bus terminus spreading from the pavement on Parker Street. The model of the scheme was published in the *Architectural Review* on 16 June 1960, and in the same issue Ian Nairn wrote, 'The biggest private development inside the Ring Road is the Piccadilly Centre, by Covell and Matthews, which is the only one of the big commercial super block schemes . . . to hold out some hopes of being a good building – good in its architectural details and good to walk around, in a fuzzily humanistic sense which is just as important.'[41] But models can be deceptive. Piccadilly Plaza, in spite of its continued support from some members of the architectural community, has never been loved by the public at large.

The adoption of brutalist techniques and aesthetics (particularly in the use of concrete) in the massive developments of the 1960s contributed substantially to the development of the feeling that modern architecture was inhuman . . . It has been argued that the disasters of the 1960s were inevitable because the modern movement was damned from the start, not only by a sterile, boring aesthetic, but by its paternalistic, authoritarian attitudes, combined with a blind worship of mass production and false mechanistic analogies.[42]

If the blight of the CDAs weren't enough, there was always the blight of the intended Road Systems. In 1961 a local Act of Parliament had been obtained to acquire land and property for the building of a number of major new highways: the City Centre, Inner, Intermediate and Outer Ring roads. Both Telephone House and St Andrew's House were set back some way from the present line of Portland Street, and this was to allow for the building of the new three-lane, dual carriageway City Centre Road which would have run 'twenty feet below the present level of Portland Street, then behind Central Station through the City Exhibition Hall in Castlefield, over the river Irwell to complete the circle in the City.'[43] The Brown's and Watts' Warehouses, of course, would have had to go, but this was the era of the road planner and history had no place in the new road scheme of things.

There was to be a huge multi-level interchange towering over Dale Street and Piccadilly, encroaching on Piccadilly Gardens and wiping out most of the buildings in an area bounded by Lever Street, Paton Street, Hilton Street and Piccadilly. The junction with Portland Street and Princess Street was to be

118] Gateway House, Station Approach, Richard Siefert & Partners, 1969

a four-acre roundabout, and Princess Street was to become a two-way major radial road with all the buildings on one side demolished. The buildings on the north-east side of Princess Street were saved only by pressure from the Victorian Society and by the listing of Gregan's Mechanics' Institute.

Vehicles were, of course, an increasing problem. In 1940 there were only 2·3 million vehicles on the nation's roads, increasing to 9·4 million by 1960, and by 2010, it was projected, there would be 30 million to 40 million. The motor car was becoming an important element in the make-up of the city. In 1942 Alker Tripp, a policeman, published a slim volume about vehicle movement and introduced the idea of the traffic-free precinct.[44] His ideas were taken up by Colin Buchanan, a civil engineer, loaned from the new Ministry of Town and Country Planning to the Ministry of Transport to undertake a study of traffic conditions. Buchanan's report, *Traffic in Towns*, was published in 1963 and became seminal in its influence.[45] Buchanan advocated the separation of pedestrians and vehicles, and, following advice given in the Buchanan Report, the City Council in the 1960s encouraged schemes which would separate pedestrians and cars by keeping cars on the streets and placing walkways linking buildings some 20 ft above the street level. A complex pattern of entrances to buildings was envisaged, with shops and other facilities incorporated into these corridors.

Many buildings in the 1960s and 1970s were designed with first-floor deck access in mind, though few examples remain: the first-storey deck access to Eagle Star House on Mosley Street (Cruickshank & Seward, 1973) is still visible; the bridge between the Arndale Centre and Marks & Spencer was destroyed by the 1996 bomb (though a new one is being built); the bridge across Deansgate from the Old Shambles was demolished only in 1999. Deck access can still be seen in the University Precinct: the upper link between the Royal Northern College of Music and the Precinct is only part of a series of aerial walkways which would have included a huge spiral ramp coming down into All Saints Square. A new walkway has been provided between the new Business School building and the Precinct.

Hugh Wilson, co-designer of the Arndale Centre and one of the university master planners, said the motor car must serve, but must not be allowed to dominate. And his was a shared vision of the New Town of the future. 'The centre will be a pedestrian precinct, with cars and warehousing at ground and/or basement level, and pedestrians on a first-floor deck. On, around, and piercing through the deck will be offices, flats, shops and public buildings, with multi-level access for servicing.'[46] The problems with deck access – not only making people use stairs and ramps, but providing hidden areas suitable for vandals and muggers – became clear in the deck access housing blocks on the notorious Hulme Estate. Only John Sheard, then a final-year architecture student, had the vision to leave pedestrians on the ground and make the cars go up and down ramps, an activity to which they are much more suited.[47]

Fortunately, little of the road scheme came into fruition, though one major part was completed. Road 17/7 was commenced in 1964 and completed in 1967 (though the spur to Sackville Street ends abruptly in mid-air), and was named the Mancunian Way after a competition among local schoolchildren – over 500 entries were received. The quadrupling of the price of oil following the oil crisis of 1973 effected major reviews of the road building programme. In 1976 the Greater Manchester Council abandoned the Inner Ring and City Centre roads, replacing them with the existing Inner Relief Road plan, and by 1977 Greater Manchester had scrapped over half its £800 million road-building programme.[48] But although the road proposals were being reviewed, the abandonment of a major highway scheme did not necessarily remove all blight, since large schemes are often replaced by smaller schemes, and there remained the blight due to speculative land-holding with the intention of realising 'hope values' by alternative land zoning.

IO

HOUSING

IN THE
POST-WAR PERIOD

I live forlorn on the seventh floor of a corporation flat
which the children have all fell from and the pigeons have beshat.
I do not mind the loneliness, the long evenings with the tellie;
but I do wish the wind hadn't altered the flight of the brick
I dropped on Jack Kelly.
[Alan Jackson, *The House that Jack Built*, 1973]

THE 1945 *Manchester Plan* had concerns about both the density and the age of its housing. About 60 per cent of Manchester's houses had been built at densities in excess of twenty-four to the acre; most of these 120,000 house were old and needed to be rebuilt, and over 69,000 were considered by the Medical Officer of Health to be unfit for human habitation. The plan, however, did not consider that putting people into high-rise blocks was the answer:

It would be a profound sociological mistake to force upon the British public, in defiance of its own widely expressed preference for separate houses with private gardens, a way of life that is fundamentally out of keeping with its traditions, instincts and opportunities . . . the advocates of large-scale flat-building greatly overestimate the proportion of people now living in the congested areas who might thereby be decently rehoused on the site. Blocks of flats to accommodate the majority of the residents in Manchester's inner districts would have to be so close together in relation to their height and capacity that the lower rooms would get little daylight, communal lawns between them would soon get trampled into bare mud, and playground noises would become intolerable. In other words, it is impossible to get rid of the effects of congested development by turning it on edge.[1]

The plan realised that, at lower densities, not enough houses could be built to accommodate the people from the slums, and advocated rehousing them in Wythenshawe and other new residential areas. Pressure from Lady Simon, the *Guardian* newspaper and the City Surveyor persuaded Manchester to pursue overspill sites rather than high-density housing in the city area. In 1946 Manchester wanted to build New Towns for its inhabitants at Mobberley and Congleton, but Mobberley presented considerable geological difficulties and Congleton was unsuitable because of the new radio telescope planned there.

Again, in 1953, Manchester sought to build 10,500 houses in Mobberley and 12,000 at Lymm, with industrial and other development. Both schemes were objected to by Cheshire County Council and the National Union of Farmers (on the grounds of reuse of agricultural land), and their views were supported by the planning inspector, 'I must assume that to save or postpone the taking of good agricultural land for building is at least as important as the maintenance by Manchester of a steady and adequate rate of housebuilding.'[2] The Housing Minister rejected both schemes, but in 1956 Manchester again returned to the Lymm site, with a requirement to build 17,000 houses for a population of 60,000. The Minister commissioned a public inquiry to investigate the Lymm proposal, and following this report refused Manchester's application.[3]

Manchester, in 1955, had 68,000 houses unfit for human habitation, yet the total number of slum houses cleared between 1955 and 1960 was only 7,737.[4] The 1949 Housing Act had exacerbated the problem by removing the phrase 'working classes' and making local authorities responsible for the housing needs of all their residents. By 1960 Manchester was building new homes at only a third of the rate of the 1950s, and, in 1961 the Council accepted an annual housing target of 4,000 homes. The pressure on the Council was not from its ineffectual Housing Committee, but from the city's Medical Officer of Health and the Town Clerk, with backing from the Ministry of Housing and Local Government. In 1962 R. Nicholas was able to write,

> In a survey taken in 1944 for the purposes of the City of Manchester Plan it was found that about 90,000 houses in the City were without baths. Today there are about a quarter of a million Manchester people – about a third of its entire population – living in 60,000 houses which were declared unfit for human habitation years ago [and the worst of these, some 20,000 homes, were built before any by-laws were invented: two-storey houses without foundations, at a density of forty-five per acre. About 700 per year were simply falling down]. The City needs about 83,000 dwellings to replace existing unfit houses and to make up for the shortage which has been caused by the recent war.
>
> The remaining undeveloped lands within the City, namely at Wythenshawe and Blackley and in areas which have been cleared under the provisions of the Housing Acts, are now being cleared for housing purposes. The Corporation's slum clearance programme is again well under way after its postponement on the outbreak of the 1939–45 war, but the shortage of land within the City makes it imperative for the Corporation to find sufficient overspill sites

to rehouse a large part of its population, and great efforts have been made, and are still being made, to secure the necessary land outside the City . . . Within the City itself a considerable amount of large scale flat development has been carried out in cleared areas, notably at St George's, Hulme and in Collyhurst.[5]

Overspill estates were created closer to the city at Heywood and Langley to the north, Hattersley to the east and Worsley to the west. Between 1954 and 1976 Manchester erected 71,000 new council houses and flats, some half of them in the overspill estates, but these numbers fell far short of the 90,000 dwellings demolished in the same period.

All this time, Manchester was losing population faster than any other major UK city except Liverpool and Glasgow, the population declining by 8 per cent between 1931 and 1951, and by a further 6 per cent by 1961. By 1985 the population of 457,500 was 41 per cent lower than the peak level of 1931, and the downward trend has continued, to 430,000 in 1997. Those who could afford to buy property were leaving Manchester for new homes in the outer suburbs. Between 1921 and 1951 the population of Prestwich had risen by 82 per cent, that of Wilmslow by 90 per cent, of Hazel Grove and Bramhall by 100 per cent, of Urmston by 156 per cent and that of Cheadle by 186 per cent.[6] As Derek Senior wrote in 1960: 'In the last four years nearly 3,000 houses have been built by private enterprise in the Cheadle and Gatley Urban District alone – more than half as many as the Manchester Corporation has managed to build on all its sites, internal and external, in the same period.'[7]

When Sir Keith Joseph became Minister of Housing in 1962 he set up a regional office in Manchester to assist local authorities with their slum clearance. 'Areas with the worst slum problems were to double and treble their rates of clearance and industrialised building methods would boost council house building in these areas.'[8] As a result, where in 1961 and 1962 Manchester had only cleared about 1,350 slum houses, from 1963 to 1967 about 4,000 houses per year were being cleared. However, although the Medical Officer of Health was demolishing huge swathes of derelict housing, little was being built to replace them. The problem (which was a national one) was recognised in 1964 with the setting up of the National Building agency under the direction of Cleeve Barr. The agency advised local authorities on improved methods, both traditional and innovatory, and dealt particularly with industrialised and system building. Subsidies were made available from central government funds for high-rise and high-density housing.

Since 1953, following the publication of the White Paper *Houses: the Next Step*, and subsequent Ministry of Housing design guides and manuals, high-rise housing had been seen as an important factor in slum clearance. Two major RIBA symposia in 1955 and 1957 dealt with issues of high-rise living. J. Lewis Womersley, an advocate of high-rise (and co-architect of the Hulme crescents), suggested that up to 50 per cent of the population wanted to live in high-rise point blocks, but then he was already designing the huge blocks at Park Hill in Sheffield.

New building techniques had been developed in Europe for mass housing – concrete frames to support the building, and cladding to protect the interior – and these were brought into the UK. Box frame (also known as 'cross-wall' and 'egg crate') construction, like Concrete Ltd's 'Bison Wall-Frame' and the Larsen–Nielsen system were also developed – load-bearing wall panels of reinforced concrete, slotted together like a house of cards. Concrete Ltd set up specialist factories throughout Britain for their system; Wates set up factories on site. The Tracoba system, imported from France by Gilbert Ash, the French Balency system imported by Cubitt, the Spacemaker system used by Shepherd and the Swedish Skarne system imported by Cruden's all used in-situ casting. All the systems used tower cranes to lift the construction units into place, and by 1954 some 200 cranes were in operation throughout the country; scaffolding and skilled workers were no longer necessary, and it was all very fast to build. In Manchester, large contracts were negotiated with Laing and Wimpey for housing blocks, and patent systems were bought in from Sweden and France for fast-build housing.[9] The Sectra system was brought from France by Laing in 1962 – in-situ casting in steel shutters allowing high-precision casting of concrete. The Ministry of Housing and Local Government was much interested in system-built structures, and when in 1965 local authorities were asked to submit their four-year housing plans, the Ministry made it clear that it would look kindly on system-built housing schemes.

All these system-built blocks tended to look alike, and their dull uniformity was boring. As an anonymous city architect in Manchester recollected, 'That nine-storey slab, you banged it down in Wythenshawe, you banged it down elsewhere, I got sick of seeing it! There it was in the drawer and you just kept reusing it! It was a pretty miserable thing to have to do . . . Then some foreman from Parks would turn up twelve months later in a lorry and say, "Right, Bill, chuck out a couple of trees here".'[10] Only after J. S. Millar was appointed City Planning Officer in 1966 did some form of design ethos emerge. Robert Stones, Chief Assistant Architect, set up, with Millar's help, a semi-autonomous Housing Development Group within the Department of Housing. From this group came socially acceptable deck-access and cottage-type schemes for Gibson Street in Longsight, Turkey Lane in Harpurhey and Wellington Street in Beswick-Bradford, of 430, 1,000 and 300 acres respectively. Only one scheme was built to the designs of the group: Gibson Street, Longsight (in 1966), a ribbon of ten-storey barrier blocks with grouped estates running out from the back of them. The estate was demolished in 1992.

Shortage of building land in Manchester focused the minds of the city, but Manchester was still broadly against high-rise building. A publication by the Housing Committee in 1967, *Urban Renewal Manchester*, stated that dwellings must not be put into 'office block' arrangements, and foresaw no buildings higher than six-storey maisonettes. The point was reinforced on 16 May 1968 by the collapse of Ronan Point in Newham, east London. This was a twenty-three-storey Larsen–Nielsen system which used large concrete slabs connected together to make the walls and floors, and there was no structural underpinning. One wall panel was blown out, which caused an entire corner of the building to collapse like a house of cards, killing five people and injuring eighty. Six hundred similar blocks had been built by Taylor Woodrow-Anglian around the country.

Ronan Point gave the reason to stop high-density housing altogether, and in 1968 the Ministry of Housing and Local Government moved toward refurbishment schemes for older houses rather than wholesale demolition and rebuilding. In most cities not enough new houses could possibly be built to house those displaced, and the areas already cleared were creating acres of derelict and vandalised land. The 1969 Housing Act encouraged the renovation of existing buildings, supported by central government grants for landscaping, car parks, play areas, etc. General Improvement Areas and Housing Action Areas created a patchwork of refurbishment, and by the early 1970s hardly any system-built housing was being erected.[11] The change in attitudes is exemplified by Colin Buchanan's observation:

> Often, when I am travelling by train, I look at the rows of fairly poor houses that back on to the railway lines . . . terraced houses with back additions and a little strip of garden – but I see bits tacked on, I see flowers in the gardens, little patches of mown grass, greenhouses, pigeon lofts, and of course, sheds, and I feel that those houses, miserable though they may be in many respects, nevertheless provide a creative outlet for the occupants in a way that a flat in a tower block, where you can't drive a nail into the wall without permission, does not and never can provide. If I had to pin it to one piece of advice I think I would say "Don't forget the sheds." A man must have a shed.[12]

Yet, just as the nation was turning away from system-built housing, Manchester's Hulme Estate commenced building in 1968, the year that Ronan Point collapsed. Hulme had suffered more than any other residential area during the air raids of 1940–41, and in the 1940s and 1950s slum clearance had taken place, and new flats were built – long, low-rise blocks in brick in the Bentley House Estate and in St George's, which also included a high-rise tower block. By the early 1960s all the remaining terraces in Hulme had been bulldozed, and few buildings were left standing. Rod Hackney pointed out,

> Hitler hadn't caused a fraction of the destruction which followed in his wake under the guidance of Alf Young – Manchester City Council's energetic chief public health officer. Like most other city officials nationwide Young obeyed the letter of the law, which dictated that anything built before 1919 was by definition a slum and had to go. The buildings had reached the end of their useful life and had to be removed to make land available for the planners and their huge estates at Hulme, Moss Side, Ardwick and Beswick.[13]

New ideas had emerged for Hulme by late 1964: visions of flats and maisonettes on interconnecting decks and friendly 'streets in the sky'. 'A new street pattern, entirely segregated from traffic roads, where all age groups can be suitably accommodated, which will have to serve the needs of five generations of Manchester people.'[14] Hulme, until 1965, already had the largest range of shops outside the city centre, as well as pubs, churches and its own town hall. Stretford Road was a major shopping street, and had been described in the

Manchester Evening News as 'perhaps the most famous shopping centre in South Manchester'.[15] But these all went in favour of the new shopping facilities in three precincts; at the Moss Side District Centre and in two smaller neighbourhood centres.

Hugh Wilson and J. Lewis Womersley, in October 1965, presented their £4 million scheme for the redevelopment of Hulme. Wilson and Womersley were already in partnership in Manchester, where, from 1964, they had been working on a scheme to create a unified education campus, bringing the university, UMIST, the polytechnic and the Manchester Royal Infirmary into one urban framework.[16] They already had experience of housing schemes: Hugh Wilson did the grey slate-roofed terraces at Cumbernauld New Town in 1956, and Lewis Womersley had been City Architect of Sheffield, where he had designed the Park Hill flats the same year. Womersley had experienced first-hand the slum houses of his home town of Huddersfield in the 1920s and 1930s, and dedicated most of his work to public housing, believing that 'if we are to design cities and not merely housing we must go beyond the individual dwelling and portray the grand design'.[17]

Work was under way by spring 1968: thirteen tower blocks; low-rise concrete blocks clad in a variety of materials, and connected together by aerial walkways; and the crescents – four long, curved, south-facing blocks of flats and maisonettes connected by walkways and bridges [**119**]. The crescents were named after the architects Adam, Nash, Barry and Kent, and Womersley justified the choice of names: 'We feel that the analogy we have made with Georgian London and Bath is entirely valid. By the use of similar shapes and proportions, large-scale building groups and open spaces, and, above all, by skilful landscaping and extensive tree planting, it is our endeavour to achieve at Hulme a solution to the problems of twentieth-century living which would be the equivalent in quality of that reached for the requirements of eighteenth-century Bloomsbury and Bath.'[18] By 1972 the redevelopment of Hulme was

119] Charles Barry Crescent, Hulme, Wilson & Womersley, 1970s

complete. 'Over 5,000 new homes had been built in less than eight years and over 3,000 of these were deck access, making Hulme the biggest concentration of this type of housing in the country.'[19] As if to confirm their isolation, the building of the Mancunian Way and Princess Road had effectively cut its residents off from the rest of the city.

Within months, problems became apparent. The buildings had been erected too quickly, and the unfamiliar building techniques had been poorly supervised; the reinforcing bolts and ties which held panels together were found to be missing, and leaks started to occur. The *Guardian* described Hulme as 'a morass in which design faults and tenants' revulsion at their environment have combined to produce staggering maintenance demands and angry howls of neglect.'[20] Poor insulation and ventilation caused condensation problems. The huge increases in fuel bills from 1973 meant under-floor heating became too expensive, adding to the condensation problems. Ducting for water pipes, wiring and under-floor heating allowed mice, cockroaches and other vermin to spread easily to all parts of the estate, which was 'Leaking without heating, stinking from back-flows of sewage . . . and badly vandalised.'[21]

The blocks were unsuitable for the elderly and disabled and for families with children – after one five-year-old boy fell from a top landing a petition was signed by 643 residents who wished to be rehoused. The lifts, when they worked, were usually filthy, and the aerial walkways became unhygienic as people refused to clean communal areas. Vandalism and burglary were rife – and the walkways provided excellent escape routes. A survey conducted in 1975 indicated that 96.3 per cent of tenants wanted to leave the crescents. 'Many people suffer from loneliness, depression and anxiety, finding the estate an intimidating place in which to live. Worry about street crime, drug abuse and break-ins makes many people, particularly women and elderly people, shut themselves up in their homes.'[22] Even the *Architects' Journal* was moved to describe Hulme as 'Europe's worst housing stock . . . hideous system-built deck-access blocks which gave Hulme its unsavoury reputation.'[23]

The slum clearances of the 1960s and early 1970s had removed over 70,000 of the city's worst dwellings. Redevelopment between 1961 and 1980 took place at lower densities, with the construction of 44,000 dwellings within the city and a further 16,800 in overspill estates. Despite this, over a quarter of the city's homes were still in need of major treatment. The bulk of the problem lay in housing which was built in the 1960s and 1970s using non-traditional building methods: 'Deck access maisonette blocks, which have suffered from a combination of structural faults, vandalism, problems with refuse disposal and cleaning of public areas, and, in some cases, problems with central heating. There are 4,720 units in such blocks. The main concentration is in Hulme and Moss Side where there are 2,960 units. (Deck access properties are no longer let to families with children.)'[24]

By the mid-1970s the programme of large-scale redevelopment was nearing its end and emphasis turned to the improvement of remaining sub-standard and older housing, and since 1976 some 40,000 dwellings have been improved. Manchester in 1978 had a modernisation programme for most of its older housing stock – 29,000 older low-rise houses, 6,300 of them in the inner area – and was either phasing out or modernising its walk-up flats. Design improvements were being made to 3,000 units in deck-access blocks.[25] In 1978 Manchester had 14,006 inner area residents on its waiting list (48 per cent of the total). Of those: 6,208 were local authority tenants seeking a transfer, 1,832 had children living in dwellings with access above ground level, 4,450 were overcrowded and 1,923 were families living with their grandparents.[26]

In the late 1970s almost half of Manchester's inhabitants lived in Council-rented accommodation, compared with the national average of 29 per cent, but government spending cuts reduced drastically the number of local authority mortgages available. Manchester's lending on local authority mortgages in 1978 was less than one-seventh of the 1974–75 level. Government investment in public housing was cut from £7·2 billion in 1978/79 to £1·6 billion in 1989/90.[27] In 1977/78 the council built 2,200 dwellings, but because of government policy only seventy-seven were built in 1986/87.[28] The number of council houses built nationally fell dramatically, from 79,000 in 1978 to 1,200 in 1992/93; investment in new housing was lower in the UK than in any comparable country, both as a percentage of GDP and in terms of the number of houses built *per capita*.

A survey by the City Council in 1987 found around 30,000 people living in homes without essential heating, 20,000 homes affected by damp, 80,000 people unable to afford a roast joint or its equivalent once per week, 20,000 households with at least one person who lacked a warm, waterproof coat, and nearly half of Manchester's residents unable to afford even one week's annual holiday. In February 1987 at least one-third of Manchester' inhabitants was dependent on Supplementary Benefit. Unsurprisingly, perhaps, Council tenants were three times more likely to be in poverty than owner-occupiers. The poorest people lived in Moss Side, Miles Platting and Cheetham Hill, where unemployment was around 45 per cent; Hulme's unemployment in 1986 was 59 per cent for adult males and 68 per cent for youths.[29]

After a decade of problems, the Council moved residents into other areas of Hulme or the city, and the flats and maisonettes were let to young childless couples, single people and students. In April 1992 the Hulme City Challenge was launched with £37·5 million of government money, and the City Council set up Hulme Regeneration, with AMEC as a partner to oversee and co-ordinate the rebuilding, and Mills Beaumont Leavey as lead design consultants. 125 acres were to be cleared and rebuilt in five years, with a private sector investment programme of £200 million. Plans were drawn up for 3,000 new homes (mostly low-rise, traditional properties), offices and community facilities. Stretford Road, once a busy shopping street, became Hulme Walk in the 1970s, a degraded inner city walkway and precinct. It is now a wide thoroughfare called the Stretford Road Development Corridor. The unsuccessful District Centre was replaced by a modern Asda supermarket and other shops.

The *Guide to Development in Hulme*, which was published in 1994, was architect-led, and ensured that future tenants were consulted. 'What distinguishes the present approach to Hulme to that of the 1960s is the degree of community involvement that has been encouraged by Hulme Regeneration, and the nature of the masterplan and subsequent design code, which must be adopted by the developers and architects.'[30] The authors of the *Guide* were concerned to create a viable urban neighbourhood, 'but we realise that such neighbourhoods generally evolve naturally, in piecemeal fashion over some time, rather than through high-speed clearance and comprehensive redevelopment. Our strategy, therefore, is to create both the appropriate framework in which new development can fit, and fertile conditions for the investment needed for the growth we seek.'[31]

For the Homes for Change Co-operative, Mills Beaumont Leavey Channon (1994–96) designed an eighteen-hour-a-day building, the form of which evolved from a series of intensive weekend design workshops with the future tenants [120]. The basis of the design is a four-sided urban block of four and six-storey buildings, forming a central courtyard, with the base and corners of the building articulated by height or distinct architectural elements. There are shops, workshops, a café and studios and performance space which form the base of the building on the west and northern façades. Their activities add a dynamic to the courtyard as well as the street. The enthusiasm of the co-operative was matched by the commitment of the Guinness Trust as the major funding partner backing the project.[32]

OMI Architects were involved in 1994 in a new £4·5 million housing scheme on Boundary Lane, for the Guinness Trust Housing Association. The 124 dwellings are a mixture of family homes, general needs homes, and homes for wheelchair users, and there are flats for the over-fifty-fives grouped around a secluded garden. A variety of forms are used, from single storey units to a gateway

120] Homes for Change Building, Hulme, Mills Beaumont Leavey Channon, 1996

five-storey turret, containing maisonettes and marking the entrance to the estate. The consultation of OMI with the tenants' association lasted seven months, and included a visit to the Byker estate in Newcastle. OMI were 'keen to hear the voice of the silent majority of the community which had been ignored in the planning of the area three decades ago.'[33] As Peter Marcus of the tenants' association said, 'When tenants have a say in everything from allocation of units, through site layouts to architectural design and interiors, it engenders social ownership, a spiritual ownership even. People are going to say "I designed that turret or that fence," and will make sure it is looked after. It is interesting to see that there has been no vandalism among the newly completed houses.'[34]

A number of private-sector building firms have also provided houses in Hulme for rent or for sale [121], among them Redwood Homes, and Bellway Homes, which has created one of largest private-sector residential schemes undertaken in the city, of 649 homes, eleven commercial units, a nursery and a park, at an estimated cost of £34 million.[35] Environmental improvements have also taken place: Hulme Park (by landscape architect Neil Swanson), opposite the Zion Centre, was the first large-scale park created in the city since the nineteenth century. The Hulme Arch (Chris Wilkinson and Ove Arup & Partners, 1997), spanning Princess Parkway, and opening up Hulme to the city, was presented with a Highly Commended award at the 1998 Structural Steel Design Awards. Hulme was one of the top regeneration projects in the country, and was one of the six finalists in British Urban Regeneration Association's annual awards in June 1996.

121] Mixed housing, Stretford Road, Hulme, 1990s

Despite all the refurbishment, over a quarter of the city's homes are still in need of major treatment, and the bulk of the problem lies in housing which was built in the 1960s and 1970s using non-traditional building methods. The *Manchester Plan* allows for a further 16,000 dwellings in the city between 1991 and 2001, which reflects the amount of land available for current and future development use, and these houses will be built in a traditional style. Greater use will be made of housing associations, such as the Housing Corporation scheme which replaced the 600 deck-access flats of Fort Ardwick.

Manchester City Council, together with Tameside MBC and Manchester TEC, has submitted a bid for resources from the Single Regeneration Budget to cover parts of Beswick, Clayton and Openshaw in Manchester and Ashton West End in Tameside. Among the aims are the renovation or removal and replacement of undesirable and inadequate housing so that the retained stock is better able to meet the needs of the community. Merseyside is the only part of England to have Objective 1 status which qualifies for maximum grant from the European Regional Development Fund and the European Social Fund (Liverpool is in first position in the National Deprivation ranking, Manchester is in third position), and the northern boroughs of Manchester have intermediate status. A new ten-year programme, 'New Deal for Communities', will tackle severe deprivation in neighbourhoods of up to 4,000 households. Liverpool and Manchester have been designated as pathfinder areas and invited to develop innovative bids for approval in July 1999. Funding will come from £800 million of new money unlocked by the government's spending review.

II

THE 1970S

DEVELOPERS
AND DEMOLITION

The built environment of today fails to satisfy, not because architects have been trying to impose the wrong sort of architecture, but because the real shapers – businessmen in the private sector – have been making their decisions with no regard for the architectural (or indeed) the human consequences. [Lance Wright in the *Architectural Review*, April 1973]

BEFORE WORLD WAR II there were few speculative developments, very few large property companies, even fewer quoted on the stock exchange, and no property press. After the war this all changed. 'The property boom began with the reconstruction of bombed-out town centres and as it secured an increasingly powerful place in the economy, development companies proliferated along with estate agents, surveyors and property investment companies.'[1] From 1971, when controls on bank lending were lifted, three times as much capital went into property development as went into industrial production. By 1974 the share value of the three top property companies exceeded that of British Leyland.

In Manchester, between 1963 and 1972, there was a 37 per cent growth in office space by rateable value, and much of this was the replacing of obsolete premises with new speculative buildings over which little planning control was exercised. By the middle of the 1970s Manchester had a considerable net over-provision of office space, at the same time as there was a decentralisation of offices to outlying towns. Bolton, Bury, Oldham, Rochdale, Salford, Stockport and Wilmslow all saw an increase in office employment, particularly in higher managerial and professional jobs.[2] The lack of car parking, congestion and a high business rate in Manchester were all contributing factors. In 1971 total office employment in Manchester was 60,220 people, but by 1977 the figure had declined to 53,170. This decline is partly explained by the fact that 39 per cent of office jobs in the 1970s were linked with manufacturing. 'But for the expansion in the national health service, education, social services and public administration, relatively few jobs would (in fact) have been created in the service sector of the Manchester economy 1971–1976.'[3]

Office employment may have been falling, but that did not stop the destruction of Victorian buildings and the erection of new office blocks in their place. One major reason for replacing old buildings with new offices was, of course, that old buildings, especially nineteenth-century ones, were perceived as problematical; their footprint was too large, they did not have enough floors, and the floors they did have were too high, their brickwork and stone needed expensive consolidation, they did not meet modern fire regulations and, in any case, clients wanted spanking-new and modern-looking buildings to reflect their image. History was somewhere to visit, not to work in. And local authorities cannot turn down applications because they are speculative or are a waste of resources or have no social context, nor can they question the profit motive, or the profits, of a developer.

> A developer is . . . in a very strong position compared with the planners or the public. He need only justify his proposals in pure physical planning terms. In addition, he will have a team of surveyors, and valuers, and ex-local authority planners who are experts at presenting their schemes to planners and councillors. The team will probably know the local area at least as well and probably better than the local authority planners. The developer's team also probably knows more about planning than the planners. It knows the local planning situation backwards because it has dealt with it so many times and of course knows how to squeeze the maximum amount of profitable space out of a development site.[4]

Opposite the Watts Warehouse on Portland Street, on a derelict site, the new eleven-storey Bank of England Regional Headquarters were being built (Fitzroy Robinson & Partners, 1971), and set back behind a little island of trees and grass [122]. Behind the old Bank of England on King Street, Cruickshank & Seward (John Sheard, 1971) were building Century House, nine storeys of brown glass and the same Spinkwell sandstone that the Town Hall was built with. This was the first speculative building with air-conditioning in Manchester, and was described by Professor Bell of Manchester University as 'one of the most gentlemanly modern buildings in the city'. Century House was itself demolished in 1996 for the new, and much larger building, at 82 King Street (Holford Associates) (see [154]).

Elsewhere, developers were simply clearing the sites of older property in the hope of realising future land values; land, unlike any other commodity, rises in value even if nothing is done to it. As an unnamed official in Manchester City Architect's Department put it in 1973, 'Land means money. Not just money – it's a gold mine.'[5] But there was growing opposition to the destruction of old buildings, and to the new developments going up in their place. Richard Sheppard pointed out, 'Both architects and their architecture are disliked by the public . . . architecture is inextricably bound up in the social fabric of society and expresses its hierarchic and symbolic functions. The real content of architecture, built up with love and care over many generations, is being thrown away for no good reason.'[6]

The image of architects (and the planning authorities they dealt with) was not helped when the profession itself came under the spotlight in the 1970s with the trial and conviction of John Poulson, a Yorkshire architect who had corrupted local authority officials and others.[7] Alan Maudsley as Chief Architect of Birmingham in the late 1960s and early 1970s had also been found guilty of corruptly received money for the issuing of contracts and certificates of work. Although only players in a larger game, it was as *architects* that they were labelled, and this called the probity of the profession into doubt. Patrick Nuttgens said,

Architects have always been self-righteous, insisting on their integrity and independence as reasons why they should lead the building team. The myth was shattered. After Poulson, there was no reason why the public, or those in authority, should take the trustworthiness of architects for granted . . . The second factor was the profession's erratic mania for self-flagellation and exposure . . . At the same time, architects became more and more preposterous in their claims for attention. They set up authorities on everything – on town planning (to the disgust of the TPI), on landscape (to the fury of the ILA), on pollution (to the irritation of ecologists), and on economics (to the utter

122] Bank of England headquarters, Portland Street, Fitzroy Robinson & Partners, 19

amazement of economists who had, uncharacteristically, observed architects' inability to control costs). They even decided to tell the BBC how to run itself.[8]

What was disliked most was not so much the arrogance of the architectural profession, or its feet of clay, as what it was building. As the city's Planning Officer said in 1972, 'The current pressure for conservation . . . results from widespread dissatisfaction with the new development that is replacing the old.'[9]

The Town and Country Planning Act of 1947 had established a framework for protecting buildings, primarily as a means to identify buildings of quality remaining after the blitzes of World War II. The 1969 Town and Country Planning Act provided for the Victorian Society and others to be consulted where Victorian or Edwardian buildings were likely to be demolished. But it was not until 1973 that Victorian buildings were recognised, and, even then, 'between 1840 and 1914, only buildings of definite quality and character qualify, and the selection is designed to include the principal works of the principal architects.'[10] 208 buildings in the city centre were listed. The Civic Amenities Act of 1967 and the 1974 Town and Country Amenities Act provided for Conservation Areas to be designated, and in these areas of special architectural or historical importance all buildings would require consent for demolition. The first ten conservation areas in Manchester in the 1970s were: the area around the cathedral, St Ann's Square, St Peter's Square, Albert Square, Upper King Street, St John Street, Whitworth Street, Chorlton Green, Victoria Park and Didsbury St James. The 1974 Act allowed the Department of the Environment itself to designate Conservation Areas, and, under the Act, the price paid by a local authority did not need to account for the development potential of the site; local authorities could execute repairs on listed buildings and buildings in conservation areas and charge the cost to the owner.[11]

Not that many local authorities in that period particularly valued their architectural heritage. Randolph Langenbach wrote about the demolition of the anonymous mills around Stockport Viaduct which had so spoilt Lowry's view, 'The destruction is so complete that one can only believe that it must have been the result of an intentional effort to expunge the 19th-century industrial image.'[12] And the permitted destruction of Victorian buildings in Manchester seemed just as intentional.

Philistine may be too harsh a word, but the works of the nineteenth century certainly did not find much favour in the council chambers of the city. In July 1971, for example, the Town Hall Committee recommended to the Council that the Albert Memorial should be preserved on its present site and provision made for its restoration and cleaning during the next two financial years. On 28 July the City Council disapproved the proposal and instructed the Town Hall Committee 'to take the necessary steps to secure the dismantling of the Memorial and to dispose of the constituent parts to the best advantage and to confer beforehand with appropriate societies and organisations with regard to its possible re-erection and retention in another location.'[13] It has also been recorded, perhaps apocryphally, that one councillor suggested using the Albert Memorial as hard core for the City Centre Road.

The Planning Committee had given consent to the National Westminster Bank for the demolition of Heathcote's Parr's Bank in York Street together with the other Heathcote and Waterhouse buildings on Spring Gardens at the top of King Street. It was intended to replace them by an eleven-storey office block with an open space in front, though in the end the bank's eleven-storey, pebbledashed building went up at the Market Street end of Spring Gardens. Princes Buildings, Oxford Street – the one Art Nouveau building in central Manchester – was to be demolished, and only its listing saved its façade, and stopped the clearance of the site all the way to Tommy Duck's pub for new office development (though Tommy Duck's was demolished overnight on 21 February 1993 by Greenall's, who were fined £1,500 for breach of building control regulations). The owner of India House was applying to demolish it, but even the council was determined to hold on to that building.

The Corporation itself still had under way the ten huge areas of comprehensive redevelopment (CDAs) which meant the destruction of much historical building: Market Street, and the replacement of all that stood between Market Street and Withy Grove by the Arndale Centre; Market Place (the Old Shambles) where new shops and offices were nearing completion; the Upper Civic Area, an on-going development from Albert Square through to Deansgate by the Heron Group; the CWS area, in which the major buildings had already been erected; Smithfield Market (1853), which was demolished, together with a few remaining late eighteenth-century houses and shops, in order to create a car park (and the city had applied for consent to demolish the 1873 Fish Market); the Corn Exchange (due for demolition for road widening); Central Station, part of a twenty-three-acre CDA, including the Great Northern Railway Warehouse; Lower Mosley Street; Byrom Street; the Rochdale Canal Basin.

1975 was European Architectural Heritage Year, its purpose being to draw attention to, and preserve, the country's historic buildings. To emphasise the continuing urban blight and plight, Colin Amery of the *Architectural Review* and Dan Cruickshank of the *Architects' Journal* wrote *The Rape of Britain*, and rightly pointed out, 'Our urban heritage is rich, but fragile, and once a building is demolished it can *never* be replaced.'[14] Exhibitions were put on by Marcus Binney to bring people's attention to the destruction of the past and SAVE Britain's Heritage was formed to publicise the fate of, among other buildings, the anonymous mills of the north of England. John Betjeman was invited to write the foreword to *The Rape of Britain*, and his evocative word picture sums up the period,

> In my mind's ear I can hear the smooth tones of the committee man explaining why the roads must go where they do regardless of the humble old town they bisect. In my mind's eye I can see the swish perspective tricked up by the architect's firm to dazzle the local councillors. I see the tailored models walking past the plate glass, bent forward against a strong breeze. Round the corner I see senior citizens and youth representatives sipping Cinzano under a striped umbrella in the hot sunshine which always lends a Costa Brava look to architectural drawings. I hear words like 'complex', 'conurbation', 'precinct', 'pedestrianisation' and that other couple of words which mean

Milne Building, Mosley Street

] Eagle Star House, Mosley
Street, Cruickshank &
Seward, 1973

total destruction, 'comprehensive development'. Places cease to have names, they become areas with a number. Houses become housing, human scale is abandoned.

We must put in something to please these tiresome people, the preservationists, and so we will leave, shorn of its surroundings, a Georgian building which has been praised in a guide book. If one of the pundits has said of a building 'not especially nice' then down it will come. And if he hasn't mentioned it there's no reason why we should preserve it.[15]

The 1840s Milne Building at 54 Mosley Street [123] *had* been mentioned by Pevsner in his *Buildings of England*, and was described by him as 'the most startling warehouse of Manchester'. It was also the only Manchester warehouse he illustrated.[16] This, however, did not stop its demolition for the long concrete and glass building (Cruickshank & Seward, 1973) [124] for the Royal London Assurance Company (now Eagle Star House). Unfortunate, too, was York House at 55 Major Street, a Lloyd's Packing Warehouse (H. S. Fairhurst, 1911). One of the most remarkable buildings erected in Manchester, and historically one of the most important, it was unique in the country in having a totally glazed rear elevation where each of the seven storeys was stepped back from the lower one and each floor had vertical and lean-to glazing running the width of the floor [125], and all done to preserve the ancient lights of buildings at its rear. It took another fifty-five years for something like this to be repeated in James Stirling's History Library at Cambridge. A public inquiry took place in 1973 regarding a large roundabout for the City Centre Road and a proposed office development on the site of York House. In spite of considerable support for its maintenance (even Walter Gropius wrote a personal appeal), York House was demolished in 1974. The road was never built, and where York House once stood is the car park which has been there since the building was demolished.

Some buildings were saved. In the early 1970s, for Williams & Glyn's Bank, Fairhurst's refurbished and restored Walters's Manchester & Salford Bank building on Mosley Street. Barker & Ellis's extension was gutted behind the retained façade, and a new large sandstone extension was built, distinctly modern but in keeping with the spirit, and the lines, of the buildings next door [**126**].

In 1973 the Watts Warehouse was bought by the Lyon Group (Northern), who intended to modernise the building and convert it into an office block. The Lyon Group were declared bankrupt in 1974 and the receiver applied to have the building demolished (maintenance was costing £12,000 per year) in spite of its Grade II* listing. A campaign to save the building was launched by Lady Eleanor Campbell-Orde, the senior surviving member of the Watts family, and in 1979 the building was purchased by the Britannia Hotels group, when outline planning permission was given to convert the building into a 338 bed hotel. The Britannia opened its doors on March 1982.

The Royal Exchange building had come under threat in the 1960s, but was rescued in 1973. The building had been sold to City Centre Properties in 1961 for the bargain price of £2·5 million, and after the 'Change ceased trading in 1968 the trading hall lay unused and undeveloped, perhaps with a view to realising its land values, for this was prime city-centre land, and the building had not yet been listed. During the Manchester Festival of 1973 the 69 Theatre Company performed inside a temporary tented structure designed by Richard Negri, their artistic director. From this came the remarkable concept of a permanent free-standing auditorium set within the space of the trading hall. A number of models of a theatre in the round were made by Negri, and the final design was used as a brief for the architects, Levitt Bernstein Associates, chosen from a list of thirty practices. Working closely with the architects were Ove Arup & Partners, structural engineers, and Max Fordham & Partners, mechanical and electrical engineers.

The artistic intention was to provide an intimate theatre in the round, with a close physical connection between the actors and the audience. A theatre

125] York House, Major Street, H. S. Fairhurst, 1911

126] Williams and Glyn's Bank, Mosley Street, H. S. Fairhurst & Son, 1968–72

was wanted as simple, honest and transparent as a Classical Greek theatre, but having a synergy with the vast expanse of the trading hall, and for this reason, as well as fire regulations, the theatre was glazed with clear glass. The fire regulations also meant the provision of a non-combustible structure, and this also harmonised with the notion of honesty. The Exchange building was listed Grade II in 1974, so its character had to be respected, with the least possible modification of the existing fabric. The floor could permit a loading of only 450 people of the intended audience of 700, and it was decided to suspend the 'acting module' from the huge brick piers of the Exchange (see [**166**]). From the four suspension points, circular, hollow-section steel trusses (diverted from an oil rig) span the 30 m between the piers, and from these secondary trusses form a square 21 m by 21 m on which the auditorium is carried. The superstructure is also made of steel members, and the upper seating galleries, lighting rigs and the transparent enclosure are suspended from the fourteen roof trusses of the auditorium.

The concept of a seven-sided auditorium came as a moment of inspiration: in a hexagonal structure, people in the corners of the angles feel remote from the actors; an octagonal structure comes too close to a circular form. Seven sides provide good acoustic relationships, and mean that people on opposite sides of the auditorium do not look directly at the audience opposite. But a purely heptagonal form would be too geometrical, so, above the ground-floor seating, each of the tiers is rotated by one-fourteenth, and a constant spiral form is set up. Not only do all 700 people have excellent sightlines, no one is farther than 30 ft away from the actors – a remarkable achievement. The seats are set in small blocks forming 'family groups', and the benches which form the front row of seating come right up to the edge of the acting area.[17] Rehearsal rooms, dressing rooms, greenroom, workshops and offices were all accommodated in the rooms off the trading hall. In the end, a remarkable theatre was designed for about £1 million, as against the cost of a new, self-standing theatre of £4 million to £5 million. It is a unique and innovative structure, a superb example of the reuse of an old and largely redundant building.

But the 1970s saw few older buildings being retained and reused; modern clients wanted modern buildings. On the corner of York Street and Fountain Street, Leach Rhodes Walker, in 1975, built the tile-clad, eleven-storey York House [**127**]. The building is set back from the building line of earlier buildings not for road widening but to give an open grassed space in front. On the corner of Quay Street and Deansgate their Overseas House of the late 1970s is a seven-storey, twelve-bay building of brick, concrete and reflective glass. Both York House and Overseas House were speculative developments. Centurion House at 129 Deansgate, ten storeys of brick and glass over a podium [**128**], was built by Leach Rhodes Walker in 1977 as part of the landscaping of Brazennose Street.

None of these replaced buildings of any particular historic value, but still added to the excess office stock in the city, and there were still huge holes in the centre, gaps left and not built on – a large amount of the centre was simply left as car parks. By 1979, in Manchester, there were some 5 million ft^2 of incomplete developments or unimplemented permissions to build new office space. John Millar, Manchester's Planning Officer, wrote, 'This, in some areas, may have had a blighting effect on other activities in that land owners have been tempted to look to unrealistically high prices for land because of the hope that office accommodation would eventually be attracted to their site.'[18] And, it should be remembered, all this development was taking place against a decline in office employment.

Manchester in the 1970s was not only losing office jobs, it was also losing jobs in its retail sector. Because the city centre had been so badly hit by bombs in the war, its shopping facilities compared unfavourably with other towns in the region, and these other centres which were developed more quickly were capturing a lot of Manchester's traditional retail trade. The city lost out particularly to Stockport in the early 1970s as the Mersey Way shopping centre was developed. 'Manchester lost 6 per cent of its turnover between 1961 and 1971, while every major peripheral centre recorded increases and in the almost totally rebuilt Stockport town centre a phenomenal 108 per cent.'[19]

Renewal of the retail market was essential, especially given the migration of work to the south-east and the loss of traditional industries. Shops, even the over-provision of shops, are necessary in view of the high percentage of employment they provide and the rates they pay. (In 1971 132,000 people, some

127] York House, York Street, Leach Rhodes Walker, c. 1975

128] Centurion House, Deansgate, Leach Rhodes Walker, 1977

10 per cent of workers, in Greater Manchester were in retailing, and shops provided over 9 per cent of all rates accruing to local authorities in the area.) As had been pointed out at the Manchester RIBA conference in June 1960, 'The City authorities, especially in northern cities, are caught between two fears: that if they do not renew the centre, offices and shops will move out, and that if they do they may not get a return on a great expenditure.'[20]

The area between Market Street and Withy Grove was ripe for development. It was seen as being particularly unattractive and congested, there were trams, cobbled streets, and behind the shops on Market Street there were still small courts like Cromford and Marsden Courts, the latter still hemmed in on all four sides by buildings. Lewis's stood at the top end of the street, and the new St Michael House at the other, but in between was little of any significance, except, perhaps, the Seven Stars Inn on Withy Grove, one of the oldest pubs in the country, having been granted a licence in 1356 – but that had to go. A Comprehensive Development Area had been designated by the City to develop the area as a whole, the development was seen as being beneficial, and the vision looked good:

> The 30-acre site bounded by Market Street, Corporation Street and Withy Grove, at present a shabby district, is due for large-scale commercial development with large stores, small shops, banks, pubs, showrooms, an hotel and ample parking space. Market Street would become a 'landscaped pedestrian way', the backbone of a system of malls and arcades. To make way for this gleaming paradise we shall have to lose some attractive little courts, some narrow twisting streets, the open-air bookstalls ... and some historic and charming old pubs. But it has happened before. Manchester's 'Second Town Plan' of 1821 was founded on the widening of Market Street.[21]

Sam Chippindale, head of the developers Arndale Property Trust, had started to buy up properties in the area from 1955.[22] In 1963 the company was taken over by Town & City Properties, who purchased much of remainder. Agreement was reached with the Corporation for the whole area to be zoned and leased to Town & City, but building did not begin until 1972, seventeen years after site acquisition. Town & City, in 1973, sold the site to the Corporation, retaining the leasehold, but by 1975 the developers were in severe difficulties, and the City Council underwrote loans of over £16 million. Later, Town & City sold their leasehold to P&O Properties, who managed the site until 1998, when it was taken over by the Prudential.

When Town & City Properties were looking for suitable architects, they were the country's largest town centre shopping scheme developers, as well as being the pioneers of the closed mall, and had already completed some twenty schemes in the UK. The Manchester Arndale was to be the largest, flagship project, and, spread over an area of fifteen acres, was some four and a half times larger than the average shopping schemes so far built. The Arndale was destined to become the largest covered shopping mall in Europe.

The firm of Hugh Wilson and Lewis Womersley was chosen (they were already involved in masterplanning the University Precinct, and had just completed the rebuilding of Hulme), given a detailed brief of a US-style scheme and told to make it work. But Kenneth Shone, a partner in Wilson & Womersley, said, 'It wouldn't work, partly because it didn't relate to the site and partly due to the demands of the planners who wanted a larger site to be developed to include a bus station, car park and market.'[23] There was also a conflict with the City Engineer, whose planned Inner Ring Road would have restricted access to the site. The architects were told that Corporation Street and High Street were to be main traffic routes, and consequently there were restrictions on pavement widths, and shop frontages on these roads were banned. Unfortunately, after the building had started, the road engineers changed their minds about both the roads and the restrictions. According to Kenneth Shone, 'That's the architect's lament. You can't do much about it except hope that in years to come when the building is modified, they will restore those streets to shopping arcades which is what we intended.'[24]

There was little fruitful communication between the developers, the architects or the City. The architects produced alternative schemes, one of which was on the European pattern, based on glazed covered arcades, but it was rejected by the developers. An American, closed scheme was eventually decided upon, against the desire of the architects. In their design report they said, 'The brief we had been given by the developer and as amended by the local authority would produce a very introverted building. And we said this would not be attractive.'[25]

Construction started in May 1972, with the mall areas of sixty shops, including W. H. Smith and Mothercare and the office block (which opened in September 1976) and concluded in 1979, with the opening of British Home Stores and Littlewood's. The costs were enormous: land £11·5 million, building £44·5 million, shopfitting £44 million – a total of £100 million. And the size was considerable; a fifteen-acre site, of 1·2 million ft^2 (115,200 m^2). On two levels of malls were 210 shop units and a two-storey market hall, there were parking spaces for 1,800 cars, a bus station in the basement and a twenty-two-storey office block and sixty flats and maisonettes sitting on the roof. 'One of the

129] Arndale Centre, Market Street, Wilson & Womersley, 1972–79

primary objectives of the development was the provision of the number of uses so that the area is kept alive and busy at night and weekends, but the primary use is shopping.'[26]

But it was never the pleasantest place to shop in. The interior was hot and stuffy, the malls were undifferentiated, and shoppers became lost. All the lighting was artificial and the sun's rays did not penetrate. Toilet facilities were meagre, and the signage was poor. But the developers thought they were doing the right thing by providing what was essentially a huge box containing shops. 'Shoppers seem to want the safety and climate of covered shopping facilities.'[27] The exits (and the car park) were a long way apart but 'one essential rule of the shopping centre game is to keep customers shifting from attraction to attraction, never from attraction to entrance–exit.'[28] Surprisingly, the exterior was clad in tiles (giving it the nickname of 'the largest public lavatory in the world') at a time when the majority of shopping schemes were being built with brick and glass façades [129]. As David Ward wrote, 'Manchester's Arndale Centre is so castle-like in its outer strength that any passing mediaeval army would automatically besiege it rather than shop in it.'[29]

Wilson and Womersley said, 'We the architects have taken all the stick and we've made a conscious policy decision to sit here and bear it . . . we're not responsible for everything in there, but we're not sorry about the things for which we are responsible. We are not particularly upset about the decisions we took as opposed to those which were forced upon us . . . I'd like to think everyone learns by experience.'[30] Thankfully, for the rest of the country, the experience was not repeated.

As important as the setting down of this huge building on the cityscape was the impact it had on the shopping patterns of the city. In 1980 a survey of shopping provision was carried out by the City Planning Department which showed that, of the tenants, 37 per cent were branches of retailers already represented in the city centre, and a further 40 per cent were retailers new to the centre. The remaining 23 per cent had transferred from elsewhere in the city centre. The move of Littlewood's from Piccadilly and of British Home Stores, C&A and 19 per cent of the smaller traders from Oldham Street to the Arndale Centre meant the almost immediate dereliction of the Piccadilly/Oldham Street area, a desuetude which has lasted almost twenty years. Oldham Street has only recently come back to life with the provision of specialist shops, niche retailing and the building of loft apartments.

Even before phase one of the Arndale was completed, change was being forced on Manchester, by the introduction of a higher-tier authority. On 1 April 1974 the Greater Manchester County Council (GMC) was superimposed on the District Councils of Bolton, Bury, Manchester, Oldham, Rochdale, Salford, Stockport, Tameside, Trafford and Wigan. The GMC was responsible for the strategic planning, major developments and transport needs of an area of over 500 square miles and a population of 2·7 million. It was the third largest metropolitan county after Greater London and the West Midlands. And, of course, the new authority had to have a brand-new building. GMC's County Hall (Fitzroy Robinson & Partners, 1974), on the corner of Portland Street and Aytoun Street, has six storeys over a ground-floor podium; bands of brick, concrete and glass with a concrete lid over the set-back sixth storey (see [26]).

The first *Greater Manchester County Structure Plan* was submitted to the Secretary of State in 1979, and among the concerns of the plan were the appropriate provision of office space and shopping facilities in Manchester. Some of the policies were aimed at preventing a repetition of the blight following the office boom of the 1960s and 1970s, and the decline of local shopping areas following the proliferation of superstores and town-centre shopping schemes. The plan was adopted in 1981, with a revision in 1986 just before the GMC was disbanded. Two important objectives were the concentration on development in the urban areas and focusing investment on areas of greatest social deprivation in the central core. Attention was to be paid to providing a more appealing environment in the city centre and adjoining parts of Manchester and Salford in order to attract more businesses and people. There was to be the removal or reuse of derelict land and obsolete buildings, and the cleaning-up of river pollution. New attitudes became apparent, and the GMC was keen to bring in private investment. The development of the redundant Central Station site and of Castlefield were seminal actions in the successive regeneration of Manchester and are worth some study.

In the 1930s 400 trains a day ran into Central Station, but from March 1967 local train services of the Midland line were withdrawn and on 5 May 1969 the station was closed under the Beeching plan for the rationalisation of the railways. In October 1972 the site was sold to Arkle Holdings, the firm of a property speculator and racehorse owner. Ownership was then transferred to English & Continental Investments, itself owned by the Crown Agents. Cruickshank & Seward prepared a major scheme to develop the site, and first outline planning approval was given in 1975. The proposal covered a twenty-four-acre site,

130] Central Station development, Windmill Street, proposals by Cruickshank & Seward, 1975

from Lower Mosley Street to Deansgate, from Peter Street to Great Bridgewater Street, reaching out toward St George's, Hulme, and would have been a major asset to Manchester, rivalling in size the later NEC at Birmingham. Even then, this development, worth about £50 million – a huge amount at the time – was being talked about as a 'gateway' scheme.

The train shed was to be glazed, revealing the restored arches, and new buildings were to be woven through the structure [130]. At the side of this exhibition hall was to be a trade and conference centre, and, towards Deansgate, blocks of offices, a 160-bed hotel and 150 flats would have replaced the Great Northern Railway Company's Goods Warehouse. Altogether 750,000 ft^2 of offices and 69,000 ft^2 of shops and showrooms would have been provided by the scheme. A thirty-two-storey tower of three interlocking drums of brown glass was to rise at the south-western end of the site – at more than 400 ft rivalling in height, and responding to, the CIS building, and reflecting the curved arches of Central Station, yet far enough away from the Town Hall to avoid competing with its tower. Four acres of the site, to be known as Central Square, were to be laid out as open space, landscaped with trees, fountains and pools. There was even to be a glazed, tubular moving walkway stretching from Deansgate Station almost to Albert Square. The developers claimed that Central Square would provide Manchester 'with not only a social focus, but a shop window for its commercial future.'[31]

The developers went out of business in 1976, and the scheme was shelved within an ace of the first sod being turned.[32] In spite of interest from the GMC, the site was sold, in 1977, to a demolition and scrap recovery firm, George Robinson (Manchester), whose intentions became clear when they stripped and demolished the Cheshire Lines Warehouse. Following court action between Robinson and National Car Parks (who were using the train shed) about mortgage arrangements, an agreement was reached so that the GMC was able to acquire the site.

Here though was the GMC's difficulty, ownership of a twenty-four-acre, largely barren site containing derelict buildings badly in need of restoration, with no positive ideas about its future, and strangely no one seemed to have remembered the earlier proposals of 1975. In 1980 the GMC set up a Joint Venture Study Group in partnership with Manchester City Council and Commercial Union Properties, with Jack Bogle of Essex Goodman & Suggitt (later EGS Designs) providing architectural expertise, to provide a scheme for the site which would involve both public and private-sector money. This led to a unique partnership being formed – joint ownership of Central Station Properties by a local authority and a commercial company – and the partnership gained support in the form of Urban Development Grants and European Community money.

Phase 1 of the regeneration started in 1982 with the total refurbishment of the Grade II* listed train shed to form the Greater Manchester Exhibition and Event Centre, then called 'Central'. The brief to the architects was to provide exhibition facilities of 10,000 m^2 which could be subdivided to provide facilities for small, medium and large exhibitions, together with all the necessary ancillary accommodation, including foyers, restaurants, administration services, public accommodation, landscaping and car parking – altogether occupying approximately eleven acres of the total development area.

The station had been badly neglected over the years, and the most urgent job was the consolidation of the brickwork. 150 men from the Unemployment Register were employed raking out and repointing the undercroft brickwork for nine months.* The main contracts were let out in 1983, and the structural work began. The two brick buildings on either side of the main gable, originally the station offices and a restaurant, together with the perimeter wall (for even this was included in the building's Grade II* listing) were demolished following agreement from the Royal Fine Arts Commission, and this allowed the front of the station to be seen for the first time. The cladding of the gable was removed, and new glazing was placed inside the existing structural members [131]. The eighteen internal 65 m span wrought-iron arches were consolidated, and externally a new aluminium roof was provided which expressed the original 'Paxton-type' ridge-and-furrow glazing. Ancillary buildings around the front and side of the train hall were supported using existing cast-iron forms, recast from original columns and brackets taken from platform extensions to the rear of the main hall. Subdivision of the hall was achieved by a retractable flexible 'sail' dividing the hall into approximately 70 per cent and 30 per cent of the whole volume. G-MEX was opened by HM the Queen on 21 March 1986.[33]

The GMC acquired the adjoining Midland Hotel in 1983 and commenced a £14 million renovation programme to consolidate the exterior, which had been badly neglected. The hotel was later bought by Holiday Inns, and the interior was refurbished to something approaching its original form. A glazed atrium now covers the enlarged reception centre in what was the light well of the building. It seems a pity, though, that the original *porte cochère* is not being used.

In the Castlefield area, too, the GMC was busy. In 1972 the clearance of houses on White Lion Street, for the intended relief road, gave an opportunity to carry out archaeological excavations in the area. The Manchester Region Industrial Archaeology Society began a photographic survey and brought to public attention the importance of the area as the earliest transport system in the country.

On 8 September 1975 Liverpool Road Goods Depot closed, and in that year the GMC carried out its own survey of the site. Although the British Rail Property Board offered Liverpool Road Station to the GMC in September 1976 for the princely sum of £1, the offer was not taken up. It was not until late 1978, following pressure from a number of groups, especially the Liverpool Road Station Society, that the station, the 1830 warehouse and adjacent land became the new home of the North Western Museum of Science and Industry.

---

* In 1983–84 sixty-five men (via the Manpower Services Commission) were employed on site for the stabilisation of the Great Northern Railway Goods Warehouse. Fifty-five men were used to repoint the Watson Street arches. In 1985–86 the brickwork of the Rochdale Viaduct, Whitworth Street, was repointed. A total work force of 700 men.

Greater Manchester Exhibition and Event Centre

131] G-MEX, Windmill Street,
~ssex, Goodman & Suggitt, 1980

In 1979 *Historic Castlefield*, published as a study and proposals document, called for the development of the Castlefield area: cleaning the canals, restoration of the remains of Liverpool Road Station, reclamation of Higher Campfield Hall as a market, and utilisation of the City Exhibition Hall. It was, unfortunately, already too late for Barry's St Matthew's Church, which had been demolished in 1951 to make space for offices and a petrol station. Castlefield was designated a Conservation Area in 1979, and regeneration began. In 1979 the City Council resolved to retain and repair the City Exhibition Hall, and in 1980 proposals were made for laying out the Roman gardens and creating a reconstruction of the north gate of the Roman fort. All these initiatives led to Castlefield being designated the country's first Urban Heritage Park in 1982.

From June 1979 work began on restoring and clearing the site for the museum. Thomas Worthington & Sons (successors to that famous name, and probably the oldest extant architectural firm in the city) were appointed by the GMC as consultants to the museum scheme. Barry Johnson, a senior partner in Worthington's, restored Liverpool Road Station and transformed the 1855 Goods Transfer Shed into what is now the Power Hall [**132**], containing what is reputed to be the world's largest collection of working stationary steam engines. The architect was responsible not only for the building but also for the layout and settings of the engines, the bases, pits and power supplies, and the rail track outside. The trademark red columns at the entrance were brought from S. Z. de Ferranti's Deptford Power Station (of 1889), in recognition of de Ferranti's first factory in Hollinwood, Lancashire, in 1897.

The first phase of the Museum of Science and Industry was completed by 1984, and the Air and Space Gallery opened soon after in the old Upper Campfield Market building. In 1985 the museum won a Civic Award for outstanding contribution to the quality and appearance of the environment. When the GMC was disbanded in 1986, Building Design Partnership[34] were appointed as architects to the museum and designed the National Gas Galleries underneath the railway arches, reconstructed the Grade I listed 1830 carriage sheds, designed modifications to the Air and Space Gallery and converted the 1880 Lower Byrom Street Warehouse into a reception area, bookshop, lecture rooms and display galleries. The warehouse conversion won a prestigious RIBA Regional Award, and in 1990 the Museum of Science and Industry won the National Heritage Museum of the Year award. In 1990 Building Design Partnership started to carry out a repair strategy on the 1830 warehouse. Up to 1995 £4·1 million had been spent on converting the warehouse to exhibition galleries, and in August 1995 the museum was awarded £1·4 million from the European Union to complete the improvement work.

In 1980 Granada commissioned Building Design Partnership to investigate the expansion of their Television Centre on the adjoining goods station, backing on to the Museum of Science and Industry. Work started in June 1982 on the Grape Street Bonded Warehouse to convert it into studios, rehearsal spaces, offices and support areas. The set of *Coronation Street* blocked access to the warehouse, and was coming to the end of its useful life, so it was decided to relocate the set on the other side of the warehouse. This gave the opportunity to rebuild the set full-size instead of the two-thirds scale of the original, providing a more flexible and realistic street. Computer modelling was carried out to ensure that the change-over appeared seamless to the viewer.

For Granada, in 1988, Building Design Partnership also developed the Granada Studio Tours, from concept to set design and procurement. This was a complex project, based on a disused railway goods yard, and incorporating 50,000 ft^2 of existing buildings, all in a restricted three-acre site, and allowing up to a million visitors per year without disrupting programme making. Tour parties can visit mock-ups of television facilities, walk down Coronation Street, drink in a specially created Rover's Return pub, visit Baker Street and New York. Behind the sets are real facilities for shopping and eating. In all, 25,000 ft^2 of new buildings were created, including a 600-seat theatre and an exhibition space of 10,000 ft^2. 'Projections', a 70 foot cinema screen with six sound channels and

132] Museum of Science and Industry, Castlefield, Thomas Worthington & Sons, 1986

computer-controlled seats that move with the action, was also designed by Building Design Partnership. Granada Studio Tours and the Museum of Science and Industry between them attract over a million visitors per year.

Under the auspices of the GMC two important and otherwise neglected sites in the city, Central Station and Castlefield, were brought into use and provided the foundation for the developments which will be discussed in later chapters. The GMC was established in a period of low economic growth and had little funding with which to carry out much work. It was abolished by the Local Government (Interim Provisions) Act of 1986, but its legacy was considerable, for it demonstrated that joint action between private funding and local government could help to regenerate a city.

12

1980 TO THE MID-1990S

ENTERPRISE
AND THE CMDC

It makes me resentful and angry that that I should be working in an era when the expectation level of the client, planners and the public is so low . . . Can't we drop this essentially moral miserableness that grips architecture and start to produce buildings that people may actually like – even something that could be described as beautiful? [Piers Gough in the *Architects' Journal*, 1977]

THE 1977 White Paper *Policy for the Inner Cities* recognised that many of the country's city centres were in a state of decline. Vacant and derelict land, falling job opportunities and reductions in public services were all having a deleterious impact and 'may well deter prospective developers who will tend to see it as evidence of the weakness of economic activity in the areas. Steps to improve the attractiveness of inner area sites and to bring land back into use must rank among the urgent tasks of the regeneration of the inner cities.'[1] Under the heading 'What needs to be done' the White Paper outlined its policies: specific commitment by both central and local government to regenerate the inner cities, strengthening their economies and improving their environment. Social problems needed to be addressed as well as unemployment. 'It is vital to preserve the firms and businesses which at present exist in the inner areas. Indigenous growth needs to be cultivated by facilitating the expansion of local firms. New sites and premises . . . are needed in order to attract suitable manufacturing, service and office firms to settle within the cities.'[2]

The White Paper led to the 1978 Inner Urban Areas Act, local authority based and designed to allow local authorities to use planning and environmental policies to facilitate the growth of employment in the inner city areas. Loans of up to 90 per cent were to be made available for commercial purchase of suitable land, for the erection and expansion of industrial buildings and to provide initial rent-free periods for factories. The Act was of benefit to the Inner City Partnership of Manchester and Salford (which had been set up in 1977 in an attempt to regenerate the cities' inner areas), and both councils used between one-third and half of their share of the money to buy land for industrial sites, building advance factory units and making loans and grants.

But the new Conservative government in 1979 was already starting to demote local authorities from their part in regenerating their localities, and began enhancing the role of the private sector. The government reduced funding to Inner City Partnerships and directed it toward Enterprise Zones and Urban Development Grants. Increasingly, the private sector was to lead the revival of the inner city. Quangos would take over many of the regeneration functions that local authorities had previously held, and the powers of local government would be considerably reduced. The impact of market forces quickly became apparent. 'In the decade from 1979, when Mrs Thatcher applied the monetarist analysis and freed the market of perceived countervailing forces, 94 per cent of all job losses occurred North of a line drawn from the Wash to the Severn. Of the manufacturing jobs lost, 70 per cent were in the North . . . More depressing still were the figures on investment – since 1979, the real value of manufacturing investment has fallen by 41 per cent in the North.'[3]

In the north-west there was a loss of traditional industries, and by the mid-1980s the textile industry accounted for only 65,000 jobs, 2·6 per cent of all employment in the region. Manufacturing's share in the GDP of the region fell from 35·6 per cent in 1975 to 30·6 per cent in 1984, and 300,000 manufacturing jobs were lost between 1975 and 1985. But the financial and service sector rose from 8·3 per cent to 12 per cent and distribution, hotels and catering rose from 13·5 per cent to 14·3 per cent in the same period.[4] The north-west region still had considerable financial muscle. 'With the exception of the South East, it [the north-west] has a larger population and contributes more to the economy than any other U.K. region.'[5] (In 1984 the region's GDP was £28·3 billion.)

To aid depressed areas, the government set up Enterprise Zones in 1980, and these permitted exemption from development land tax, included a tax concession of 100 per cent capital allowances on industrial and commercial properties, and allowed zero rates to be paid for a period of ten years, the lost revenue being made up by the Treasury. Most Enterprise Zones were designated for derelict or vacant land, since the government did not want existing firms to benefit from these financial incentives. In 1981 Salford and Trafford both bid successfully for Enterprise Zone status for the Ship Canal docks and Trafford Park industrial estate respectively, and both these developments were to have an impact on the city and region.

In 1981 a small part of Salford docks was incorporated into an Enterprise Zone: 150 acres, around the area from Dock 9 to Dock 6. The council purchased the whole of the docks for £1·6 million, comprising 160 acres of land plus seventy-five acres of water (and three miles of waterfront). After an abortive attempt in 1982 to develop the area – which was, basically, a featureless plain with fingers of water running through it – Salford Council approached the Department of the Environment for a Derelict Land Grant with which to purchase and reclaim Dock No. 6. The grant, funded by central government, was available only for capital expenditure on development projects designed collaboratively between local authorities and the private sector, and was designed to lever in private funding with minimum local authority contribution. Of the fourteen Derelict Land Grant bids also made by Manchester City Council at the time, only three were successful. The extension of the Moss Side brewery went ahead, but although the other two schemes – to convert city-centre buildings into flats – were approved, the developers decided not to proceed.

It soon became clear that the £10 million Derelict Land Grant given to Salford was insufficient, and it was eventually agreed that Urban Programme funding could be used to cover on-site work (the quays) and the Derelict Land Grant to cover off-site work (the basins), possibly the first time that a Derelict Land Grant had been used for water rather than land. Dock 6 and adjacent land was sold to Edward Hagan's Urban Waterside on condition that Urban Waterside secured £4·5 million of development to match the £4·5 million Derelict Land Grant within three years. Hagan managed to secure the funding (including remortgaging his own £500,000 house) on New Year's Eve three years later, days before the deadline. The first buildings went up on Dock 6, renamed Clippers Quay: a £3·5 million multi-screen cinema, the four-star Copthorne Hotel, a public house and restaurant, and, later in 1988, 200,000 ft^2 of office space, built by Urban Waterside, including Regatta House for Compaq Computers (Mills Beaumont Leavey).

It was evident that developing Dock 6 alone would not be viable, and in 1985 a comprehensive development scheme for the whole dock area, the Salford Quays Development Plan, was drawn up by Shepheard Epstein Hunter (architect-planners who had been involved in the earlier 1982 scheme) with Ove Arup & Partners as consultant engineers. Central government gave approval for £25 million of assistance. The Development Plan covered four main areas: water quality, roads and services, public access and landscape. Dams were constructed across the mouths of docks to keep out polluted water. 'Heloxors', to oxygenate the water, were installed in the basins and fish were introduced. Bunds were thrown from the sides of the quays to vary and humanise the scale of the water areas; new canals were cut through the quays to link the basins. Obelisks and cargo cranes were relocated. Bridges were thrown across canals; a disused railway swing bridge of 640 tons was moved three-quarters of a mile to cross Dock 9.

A vocabulary of design elements was created to give design consistency. All water edges were lined by trees and lamp posts. There were changes of level and vertical emphasis: many quayside sites are at two levels; steps combine two rhythms, full-size and half-size. There were long ramps for the disabled. Houses and flats started to be built, and by 1995 there were 450 homes in the Merchants' Quay, Grain Wharf and Anchorage Wharf developments.

At the beginning of 1989 investment in Salford Quays by the private sector reached £65 million; committed development was more than £260 million, and the total investment was foreseen as £350 million to £400 million. By 1991 4,000 jobs had been created. Enterprise Zone status was to end in 1991, so there was

3] The Victoria, Harbour City,
lford Quays, Fairhurst's Design
Group, 1991–93

a rush of office developments to gain tax benefits. Peel Holdings developed the Victoria, Harbour City (Fairhurst's, completed 1993) [133], on their land on the north side of Dock 9, for offices, retail outlets, restaurants and studio accommodation. This large structure of ten storeys and 115,750 ft^2 of floor space was designed as a speculative building for corporate headquarters, and because there were no land charges, and since the Enterprise Zone allowed a 30 per cent kick-back on taxes, the building could be expensive at £22 million. The Victoria is phase 1 of Harbour City, which will eventually comprise over 250,000 ft^2 of office space.

At the end of Dock 9, Salford Council took over the land and with AMEC developed the Anchorage (Percy Thomas Partnership) [134], a development of 234,000 ft^2, let to BUPA, NatWest, Barclay's, Halliwell Landau and the Inland Revenue. And at Exchange Quay, the largest single office development in the north-west, 520,000 ft^2 was developed by the Charter Group and let to Barclay's Bank and Pitney Bowes. Other lettings on the Quays were for the regional headquarters of Parcel Force and of Royal Mail Post Office Counters.

During the ten years that Salford Quays enjoyed Enterprise Zone status, Salford Council and the developers took full advantage of the difficulty of finding sites for large stand-alone offices in Manchester. Both the Greater Manchester Structure Plan of 1981 and the City Centre Local Plan of 1984 had recognised the importance of Manchester as the regional centre and as the second financial centre in the country, yet both were aware of the problems which had been caused by the decentralisation of offices. The city needed to promote itself, and to be made more attractive to create a suitable atmosphere for inward investment for smaller office developments and for the specialist and comparison shopping facilities (absent in Salford Quays) which were a vital factor in the make-up of the city.

The City Council set up a successful promotional campaign for city-centre shops in 1982 and 1983, and commenced the pedestrianisation of King Street, Market Street, Albert Square and St Ann's Square, all with a view to enhancing the city's image and to enticing businesses and shoppers into the centre. Market Street, Britain's second busiest shopping street, was stopped to traffic in 1981 and repaved. But the vehicle ban was not enforced, and the street furniture was badly designed and co-ordinated. There was a limited design competition in 1993 which provided new street furniture, and at the east end of the street a 45 ft high, thirty-tonne marble obelisk was erected which quickly became a gathering place for homeless young people and their dogs. The obelisk, which had cost £80,000, was removed on 28 October 1997, to be re-erected in Crumpsall Park two years later.

St Ann's Square, in 1984, saw the first proper attempts at pedestrianisation, with a few litter bins, some scrawny trees, no seats and restricted vehicle access which was seldom enforced. The scheme, needless to say, was not successful. The present refurbishment, which won the Pedestrianisation category of the 1995 National Street Design Awards, with new paving, stone seats and large granite balls, designed to protect both the square and its statuary from motor vehicles, is of 1993, and was designed by Warren Marshall of the City Planning Department.[6] The cost of almost £1 million, excluding the cotton-bud sculpture, was part-funded by MEPC property developers and the Prudential Assurance Company.

The model of the cotton bud, designed by Peter Randall-Page, was unveiled on 28 July 1995. The sculpture cost £300,000 and was funded by the City Council, MEPC, the Prudential and the European Union. The then leader of the council, Graham Stringer, said, 'The overall objective has been to ensure that

134] Anchorage 1, Anchorage Quay, Salford, Percy Thomas Partnership, 1990s

St Ann's Square is an attractive area which will stand the test of time for people who visit, work and shop in the city centre and the new water feature will make a considerable contribution to this.'[7] Only two years later, city centre boss Councillor Pat Karney said, 'We have made mistakes in the past and we've taken a lot of stick over it, but no more. We want traditional fountain areas and no more of this arty stuff.'[8] *O tempora! O mores!* Following the upgrading of St Ann's Square, the area around the church was refurbished in 1997 as part of Leslie Jones Architects' remodelling of the rear of 35 King Street.

The refurbishment of Albert Square commenced in 1984, and was completed in 1987, with new granite setts and stone paviours, and the square was softened by trees donated by the *Manchester Evening News*. The fountain which had been designed by Worthington in 1897 to commemorate the opening of the Thirlmere viaduct was brought back from Eaton Park, restored and re-erected in 1998. Albert Square has increasingly become the civic square, with special events and promotions, especially at Christmas time.

In Chinatown, in recognition of the importance of the largest Chinese community outside London (over 30,000 people of Chinese descent live in Manchester), Europe's first true imperial Chinese arch [135] was built in 1987 by twelve craftsmen from the People's Republic of China. Construction costs were £350,000 with contributions from the Council, the Department of the Environment and the Chinese community. Manchester was recognised as a 'Dragon City'. With support from the Council, there has been considerable conversion of old warehouses into restaurants, shops, supermarkets, banks, medical and educational facilities and residential accommodation in the area.[9]

The landscaping of parts of Manchester helped to provide a better image of the city, and coincidentally there was a boom in office building in the city in the mid-1980s, though still without sufficient tenants to fill the space created. In 1985 7·2 million ft^2 of floor space had been on the market for over eighteen months, equalling 46 per cent of all available floor space.[10]

At 50 Fountain Street a new building for Barclay's (Fairhurst's) was being erected: three storeys of plain brick and two storeys of offices contained within the roof structure, which continues as an extension on to the refurbished Victorian warehouse on the corner of Spring Gardens (see [34]). At 136 Deansgate, turning the corner with Bridge Street, the monolithic dark red brick Halifax House (Turner Lansdowne Holt, 1983) was built [136]. At 32 Charlotte Street is Hanover House (Spratley & Cullern, 1983), another brick building but this time in imitation of a Victorian warehouse, appropriately enough, perhaps, since it is surrounded by Walters's originals.

The buildings opposite the Town Hall had been demolished in the mid-1970s, leaving two large holes in the ground at the top of Brazennose Street. Concerned with the blight on their doorstep, discussions took place between the Council and the developers and it was agreed that, if the left-hand site was developed, the City Council would take a good part of the lease at an agreed £5 per square foot (about twice the average rental for the area). The confidence of a pre-let persuaded the developer to erect the building (Heron House, Leach Rhodes Walker, 1979–82) [137], and by time the building was erected and

135] Chinatown arch, George Street, 1987

136] Halifax House, Deansgate, Turner Lansdown Holt, 1983.

[▼] View down Brazennose Street
with Heron House, Leach Rhodes
Walker, 1982, and Commercial
Union Offices, Kingham Knight
Associates, 1983

occupied £5 per square foot was a reasonable rental. The development of Heron House stimulated interest in the site on the other side of Brazennose Street, and offices for the Commercial Union Assurance were erected (Kingham Knight Associates, Liverpool, 1983).

In the early 1980s brick was the characteristic building material, for it was the inclination, if not the policy, of the Planning Department to allow only brick-clad buildings to be erected, no doubt as a reaction against the concrete buildings of the 1960s and early 1970s. Developers, too, were unwilling to put forward more adventurous buildings which might be rejected by planning committees and have to go to appeal. But at the other end of Brazennose Street, Lincoln House, 127 Deansgate (Holford Associates, 1986) [138], is one of the buildings which marked a change from the serried ranks of brick, for this large nine-storey building is completely clad in glass (and demonstrates the latest glazing technology and improvements in neoprene sealants). When the plans were submitted in 1985 the deputy to Ted Kitchen, then Planning Officer, is reputed to have said, 'Hey, Ted, look at this before we turn it down.'[11]

The other building which, though built outside the centre, had an impact on future developments within the city was the new Sir William Siemens House (Mills Beaumont Leavey, 1986–89), a headquarters building for the Energy and Automation Division of Siemens plc, and the first phase of a development on an 8 ha greenfield site. This is a startlingly white building set amid the traditional brick houses of Princess Road [139]. The façades are in the form of a light pierced skin of self-cleaning, aluminium rain-screen cladding, and the linear forms of the offices, combined with a four-storey circular element, contribute to a strong technical image, appropriate to the technical nature of the company. The white cladding and glazing provided Manchester with a modern building with its roots in the Miesian tradition.[12]

138] Lincoln House, Deansgate,
Holford Associates, 1986

139] Siemens House, Princess
Parkway, Mills Beaumont
Leavey, 1989

Lincoln House and the Siemens building marked a change in attitudes toward the built form, and architects and property agents alike were becoming more adventurous and more confident. The commercial outlook seemed buoyant, and in April 1986 Grimley & Sons reported that Manchester's central office market was at its most active for ten years.

The Manchester Phoenix Initiative was set up in 1986, a non-profit-making organisation comprised of businessmen, union leaders, architects and developers, acting as a catalyst for the regeneration of the inner city and helping to bring in public funds in the form of Urban Regeneration Grants. Phoenix, with the City Council's support, went into action in January 1987 in the Whitworth Street corridor, and by November 1987 £250 million of new developments at five different sites were under way. In the Gaythorn area, discussions were taking place between Phoenix, British Gas and a leading developer to promote new building on the site of the old gasworks. The railway arches on Whitworth Street West were converted for small businesses, showrooms and studios, and still active under the arches is the Green Room, an independent *avant-garde* theatre company. The conversion of Granby House into flats for sale (the start of Halliday Meecham's creation of Granby Village for Wimpey, 1989–95), came from the Phoenix initiative, as did the conversion of India House into letting apartments by the Northern Counties Housing Association, and the conversion of Corson & Aitken's warehouse into the Dominion Hotel. The transformation of Manchester's Victorian warehouses began in Whitworth Street.

However, on Friday 6 November 1987 the Refuge Assurance Company left its premises on the corner of Whitworth Street and Oxford Street for a greenfield site in Wilmslow, to a new building designed by Building Design Partnership. The company had been in discussion for a year with Bob Scott about a plan to turn the Refuge into new home for the Hallé, but the £3 million needed was not forthcoming. One of the most prestigious and expensive buildings in Manchester lay forlorn and empty except for a caretaker and the ghost on its staircase, and it was not until the 1990s that its conversion into the Palace Hotel commenced. Despite the work done by the Phoenix Initiative, older buildings were still not finding much favour with office developers: in Greater Manchester, between December 1983 and June 1985, almost 5 million ft^2 of floor space of old industrial buildings had been demolished. And derelict land continued to be a major problem: the north-west had 24 per cent of all the derelict land in the country, and there were 4,035 ha in Greater Manchester alone, over twice as much as in Greater London, even though between 1974 and 1982 more had been done in the north-west than any other region to reclaim it.[13]

In 1988 the Central Manchester Development Corporation was set up, with a remit to develop the area already covered by the Phoenix Initiative, and Manchester Phoenix, in common cause with the City Councils of Manchester and Salford and the Salford Phoenix Initiative, transferred its attention to the neglected area bounded by the Cathedral and Chetham's School and the Church of the Sacred Trinity in Salford. AMEC Regeneration were selected as the development co-ordinators for the project, and Fairhurst's were appointed as architects to the 'Northern Gateway Study' with the commission to generate ideas for the area. A visit by John Crowther and John Lynch of Fairhurst's to Norweb got backing for the study in twenty minutes.

The area to be regenerated had major drawbacks: it was intersected by major traffic routes; the redundant railway land of the old Exchange Station at high level dominated the area; the administration of the area was split by Salford and Manchester City Councils; most important, having been neglected for years, there was no sense of 'place'. It was necessary, therefore, to establish an increased awareness of the river, of the Cathedral and Chetham's, and to create a pleasing sense of place for the area. This would be realised by stressing the heritage aspect of both the Cathedral and Chetham's School, by utilising the Riverside park on the Salford side of the Irwell and by use of the Cathedral underbank – the arches overlooking the river. The physical environment would be improved, new open spaces provided, the changing levels of the site would be exploited, buildings would be cleaned, the transport infrastructure improved and a design philosophy implemented [140]. All the improvements would attract commercial development to subsidise the non-commercial parts of the scheme. The report was produced in November 1988,[14] and although

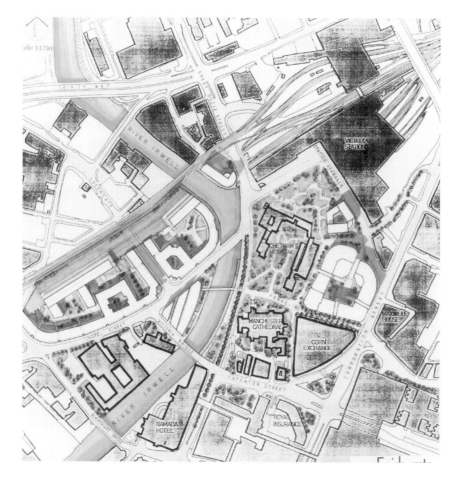

140] Phoenix Initiative, part of th proposals for the regeneration of the mediaeval quarter

little was done at the time to implement its proposals, the rebuilding of the area ten years later seems to share many of the report's ideas. The greatest value of the Phoenix Initiative was, however, its influence on the thinking of the City Council, and the bringing together in partnership of the public and private sectors.

The government was still promoting private enterprise, and in 1987 the Urban Regeneration Grant was introduced to complement the Urban Development Grants (set up in 1981), under provisions of the Housing and Planning Act of 1986. The grant was payable direct via the Department of the Environment to private developers without their having to go through local authorities, and without the proposed development having to receive local authority approval. In May 1988 the City Grant was introduced to support capital developments by the private sector where the return on investment would otherwise be marginal. It replaced both the Urban Development Grant and the Urban Regeneration Grant. In the same year the government imposed the Central Manchester Development Corporation on Manchester.

Urban Development Corporations (UDCs) had been created in 1980 by the provisions of the Local Government, Planning and Land Act, which gave the Secretary of State the power to establish them if 'expedient in the national interest to do so.' Thus the UDCs were answerable to the Secretary of State and were firmly outside the control of their local authorities. A UDC's powers were considerable, and it could 'grant planning permission for developments in its area; acquire, hold, manage and dispose of land in its area; provide water, electricity, gas, sewerage and other services; provide various forms of grants and financial aid to developers'.[15] The UDCs were set up as partnerships between central government and the private sector, with local authorities, at best, ignoring them, and at worst trying to hinder them. The UDCs were market-led, and were meant to gear in private finance at a ratio of 1:4, public to private, although the figure was seldom met: of the first two UDCs set up in 1980, London Docklands DC's gearing was 1:12, but Merseyside UDC's was 4.3:1.

> The function of Urban Development Corporations in particular . . . was to create greenfield sites within cities, safely circumscribed places which have been cleared of all local influence, both economic and political . . . First . . . it has to be pointed out that many of the new developments in city centres, and certainly those in the areas controlled by UDCs and Enterprise Zones, are not taking place unaided. They are happening on the back of very consider-able state subsidies . . . 'Leverage' is simply another word for subsidy . . . this money is spent on these high-visibility schemes while local authorities in the same areas are being starved of resources for the provision of basic services.[16]

And, of course, most of the public subsidy as well as private investment went to London, as Michael Middleton observed. 'Break down the £800 million allocated to the Corporations and you will find over £500 million of it going to the richest – London Docklands. In November 1989 the government announced a 37 per cent increase in expenditure on regeneration over the next two years;

of the additional £420 million involved, no less than £359 million was earmarked for the LDDC.'[17] Middleton pointed out that in September 1989 the Department of the Environment was admonished by the Audit Office for its failure to ensure that its £4 billion per annum was going to areas of greatest need.

Trafford Park Urban Development Corporation was established in February 1987,[18] with £160 million to spend over ten years, with the objective of securing the economic and physical regeneration of the area. About one-third of Trafford Park was lying derelict, and Trafford Council was having to spend £1 million to £2 million per year (10 per cent of its capital budget) on maintenance alone. There were still 600 firms in Trafford Park, including important names like CIBA-Geigy, Kellogg, GEC, GKN, Shell, Massey-Ferguson, Brooke Bond Oxo, Procter & Gamble, ICI, the *Daily Telegraph* and *The Times*, but they provided employment for only 24,500 people, less than a third of the number at the peak of employment. Only forty people were resident in Trafford Park, but 45,000 unemployed people lived within a five-mile radius, and regeneration of the Park would create job opportunities.

'In some respects its task could be seen as the management of the UK's largest industrial-improvement area and it could have been expected to attract a mix of activities similar to those already existing, namely manufacturing and distribution.'[19] The problem was that the Park was surrounded by Enterprise Zones in Trafford and in Salford, as well as having proximity to Manchester city centre. The developments at Salford Quays across the canal suggested an alternative, the concept of Trafford Wharfside, 250 acres of land lying between the Ship Canal and Bridgewater Canal, and described somewhat extravagantly in the Trafford Park Development Corporation brochure as 'Europe's most spectacular waterside development'.[20] By 1990 Trafford Park UDC had reclaimed 620 acres of land, built 1 million ft^2 of new buildings, with a further 2 million ft^2 under construction, and had created 2,000 jobs. Trafford Park UDC closed in March 1998, but its input of £43 million had generated over £380 million of inward investment, and had helped to bring in an extra 1,000 companies and 30,000 jobs to Trafford Park in its ten years.[21]

In March 1988 the government launched its £3 billion 'Action for Cities' package. Ministers armed with glossy brochures toured the country having working breakfasts with businessmen, preaching the message that 'regenerating the cities was a job for the private sector and that local authorities would be relegated to a minor role in which the damage they could do could be controlled'.[22] No new policies were announced, and responsibility for the inner cities was in the hands of an individual Minister rather than a Ministry. The proposal brought together, for the first time, crime, education and tourism as aspects of the regeneration of the inner city, although the package said nothing about health or social services, education (other than training), welfare, poverty or deprivation. In the same year the CBI review *Initiative beyond Charity* stated, 'Cities will . . . have to spring from sound economic development, driven by private sector investment decisions taken on the basis of the commercial returns available, not from a sense of charity.'[23]

141] Direct Line offices,
Peter Street, Fairhurst's
Design Group, 1988–90

The year 1988 saw the establishment of smaller UDCs in Bristol, Leeds, the Don valley in Sheffield and central Manchester. The Central Manchester Development Corporation (CMDC) was established by Westminster on 30 June 1988 (and financed under the Action for Cities programme), with the task of developing a 470 acre (187 ha) crescent to the south and east of the city centre as 'The Ideal Business Location'. It was the first city-centre UDC, and the smallest.[24] Among the objectives of the CMDC were: bringing land and buildings back into effective use; encouraging the development of existing and new industry and commerce; creating an attractive environment; ensuring, where appropriate, that housing and social facilities were available to encourage people to live and work in the area; levering private investment into the area; playing a full part in reinforcing and promoting central Manchester's role not only as a regional centre but also as a national and international resource.

Major components of CMDC's strategy included: environmental improvement – the removal of dereliction and blight and building upon the environmental assets of the area, particularly the waterways; promotion of the 'Mill Demolition Scheme' which gave grants toward the cost of demolishing obsolescent industrial properties, and grants towards feasibility studies to assess new uses; development for new activities – bringing into the area new types of economic and development activity such as city-centre housing and tourism; development for specialist activities – the provision of specialist facilities for commerce and industry that build upon the area's location and complemented activities in the city centre.[25]

The first new building to be erected in the CMDC area was 44 Peter Street (Fairhurst's, 1988–90), a small but prestigious building on a prime site next to the Free Trade Hall, and stone-clad to respect its neighbour [141]. In 1989 British Gas began actively to market the redundant Gaythorn Gas Works site.

Building Design Partnership carried out an initial site analysis and prepared three generic options for 200,000 ft^2 of office developments, and the name 'Grand Island' was coined for the site. With the aid of the CMDC and Grimley & Sons, British Gas secured the British Council as a pre-let tenant of considerable status and significance with an occupation date of end-December 1991.

At this point, details of what lay below the surface came to light. Gone were the seductive marketing options and in came the reality of a site located among nineteenth-century tar wells, the foundations of a massive coking plant, gasholder bases, the culverted rivers Medlock and Tib, a network of gas mains up to 36 in. in diameter, retort bases, methane and generally contaminated earth. Above ground was the almost sculptural pressure reduction station.

The specific requirements of the British Council for a column-free exterior and offices 18 m deep, and with 20,000 ft^2 of office space per floor, had an overwhelming influence on the plan and massing of the building. During the design process the British Council appointed three different consultants to ensure that its requirements were achieved, and one of these, Max Fordham, insisted, on environmental grounds, that the windows should represent no more than 40 per cent of the external wall area from floor to ceiling. This caused great difficulties in the design of the building's fenestration, and it gave the building a heavy solid-to-void character.

The building is a pre-cast concrete frame and floor building with a regular plan of 54 m by 48 m overall, six storeys in height, with accommodation arranged around a central 18 m by 21 m atrium [142]. Externally there is a grey, powder-coated, metal rain-screen cladding. Just a few months earlier the Siemens building had been completed, but it was felt inappropriate to use all-white cladding in the city centre. The original proposal was for silver-grey cladding but at the time no guarantees could be given of the longevity of that particular finish. This left the choice, in reality, to the greys and the stone colours. Stone-coloured powder coating was not acceptable and therefore the team of British Gas, the British Council and Building Design Partnership toured Europe visiting rain-screen-clad office buildings in Belgium, Holland and Germany. The

142] British Gas Building, Grand Island Site, Building Design Partnership, 1992

consensus was the adopted warm grey which came in for some criticism but is a similar colour to that later used on the Concert Hall and Victoria Arena. Without the phase two building the site remains incomplete, leaving the existing building in splendid isolation. The British Council, after suffering large staff reductions in 1998, moved to Bridgewater House on Whitworth Street, and the Grand Island site has been taken over by British Telecom.

Even as the CMDC was being created the signs of recession were becoming apparent, and although a number of sites in the city had been earmarked in the 1980s for potential development, most of them remained as derelict brownfield sites or car parks, and the nearest these schemes came to realisation was the artist's vision painted on the hoardings which surrounded the site. Land values collapsed in 1989–90, and in 1990–91 even the CMDC made a loss of £8·3 million on land transactions.[26] Outside the CMDC's sphere of operations most of the city centre schemes were developer-led, and with the down-turn in the market they suffered.

What building work remained was on a small scale, like the development in the late 1980s of Prince's Building on Oxford Street and Oxford Court behind it. The site had lain undeveloped for some seven years, and attempts were made to persuade the owners to develop the site. Counter-proposals by the owners to demolish were rejected. The developers went into liquidation, and the building was sold off to the Miller Group from Scotland. All that remained of Prince's Building was the façade (its beautiful Art Nouveau front door was stolen one weekend), and behind this Leach Rhodes Walker built a shallow two-storey building, now occupied by the Northern Counties Housing Association. On either side of Prince's Building the developer wanted to erect two-storey buildings, but the Planning Department insisted (uniquely for a listed building) on the buildings on either side being built to a different architectural form and as high as the Prince's Building's façade. On either side are now similar, but not identical, square brick buildings with stone detailing, parts of which echo, but do not copy, the terracotta decorative panels on the listed building. The flanking buildings consciously reflect the brick and stone of traditional Manchester warehouses.

Behind Prince's Building, on a derelict bombed site, Oxford Court (Leach Rhodes Walker, 1987–89) was developed as a series of small, self-contained offices, in emulation of Georgian houses [143], a concept taken from the houses in St John Street, which had long been used as offices by professional people. The three-storey office contained within vertical walls with its own front door was suitable for professional tenants who wanted a small space and might wish to buy their own buildings, and created fewer problems for security and maintenance than conventional office blocks. The small scale of this development was indicative of the state of the market – the developer was sensibly hesitant about putting up a large office block.

A £100 million development was planned in 1991 by Shudehill Developments, a company formed by the CWS, CIS and Bishopsgate Properties (part of the Maxwell empire). The Shudehill Shopping Centre, a ten-acre site at the side of Withy Grove and Shudehill, would have featured a glass-topped Galleria like Milan's Galleria Vittorio Emmanule and a dome higher than the nave of St Paul's, and with squares based on Covent Garden. It was to have rooftop parking and its own Metrolink station. Stephen Wood, director of Shudehill Developments, said, 'The city centre has to a large extent stagnated in retail terms. There's been no major development in the city centre in the last 15 years. The need for more shopping has been emphasised at several public enquiries in recent years. Shopping trade will continue to leak away from Manchester city centre unless new large-scale retail development can be provided.'[27] Although the Shudehill scheme did not go ahead, this was a significant comment in view of the later building of the Trafford Centre. The Maxwell empire collapsed after the death of Robert Maxwell, but there were deeper underlying reasons why development did not go ahead. The effects of high interest rates, rapidly rising inflation and a slow-down in both manufacturing and the service industries were being felt in the city.

> The problem which Manchester faces is typical of many northern industrial cities in the UK. As the rate of growth in the economy improves it is first manifest in London and the South-East and only subsequently trickles down to other regions. However, just when the effects are beginning to be felt in the peripheral regions, the national and South-Eastern economy overheats and the government has to apply the brakes. Consequently, the boom for cities like Manchester is soon over.[28]

By the early 1990s the boom was over for everyone. The recession was deeply felt in the building industry and the figures for the major construction companies show how much the whole sector was suffering. At the end of 1993 only Laing made profits, of £11 million, largely due to some clever reorganisation, the next best performer being Higgs & Hill with a loss of £11 million. Mowlem lost £27 million, Taylor Woodrow £66 million, AMEC £87 million and George Wimpey £112 million[29] Although the losses were partly due to a recession in

143] Oxford Court, Oxford Stree
Leach Rhodes Walker, 1989

144] 15 Quay Street, Stephenson
Bell, 1992

the housing market and the virtual moratorium on local authority housing, the construction of large-scale projects had also virtually ceased.

Large-scale building in the region was still going on at Salford Quays, taking advantage of tax breaks before its Enterprise Zone status ended, and a number of the larger architectural practices were involved there and in Trafford. In Manchester some buildings were being erected, but on a small scale, for money was tight. The significance of these new inner-city buildings was the opportunity they gave, especially for the smaller and younger practices to demonstrate their expertise. All the younger architects were passionate about their city, many had been to architecture school together, and not a few of them had cut their first teeth working for Building Design Partnership. A new Manchester spirit, if not a new vernacular, was slowly starting to emerge, and by the end of the decade, developers had come to realise that good-quality architecture could command high rents; but it was all to take time.

At 15 Quay Street, in 1992, Stephenson Bell designed a small five-storey brick building which, by means of a stone-clad corner tower [144], cleverly bridges two old buildings (the old Post Office and the Hospital for Skin Diseases), each of a different height and building line, and manages to double the accommodation on the site. The apparently simple design was clever enough to win both a Civic Trust commendation and an RIBA Regional Award. In the same year Mills Beaumont Leavey built 49 Peter Street (for Grand Metropolitan), a concrete-framed building clad in polished granite [145], and this too bridges two existing and very dissimilar buildings (in this case a curtain-walled building of the 1960s and a nineteenth-century brick warehouse) by clever cutting back of wall surfaces and reducing the number of storeys from seven on one side to five on the other.

Stephenson Bell, in 1993, remodelled the interior and entrance of what had been Lamb's Showrooms at 16 John Dalton Street. Trinity Court [146] has been described as one of the best interiors in Manchester, and Salomon's beautifully detailed polychromatic façade of 1865 was retained, not just because it was then listed, but because both architect and clients (Barlow plc and the Church Commissioners) valued it. The conversion, done in conjunction with structural engineers YRM Anthony Hunt Associates, won a Civic Trust award in 1993.

In 1993 the refurbished St George's Building was opened. In 1988 the Grade II YMCA building had become too small for the Association, and it was sold to the millionaire Pyarali Lakhani for the bargain price of £1 million. The building was leased back to the YMCA until it moved into new premises in 1990. The present developers, Eagle Star Properties, paid £2 million for the building, and for them a new atrium has been built, through which two wall-climber lifts run to the new floors rationalised to meet modern requirements for open, unencumbered office spaces (Austin Strzala Turner and Ove Arup & Partners, 1993). It is now known as St George's House, from the reproduction of Donatello's St George on the third floor.

In the following year the Manchester Metropolitan University commissioned Mills Beaumont Leavey Channon to design its new library at Aytoun Street

145] Offices, Peter Street, Mill Beaumont Leavey, 1992

146] Trinity Court, John Dalton Street, Stephenson Bell, 1993. The atrium

7] Manchester Metropolitan
University Library Building,
Aytoun Street, Mills Beaumont
Leavey Channon, 1994

[147]. Against the drab bulk of Besant Roberts's 1960s rectangular concrete and glass block, the new steel-framed building's cladding of white aluminium rain-screen panels and ceramic-faced blocks, and the *brise soleil* running round its curved form, make a landmark statement.[30]

Farther along Aytoun Street is one of the few public-sector works of the period, the refurbishment of the Crown Courts in Minshull Street, by the Hurd Rolland Partnership for the Courts Service, and completed in 1996. The brief required the restoration of the original Minshull Street building fabric, and the repair and alteration of the four Victorian courts to their original condition. The opportunity was taken for a radical reordering of the ground floor of the original building to provide four new courts, with two additional courts in a new building along with supporting accommodation. The constraints of the site and internal circulation demanded a new entrance at Aytoun Street via the new building [148].

Internally the building is extremely complex, as there are several strands of circulation which, for security and safety reasons, have to be kept entirely separate, varying from security for defendants to free movement of the public. The resolution of the circulation problems led to the main design feature – the central atrium area [149], utilising what had been the original Victorian courtyard, and representing the links between the old and the new. The site available for the new building was a very small footprint compared with the existing one, and appropriately it continues the rhythm of the existing building's silhouette, using a limited palette of materials, including slates, stone and brick. The new work is sympathetic to Worthington's original building without being a pastiche, and although the final design is unmistakably contemporary it accepts the dominance of the existing building.[31]

By the time the draft Manchester Plan (*The Unitary Development Plan for the City of Manchester*) was published in 1992, the City Council was committed to working in partnership with the private sector and the CMDC. Among the aims of the plan were to protect the best of the city's architecture, get as many jobs as possible into the city without spoiling the environment, maintain and enhance the commercial and shopping role of the city centre, ensure that the growth of the airport brought benefits to the people of Manchester, and continue to encourage the important regional role of the city centre in providing for business and leisure. 'A primary function of the Regional Centre is its role as a commercial centre in serving not just the City of Manchester and the Greater Manchester conurbation but the north-west region and beyond. The banking, insurance and related sectors need a City Centre location with the benefits of accessibility, interaction and prestige which this brings.'[32] The Manchester Plan was officially adopted in 1995.

The Central Manchester Development Corporation was disbanded at the end of March 1996, but in its eight years of operation it generated a total investment of £430 million, built 2,583 housing units, provided 97,904 m² of office space and created thirty-eight leisure schemes.[33] Not least among its achievements was its promotion, jointly with the City Council, of a new home for the Hallé

148] Crown Court, Aytoun Stre
Thomas Worthington, 1867–7
and Hurd Rolland Partnershi
1987–96. The new entrance

149] Crown Court, Aytoun Stre
Thomas Worthington, 1867–7
and Hurd Rolland Partnershi
1987–96. The atrium

PLATE 29] G–MEX, Windmill Street,
sex, Goodman & Suggitt, 1980

PLATE 30] Lincoln House,
Deansgate, Holford Associates,
1986

PLATE 31] View up
Brazennose Street

PLATE 32] Direct Line offices,
Peter Street, Fairhurst's Design
Group, 1988–90

PLATE 33] 15 Quay Street,
Stephenson Bell, 1992

PLATE 34] MEN Arena,
Austin–Smith:Lord, 1995

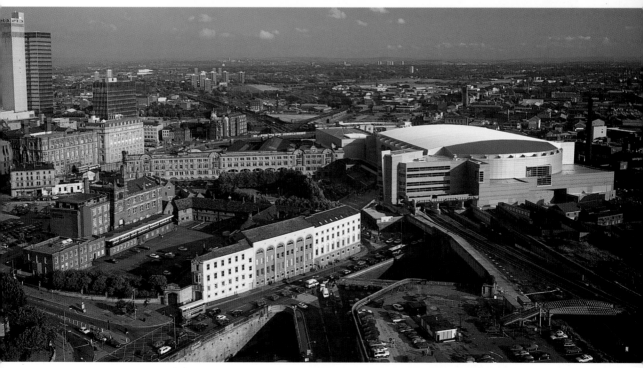

PLATE 35] Bridgewater Hall
Renton Howard Wood Levi
Partnership, 1990–96

PLATE 36] Bridgewater Hall
Auditorium, Renton Howard
Wood Levin Partnership,
1990–96

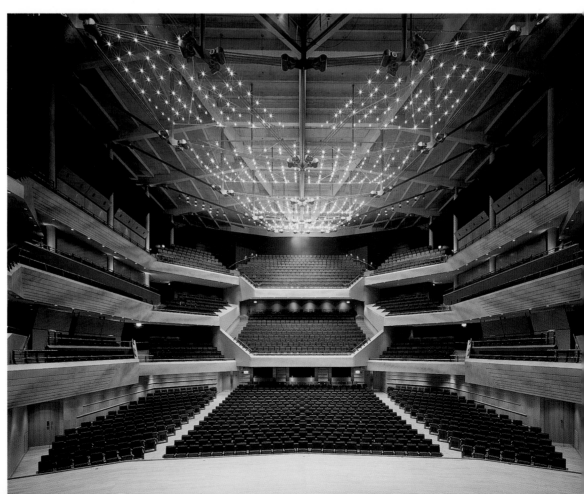

PLATE 37] Offices, Barbirolli Square, Renton Howard Wood Levin Partnership, 1990–96

TE 38] MMU Library Building, toun Street, Mills Beaumont Leavey Channon, 1994

TE 39] 201 Deansgate, Holford Associates, 1997

© HAYES DAVIDSON 1999

PLATE 40] Commonwealth Ga
Stadium, Arup Associates a
Lobb Sports Architecture,
1999–2002

PLATE 41] Velodrome interio
FaulknerBrowns. Track desi
by Ron Webb, 1994

ATE 42] Royal Exchange Theatre,
Levitt Bernstein Associates,
1998–99

PLATE 43] Marks & Spencer before the bomb

PLATE 44] Marks & Spencer, St Mary's Gate elevation, Building Design Partnership, 1998–99

PLATE 45] Marks & Spencer, detail of structure

PLATE 46] Marks & Spencer, Exchange Square elevation, Building Design Partnership, 1998–99. The 'windmills' by John Hyatt of Manchester Metropolitan University

PLATE 47] The Old Wellington I
and Sinclair's Oyster Bar
relocated on Exchange Square

PLATE 48] Exchange Square,
Martha Schwarz Inc, 1998–2000
Water feature by the Fountain
Workshop

PLATE 49] Triangle at the Corn Exchange, Ball & Elce, 1889–90, and Potts, Son & Pickup, 1904–14. Refurbishment, Ratcliffe Partnership and Mountain Design, 1999–2000

PLATE 50] New Arndale frontage on Corporation Street, Ratcliffe Partnership, 1999–2000

PLATE 51] New bridge over Corporation Street, Hodder Associates and Ove Arup & Partners, 1999–2000

PLATE 52] Great Northern Square,
Leslie Jones Architects, 1998–2000

PLATE 53] Urbis, Ian Simpson
Architects, 1999–2001

PLATE 54] Trinity Bridge, St Mary's Parsonage, Santiago Calatrava, 1994

PLATE 55] Interior of Trafford Centre, Chapman Taylor and Leach Rhodes Walker, 1995–98

PLATE 59] Quay Bar, Bridgewater
Viaduct, Stephenson Bell, 199[...]

PLATE 60] Merchants Bridge,
Whitby & Bird, 1996

Orchestra. The development of the Bridgewater Hall and office complex on Lower Mosley Street provided the opportunity for a major commercial development and a building which would add prestige to the city. Work started in 1993, but the history of the site stretches back over twenty years and demonstrates the difficulty of getting major developments off the ground.

Tom Marshall, now chief executive of Lambert Smith Hampton, was asked in 1974 to acquire the land for Gerald Ronson's Heron Group, for the Manchester Heron Centre, but the scheme came to nothing. In 1988 the five-acre site came on the market, and Beazer, who were then developing Chepstow House, bid, along with twenty-seven others, for the right to develop the scheme, in a developer/architect competition set up by the City and CMDC. Here was an opportunity to regenerate a run-down site (used primarily for car parking) and to provide a new home for the Hallé Orchestra.

The 'Bridgewater Initiative', for the concert hall and offices, was won by Beazer as a design-and-build contract in January 1990, the architects being Renton Howard Wood Levin Partnership (RHWL), an experienced practice, with more than eighty theatre and concert hall projects behind them. Beazer, however, were shortly after taken over by the Hanson Group, and as Marshall explained, 'Confidence gave way to gloom. There was never the remotest chance that Hanson would be interested in developing this scheme. The grand vision of placing Manchester's commercial heart up amongst the very best in the world was now in very real danger of looking like no more than another great and glorious folly.'[34]

Fortunately, AMEC Developments stepped in and part-funded the office scheme with pension fund managers Hermes. The contract for the Concert Hall was put out to design and build with Laing North West, who continued with the original architects RHWL (and Ove Arup & Partners as structural engineers). Planning permission was granted in 1992, and funding, which included £42 million from the City, the government and the European Union, was in place by 1993.

The form of the Concert Hall was generated from the requirements of the auditorium, and, as the first stand-alone auditorium to be built in the country since the Royal Festival Hall in 1951, it needed to have presence and to be on a large enough scale to stand up against the looming bulk of G-MEX. The base of the building is a deep plinth of red sandstone blocks and above this rise walls of metal cladding and glass which shield the Jura limestone-clad auditorium [150]. A stainless steel roof comes to a point over the prow of the glazed foyers and entrance.

The suspended glass curtain of the foyers, which appears to pierce through the flanking walls of silver metallic panels, forms the external focus of the building on the plaza of Barbirolli Square, and provides a sense of arrival to the concertgoers. Behind the glazing are the four levels of foyers and bars beyond which is the huge slope of the auditorium wall. The Lower Mosley Street side of the Hall is noisy, and on that side are the box office, shops and offices and minor entrances (and the rehearsal rooms for the percussionists). On the other side of the Hall, glazing from roof to floor allows views from the foyers on to an arm of the Rochdale Canal (specially opened for the development), and on this quiet side are the rehearsal rooms and suites for corporate entertainment.

The auditorium is the heart of the building, and is entered on each level through wide bronze doors which symbolise the movement from the light, ephemeral space of the foyers to the serenity of the auditorium. In most concert halls the design is driven by acoustic requirements, but here the architects agreed with the acoustic designers, Arup Acoustics, to create a balance between the aural and visual criteria. The designers wanted to create a sense of intimacy and involvement with the orchestra, and this was achieved by breaking down the audience of 2,500 (250 more than the Free Trade Hall held) into small groups located in carefully defined spaces on multiple levels of tiered seats and galleries [**151**]. The focus of all the seating is on the performing area and on the great organ which rises behind the orchestra; the organ was designed by the architect (Nicholas Thompson) in conjunction with Thomas Trotter, who wrote its specification for the manufacturer, Markussen of Denmark. The surfaces of the tiers and galleries, coupled with the overhangs, provide the critical lateral acoustic reflections. Even the seats were designed so that the acoustics are the same whether the auditorium is full or half empty. Individual under-seat ducts, fed from the plant tower in the corner of site, provide the necessary ventilation.

The auditorium is finished in natural materials: oak floors, cherry-veneered panelling, bronze handrails, with a background of rich indigoes and Indian reds, and the colours were inspired by autumn leaves collected by the architect from Kew Gardens. The colour of the auditorium is contrasted with the white

150] Bridgewater Hall, Barbirol Square, Renton Howard Wood Levin Partnership, 1990–96

151] Bridgewater Hall, Renton
Howard Wood Levin
Partnership, 1990–96.
The auditorium

and blue of the foyers, where the specially designed carpet was based on Monet's lily paintings.

Columns rise from the upper elements of the bowl of the auditorium to carry the elegant large-span roof, whose structural members are clearly expressed behind a myriad of tiny lights, designed by Lighting Design Partnership. The Metrolink runs immediately to the side of the building, and acoustic separation from street noise is provided by the roof insulation and the walls of the auditorium, and by the foyers and offices around the outside of the auditorium. To isolate the auditorium from low-frequency noise the whole building is mounted on 270 giant vibration isolation bearings, manufactured by GERB of Germany, and developed originally for buildings in earthquake zones. It was their first use in a concert hall. No part of the auditorium actually touches the ground, and the gap between the Concert Hall and the ground is clearly seen from the basement. (Tours of the building are available on payment of a small fee.)[35]

The first-year ticket sales, in 1996, were £4 million (by comparison, in the last year in the Free Trade Hall sales were only £1 million); 40,000 concertgoers visited the Hall, 76 per cent of whom had never gone to the Free Trade Hall. The Hallé needs to attract a good audience, since it is one of the lowest-funded of all the provincial orchestras. It is fortunate that the Concert Hall has no outstanding debt from its construction, and that is because of the building and pre-letting of the two office blocks on the other side of Barbirolli Square. By locating the Concert Hall in a focal position, to be seen from both Albert Square and St Peter's Square, the north side of the site became available for the commercial development, which also obscured the view of the backs of buildings on Oxford Street from the Concert Hall foyers.

The competition stage model was developed as a metal-clad building for Beazer, the original developers, and subsequently brick-clad buildings, reflecting Manchester's warehouse tradition, were developed for AMEC Developments. In an attempt to establish funding and a high pre-let percentage of the scheme, RHWL examined a variety of alternative designs ranging from single high-rise structures to more traditional brick ones. The final version of the scheme provided for two similar, but not identical, buildings and reversed the access to the buildings, which now had their entrances facing the Concert Hall. Stone cladding was a specific requirement of the tenant consortium, and a polished Sardinian grey granite was selected to provide, with the semi-reflective glazing (for reduced cooling loads), a smooth-skinned envelope [152] that would blend with the tones and textures of the surrounding buildings and the materials of the Concert Hall.

152] Bridgewater offices, Barbirolli Square, Renton Howard Wood Levin Partnership, 1990–96

153] The Observatory, Cross Street, Holford Associates, 1995–96

154] 82 King Street, Holford Associates, 1996

It was agreed with the tenant consortium to place the higher, nine-storey building on the Chepstow Street side of the site, so that, when seen from Lower Mosley Street, both buildings appeared to be of equal status and prestige. The two buildings are similar in size, height and plan shapes, but the stronger horizontal banding and recessed curves of the lower building contrast with the projecting bays and expressed verticality of the taller building behind. Both the buildings are arranged with diagonally positioned cores which allow flexible letting arrangements for potentially two tenants per floor. The scale and mass of the new buildings were designed to form a visual bridge between Peter House and the Concert Hall.[36]

Barbirolli Square itself forms a link between the Concert Hall and the office buildings. York stone paving, shot through with bands of granite originating from the grid of the office buildings and the radiating axes of the Concert Hall, creates a relationship between the buildings; the red sandstone plinth of the Concert Hall is continued round the quayside and rises again in the form of piers which enclose the waterside restaurant which forms the base of the belvedere from which the offices rise. The scheme is softened by tree planting – London planes at street level and willows and trained lime trees at quay level – and by the £200,000, eighteen-tonne marble pebble by Japanese artist Kan Yasuda.

By 1996, coincidentally with the opening of the Bridgewater Hall, confidence had returned to the city, and developers were again commissioning larger-scale buildings. The Observatory, Cross Street (Holford Associates, 1995–96), on the site of the Cross Street Chapel, had been designed during the recession, but the City Council had blocked plans for the development by refusing to sell back to the chapel a strip of grassed land fronting the building which had been sold to the council in 1959 as part of a potential road-widening scheme. The trustees of the chapel, who had asked AMEC to develop the site, were keen for the building scheme to go ahead, because they would get a new chapel to replace the old one, described by the Reverend Denise Boyd as 'a barn with all the atmosphere of a garage'. The Council eventually relented and the Observatory commenced building in 1995 [**153**]. Eight floors of offices, providing 55,000 ft^2 of lettable floor space, rise above the circular chapel rebuilt on the ground floor, and are clad in red brick, sandstone and granite, familiar city-centre materials, and these contrast with the modern materials of curtain walling and metal to dramatic effect. At the Cross Street and Cheapside corners are towers, a characteristic of so many of Manchester's historic buildings. The bodies buried at the rear of the building were re-interred in Southern Cemetery. No one has been buried at Cross Street for 150 years.

On 82 King Street, Holford Associates in 1996 provided a stone and glass building rising fifteen storeys behind Cockerell's Bank [**154**]. This is a building to which a number of people have raised objections particularly because

155] 201 Deansgate, Holford Associates, 1997

156] St James's House, John Dalton Street, Fairhursts Design Group, 1997

157] Fountain Street, with an office block by Spratley Cullearn Philips, c. 1996, and Fountain Court, Fairhurst's Design Group, mid-1990s

158] 81st on Fountain Street, Holford Associates, mid-1990s

its tower competes with the tower of the Town Hall. But a number of factors had to be taken into account by the designers. The design brief, from Friends' Provident, was to optimise the site of 82 King Street (Cockerell's Bank of England) and 7 Tib Lane (which required the demolition of the handsome Cruickshank & Seward building of the 1970s referred to in the previous chapter), creating economically viable commercial office accommodation of the highest technical specification.

The bank, a Grade I listed building, was restored and the banking hall made the focus of the redevelopment, acting as both office entrance hall and public foyer with retail at the sides. But it could offer relatively little usable space, with its circulation and floor space compromised by the external architecture, so the poor nett-to-gross areas in the bank had to be absorbed over the larger project – and this entailed a tall building. And as has been pointed out by another architect, 'It is true that the developer tries to get maximum allowable space on his site: after all, if town planning conditions permit certain sizes of building to occur, then it is ridiculous for anybody not to develop the site for its fullest potential. There is no point in under-developing on valuable land.'[37]

King Street already had a number of tall buildings, rising above the general plateau of building heights, and in this context the architects felt it appropriate to create a building of significant scale and presence, a landmark building complementary to those already standing. The new building is a tower composition clad in stone and glass, designed to be revealed in partial views from the surrounding streets. The major set-back on the tenth floor reflects the changes in the architectural mass of both Ship Canal House and Lutyens's Midland Bank.

In contrast, on a brownfield site (part of which had been the Quakers' Burial Ground in the nineteenth century) at 201 Deansgate, in 1996–97, the same architects designed a smaller building for Chestergate Seddon [155]. This was built on an L-shaped site of derelict land, with a narrow frontage to Deansgate. The external form of the building employed the texture and patina of familiar city-centre materials – red brick, steel, glass and sandstone – and the approach to detail on the building was industrial in spirit. Simple square punched window openings are spanned by exposed fabricated steel lintels. Courses of bricks are recessed at intervals to provide a simple and unobtrusive articulation of the surface. Red Halldale sandstone is used to highlight significant features of the architecture – the projections at key heights and the corner columns; the column at the entrance alone cost £20,000. There is a four-storey entrance atrium, and next to it the lifts and staircase tower rise through six storeys (capped by a staircase lantern) to give a strong vertical emphasis. The building won a Civic Trust award in 1998.[38]

159] 'Clock House', Royal & Sun Alliance, York Street, Cassidy & Ashton, 1996

In 1994, the year the city hosted the Global Forum, Manchester was made UK City of Drama, in recognition of the number and quality of its theatres (it has more theatres *per capita* than any provincial city), and a certain pride in the city was evident in a way that had not been seen for a long time. In the same year the *City Pride* prospectus was published. The prospectus, which covered Manchester and parts of Salford, referred to the area becoming by the year 2000:

- a European regional capital – a centre for investment growth, not regional aid;
- an international City of outstanding commercial, cultural and creative potential; and
- an area distinguished by the quality of life and sense of well-being enjoyed by its residents.

The vision rested on 'the marrying of an enhanced international prestige with local quality and benefit. Neither can be achieved without the other'.[39] Manchester was in a confident mood.

13

THE 1990S

BIDDING FOR
THE GAMES,
AND A BOMB

To hear footfalls, laughter, bird-song in the very heart of cities is a real recapture of territory lost to civilisation, and the fact that the surrounding architecture is generally mediocre and sometimes absurd does not seem to matter and confirms once again the truth, often proclaimed by architects, that urban design is about the creation of spaces and not about the particular decor of the façades that wall them in. [Lionel Esher, *A Broken Wave*, 1981]

ONE OF the most important reasons for growing confidence in the city, and which brought in much-needed finance, was the bidding for the Olympic Games. The bidding process was important to the city, not only in generating inward investment but, as important, in raising its profile externally and, internally, engendering a sense of pride.

Manchester's first bid in 1988 for the 1996 Olympic Games had very little to show; there were no buildings under way, and all that Manchester had to offer was models and drawings of proposed structures. The major venues were to be in Dumplington, with other facilities scattered around the north-west in Liverpool, Wigan, Chester and north Wales. Support from both the British Olympic Association and the government was lukewarm, and the City Council was not involved. It surprised no one that Atlanta won the Games, but valuable lessons had been learned. The City threw its full weight behind the second bid for the 2000 Olympics, and Graham Stringer, leader of the Council, with Bob (later Sir Robert) Scott, chairman of the bid committee, managed to engage the personal involvement of Prime Minister John Major and the support of the Conservative government. It was clear from the first bid that the International

Olympic Committee favoured compact sites, and a brownfield site in Bradford in east Manchester (renamed Eastlands) was selected as the site for the athletics stadium and other major facilities, to a master plan designed by Sir Norman Foster & Partners. Twenty-one of the twenty-five Olympic venues would be situated within the so-called 'Olympic Ring' and ten of the proposed venues would be within ten minutes' walk of the Olympic Village.

The bidding for the Games would provide a means of regenerating a particularly run-down sector of the city. In earlier decades there had been a huge downturn in the economy of Bradford, Beswick and Clayton, an area once given over to heavy industry. Johnson's Wire Works, Manchester Steel, Renold Chains and Crossley Motors had all closed, throwing tens of thousands on the dole. 'That area became 146 acres of nothing. Bradford just died when all the heavy industry shut up and moved away.'[1] In 1992 the East Manchester Regeneration Strategy was published, with the objectives of stimulating economic and business development, securing effective land use and environmental and infrastructure improvements, encouraging diversity in housing and developing a skill base in local communities. All this would be led by the provision of the major sporting facilities. Ten thousand new jobs and 2,000 new houses would be provided by encouraging inward investment in the area.[2]

The potential for income into the city and region was enormous. Staging the Games would have cost over £2 billion, but income from television rights, sponsorship and other income would have produced a £65 million surplus. Running the event would have generated £1·5 billion, including sponsorship, media and merchandising revenue and £250 million of new tourist spending.[3] The Games would have generated £4 billion of new expenditure in the northwest, and a capital investment programme of up to £2·5 billion. Barcelona had completed twenty years of development and reconstruction in just five years after it was awarded the 1992 Games, and there was no reason why Manchester could not do the same.

It was essential for the International Olympic Committee to see facilities under construction when they visited Manchester in 1992/93, and on the Eastlands site the Velodrome was being erected. A design-and-build contract by AMEC, with architects FaulknerBrowns and concept design by HOK Sports Facilities Group, its focal point was the Ron Webb-designed 250 m Siberian pine cycle track. The track has complex geometry with banking and curves designed to catapult the cyclist down the straights with gravity forces of up to 4G, and it was the configuration of the track which defined the shape of the building [160].

The geometry of the track and the need to provide unrestricted sightlines for spectators gave rise to the main internal feature of the structure, a 20 m wide central steel box-truss arch (by Watson Steel) spanning 122 m from end to end of the building, springing from four huge concrete thrust blocks each weighing 310 tonnes. The arch creates a skeletal backbone to a domed structure of 600 tonnes of steel. With an enclosed ovoid area approximately 120 m by 100 m in size, the Velodrome can accommodate up to 3,500 people. Externally the oval form, evoking speed, movement and fluidity, is provided by subtly coloured blue cladding bricks, a band of metallic cladding and blue-tinted glazing, covered

by an aluminium roof – all evocative of cycle handlebars and a cycling helmet [**161**]. The £9 million National Cycling Centre – the UK's first purpose-built cycling stadium and now the headquarters of the British Cycling Federation – opened in September 1994.[4]

In 1989, just a year after the Phoenix study of the area, the Manchester-based developer Vector Investments, assisted by Bovis North, had identified part of Manchester Victoria station as a potential development site for office accommodation and a small indoor arena. When Manchester announced its intention to bid for the 2000 Olympic Games, the landowners, British Rail, issued invitations to bid for the redevelopment of the fourteen-acre Victoria Station site, to include an Olympic-standard arena, and the Vector/Bovis proposal was accepted. The architects Austin-Smith:Lord developed the master plan and led the project, DLA Ellerbe Beckett, specialists in arena design, carried out the design of the Arena, and Ove Arup & Partners provided the structural design and service work. Bovis Construction was the principal contractor.

The contract was announced on 24 December 1992 by John Redwood, Secretary of State for the Environment, with a grant of £35 million, then the biggest-ever grant for a single sports facility. The station had to operate throughout the building work, and before construction of the Arena could begin in earnest eight of the existing railway lines had to be removed and four new platforms constructed. Demolition of part of the existing station took place during Christmas 1992, and by August 1993 two new railway lines were operational.

The redevelopment scheme was designed to attract people on a substantial scale, to create employment and provide leisure and retail facilities that would enhance the station and animate the area during the day and night. The major elements of the proposal were the Arena, the City Room (a retail and circulation space) [**162**], Arena Point (office accommodation), a multi-storey car park and a multiplex cinema. In phase two the City Room is intended to be extended into a major retail development. A multi-storey tower with offices and restaurant, rivalling the CIS building, was intended to complete the site, though it is doubtful whether it will be built.

The architectural language of solid, heavily articulated masonry walls contrasting with lightweight metal and glass elements drew its inspiration from the Victorian station buildings and the spirit of railway architecture. The Arena itself is constructed of reinforced concrete rather than steel, to reduce noise

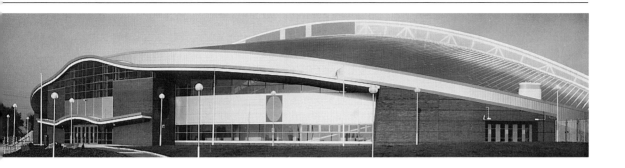

161] Velodrome, Eastlands,
FaulknerBrowns, 1994

transmission, and a concrete transfer deck which incorporates sound insulation spans the railway tracks and platforms and forms the floor of the concourse, Arena Point and the City Room. The roof of the Arena covers an enormous area of 1·52 ha, and a large steel truss spans 105 m across the event floor, with orthogonal trusses at each end to form a curved upper surface. On a roof of this size, thermal expansion is of major significance: only the centre point of the roof remains static, and at the four compass points of the roof are bearings on which it slides as it expands and contracts.

The Arena, which has a permanent ice floor suitable for ice hockey, is the largest indoor entertainment centre of its type in Europe [163], with 16,500 seats for sports, and a 20,500 seat capacity for other centre-stage events like concerts.* The Arena, originally sponsored by Nynex, is now sponsored by the Manchester Evening News.

In October 1993 the Olympic dream crashed. The Games were awarded to Sydney by two votes – an attractive bid from an attractive city, and Sydney would probably have beaten runner-up Beijing even without the offer of sports development funds to two African countries. Manchester was still suffering from its image as a bleak industrial town, peopled by Lowry's 'matchstick men' soaked by constant rain, and even Linford Christie said he would rather run in Sydney. Nonetheless, more than £200 million extra public and private investment came into Manchester during the bidding process, and the provision of £75 million of resources toward the building of the Velodrome, the Arena and clearing the Eastlands site was Britain's largest single city urban regeneration package.

In Manchester commitment and enthusiasm were undiminished. The city was feeling bullish, and within a month of the Games being given to Sydney it was invited by the Commonwealth Games Council for England to bid for the 2002 Commonwealth Games, in the year of the Queen's jubilee, and the first Games of the new millennium. On 2 February 1994 Manchester beat London by seventeenth votes to seven to the right to bid, and on 3 November 1995 the

---

* On 19 February 1998 the Nynex Arena established a record for the largest crowd to attend an indoor team sports event in Britain when 16,000 people watched a Manchester Storm ice-hockey match. Incidentally, ice hockey took place until 1948 in the Manchester Ice Palace, Derby Street, Cheetham, just north of Strangeways, on 14,000 ft² of ice.

Games were awarded to Manchester. Paul Taylor, the DoE inspector who presided over the public inquiry into the Eastlands site, said:

> The proposed complex would produce substantial employment, economic and environmental benefits . . . I consider that it is possible to be reasonably confident that the necessary resources will become available to enable the leisure and sports complex to be built, irrespective of whether Manchester hosts the Commonwealth Games. The presence of the impressive Velodrome does, in my view, give confidence about the potential of Eastlands as a major centre for leisure and sport.[5]

For the Commonwealth Games almost all sports will be held within twenty minutes drive of the Sports Village. At Eastlands there will be athletics in the Millennium Stadium, badminton in an adjacent stadium, cycling in the Velodrome. The stadium will be the anchor building of a proposed 'Sport City' which will have a £3·5 million Indoor Tennis Centre and a £10 million Sports

162] Victoria Station development
Austin-Smith:Lord, 1995.
The architect's proposals

163] MEN Arena, Austin-
Smith:Lord and DLA Ellerbee
Beckett, 1995

Academy. A sports injury clinic is also to be built in Eastlands. The Commonwealth Games open on Thursday 25 July 2002 for ten days.

The athletics stadium is, of course, central to the Games, but this structure has already had a chequered career. In July 1992 outline planning permission was granted for a stadium for the Olympic Games bid, and in March 1993 a worldwide competition for the stadium design was won by Arup Associates. Designed in association with HOK Sports Facilities Group, the spectacular International Stadium, with a circumference of 1 km and seating for 80,000 spectators, was intended to create a distinctive landmark for Manchester.

In spite of losing the Olympic Games, at the beginning of 1995 there were hopes that Manchester would be given the National Stadium, the 'Wembley of the north', something which the City Council thought both the Premier League and the Rugby League would support. Manchester faced competition from Birmingham and London, and in October 1995 Manchester was shortlisted with Wembley Stadium. For the National Stadium bid the design was scaled down to a 65,000 seat stadium, but after considerable delay to allow London to become organised, Wembley unsurprisingly gained the prize. Such was the lure of the famous twin towers that even the Rugby League said that it preferred its finals to be held there.[6]

On 2 September 1998 came the announcement of a new stadium for Manchester, a permanent 48,000 seater, to be built using £77 million of lottery cash from the English Sports Council plus £13 million from the City Council's fund for major projects. The design for the new City of Manchester Stadium was by Ove Arup & Partners in Manchester, Arup Associates in London and Lobb Sports Architecture.

The stadium [164] has been designed to enhance sightlines and create visual proximity to the sporting events. A circular seating plan combined with an oval arena creates elevations that sweep up from the north and south to contain four key levels on the east and west. The dramatic sweeping form moderates the bulk of the building. The high sides provide protection from prevailing winds and low sun angles while providing a concentration of seats and supporting accommodation in the areas most favoured by spectators; the low sides allow sun on to the grassed arena and give a human scale to the structure. Glass walls, a cable-supported series of steel masts, ramp access and exit routes, concrete seating bowls and a steel structure can all be built independently to speed construction. Seating will expand from 38,000 seats for the Games to 48,000 for football, with up to 60,000 for pop concerts.

By 2003 Manchester City Football Club will have taken over the stadium. Many people have objected to the eventual loss of a major athletics stadium in the north-west, but there are few international athletic events which could attract the crowds to support the investment, and, of course, there are already excellent facilities at the Don Valley complex in Sheffield.

The fourth structure built for the Commonwealth Games is the new 'Manchester 50' swimming pool (FaulknerBrowns, 1999–2000) [165], on Oxford Road adjacent to the universities. It consists of a 50 m competition pool, a 25 m diving pool and 200 m^2 of leisure waters with flumes and bubble pools. In

164] Stadium, Eastlands, Ove Arup & Partners, Arup Associate and Lobb Sports Architecture, 1999–2001. The architect's drawings

165] Swimming Baths, Pool 50, Oxford Road, FaulknerBrowns, 2000. The architect's drawing

the basement is an additional 50 m training pool, which will be used by elite swimming squads. There are also dry sports activity spaces, a poolside cafe and a crèche. There are 1,500 permanent spectator places with additional seating for the Games. The design features a curved metal roof with glass end walls, and on the Oxford Road side these are transparent to a height of 10 m, giving a view into the main pool hall. All three universities in Manchester are contributing to the capital and running costs. A new, and brutally ugly, multi-storey car park (FaulknerBrowns, 1998–99) to serve the pool has been constructed on the corner of Booth Street and Upper Brook Street.

Manchester was the only city that actually bid for the Games, which, of course, have a much lower international profile than the Olympics. The Commonwealth Games are the second largest event in the sporting calendar but, since only the Commonwealth is involved, television companies have little interest, and sponsorship is consequently harder to come by. Whether the Games will make a profit or a loss remains to be seen. Nonetheless, it is estimated that £125 million to £150 million will ultimately be spent in Manchester on the Games, and it has been calculated that sport has attracted £100 million to £200 million in the city in past ten years.[7] Bidding for the Games gained Manchester urban regeneration money that it otherwise would not have received. Manchester even got its own line in the DoE's spending allocations, the only city to have done so – £30.2 million for 1994–95 at its peak. Perhaps more important, bidding for the Games brought the City Council and the private sector together in a partnership which otherwise might not have happened. It also instilled in Mancunians a greater sense of pride in their city. As Ian Simpson, an architect closely involved in the Games bids, has commented, 'We competed for two Olympics and in the process council members and executive officers visited other cities like Barcelona and brought the lessons home with them . . . People at the top from the Council Leader through to the Planners really want Manchester to be a great city. There aren't many cities which have anything like this enthusiasm and commitment to move forward, do things and change.'[8]

Just as confidence was returning to the city, at 11.20 a.m. on Saturday 15 June 1996, came the devastating explosion of a 3,300 lb IRA bomb, the largest explosive device set off in mainland Britain. More than 200 people were injured, mostly by flying glass, and only through good fortune and the considerable efforts of the police to clear the area was no one killed. The morning was hot and sunny, and the city centre was crowded. At 9.41 a.m. a warning was telephoned to Granada Television, and within the hour police had cleared some 80,000 people from Marks & Spencer, the Arndale Centre and the streets around.

The explosion, when it occurred, damaged buildings up to a quarter of a mile away. Marks & Spencer took the full brunt of the blast, together with Longridge House and the Arndale Centre – the rumours that the Arndale was collapsing at 4 ft per hour and would have to be demolished were, unfortunately, fallacious. Forty-nine thousand square metres of shops and 57,000 m^2 of offices were damaged. The domes of the Royal Exchange and the Corn Exchange were both severely damaged. The Cathedral had its windows blown out, some masonry collapsed and the roof of the Song Room was lifted – repairs to the glass alone cost £150,000. St Ann's Church, which had just completed a major refurbishment scheme, had much of its glass blasted out and repairs cost £125,000. In Chetham's School students and visitors who had been listening to a concert had left the school hall for a refreshment break only minutes before the blast blew in its windows. The blast reached as far away as the Co-operative Bank in Balloon Street, the buildings in King Street and Lewis's and Debenham's on Market Street, and all lost part of their glazing. Streets were strewn with glass and rubble, and shards of glass were embedded in walls. Glaziers from all over the country descended on Manchester, even before the alarm bells stopped ringing.

The destruction displaced 670 businesses and caused financial difficulties for a further 3,000. The Lord Mayor's Emergency Appeal Fund was set up on 19 June to help them, and by 27 June Sir David Alliance and John Zochonis had contributed £600,000, and the government had contributed the 'spontaneous' sum of £50,000. By 10 January 1997 £2·5 million had been contributed. Some traders in the Arndale Centre were allowed back after three weeks and by June 1997 three-quarters of the traders had returned. The residents on top of the Arndale moved back only after four months, and this included the two residents who remained in their flats during the blast. Traders in the Corn Exchange were not allowed back until 22 July because of the danger of falling glass, and most of them went on to open new shops in the Coliseum on Church Street, on a site where John Wesley had preached and L. S. Lowry had been a rent collector. The Royal Exchange Theatre Company moved to a temporary site on Upper Campfield Market. On 1 November 1996 Marks & Spencer reopened in Lewis's store and in a new food hall on Spring Gardens. The project took 138 days and 500,000 man-hours; 2,000 tins of paint were used and over three acres of carpet laid. A new escalator was built and installed in Lewis's in six weeks.

On 1 July Manchester Millennium, a consortium of city leaders and businessmen, was set up to oversee the rebuilding and recovery process, and on 3 July a £21 million aid package was unveiled by the government, though it came from the UK's allocation of the European Structural Fund for the Greater Manchester, Lancashire and Cheshire programme area. On 10 February 1997 the government announced a £43 million grant to help rebuild the city centre.

On 17 July 1996, at the instigation of the Deputy Prime Minister, Michael Heseltine, an international urban design competition was launched for the master planning of the city centre. The competition was funded by £1 million from the European Structural Fund (money that would not have been spent if it were not awarded to Manchester) matched by the City, plus another £150,000 from the government. The competition attracted twenty-seven entries, from which five teams were shortlisted and given £20,000 and six weeks to prepare more detailed schemes. Each of the teams had provided a range of suggestions to improve the centre of the city, from better public transport, more pedestrianisation and more green spaces to an expanded central shopping core. New considerations for the design teams were that Marks & Spencer's would be demolished and rebuilt, Longridge House would be demolished and the Arndale Centre would remain as an important shopping centre but could benefit from several changes. The

Arndale bus depot would not reopen, so consideration had to be given to how buses travel round the city centre. Here was a chance to develop the centre, and to bring into the retailing sector the neglected area around Victoria Station.

The schemes were submitted by 18 October 1996, and the winning team of EDAW, Ian Simpson Architects, Benoy, Johnson Urban Development Consultants and Alan Baxter & Associates was announced on 5 November 1996.[9] They offered a pragmatic and strategic vision of the rebuilding and, rather than trying to rebuild the city centre, provided a concept of how to work with what was left. Particularly important to the scheme was the opening up of a strategic route to the Cathedral area. 'It would provide the city with a compelling new series of linked pedestrian spaces joining St Ann's Square to the entertainment district proposed for Shudehill. These features combine to make a simple, yet memorable, future city centre.'[10] Building Design Partnership, which had already been commissioned by Marks & Spencer for their new building, was retained to develop the area around the Cathedral and the river Irwell.

In the Royal Exchange the blast – a pressure wave followed by a vacuum – had ripped through the building, severely damaging the dome, lifting it and setting it down in a slightly different position. Fears for the structural integrity of the building, including rumours that the columns had shifted, were, however, unfounded. The office windows and their frames were, of course, damaged, and work was quickly put in hand to restore the Exchange building (Holford Associates with the Broadhurst Partnership as structural engineers).

The Royal Exchange Theatre itself escaped damage. Because the theatre is suspended on a structure that sits on sliding pads inside the supporting piers, and the bottom gallery A frames rest on shock absorbers, the auditorium itself was rocked but undamaged by the blast – even the large glazing panels were unbroken. A National Lottery application had already been made in 1995 for the refurbishment of the theatre and the building of a new acting space, and Lottery funds were applied, together with insurance money, to the refurbishment of the trading hall and redesign of the theatre. Levitt Bernstein were reappointed as architects, again with Ove Arup & Partners and Max Fordham & Partners as the engineering consultants.

The primary space-frame structure of the auditorium was completely rebuilt, and the roof of the module was raised, allowing the installation of a new flying and lighting grid [166]. Major enhancements of the technical performance of the theatre were made, including improved sound, lighting and acoustics, and new seating and air-conditioning have been provided. A new opening roof to the auditorium allows the mixing of the acoustics of the hall and theatre. The theatre is now one of the most technically advanced in the country.

In the trading hall, the maple and black walnut wood-block floor has been relaid, with oak blocks incorporated in a geometrical pattern to respond to the geometry of the theatre, the domes have been restored and reglazed with blue glass, and the columns have been refurbished. Seven sulphur plasma lamps, suspended from the soffit of the hall, reflect light downward via circular glass discs to provide a random pattern of spots on the floor. Amber Hiscott has designed the new coloured glass in the hall and at the entrances, John Fowler

166] Royal Exchange Theatre,
Levitt Bernstein Associates,
1997–98

has created seven tall figures representing the arts for the new Café Exchange and Peter Freeman was responsible for the neon artwork.

A new two-storey, 120 seat studio theatre, the 'Selfridge Studio', has been added to the side of the trading hall for cutting-edge writers and new talent, and all the bars, cafés, booking and backstage facilities, the Craft Centre and Waterstone's bookshop have been redesigned. The main entrance from St Ann's Square has been enclosed in a glass screen, and a glass lift rises to glazed bridges at each level of the building. The total refurbishment bill was around £30 million, of which £20 million came from the Lottery via the Arts Council, £7 million from insurance claims and the theatre's own appeal; the rest came from Europe. The sixty-seven retailers below the hall started to move back in during the summer of 1998, and on 30 November 1998 the theatre reopened, appropriately, with *Hindle Wakes*, the play being performed the night before the bomb.

Next to the Royal Exchange is the new £85 million Marks & Spencer store which opened in December 1999. This flagship store covers the site of the former store and Longridge House (the site was bought within a month of the explosion), and is the largest Marks & Spencer in the world: 25 per cent larger than their Marble Arch store, and with 32,500 m^2 of shopping area over four floors [**167**]. For the architects, Building Design Partnership, the sheer size of the building was one of the factors that determined the built form. The building has a footprint of 65 m by 100 m, about the same size as the Royal Exchange, and internally there are huge floor plates, each floor being 70,000 ft^2 gross and 55,000 ft^2 net. The building is constructed of in-situ concrete (as good in quality as most fair-faced work) and steel. The steel framework, weighing 4,200 tonnes, rises 26 m above the pavement, and the four upper and two basement floors of steelwork were erected by Bovis, the main contractor, in just four and a half months. Because of the size of the scheme, Building Design

167] Marks & Spencer,
Corporation Street, Building
Design Partnership, 1998–99

Partnership used computer-aided design in order to complete the necessary
work within a two-year period; designing the building manually would have
taken the better part of four years.

Externally the building has a rain-screen cladding of Jura limestone, rough
on the ground floor, and polished on the upper floors. But the appearance is
primarily of a glass building, and looking out on St Mary's Gate and on to the
newly created Exchange Square are glazing panels running the height, and
most of the width, of the building. The individual glazing panels are 3,200 mm
by 1,900 mm made up of thick laminated glass. Glass of this thickness and
make-up would normally have a greenish tinge, but specially transparent glass
was made to afford maximum views into and out of the building. Meticulous
care has to be taken in the design of glazing over such a large area, and even
the external metal fixings of the glazing panels have a pitch calculated so that
pigeons cannot perch on them. Unusually for a department store, the building
has four major glazed façades, and the other two façades on Corporation Street
and New Cathedral Street have tall glazed entrance bays, flanked by wide bays
of frosted glass, jutting out from the Jura limestone cladding, with corners of
clear glass for display. The whole of the glazing system is from Italy, and the
elevation cladding is as expensive as anywhere in the country. In recognition
of the site of the building between the Royal and Corn Exchanges, its cornice is
the same height as the Royal Exchange's, and the façade on the New Cathedral
Street side is gently curved to reveal views of the Corn Exchange.

Good permeability was a major design factor and was achieved by means of
a glass-covered *galleria* running through the centre of the building, connecting
Corporation Street and New Cathedral Street. Around the central light well
four wall-climber lifts and fourteen escalators work to each floor. Six staircases
and four customer lifts are placed at the edge of the building, and on the front

face are scissor stairs. Specially adapted lifts, tactile flooring and an induction hearing loop are part of the barrier-free design. Part of the second and third floors will be left empty for future expansion but, even so, there are some 650 staff serving a large customer base. As the shopping population at any one time is expected to be around 11,500, customers need to find their way round easily, and there must be good provision of fire exits. Exceptionally, the whole envelope has been designed to meet fire regulations, thus avoiding the need for fire doors on each floor, problematical in such an open building. This special case, developed with the Fire Research Station at Warrington, is the first of its type and could become the standard for future large stores. That Marks & Spencer have decided to keep a location in the city centre shows loyal determination, though it may be remembered that Lord Sieff was an old boy of Manchester Grammar School.

Running past the side of the new M&S store, New Cathedral Street links St Ann's Square with the Cathedral, and is set to become the backbone of the new city centre. High-quality street furniture, paving of York stone and granite and specially designed lighting reflect the status of what is likely to become one of the country's most expensive shopping streets. The design is by Urban Solutions, a partnership of MEDC, the Council's Engineering Design Department, the Council's Landscape Architecture Department and Jim Chapman of architects R. James Chapman. A large basement area, suitable for articulated vehicles, has been built underneath the Street for loading goods into Marks & Spencer and the shops in Shambles West. A lower basement is used for car parking for M&S and the Shambles West shops.

On the other side of New Cathedral Street, in spring 1999 Prudential Assurance commenced the development of the 1·1 ha site of Shambles West, to replace the concrete square of the 1970s. Here, by Christmas 2001, will be 32,515 m^2 of retail and catering space, 16,700 m^2 of offices and leisure space and eighty-two new homes on fourteen floors (Ian Simpson Architects). A new four-storey department store is to be built on the corner of New Cathedral Street and Exchange Square.

The new civic space of Exchange Square lies on the northern side of Marks & Spencer, bounded by the Cathedral, the Corn Exchange, M&S and the Arndale Centre. The new square, with metal tracks, symbolising the importance of railways in Manchester's history, and glass strips illuminated at night, meets a series of gently graded ramps leading to the Corn Exchange, and links the retail sector with the mediaeval Millennium Quarter. A river bed feature following the line of Hanging Ditch indicates the transition from modern to mediaeval. Seats on the square and the ramps provide resting and meeting places. The square, it is hoped, will become a natural venue for festivals, fairs and other cultural activities. The design was awarded to Martha Schwartz of Massachusetts, who, apparently unaware that palm trees cannot grow in Manchester, had planned stainless steel trees to soften the edges. Corporation Street, too, will become a major walkway with (real) trees, and has been redesigned to take buses, taxis and pedestrians. The street will be opened up to cars at night, to avoid the social problems that come with quiet pedestrianised areas.

168] Corn Exchange, Cannon Street, Ball & Elce, 1889–90, and Potts Son & Pickup, 1904–14

The Corn Exchange [**168**], now called 'The Triangle at the Corn Exchange', has undergone a major restoration which included the replacement of 800 window frames and 1,700 m² of glass for the shattered dome. Repairs to the roof alone required seventy tonnes of steel and the removal of 4,200 m² of slate, 60 per cent of which were reused; 20,000 new slates. The £8 million reconstruction required a 10 km web of scaffolding, and was completed in 500 days. A new interior (and an additional glass dome), designed by Manchester-based architects Ratcliffe Partnership and Mountain Design of Glasgow in close partnership with English Heritage, has a ground-floor atrium and glass escalators rising to a galleried development on five floors. Fifty-five retail units on three floors provide more than 100,000 ft² of high-quality retail space, with a concentration on 'lifestyle retailing', clothes, books and homewear. Frogmore Estates, owners of the Corn Exchange, have also developed the 'Gateway' on the former Jonas Woodhead factory area, between Cheetham Hill Road, Lord Street and Red Bank. The shops looking on to piazzas with cafés, the car park with space for 1,000 vehicles, the Metro and the bus links provide a focus for the long-neglected area north of Victoria Station.

Next to the Corn Exchange, on the corner of Cateaton Street and Cathedral Street, are the two old pubs removed from the Shambles, the Old Wellington Inn and Sinclair's Oyster Bar. The dismantling of the pubs was completed in March 1998, and their rebuilding was completed late 1999. Twenty-five thousand bricks, hundreds of pieces of timber, seats, staircases and panelling were carefully taken apart, and every item was colour and letter-coded, numbered, photographed and stored on computer before removal started. Four carpenters worked constantly on the reconstruction, with Richard Bannister, project manager with Mace, overseeing the £2.5 million removal. The reconstruction and renovation were carried out by William Anelay, a 250 year old specialist company from York. On the other side of the Crown & Mitre hotel, in Hanging Bridge Chambers and 10–12 Cateaton Street, a Visitor Centre has been designed to support the work of the Cathedral, and by October 2001 it will contain a lecture space, a café, bookshop and the Living Cathedral and Mediaeval Exhibitions.

Behind the Corn Exchange, the new City Park is to open in September 2001, and rising from it will be the iridescent glass building of 'Urbis', the building of the modern city. This £28 million building (£20 million came from the Millennium Commission), designed by Ian Simpson Architects, was the winner in an another international competition, and will form a visual and symbolic bridge between the first industrial city and the rebuilding of the centre. From its low entrance to the north this futuristic, glass-clad building rises like the prow of a ship thrusting into City Park. Six floors will be used for exhibits on the history and future of the city. There will be cafés at ground level, and a tower rising through the centre to a top-floor restaurant with views over the city; the foyer will have interactive touch screens and video projections, and an optical camera obscura. Urbis will be fronted by a plaza which will provide an intimate setting for performances associated with Chetham's School, the Cathedral and Urbis itself, and the building will be the focal point of the Millennium Quarter, a £41 million project for land bordered by the Irwell, Corporation Street, Victoria Station Approach and Hunt's Bank.

From the side of the City Park, between the Cathedral and Chetham's School, lawns will stretch to the banks of the Irwell, from which will be a view of the new River Irwell Park and 250 new homes on the Salford side of the river. The new landscaping, developed by Building Design Partnership, will provide much-needed green and open space. Fennel Street will be landscaped to provide a pedestrian route between Urbis and the river. Victoria Street will be narrowed to create a wider pedestrian area, and the arches beneath Victoria Street will be converted into riverside cafés, restaurants and shops.

The Arndale Centre, of course, still stands, and is still one of Europe's largest covered shopping centre at fifteen acres and 1.25 million ft^2, and is visited by

750,000 shoppers per week. It was purchased by the Prudential in January 1998 for £315 million. The refurbishment of the Arndale will provide greater permeability: a new part-glazed roof will create a winter garden on Cannon Street, which will become an all-weather shopping street; the internal 'streets' will be improved and opened up to more light. The face-lift for the interior of the Arndale is to be carried out by Rodney Carran of Chapman Taylor Partners, the architect of the Trafford Centre. Already Boot's (the first store in the Arndale to reopen after the bomb, and the first to complete its rebuilding) have refurbished and enlarged their store and their £14 million renovation has created the largest Boot's in the world.

The new frontage of the Arndale on Corporation Street, designed by the Ratcliffe Partnership, is clad in red brick, sandstone and granite, with metallic panels, glazed walls, glass blocks and high-tech glass and steel canopies. The yellow tiles on this façade, at least, have been banished to memory. The bridge that used to link the Arndale Centre and Marks & Spencer had to be demolished after taking the full force of the bomb blast. A new tubular, twisting glass and steel bridge (Hodder Associates and Ove Arup), using new technology, was erected over Corporation Street in September 1999, and symbolised Manchester's recovery from the events of 1996.

The last piece in this rebuilding jigsaw has been the £110 million conversion (by RTKL Architects) of the area behind the façade of the old Maxwell House building on the corner of Withy Grove into the 'Printworks', a leisure and entertainment centre. In a deal signed in July 1997 developers Don & Roy Richardson, who had already built the Merryhill shopping complex in the West Midlands and Atlantic Wharf in Cardiff Bay, bought the site for £10 million from Shudehill Developments (a joint venture by the CWS and CIS). What was once the largest newspaper printing works in Britain[11] has been transformed into a 300,000 ft^2 site with a twenty-screen UCI cinema multiplex including the north-west's first Imax 3-D cinema, a Virgin family entertainment centre, cafés, twenty-four-hour bars, themed restaurants, shops, a health and fitness centre and a basement night club which holds more people than the Apollo and Palace Theatres put together.

The leader of the City Council, Richard Leese, said, 'We placed a very strong emphasis on developing cultural and entertainment opportunities to broaden the interest and attraction of the city centre. We saw the Shudehill site as a prime location for a large regional leisure and entertainment facility. It will add massively to the diversity of the area, its attractiveness as a place to visit and will enhance its competitive edge.'[12]

A new cobbled street, complete with special weather effects, runs through the Printworks complex, linking the main entrance on Withy Grove with a proposed transport interchange on Shudehill. The transport interchange, bounded by Shudehill, Dantzic Street and Hanover Street, is due for completion in November 2000, and will comprise a bus and coach station and a new Metrolink station with, above, a six-storey car park for 1,000 cars. The building, seen by many as alien to the character of a conservation area, has provoked cries of outrage and calls for a public inquiry.

The rebuilding of Manchester's centre has been a vast undertaking. In the new city centre, by the year 2002, 800,000 ft^2 of retail space, 168,000 ft^2 of office space, 380,000 ft^2 of leisure space, 80,000 ft^2 of cultural and civic space, 283 new homes, twelve acres of new public spaces and 1,020 new jobs will have been created. Moreover, it will have taken £83 million of government and Lottery money, and £350 million invested by the business community, making it the largest renewal project undertaken by any city since World War II. For this work Manchester Millennium and the City Council were awarded the 1998 Royal Town Planning Institute's Queen's Silver Jubilee Cup and the North West Royal Town Planning Institute's John Coaker Cup.

While the terrorist bombing has to be deplored, it provided a unique opportunity to create a brand-new heart and to bring into better use the area around the Cathedral and Victoria Station, and it is significant that design and international competition have played such a large part in the rebuilding of the city. However, it is a pity that it took such a dreadful event to generate a coherent design scheme for the city centre. Birmingham by 1990 had a City Centre Design Strategy which has already produced a vibrant inner city regeneration, and Glasgow followed with its City Centre Public Realm Strategy. But Manchester's *City Development Guide*, based on the *Design Guide for Hulme*, was not published until 1995 and then in only in draft. The *Development Guide* was not followed up, and the IRA bomb supplanted it. The *Supplementary Planning Guidance for the City Centre Bomb Damaged Area* is a technical document rather than a design document. The *Design Guide for Hulme* dealt, of course, with a site with single ownership by the City, but elsewhere in the city multiple ownership means that many of Manchester's planning measures have, of necessity, been piecemeal and concerned with prestige projects. Developments are taking place but are commercially led and there is little sense of an overall design structure being put in place.

At the other end of Deansgate another major leisure and entertainment centre development is taking place – the Great Northern Railway Warehouse project. The 'Great Northern Experience', when completed in 2002, will be one of the country's largest entertainment complexes at 500,000 ft^2. Merlin Great Northern were given the go-ahead by the CMDC in March 1996 to turn the Grade II* listed Great Northern Railway Warehouse site into a business and shopping park, with a new convention centre. CMDC chief executive John Glester said, 'It is the Corporation's clear view that the comprehensive regeneration of the Great Northern site, which has lain largely disused or underused for more than 60 years, is at last achievable through these proposals.'[13] This £100 million development is being carried out by Morrison Developments and Merlin International Properties in conjunction with English Partnerships and Manchester City Council, and provides a leisure and entertainment centre covering more than ten acres. Here will be 70,000 ft^2 of leisure and retail, pubs, cafés, restaurants, 1,000 car-parking spaces and a 40,000 ft^2 civic square.

Objections to the scheme were raised by the Newcomen Society, the Inland Waterways Association, the Council for British Archaeology, British Waterways, the Institution of Civil Engineers, the Railway & Canal Historical Society and

the Victorian Society; it even featured in *Private Eye*'s 'Nooks and Corners' column, 3 November 1995. The development has meant demolishing the Grade II listed carriage ramp, three-quarters of the listed connecting railway viaduct and many buildings in Peter Street. Council leader Graham Stringer said, 'These proposals are bringing more than £100 m worth of investment into the city. If you want to bring investment into a city you have to change things. Just to preserve buildings that are no longer of economic use is not something we should be doing. How many of these protesters actually live in Manchester? How many of these people are unemployed, and what are they doing to bring jobs to Manchester?'[14]

The site was hidden behind buildings on Peter Street and the long façade on Deansgate, which may lay claim to be the longest continuous Victorian façade in the country but offered an impenetrable wall. The demolition of the buildings on Peter Street has opened up the site and now allows views to G-MEX and the Bridgewater Hall [**169**]. On Deansgate the shops and arches have been maintained, and a new opening opposite Camp Street provides access from the west. On the corner of Peter Street a screen wall-tower helps to brace the Deansgate wall and provides a fire exit for the new construction over the arches, including the 10,650 ft^2 Screen Wall Café.[15]

Phase I, the enabling works package for Deansgate North, provided for the refurbishment of the shops on Deansgate, the 10,000 ft^2 Bar 38 café bar and the Great Northern Square, a sunken amphitheatre for open-air performances, operational in 1999. The Great Northern Warehouse itself provides two lower floors of shopping and leisure facilities, with the upper floors used for car parking. Phase II, for Deansgate South, operational by spring 2001, will see the creation of a new 150,000 ft^2 'leisure box' to the south of the warehouse, with a multiplex cinema, leisure and car parking. The ten-storey Great Northern Tower, 100,000 ft^2 of offices on Windmill Street, will be finished by March 2002. Phase III, due for completion in 2002, will see the creation of an hotel on the south end of the site and the refurbishment of Whitworth Street West arches for car parking.

National Car Parks will generate much of the rent for the development, and cinema giant AMC, which promised to provide 'a unique and enthralling out-of-home entertainment experience',[16] signed a deal in December 1998 for a twenty-four-screen, 5,200 seat multiplex, and has thus provided the site with a 200,000 ft^2 anchor tenant. The multiplexes at the Great Northern Experience and the Printworks, together with all the other multiplexes, have made Manchester one of the best provided cities with cinema screens – one screen to each 5,200 residents, compared with Newcastle (9,477), Bristol (10,246) and, bottom of table, Leeds (25,000).

In 1997 the Millennium and Copthorne Hotels Group applied for planning permission for a 219 bedroom, five-star hotel to be erected within and rising from the Free Trade Hall. The architects, R. James Chapman, designed sixteen storeys set in a rectangular block running at an angle of about 45° across the top of the hall, but set back so as to be virtually invisible from Peter Street. English Heritage, the Civic Society and others (including *Private Eye*'s 'Piloti') objected and were branded 'historical hysterics' by the leader of the Council.[17]

The new architects, the Anthony Blee Consultancy, responded with a more sensitive solution, enlarging the size of the hotel by 50 per cent, increasing the number of floors to twenty-four and the beds to 300, but this time set in a cylindrical building 270 ft high, just a little shorter than the CIS tower. The shape was chosen to reduce the apparent bulk; the tower was to be stone-clad to reflect the stonework of the Free Trade Hall. Councillor Leese called it 'an exciting new use for a building that is very dear to many people in Manchester'.[18]

The Civic Society, the Victorian Society, the Royal Fine Arts Commission and others again objected, and as a result of the strong objections put forward by English Heritage, a public inquiry was set up on 21 April 1998. The hotel scheme had the unequivocal backing of Manchester's five MPs, and Tony Lloyd, then Foreign Office Minister, giving evidence to the inquiry, said, 'We believe that the development of the Free Trade Hall as a high quality hotel is totally consistent with the regeneration strategy. The provision of high quality hotel accommodation is a fundamental component of an international standard complex. It will maximise job creation and not require uncertain public subsidy in the short or long term.'[19] Anthony Blee said that architectural interest in the building was only skin-deep, and, as supporters of the scheme have pointed out, only the Peter Street façade is original, the rest was rebuilt in 1951.

However, it was the historical association that the advocates of the development ignored. The very name of the Free Trade Hall marks a significant chapter of England's economic history; it was built on the site of Peterloo; in the Hall in 1905 Christabel Pankhurst and Annie Kelly campaigned for women's emancipation, and from its stage have spoken General Booth, Keir Hardy, Chamberlain, Asquith, Lloyd George and Winston Churchill. So important was its symbolism that in 1920 the Free Trade Hall was bought for £90,000 by the Corporation 'so that the hall should not be lost to the citizens' and, symbolically, it was the first building reconstructed in Manchester after the war. It was the commercialisation of an historically significant site as well as the conversion of the building itself that gave rise to so much concern – one can hardly imagine another city allowing it to happen.

The Deputy Prime Minister, John Prescott, determined against the scheme, and the Free Trade Hall went back on the market. The difficulty remained of finding an appropriate and acceptable use. It has been pointed out that there is no public lecture hall in Manchester, and none of the major learned or professional societies has rooms – but such uses would not pay for the upkeep of so large a building. A museum of Manchester's history has been proposed but, again, the income would probably not meet the costs. The Royal Fine Arts Commission said that hotel use was inappropriate for a building of such historic importance and resonance and suggested turning the Hall into a conference centre, but a brand-new conference centre has been built immediately behind it. It may be asked why the roles of both buildings could not have been reversed. The Free Trade Hall could have been turned into a 1,200 seat conference centre (as had been proposed in 1993 in the *North West Insider* magazine), and many have argued that the 800 seats of the new centre are not sufficient. There is, presumably, logic in it somewhere, and planning considerations are, hopefully, not based solely on the profits to be made from selling important historical sites.[20]

The new International Convention Centre (Stephenson Bell, 1999–2000) is City-driven, and is leased by the Corporation to G-MEX. G-MEX lost out to the Nynex Arena (later changed to the M. E. N. Arena) for pop concerts, and in future will concentrate on international exhibitions and conferences. The new centre links G-MEX and the 500 seat seminar centre designed by Nick Bogle of EGS Designs. It is the UK's first purpose-built convention centre to be linked to an exhibition complex in the heart of a major city centre, and is intended not to rival Birmingham's National Exhibition Centre (that opportunity was lost in 1975) but to rival Glasgow and Harrogate. The centre has a 2,000 m^2 multi-purpose hall and an auditorium of 800 seats. Externally [**170**] the building has a cladding of pink/red sandstone, to reflect the architecture of the Bridgewater Hall, and metal to mirror the architecture of G-MEX.

Lying between the new developments at either end of Deansgate, the old *Manchester Evening News* offices and Crown Square are due to be developed from 2000 onward, by Allied London, in one of the city's largest single development schemes. The twenty-acre site will mean moving the education offices, the legal offices (already vacated), Manchester College of Art and Technology, the *Manchester Evening News* and the Magistrates' Court. Only the listed Crown Court will remain. A new Magistrates' Court will be built on the site, together with a 300 bed, five-star hotel, shops and 60,000 ft^2 of new offices and restaurants. Hardman Street will become a tree-lined boulevard stretching to the river Irwell.

The new developments mean that over 30 per cent is being added to the city's retail stock, and the potential problem with all these new undertakings is that the focus will shift from Piccadilly to the new city centre and the Deansgate corridor. The Corporation is aware of the problem, and in 1997 issued its *Piccadilly Regeneration Study* covering Piccadilly Gardens, Piccadilly Station and the Rochdale Canal and Ashton Canal basins. Schemes by the Council and Railtrack are already under way to develop the station area, to make the station more approachable and to link it with the city centre by a tree-lined boulevard. A new park is planned, along with student housing and shops, all as part of a fifteen-year strategy; Railtrack's £20 million restoration of the train shed was completed in 1999.

Landscaping has already been carried out on parts of London Road, and the refurbishment of the old Joshua Hoyle Building [171] into the four-star 120 bed Malmaison Hotel (Darby Associates, 1998, stonework by Cameron (Northern)) has made a significant improvement to the corner of Piccadilly and Auburn Street. The go-ahead for the development was given by the CMDC in 1996, in spite of complaints that the scheme would mean demolishing the Imperial Hotel, the birthplace of the Professional Football Association. The landscaped gardens at the corner of Gore Street were carried out by So What Arts, supported by English Partnerships, which met the regeneration costs of £2·4 million.

The major objectives of the *Piccadilly Regeneration Study* were 'to significantly upgrade the major area of public space at Piccadilly gardens; to undertake modifications to Piccadilly Plaza to improve its appearance; to make it more manageable and accessible; and to introduce new activity.'[21] The study recommended that the Gardens should be treated as a single entity from Piccadilly Plaza to the north side of Piccadilly and from Lewis's to the Portland Hotel. The space, which should be welcoming, usable and safe, should contain areas for special events and facilities such as an ice rink. Opportunities should be sought for facilities such as cafés, bars and restaurants. Safe pedestrian linkages must be provided, especially to shopping and office areas. To enhance pedestrian flow, an island Metrolink has been provided on Market Street to replace the

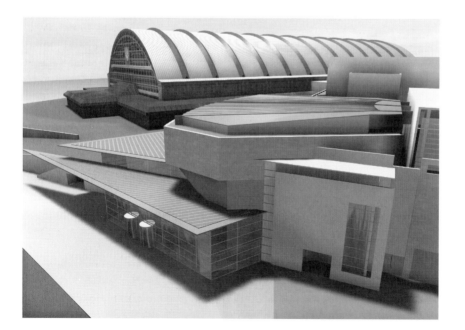

170] International Convention Centre, Windmill Street, Stephenson Bell, 1999–2000. The architect's drawing

171] Joshua Hoyle Building
(Malmaison), Piccadilly,
W. Beaumont & Son, 1906,
and Darby Associates, 1998

original split platforms outside Lewis's and Debenhams, though the Metro still criss-crosses the city's busiest pedestrian street. 'Piccadilly Gardens should be developed as a first class area of public open space. An international design competition can be held to ensure that a space worthy of a major international city is created.' Piccadilly Plaza, said the report, was unlikely to be entirely redeveloped, but steps should be taken to modernise the buildings. 'The podium is considered to be the most negative feature in urban design terms, inhibiting movement and presenting an unattractive, oppressive appearance at street level. Consideration must be given to the economic and technical possibility of removing the podium to the building with access to Piccadilly Hotel, Sunley Tower and Bernard House being brought down to street level.'

This indeed is just what is being done in the Plaza's redevelopment, in the work due to commence in 2000. The Plaza has been bought for £22 million by London-based Portfolio Holdings in what was described by Tom Marshall, deputy chairman of Lambert Smith Hampton as, 'the most significant property transaction in the city in the last five years'.[22] On this two-and-a-half-acre site is an enormous 640,000 ft^2 of lettable space, and the site has been bought on the back of existing income, particularly from the Jarvis Hotel and Sunley Tower, where government offices take up 80 per cent of the floor space and have a lease until 2005.

The architects, Leslie Jones, have drawn up a master plan to restore the Plaza as a landmark property, developed as part of a wider regeneration of the area. The podium will be opened up by means of arcades at ground level, and the polycarbonate roof lights of the 1960s will be replaced by modern glazing. Three floors of retail space will be created in the podium, and the Parker Street shops will be refurbished and upgraded. One of the most significant aspects of the development will be the new major arcade which will open up a new route through the building from Parker Street to York Street. The 40,000 ft^2 Bernard House will be demolished, and Sunley Tower will be overclad. The £50 million refurbishment of the renamed 'Piccadilly Exchange' is unlikely to be completed before 2005.

Piccadilly Gardens, the largest area of open ground in the city centre, will be transformed into a paved area with a fountain, a tree-lined boulevard and a wood (or *bosque*, as the designers prefer to call it), lawns and a horticultural area (flower beds, as they used to be called) and a Gardens Pavilion linked to Piccadilly by a walkway. The designs are by EDAW, Ove Arup and the renowned Japanese architect Tadao Ando. And all these improvements are to be paid for by the erection of a large office block on the Portland Street side of the Gardens, to be built on space given in perpetuity to the citizens of Manchester by Oswald Mosley in the 1750s. The new prestigious office building, which will cut off the view of the Gardens from those arriving from Piccadilly Station, will, according to the Council, 'shut out the noise of car traffic from the Gardens.'[23] Radical redeployment of the buses is to be obtained by rebuilding the bus station on a central reservation on Parker Street, and the Metro lines will remain. It is hoped that the refurbishment of the Gardens will be finished in time for the Commonwealth Games in 2002.

Many people have wanted to pull down Piccadilly Plaza, but in a plea for its survival as an important landmark for Manchester the architect Roger Stephenson has written,

> It is the ultimate act of urban regeneration to take a tired old Victorian warehouse with dry rot, rising damp, dodgy foundations and a leaking roof, and nurture it back into a new life, all for a cost not dissimilar to that of a new building. And yet our society gladly sanctions the demolition of 20-year-old structures for symbolic reasons, with not a thought to the possibility or reworking them or, indeed, the enormous waste of energy and materials caused by such destruction.[24]

But there have been few voices raised in support of the Plaza; the pendulum of history has swung firmly toward the preservation of older structures, and it is the intended reuse of Victorian buildings like the Free Trade Hall and the Great Northern Railway Company's Warehouse that has caused greatest concern among conservationists. And there have been objections to the destruction of buildings in less prominent positions in the city.

On the south-east side of Kennedy Street there are nine listed buildings, including the Grade II* Law Library and the Grade II City Arms and Vine inn, both converted from Georgian town houses. Nos 7–9 Kennedy Street are a Grade II listed building owned by the CIS and in good repair. Nos 28–36 are owned by Trafford Park Estates, have all been empty for over ten years and are in a state of dereliction. On the side of the street where no building is higher than four storeys, a new seven-storey office building (Butress Fuller Alsop Williams), of sandstone, brick and recrystallised glass cladding, is to be erected on the site of these buildings; No. 36 (a charming stone-clad Gothic Revival building, listed Grade II) will be retained, but Nos 28–30 (a four-storey brick warehouse whose only distinctive feature is the sculpted stone heads over the ground floor openings) and 32–4 (the only building in central Manchester with pargeted plasterwork, and listed Grade II, but in very poor condition) will be demolished. According to the architects, it is not possible to keep both listed buildings because existing sill levels would have caused difficulties in aligning with the proposed floor levels. Nonetheless, the demolition of these buildings, and particularly the change of scale on the south side of the street, have caused much concern to preservationists: the north side of Kennedy Street has already been marred by the overshadowing backs of the 1970s buildings erected on Booth Street.

Yet the pressure to upgrade and replace buildings for commercial exploitation has been as strong at the end of the 1990s as at any time. Although there had been a slow-down in office rentals in 1998, a survey based on prime rents in 448 in-town and regional locations across the UK by Colliers Erdman Lewis, London-based property consultants, showed Manchester to be the most expensive and desirable spot outside London, with top sites commanding up to £275 per square foot.[25] But it is particularly in the retail sector that the city has been attracting high rents, and the rent boom adds weight to the forecasts that central Manchester is in line to increase shopping turnover by 41 per cent by 2003 to almost £1·5 billion per year.

However, lack of floor space has long been a problem, and Manchester has had some difficulty in attracting top retail firms because King Street, a preferred site, was virtually full. Many of the ground floors of the banking and insurance buildings in east King Street have been turned into quality clothing retail establishments. The ground floor of Waterhouse's Prudential Assurance Offices, now renamed 'King's Building', has been turned over to clothing retailers DKNY and Jigsaw; Joseph & Patrick Cox have taken the ground floor of the Manchester Club; Emporio Armani is in the old Sun Fire & Life Office and Collezione Armani has taken over the Atlas Building. More retailers are in the ground floor of Cockerell's Bank of England. Casson's NatWest Bank building opposite has been sold to Orbit Developments and is being converted into 40,000 ft^2 of retail and leisure space and 65,000 ft^2 of offices.

On the other side of Cross Street, at 35 King Street, Leslie Jones Architects have converted (1997) a former Grade II* listed bank into two modern retail units for Lincoln National. The original building was retained, the former proportions of the rooms were re-established and a new floor was added to provide three floors of retailing (Red or Dead and Capolito Roma) and one of offices [172]. The building originally had a yard around it, and the modern metal and glass extensions on either side reintroduce an open element. At the rear of the building the architects opened up and repaved the area between the building and St Ann's Church.

Next door, at 41–3 King Street, Buttress Fuller Alsop (1994) designed a new building to replace a listed Georgian building. The existing interior had little of any quality, either spatially or in its details, and the building was not in good structural condition. There was much discussion about keeping the façade, but it was discovered that the Georgian 'plaster' mouldings around the windows referred to in the listing were, in fact, fibreglass of the late 1950s. The new building [172], of grey sandstone with red stone banding, respects its neighbours without being a pastiche, and its 'cornice' and upper two storeys (metal-clad and with stone columns supporting a balcony) bridge the different heights of the buildings on either side – here is a building with a good contextual relationship with the rest of the street.

Manchester, according to Dr Richard Doidge, head of retail research at Colliers Erdman Lewis, is one of Britain's 'super prime centres' for retailers. 'They want to be where the spending is, and the bigger centres like Manchester are getting bigger at the expense of their smaller neighbours.' CEL's figures show the gap between Manchester and surrounding towns widening, though Oldham also saw a 15 per cent growth in rents in 1998. 'Ultimately, the Manchester area could end up with the best of both worlds – the most successful out-of-town shopping scheme in the north of England at the Trafford Centre and the city centre reinforcing its position as the most in-demand retail location outside London's West End.'[26]

The opening of New Cathedral Street and the rebuilding of Crown Square will provide new retailing opportunities, and these are important, for Manchester, together with all the surrounding towns, has to fight for trade in the future with one of the country's largest out-of-town shopping centres. The challenge of the Trafford Centre has probably caused the greatest amount of concern in Manchester and the neighbouring towns.[27]

The Trafford Centre was conceived in 1984, and the Manchester Ship Canal Company (MSCC) submitted a formal planning application to Trafford Metropolitan Borough Council in 1986.[28] The Secretary of State called in the application (as he was obliged to do for any scheme over 250,000 ft^2) and called for a public inquiry into this and two other proposed schemes at Barton Locks and Carrington. In his report of August 1989 the inspector recommended the Trafford Park scheme. 'Any development which provides jobs, and stimulates investment near to those [economic and social problem] areas, is beneficial. In the case of the three main proposals . . . very little or possibly

172] Contextual architecture, King Street. Buttress Fuller Alsop 1994, and Leslie Jones, 1997

no public investment would be required. Surely such an opportunity cannot be turned down.'[29] The Ship Canal Company, after all, was willing to invest £150 million without public subsidy. There were 35,000 unemployed people within a five-mile radius, and the Centre would create some 6,500 permanent jobs (though probably 55 per cent would be part-time) as well as 2,000 construction jobs.

In spite of earlier failures to determine in favour of the application because of the potential congestion on the M63 (now M60), the Environment Secretary, Michael Howard, eventually gave the go-ahead in 1993. His decision was contested in the High Court by the opposing Greater Manchester authorities, but the court found in favour of the development. Appeals went to the House of Lords, which decided in favour of the scheme in May 1995. The retailing climate was less secure in the early 1990s than when the public inquiries took place, and government attitudes changed subsequently, and it is unlikely that another out-of-town centre of such a size will ever be built.[30]

The scale of the Trafford Centre [173] is enormous: 1·9 million ft^2 of space, three miles of shop fronts, thirty restaurants and bars (though it can take up to forty minutes of queuing to get served), a 1,600 seat food court, a twenty-screen cinema, nineteen escalators and forty-three hydraulic lifts. Structurally the Centre is a steel-frame building, designed for speed of fabrication, and the 19,000 tonnes of structural steelwork were erected, by Bovis Europe, in twelve months. The floors are of steel decking with in-situ concrete slabs. The malls are covered by steel arches with double-glazed roof lights, and the central feature dome is 23 m in diameter and 55 m high. The building is clad with over 2 million facing bricks; the floors are covered with 45,000 m^2 of granite and marble from Montignosa and Querleta in Italy, which alone cost £5·8 million.

The Trafford Centre is not a building which will appeal to purists. The rapid succession of architectural styles in the interior – Aztec, Chinese, Classical, New Orleans, Ocean Liner – is bewildering. The retro-classicism of the twenty-two life-size statues by Guy Portelli on the colonnade at the main entrance; the mythical griffins, symbols of the Trafford family, which clutch awkwardly at the rain spouts; the dome murals by Christopher Boulter and Ian Bearman; the Roman triumphal arch with windows and balconies (it's true), are monstrously theatrical. But the theatre has been designed consciously to pull shoppers in – some 30 million per year are expected (only 9 million fewer than the Arndale) – and the Centre has attracted over 300 retail stores, its anchor stores including BhS, Debenham's, C&A and Boot's. Selfridge's have opened their only store outside London – around 200,000 ft² and £20 million, with an ornate central *Gone with the Wind* style staircase.

Rodney Carran of Chapman Taylor was the concept architect, working on the design for twelve years. Carran has designed over thirty shopping centres, including Sheffield's Meadowhall and Lakeside in Essex, and his next project will be redesigning the interior of the Arndale Centre. Leach Rhodes Walker, who won the job in a tendered competition, were the administrative architects developing the contract past the general development and design stage, and had themselves been working on the scheme for seven years. For the Trafford Centre, the architects produced over 3,000 drawings and specifications and had twenty-four people (including interior designers) on site for twenty-seven months. The Trafford Centre opened on 10 September 1998, and cost over £600 million.

There is parking for 10,000 cars, and 'the location, cost and quality of car parking is one of the most significant determinants in influencing where and when people shop. Although public transport can help, the vast majority of customer decisions will centre on the ease and cost of using a car.'[31] The cars have, however, caused enormous congestion on the roads to the Trafford Centre, and a £20 million Metrolink extension has been turned down by the Environment and Transport Secretary, John Prescott, who overruled the planning inspector in spite of his expressed concern to reduce private motoring.

Across the road from the Trafford Centre, the Ship Canal Company intends to build a thirteen-acre Regional Sports Centre, with a large tennis and fitness centre, and the largest indoor five-a-side football pitch in Europe; the £8 million arena will have around twenty pitches. Potential additions will be a hockey or rugby stadium and a golf driving range.

Peel Holdings, the parent company of the Ship Canal Company, are also aware of the development potential of both the Manchester Ship Canal and the river Irwell, and foresee the establishment of a 'little Venice' between the Cathedral and the Trafford Centre. The Irwell, Manchester's main river, has always been hidden from view behind buildings, and as A. P. Simon wrote in 1936, 'It is extraordinary that we have so long tolerated what is no more than an open sewer, but by masking its unsavoury aspects with buildings on its banks and high palisades on its bridges we have quite successfully managed to ignore its existence.'[32] The river is becoming cleaner, and has the capacity to become, as the Thames has, a river highway. As in the nineteenth century, there could be a landing stage at Cathedral Steps for a twentieth-century equivalent of steamers to Trafford Park and Throstle's Nest pleasure gardens. The Irwell and the Ship Canal have the potential to unite rather than divide Salford, Trafford and Manchester.

Already, Manchester and Salford have a new footbridge spanning the Irwell – by Dr Santiago Calatrava, the only bridge by this eminent Spanish architect in the country [174]. Trinity Bridge, with its 41 ft pylon and cable stays, was

174] Trinity Bridge, St Mary's Parsonage, Santiago Calatrava, 1994

175] Trinity Bridge House, Chapel Wharf, Salford, Leach Rhodes Walker, 1998–99. On the left, Aldine House, Leach Rhodes Walker, 1967

commissioned as a result of a joint initiative from Salford City Council and the Salford Phoenix, and was formally opened on 25 September 1995 by the Lord Mayors of Salford and Manchester, symbolising a new and important link between the two cities.

The reason for the new bridge was to help develop the derelict land lying on the Salford side of the Irwell between the river and the railway viaduct, and on this land new offices have been built for the Inland Revenue [175]. Trinity Bridge House, Chapel Wharf, provides over 200,000 ft^2 of office space, and was the first government office project in the country to be completed under the Private Finance Initiative. The building was value-engineered for cost and speed, and it was built and fitted out in just sixteen months. The architects, Leach Rhodes Walker, it may be remembered, also designed the earlier Aldine House complex next door in 1967.

On the side of the Ship Canal in 1998 'The Lowry' commenced building, on twelve acres of ground on Pier 8 of Salford docks. This complex building, by Michael Wilford & Partners and the late Sir James Stirling, will become a notable addition to the area, and is designated as the National Landmark Millennium Project for the Arts, to be completed by mid-2000 [176]. Supported by the Arts Council, the Millennium Commission, the Heritage Lottery Fund, a European Regional Development Fund, English Partnerships, the City of Salford, Salford University and the Trafford Park Development Corporation, the building has attracted a total of £127 million from Lottery, EU and UK public funds and the private sector.

There will be two theatres seating 1,730 and 450 people, three art galleries, one of which will house the world's largest collection (330) of Lowry paintings, as well as facilities for conferences and banquets. A new plaza has been built in front of the Lowry, and on the other side of the plaza the Digital World Centre is being built as an international centre for showcase technologies. The Lowry

176] The Lowry, Salford, Michael Wilford & Partners, 1998–2000. Photograph of the architect's model

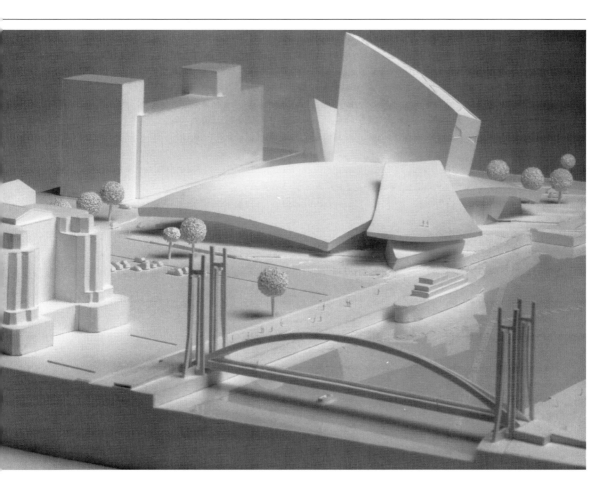

177] Imperial War Museum, Trafford, Daniel Libeskind, 1999–2002. Photograph of the architect's model

project will include a substantial commercial development, including a new hotel, shops, apartments and a unique cinema concept by Warner Villages. The Lowry, it is estimated, will draw up to 2·5 million visitors per year, generate £100 million in private investment and boost the local economy by £4 million per year. The developments on the Quays will also create 6,500 local jobs, and an estimated further 11,000 new jobs in related arts spending.

Opposite the Lowry, a lifting footbridge has been built over the Ship Canal to Trafford Wharf, and it is here that the Imperial War Museum of the North is being built. A remarkable design by Daniel Libeskind, one of the world's most exciting architects (with structural engineers Ove Arup & Partners), the building symbolises a world shattered into fragments by war [177]. The fragments – shards – represent war on land, sea and in the air. The Earth Shard will house the main exhibition area, which will include weaponry and artefacts, media coverage of war from newsreels and television, interactive exhibits and personal stories of people involved in wars. Images of war and peace will be projected on to a 58 m high projection screen on the Projection Shard, which will also house debates, lectures and education facilities. The Water Shard will have a deck-like platform for restaurants and cafés and views to the Lowry. The architect said, 'It is intended to be an enduring memorial to our past and to our future. I wanted to create a building that people find intriguing and wish to visit, yet at the same time also reflects the serious subject of a war museum.'[33]

Trafford beat seventy-one other locations for the museum and its proposals were said by Robert Crawford, director-general of the Imperial War Museum, to be streets ahead of the rest. But after delays and a change of government the Heritage Lottery Fund refused funding 'for the time being' in spite of Trafford's having met all the criteria and having secured more than half the total cost of £36 million from private funds and the European Union. Even Jonathan Glancey in London was concerned at the potential loss of this building:

> It would get people going to Manchester in ways that no amount of fashionable bars and Cool Britannia youth culture could ever do . . . Contemporary Britain, for all the talk from on high about cool, hip, hot, happening design, is awash with polite, dull architecture. We are foolish if we let some of the most inspired designs offered us drop from our limp and slightly damp hands. We have already lost Hadid in Cardiff; let's not lose Libeskind in Trafford.[34]

Eventually the project, which had the support of forty-four local authorities and more than seventy MPs and MEPs, was awarded Lottery funding in January 1999, after the cost had been reduced to £28 million, and a further £10 million was injected by Peel Holdings.[35] Libeskind's Jewish Museum in Berlin attracted huge crowds throughout its construction even before its exhibits were installed, and Frank Gehry's Guggenheim Museum in Bilbao has already had a major impact on that city's tourist trade. The Imperial War Museum will do the same, attracting at least 400,000 people annually. As a result it will generate an estimated £25 million a year in net revenue for Greater Manchester's economy, and create 1,000 new jobs as well as the 350 jobs in its construction. Next door to the War Museum it is hoped to build a museum in memory of the victims of the Holocaust. The Shoa Centre, also designed by Libeskind, will bring together archives preserved by the Manchester Jewish Museum, the National Sound Archive of the British Library and the War Museum, as well as the archives of the local press, in particular the *Manchester Guardian*.

Manchester is also fortunate in having its own attraction, the extension of the City Art Gallery, designed by Michael Hopkins & Partners [178], and won in a competition run with the RIBA (132 architects submitted schemes). This £24 million expansion scheme includes £15 million awarded from the Heritage Lottery Fund, the largest grant outside London. The expansion will give twice as much display area, a new gallery for special exhibitions, and will include the refurbishment of the City Art Gallery and Athenaeum. Included in the work are improvements in the environmental control which will allow much of the gallery's works on paper, including more than thirty Turner watercolours, to be seen, a new shop and a bigger café. The extension, due to open in 2001, is unlikely to add to the job market, but it will add to the cultural prestige of the city.

Manchester is being marketed as the arts and culture capital of the north, and with some justification, for Greater Manchester has thirty-nine art galleries

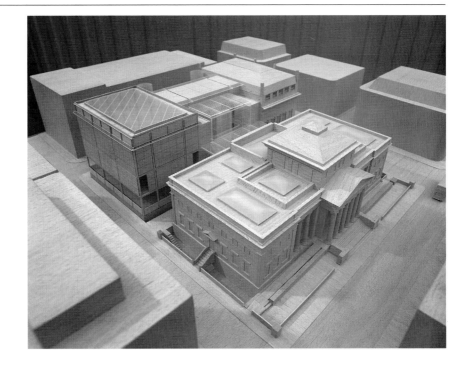

and museums, and permanent collections of film, photography, labour history, Jewish culture and the industrial past. Although the Lowry is being built in Salford, and the Imperial War Museum of the north in Trafford, both buildings will bring enormous tourist income into Manchester itself.

Manchester's Visitor and Convention Bureau has a vision to establish Manchester as a world-class tourism destination, and has the aim of generating substantial economic returns through tourism for the city region. Surprising as it may seem, Manchester is one of the country's top ten tourist spots, with an economy worth more than £419 million per year,[36] and, of the provincial cities, it is now third for tourists, behind Birmingham and Oxford. Granada Studios Tour brings in 750,000 visitors per year, the Museum of Science and Industry attracts 323,690 visitors, the City Art Gallery 231,194 and the Manchester United Tour and Museum 145,150, though these figures pale beside the number of visitors to: Blackpool tower, 1,200,000; Windermere Lake Cruises, 1,131,932; and Chester Zoo, 889,222.

In 1995 the city attracted 520,000 overseas visitors, an 11 per cent increase over 1993, and the spending by overseas visitors leapt by 71 per cent compared with the 1993 figures. But the city needs to attract more wealthy home and overseas overnight visitors: the average day-tripper spends only £11 in Manchester, compared with an average for UK-based staying visitors of £94 per visit and a substantial £408 per visit by overseas guests. The conference market is currently worth £80 million a year to Manchester, and is growing. Conference visitors are worth having; according to the British Tourist Board, the average conference delegate spends £132 per day.

One problem has been that hotel provision has been lacking until recent years. Currently there are only 2,527 three or four-star hotel rooms in the city centre, providing 4,773 beds, and occupancy rates stand at 76 per cent, higher than many European cities like Paris and Brussels. Over the past three decades, city-centre hotels have been created from older commercial buildings, and there has not been a purpose-built hotel in the centre since the Piccadilly Hotel in 1965. However, new hotels are being erected, in recognition of the rapidly increasing demand for accommodation, and these new hotels will double the number of rooms. On the site of Tommy Duck's public house Greenall's have built the Bishopsgate Development, a Premier Lodge hotel (Garnett Netherwood Architects) with 147 bedrooms, a 15,000 ft^2 health club, a 7,000 ft^2 family restaurant and café bar. Jury's Hotel Group have built a 260 bedroom hotel behind the Bridgewater Hall at a cost of £14 million. Even Manchester United has taken advantage of the boom by opening a £5 million 110-bed three-star hotel on land opposite Samuel Platt's off Sir Matt Busby Way. United have invested £500,000 in a 25 per cent stake in the hotel and a £4 million museum of football memorabilia.

Due to be built in 2000, on the brownfield site next to the Odeon in Oxford Street, is AMEC Development's 'Circus', a 240 bed budget hotel with leisure and restaurants below, and a 25,000 ft^2 basement for a health club. The architects, Leslie Jones, have developed a scheme which integrates the façades of the listed (and at present empty) buildings on Portland Street and Dickinson Street with a new façade of brick with stone detailing and exposed steel. In contrast, on the Chapel Wharf site next to Calatrava's Bridge, Rocco Forte is to build Manchester's (or more properly, Salford's) first five-star 160-bed hotel, designed and built by Jarvis Construction UK.

Other hotels are in the pipeline: a Regent Inns development on Quay Street; a 270 room hotel on Whitworth Street West; a 167 room hotel on Faulkner Street; on Princess Street, a 123 bed, four-star hotel, a 250 room development in Asia House, a 126 bed Ibis Hotel in the Marton Building on the corner of Charles Street; on Deansgate a 300 bed hotel based on Northcliffe House; and discussions are under way to turn Telephone House, Portland Street, into the city's first five-star hotel. Councillor Karney, chair of the City Centre Committee, said, 'the developers have done their surveys on market growth and demand and decided that Manchester is the right place to be. There's serious money moving into Manchester and it's becoming a major tourist destination.'[37]

14

INTO THE
TWENTY-FIRST CENTURY

A EUROPEAN CITY

When and if Manchester becomes city-conscious and city-proud, with clean streets, open spaces, clear unpolluted air, with full use of existing amenities and the carefully planned provision of others, Manchester people will want to live in their City once more. [A. P. Simon, *Manchester Made Over*, 1936]

'MARKETING MANCHESTER' was established in April 1996, with backing from Manchester Airport, the Association of Greater Manchester Authorities, the Manchester Chamber of Commerce and Industry, the Visitor and Convention Bureau and Manchester TEC. Peter Heginbotham, a director of Marketing Manchester, said, 'It's impossible to sell the concept of the North West to anybody. Manchester is a brand name, so why not use it? And if it brings in business to Cheshire, Lancashire or even Yorkshire, that doesn't matter. But if you wait for something to happen at regional level, you could wait ten years.'[1]

Manchester has been successful in the 1990s in attracting the right sort of firms and people, and has consolidated the long-held view that Manchester is a stable city in which to invest. The 1990s have seen Manchester re-establish itself as Britain's unofficial second city. 'What is now recognised as the second financial centre in the UK . . . Manchester is now the UK's second city for insurance, leap-frogging Leeds and Birmingham . . . It used to be said that Leeds was the North's major legal marketplace: but not any longer.'[2]

In 1992 a survey of Europe's top twenty-eight cities ranked Manchester third best for availability and value for money of office space and fourth best for cost and availability of staff.[3] The international property magazine *Corporate Location*, in 1993, ranked Manchester second only to Berlin as a favoured business location. In the same year DATAR, the French government's agency for regional development, identified Manchester as eleventh out of 165 cities across Europe in terms of economic importance, ahead of Copenhagen, Hamburg, Stuttgart, Rotterdam, Lyons, Turin and Geneva.[4] Manchester, by 1998, was ranked among the top ten cities in Europe in which to do business, and this made it the only UK city outside London to take its place in the premier league alongside Paris, Madrid, Barcelona and Milan.[5] It appears that one of the aims of the *City Pride* prospectus is being fulfilled: making Manchester a European regional capital – a centre for investment growth, not regional aid. However, Manchester is right on the end of the 'blue banana', the crescent of economically important European cities, and, being on the edge of Europe, needs to ensure its profile is maintained and enhanced.

One of the most important catalysts for the regeneration of the city has been the growth of urban living, but, unlike most major cities in Europe, or older cities in the UK, Manchester's resident city-centre population is still very small. The city lost its urban population during the nineteenth century, and it has taken a long time to get people to return. Ian Nairn wrote in 1960,

> Manchester's mayor may well live in the centre of his city, but he is about the only Mancunian who does . . . [But] the opportunity is there, begging to be used; surely public and private enterprise could combine to create an area that would be not only 'urban renewal' (which so often means replacing lively old dirt by dead new cleanness) but urban awakening. For fifty years now Manchester has been a nine-to-five city . . . it is elegant enough and humane enough to deserve a better fate than that.[6]

Having, in 1960, extolled the use of the Georgian houses in the St John's Street area for use by the potential city-loving population of television actors, producers and executives, Nairn noted in a postscript of 1967 that these houses had indeed been utilised, but as offices for professionals. Manchester's opportunities for living in the city had still not been taken.[7]

There were difficulties in the late 1960s and 1970s in obtaining mortgages in inner-city areas; lenders were reluctant to offer mortgages on any pre-1919 housing. There were no new properties until 1979, when Wimpey created 172 private dwellings at St John's Gardens, on Council-owned land between Byrom Street and Deansgate, close to Granada Studios. It was hoped that this would become Manchester's Mayfair, attracting businessmen, and media people, particularly from Granada. On top of the Arndale Centre sixty flats and maisonettes were built, and, off Tib Street, the Council built a small housing complex. But, apart from these three schemes, there was little inclination or opportunity to live in the city centre for a further ten years.

In 1989 Halliday Meecham Architects designed Granby Village, off Whitworth Street, for Wimpey Homes [179]. Granby House, a former cotton warehouse, was converted into sixty-two apartments, and became the focus of an £11 million scheme, part funded by an Urban Regeneration Grant, which provided 211 homes in three converted buildings and two new six-storey mansion blocks, all set round four squares. At the same time the Northern Counties Housing Association converted India House into rented apartments. On Chepstow Street, Beazer Homes was transforming Sam Mendel's old warehouse into Chepstow

179] Granby House and Orient House, Granby Row, G. H. Goldsmith & Son, 1911 and 1914. Part of Granby Village, Halliday Meecham, 1989–95

House; underneath two new atria, seventy-six apartments on five floors were created in seventeen different designs, each named after a British painter.

These three schemes were created as initiatives by the CMDC, and the first grant-aided scheme from CMDC to get under way was Piccadilly Village (Halliday Meecham, 1990–94), by Moran Holdings and Trafford Park Estates. Between Piccadilly Station and Great Ancoats Street 125 houses, fifteen craft studios, six shops, 16,000 ft^2 of offices and a public house were erected on a secure site overlooking the Ashton Canal basin.

Since the mid-1990s city-centre living has become increasingly fashionable, and large numbers of disused buildings throughout the city are being converted into apartments for sale. Typically, for Baltic plc, Ian Simpson Architects have converted the former Grand Hotel in Aytoun Street (once the Collie & Co.

warehouse, and an hotel from 1880 until the early 1980s), into the Grand, with apartments ranged round a glazed atrium above the former ballroom. Galleries around the atrium have views down to a courtyard garden. Prices ranged from £50,000 to £300,000 (almost the price of a new five-bedroom detached house in Altrincham), and people queued overnight to ensure their place.

At 109 Princess Street, Stephenson Bell converted an 1863 Clegg & Knowles warehouse into thirty apartments for Crosby Homes (see [30]). The first-floor flats are *pieds-à-terre*, but, to take advantage of the 4·1 m ceiling heights, the architects have inserted a mezzanine 'servant pod', with integrated kitchen, bathroom, bed deck and wardrobe. The fourth story was too low for accommodation, so a raised metal roof runs round the building like a continuous dormer, with windows or cut-backs for balconies for penthouses. On the ground floor are retail outlets and, of course, a bar.

In 1998 Manchester had over 1 million ft^2 of empty space in old office blocks, and increasingly these have been converted into apartments as the demand for offices has slowed. In the former Royal & Sun Alliance building in St Mary's Parsonage, and in the adjoining National Building and its 1968 glass-fronted addition, Century House, Nicholson Estates (design, Assael Associates) have created luxury apartments which include the most expensive in the city – in the summer of 1999 a two-storey, two-bedroom penthouse was being offered for £1 million. New homes, too, have been erected in the city centre, like Bridgewater Bank, Great Bridgewater Street, Bellway Homes' flagship development.

City-centre living has now become the *dernier cri*, particularly with young professionals, the DINKYs (dual income, no kids yet). It has been estimated that between 1993 and 1999 more than £100 million has been invested in residential city-centre property, and more than £150 million worth of new city homes are under construction. More than 5,000 new homes in the city centre, and 11,400 within a two-mile radius, are possible by the turn of the century.[8] There is even a local newspaper, the *Manchester Resident*. For the first time in over 150 years the city is being reclaimed for people, and Manchester's regeneration can stand comparison with anywhere.

Manchester is being marketed as a vibrant, exciting, appealing city region with a strong, managed image, and by the time the Commonwealth Games are staged it intends to become a twenty-four-hour city. It has long enjoyed a buoyant night life, not least because of its enormous student population – at over 45,000, more *per capita* than any city in Europe. The night life until the mid-1990s centred on the clubs, and the pre-club pubs. But that has changed. Manchester's music scene may not be as vibrant as it was in its heyday in the 1980s, when Rod Stewart claimed Los Angeles, London and Manchester as the best music venues in the world, though it is still thriving. The icon of 1980s music, the Haçienda, closed in June 1997, when its licence was revoked following a series of drug-related attacks on clubgoers. Rob Gretton, who owned the building, put it up for sale at £1·2 million and it was bought in August 1998 by G. R. Morris Construction, the company responsible for building the Quay West development in Trafford Park. The old Haçienda building is to be converted in 2000 under a £5 million scheme into thirty-one apartments, with the obligatory penthouse on top, offices, restaurant and café bar. It is this change from night club to restaurant and café bar which is illustrative of recent trends in the city. What more than anything has marked out the 1990s is the proliferation of places to eat and drink.

The year 1989 was significant, for it marked the opening of Dry 201 and Manto's, the first café bars in Manchester. Ben Kelly designed Dry 201 in the same bare, industrial style as his design for the Haçienda, and here on Oldham Street was the first regeneration of an area which had lain underused and unloved since its shops moved to the Arndale.

Manto's, another conversion of an older building (Benedict Smith Architects), was provided with a balcony and large doors and windows to see out and to be seen in [180], and its customers spilled out on to tables and chairs in Canal Street – Manchester's first step toward a Continental café life. The Rembrandt and the Union public houses have had a gay clientele since 1940, and the licensee of the Union was imprisoned in 1965 for 'outraging public decency' by

180] Manto's, Canal Street, Benedict Smith Associates, 1989

running a public house in which gay men were welcome. It was renamed the New Union after his release. Napoleon's night club became the headquarters of the gay scene in the 1970s, but it was not until the Central Manchester Development Corporation repaved the streets, improved the lighting and provided grants for cleaning the buildings on Canal Street that the Gay Village started to form its present identity. That there has been strong support from the CMDC and the Council is unsurprising, since the village has 20,000 visitors every weekend, and the August Mardi Gras attracts well over 100,000 visitors – the pink pound is worth a lot to the city.

By 1999 the village had over 2,000 permanent residents and the first gay shopping mall in the UK, the Phoenix Shopping Centre. It is a sense of identity and place that has created the village, and the increased number of people using the area has in turn created commercial interest. On Canal Street, Greenall's, who already owned Churchill's pub on Richmond Street, built Via Fossa (and are building another pub on Bloom Street) and this was joined by Castro, Velvet, Bar 38, the Belgian Mussel Bar and Hale Leisure's Prague V, who also opened their Berlin Bar on Bloom Street. Oliver Peyton's Mash and Air (designed by Marc Newson and Harrison Ince) was opened on Chorlton Street in 1996. There are already twenty pubs, restaurants and café bars in the village, and Carol Ainscow, who owns Manto's and Paradise, is to develop a £10 million mixed development on Sackville Street which will include twenty-five new apartments, a gym and health club, hotel and art gallery, a small café bar and four new restaurants.

The growth of leisure outlets throughout the city has been remarkable; café bars, restaurants or pubs (the boundaries between them are becoming increasingly blurred) have been inserted into the ground floor of almost any building with space, and what characterises them are large windows and, where there is room, tables and chairs set out on the street. Café life in the European manner has come to Manchester, and these new outlets are earning money for their landlords. On Peter Street, which already had a Prenez, Joop and Hullabaloo, three new bars have been created, undoubtedly to take advantage of the opening of the Great Northern Experience opposite. Albert Hall (once a Methodist Hall) has been refurbished for Chestergate Seddon and they have leased it for twenty-five years, at a commencing rental of £220,000 per annum, to First Leisure. This new Brannigan's bar, a cross between bar and night club, is seen as a complementary operation to their Royales Discotheque farther up Peter Street.

Chestergate Seddon also acquired the adjoining property, the Grand, and pre-let it to Marsden Thompson Evershed plc and Life Restaurants on a twenty-five-year lease, at £170,000 per annum, for a new Life Café (architects, Downs Variava). The Fourth Church of Christ Scientist, which used to be in the building, moved to 40 Peter Street opposite, another Chestergate Seddon building. The Albert Hall and the Grand were both forward sold to Abbey Life Assurance for £5·7 million. Next door a theme bar, The Square, was built by Greenall's on the site of the former Bauer Millet car showroom.

Brewers have poured a massive amount of money into Manchester: Bass, Greenall's, Wetherspoon's, Whitbread and Yates have investments which run into millions of pounds. Wetherspoon's Moon Under Water, converted from the former Deansgate Cinema, is in the *Guinness Book of Records* as the largest pub in Britain; the 820 m^2 pub can cater for 1,700 customers and employs sixty staff. The number of clubs in Manchester fell from a peak of ninety-five in 1987 to sixty-seven in 1997, but the number of restaurants rose from 204 to 269 in the same period, and there were almost a hundred more pubs. There were, in 1997, 365 inhabitants to every on-licence (in a population of 430,818), and the number of restaurants, cafés and pubs has increased significantly on these figures since. Manchester's diners, pubs and clubs already account for more than 5,000 jobs and generate an annual turnover of more than £140 million.[9]

More people are eating out, and this is a reflection both of the increasing spending power of the people who work and live in the city, and the availability of places to eat. Manchester is on a roll, according to Paul Heathcote, who took over Elliot House in 1996 for his restaurant, Simply Heathcote's. 'Manchester has changed in the last ten years: quality and excellence have always been wanted but only a few had been able to deliver. Now things are changing fast, Manchester's expectations are great, and the restaurants and bars of the city are growing with them.'[10]

Bruntwood Estates, who refurbished Elliot House, have also restored the Reform Club; it is now called the Manchester Club, and is home to Bernard Carroll's Reform Restaurant, designed in conjunction with Spice Design of London (Bernard Caroll is the brother of Francis Carroll, who ran the successful Brasserie St Pierre on Princess Street). Some smart London names have already joined the Carrolls, Paul Heathcote and Oliver Peyton in Manchester: Mark Jason Holmes, Young Chef of the Year in 1987, is running the Royal Exchange Restaurant, Gary Rhodes is in charge of the directors' restaurant at Manchester United's ground and the restaurant in United's new hotel. Although Bill Wyman closed his Sticky Fingers restaurant in 1999 in order to concentrate on his London outlet, there will be a Hard Rock café in the Printworks, and Sir Terence Conran will open a large restaurant in the Triangle at the Corn Exchange.

It is round the edges of the centre, however, that some of the most interesting restaurants and bars have been set up. In 1992, in the old Library and Market Building on Deansgate, Dimitri Griliopoulos took a gamble in opening his Greek restaurant and café bar, and has now been joined by Jowata, Manchester's only African restaurant. For the Atlas Bar, under the railway arches next to Deansgate Station, Ian Simpson Architects, in 1994, converted a car repair shop into a café bar/restaurant [181] using simple plywood cladding to the arches and reclaimed floorboards which run through to a small terrace at the rear of the bar, designed by Landscape Projects. The bar is part owned by Ian Simpson and Nick Johnson, both members of the master-planning team for the new city centre. On the other side of Deansgate is their newly opened Delicatessen, one of only two in the city centre, worth visiting for its smells alone.

At the side of the Bridgewater viaduct, and signalled by its tower block, which contains flats for the bar manager and landlord, is Quay Bar (Stephenson Bell, 1998, for Banks's Brewery), one of the few new bars in Manchester to

181] Atlas Bar, Simpson Associates, 1994

182] Quay Bar, Bridgewater Viaduct, Stephenson Bell, 1998

be built as a contemporary building [**182**]. The steel-framed building sits on steel beams spanning the Duke of Bridgewater's tunnel, and on the canal side of the building glass panels, set in horizontal steel members, rise through the double-floor height of the bar area. The glass panels are set out at angles, using gnomic geometry – the geometry that shapes nautilus shells – and the returns of the angles are made of coated stainless steel panels. Huge doors open from each of the metal-clad returns. All this was very expensive, but the choice of materials and shapes reflects the canals, bridges and viaduct, paying heed to the nineteenth century, but not copying it.[11] Quay Bar won the 1998 RIBA Award for Architecture, and in 1999 the building was short-listed for the RIBA's Stirling Prize, the most prestigious architectural award on offer – a notable achievement, beaten in the north-west only by Steve Hodder's winning of the prize in 1997 for his Centenary Building for Salford University.

183] Barça, Catalan Square, Harrison Ince, 1996

184] Eastgate Building, Castlefield, conversion by Stephenson Bell, 1992

In Castlefield's newly created Catalan Square is Barça, a bar designed in 1996 by Harrison Ince for Mick Hucknall of Simply Red [183]. Built under a railway viaduct, and in keeping with its industrial surroundings, Barça uses steel, brick and glass blocks to create a two-level modern Manchester bar, though the Spanish name belies its contents. Situated on Lock 92, Duke's Lock, at the junction of the Bridgewater and Rochdale Canals, Jim Ramsbottom has created a public house, Dukes 92 (Stephenson Bell, 1992), from the stables of the Merchants' Warehouse.

Jim Ramsbottom has been one of the most influential figures in the development of Castlefield. An ex-bookie turned property developer, he developed the Eastgate office complex from Lamb's old furniture manufactory (Stephenson Bell, 1992) [184], and foresaw the potential of the area long before anybody else.[12] Ramsbottom bought the Merchants' Warehouse – the oldest extant canal warehouse in the city – in 1983, for £25,000, the scrap price of the bricks and timber. In 1996, with £4 million in grant aid (from the CMDC, English Heritage and the EU Regional Development Fund) and private money, the building was converted into studio spaces and offices by Ian Simpson Architects (see [6]). The internal structure was maintained, the catheads on the street side and the shipping holes on the canal side were glazed, and new glazed extensions were added at the sides to provide stairs and lifts.

On an arm of the Bridgewater Canal, the Middle Warehouse, now called Castle Quay [185], was restored in 1992 as flats, offices, retail units and a café. In this £6 million scheme the loopholes have become balconies, and the catheads have been restored and glazed. Behind the elliptical strainer arch with its two shipping holes is the home of Piccadilly Radio.

On Slate Wharf are Bridgewater House and Irwell House, new developments by Macbryde Homes, and in a converted warehouse is Greenall's Jackson's Wharf, opened in August 1998, and internally like a smaller version of its Via Fossa on Canal Street. Linking Slate Wharf with Catalan Square is the unique

65 m long thin, curved torsion structure of Merchants' Bridge [**186**]. The bridge was commissioned by the CMDC, and a key paragraph of the brief was that 'The new bridge . . . should be unambiguously a design representative of the late 20th century which will contribute another stratum to the historic layering which is a feature of Castlefield, and which will reflect the changing pattern of uses that the area is now undergoing.' It is all the more gratifying that this bridge, designed by structural engineers Whitby & Bird, has been selected for a Millennium Product Award.[13]

At the very edge of Castlefield, off Hulme Road, Urban Splash (who have been involved in almost £100 million of housing projects) have converted Britannia Mills – six original buildings of an emery-paper factory clustered round a central courtyard – into a complex of 125 loft-style apartments. And city-centre living now extends far outside the centre. At 384 Chester Road (ten minutes' walk from Castlefield) NSJR Architects completed their conversion of a Victorian warehouse, in March 1999, to loft-style apartments complete with a cobbled courtyard, fountains and a spiral staircase.

At Castlefield a brand-new community has grown on ground where no one lived before. The area was first identified for development in 1979, but it was not until 1993 that Building Design Partnership was appointed by the CMDC to prepare a regeneration framework incorporating the canals, railway viaducts, the Museum of Science and Industry and Granada Studio Tours. The framework was intended to help revitalise the area by promoting tourism, creating new jobs, establishing a vibrant residential community and using and refurbishing historic buildings. Castlefield had the advantage that it lay neglected and fallow for most of fifty years – consequently the developments of the 1960s to the 1980s had passed it by. It is now an important part of the renaissance of the city; between 1988 and 1995 more than £60 million of private and public-sector money was spent on Castlefield, and the area now attracts more than 2 million visitors per year.

Next door to now trendy Castlefield is Knott Mill, for long one of the forgotten parts of the city, but where, significantly, Paul Butler Associates, James R. Chapman, Harrison Ince, Hodder Associates, Johnson Urban Developments, Ian

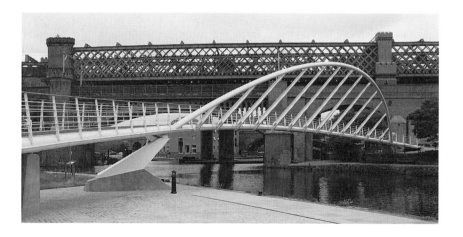

186] Merchant's Bridge, Castlefield, Catalan Square, Whitby & Bird, 1996

Simpson Architects and Stephenson Bell all have their practices in converted Victorian warehouses. In Knott Mill the refurbishment by these local practices of old premises into offices, apartments and even a recording studio is bringing life back into the area.

And there are signs that bigger players are now becoming interested. On Knott Mill Bridge, Crosby Homes are building 104 new apartments in four blocks, connected by glass atria, and spanning the Old Basin of the Bridgewater Canal on the site of the original Duke of Bridgewater's Warehouse [187]. Stephenson Bell have designed a complex of glass, brick, red terracotta rain-screen panels and stainless steel having a resonance with the industrial archaeology around and a family relationship with their Quay Bar on the other side of the Bridgewater viaduct. This is a difficult site, but it is precisely the sort of area which needs to be developed if new life is to be brought back into the city centre.

On Whitworth Street West is the Deansgate Locks Project, the conversion (by EGS Designs for Westport Developments, and supported by English Partnerships), of eight railway arches into a boardwalk of yet more bars, shops and restaurants. This project will help to link Knott Mill with the rest of the city centre.

In the past, developments in the city have mostly been around the commercial and shopping cores, but now it is areas like Knott Mill and the 'Northern Quarter' which are slowly being revived, and the pace of their regeneration is quickening. The Northern Quarter, an area bounded by Back Piccadilly, Shudehill, Great Ancoats Street and the Arndale Centre, has, like Knott Mill, for too long been a fringe location. Yet it has a vibrant community, with five café bars, of which Café Pop is possibly the only non-alcoholic café in the city, four restaurants, including the Market Restaurant (mentioned in the *Good Food Guide*), five pubs, which include the Hare and Hounds and Smithfield Hotel (both in the CAMRA *Good Beer Guide*), a delicatessen, specialist shops (housing many of the traders who were forced out of the Corn Exchange), a Craft Centre (in the remaining trading hall of the 1872 Fish Market), jazz clubs, Alcoholics Anonymous and the headquarters of the *Big Issue*. It even has its own resident artist, Liam Curtin, who has led the creation of thirty-four works of public art in the quarter for rather less money than the cost of the cotton-bud in St Ann's Square.

187] Knott Mill, housing, Stephenson Bell, 1999–2000

The Northern Quarter Association (NQA) was formed in 1993 from a group of shopkeepers, artists, night-club owners and residents, and is chaired by an architect, Dominic Sagar. After members of the City Council were invited to visit the regenerated Spitalfields in London with members of the NQA a £10,000 viability study was undertaken which eventually resulted in a brief being sent out to developers to tender for the site of the former Smithfield Market (once of a size to rival London's Covent Garden, and demolished in the 1970s for car parks). To the credit of the Council, the NQA was involved in drawing up the brief, undertook consultations on the shortlisted proposals, and its chair even had a vote on the final selection panel. Urban Splash put a scheme forward, as did Harrison Ince, who proposed an energy-efficient housing scheme which would use surplus energy from the CIS building. The chosen developers were Crosby Homes and AMEC Developments, who have committed themselves to work with the local community to provide a mixed-use and innovative development. At the time of writing, building work has yet to commence.

There has already been a successful transformation of a building on Oldham Street. Opposite Dry 201, the Smithfield Building has been converted into loft apartments for Urban Splash (Stephenson Bell, 1998). Originally the old Affleck & Brown premises, and then British Home Stores, there were nine separate buildings, clustered around a rectangular court. It has been turned into an atrium space, or winter garden [188], which, because of its natural ventilation, is designated for fire and building regulation purposes an external space. This has allowed the bedrooms to open into the internal access galleries, overlooking the internal 'street'. Here are eighty loft apartments of one to four bedrooms with double and triple-height spaces. On the ground floor are thirty-one specialist shops, in the basement is a gym, and an upper walkway connects a multi-storey car park. For this £10 million conversion (including a £3 million grant from English Partnerships) Urban Splash won the *Sunday Times/What House* Best Urban Renewal Company award, a British Urban Regeneration award, and the architects were awarded the 1998 Housing Design Award.

Next to the Northern Quarter, in a 5.5 ha scheme bounded by Ducie Street, Great Ancoats Street and Dale Street, Ian Simpson Architects have submitted a mini-Castlefield development, with five retail units, 143 flats, shops, a pub and 976 car-parking spaces, all centred around the Rochdale Canal basin. Two Grade II buildings, Brownsfield Mill and Jackson's Warehouse, would be refurbished, the canal would be restored and new housing built round the canal basin with space for mooring boats. The proposals have been approved by the Planning Committee but are still (in 1999) awaiting a decision by the Secretary of State for the Environment.

On Great Ancoats Street, in a very different development, Manchester Ship Canal Developments have been granted permission for phase two of the Central Retail Park, a mixed retail and leisure scheme, including a sixty-four-bed hotel, and drive-through and fast-food restaurants.

All these projects are in the so-called 'Crescent of Change' which links the developments around Victoria Station with the Eastlands site of the Commonwealth Games. A successful £5.7 million Single Regeneration Budget II bid

88] Smithfield Building, Oldham Street, Stephenson Bell, 1998. The 'winter garden'

prepared by the Miles Platting Ancoats and Northern Quarter Regeneration Partnership will push forward the development of the area over the next few years and seed investment where it is desperately needed. Although huge amounts of public and private-sector money have gone into the regeneration of parts of the city, it is worth remembering that Manchester is still third in the National Deprivation rankings and, outside the central core, still has a large urban poor.

There has already been massive capital investment in the Ancoats Conservation Area by Express Printers, especially in their refurbishment of the *Daily Express* building (see [92]). The building became redundant in the mid-1980s, but Peter Pemberton of Express Printers decided to stay, still employs 200 people and prints 7 million newspapers per week. The Grade II listed building (one of few modern buildings to be listed) was refurbished inside and out to create a 75,000 ft^2 office complex over seven floors. Thirty million pounds was invested in new plant and buildings at the rear. The building itself has taken £7 million, including £2 million via a City Grant, to refurbish internally and externally: new internal light well and enlarged floor plates, new black double-glazing.

In 1998 the Prince of Wales, addressing the Urban Village Forum in Manchester, said, 'There is a great deal of talk about so-called sustainable development these days, and I'm pleased that this is so. Yet it is so very much more important to turn words into action, and to demonstrate to a still sceptical planning, property and financial world, that our villages, towns and cities can be wonderful places to live, work and play, if only we take care to plan for a human scale of activity.'[14] Architect Ian Finlay (whose office is in Ducie Street) has a vision of an urban village for Ancoats, the restoration of a lively community in the longest-ignored and still the poorest part of the city. His concept is shared by planners Paul Butler Associates and Marylin Steane, one of the best champions Eastside Regeneration has had. New uses will be encouraged, ranging from residential and commercial use on the upper floors of buildings to retail, cultural and leisure uses on the ground floors to encourage street activity. The Beehive Mill, Jersey Street, has already been converted (Provan & Makin, 1996, for Joseph Sternlight, who purchased the mill in the late 1980s) for use by the media and music industry, and is home to Eastside Regeneration. But that is just the beginning. The area fronting the Rochdale Canal, where many of the historic mills are located, will be the key to the development of the village [189]. The central part of Ancoats will be regenerated by the development of 'Little Italy', in commemoration of the Italian community which became established in the 1880s,[15] and a key step will be the creation of two *piazzas* around Blossom Street [190] and centred on Isaac Holden's now disused St Peter's Church.[16]

From being the most neglected, run-down and poverty-stricken area of Manchester, Ancoats has already taken the first steps toward regeneration and recognition. Royal Mill, New Mill and Paragon Mill have been placed on the Buildings at Risk Register (together with the Islamic Academy in Chorlton-on-Medlock and the Victoria Baths, Longsight).[17] Clare Hartwell, of English Heritage, chose Gorton Monastery (E. W. Pugin, 1863–67) to launch the list on 29 May 1998. The Duke of Bridgewater's canal at Worsley, Ancoats and Castlefield has been proposed by the government to UNESCO as potential World Heritage Sites. It is significant that the very structures which helped to create

189] The mills on Redhill Street, Ancoats, as they may become. Ian Finlay, 1996

190] Little Italy, Ancoats. The vision. Ian Finlay, 1996

Manchester's early wealth are now being given such prominence as symbols of its past, and it is fitting that this study ends on the buildings with which it began.

This chapter does not mark the end of change in Manchester. There are developments which are still under wraps, though they will not be on the same scale as the changes of the 1990s. What impact the new Regional Development Agency will have on future funding is unclear. Whether the Commonwealth Games will add to the prestige of the city, or will merely leave a legacy of debt, will not be known until after 2002. The need for the city centre to be re-created will, hopefully, never occur again, here or anywhere. This book was stirred into life by that event, yet there has probably not been a better time to write about the city since the end of the nineteenth century; it is today as vital, enthusiastic and forward-looking as it was then. Only time will tell whether the momentum will continue. Meanwhile:

> Manchester is beginning to look and feel like a European city. Magnificent warehouses from an earlier age are being converted into modern loft apartments and offices. Railway arches are being turned into café bars and shops alongside the canals. The city centre trams give a continental European look. Residential developments in areas such as Castlefield on the edge of the city . . . are luring people back into the city to live. Manchester is shaking off its dirty industrial image . . . Business people outside the city are already saying it is an attractive place to invest.[18]

NOTES

CHAPTER 1   AD 70–1800: FROM THE ROMANS TO THE CANALS

1 For a detailed account of the site see G. B. D. Jones and D. Rhodes, *Historic Castlefield*, 1979.
2 *The Manchester Historical Recorder*, 1875, p. 11. The requirements were repealed by an Act of Parliament in 1759.
3 T. S. Willan, *Elizabethan Manchester*, 1980, p. 6.
4 Quoted in *The Manchester Historical Recorder*, 1875, p. 24.
5 Daniel Defoe, *A Tour through the Whole Island of Great Britain*, [1724–26] 1971, p. 544.
6 Details of the Infirmary are given in the *Builder*, 19 September 1846, p. 452.
7 *Ibid.*, 9 December 1848, p. 589 refers to the new site.
8 A history of St Mary's is given in Penny Leach, *St Mary's Hospital, Manchester, 1790–1990*.
9 J. Aston, *A Picture of Manchester*, 1816, p. 136.
10 The design may have been by William Blackburn, who built radial prisons in Ipswich (1785–90) and Liverpool (1787–89), both based on the Maison de Force, Ghent, which had been described in detail by John Howard in *The State of the Prisons*, 1777. Howard Colvin's *Biographical Dictionary of British Architects*, however, does not list Manchester among Blackburn's work.
11 In 1720 an Act of Parliament was passed for making the Irwell and Mersey navigable to Liverpool. Between 1720 and 1730 the Mersey and Irwell were made navigable up to Hunt's Bank. The Mersey & Irwell Navigation Company was taken over in 1779 by the Bridgewater Canal Company.
12 Aston, *Picture*, p. 226 n.
13 For the social history of the early canal buildings see Derek Brumhead and Terry Wyke's ' "The Duke's Agents have made a Wharf": Castlefield and its Warehouses', in Robina McNeil and A. D. George, eds, *The Heritage Atlas 3: Warehouse Album*, 1997, and *A Walk round Castlefield*, 1989, by the same authors.
14 Ronald Brunskill, *Brick Building in Britain*, 1997, is an invaluable book.

CHAPTER 2   1800–40: THE OPEN TOWN

1 See Mike Williams, *Cotton Mills in Greater Manchester*, 1992, pp. 51, 52. Mike Williams and his collaborators have provided a comprehensive discussion of mill construction in Manchester, and the author is indebted to this source.
2 Quoted in Michael M. Edwards, *The Growth of the British Cotton Trade, 1780–1815*, 1967, pp. 188–9.
3 Records of the firm are preserved in the John Rylands Library, but see also C. H. Lee, *A Cotton Enterprise 1795–1840*, 1972 and McConnel & Co., *A Century of Fine Cotton Spinning 1790–1906*, 1906.
4 Edwards, *Growth*, p. 13.

5 Quoted in Lee, *Cotton Enterprise*, p. 102.

6 Quoted in Edwards, *Growth*, p. 22.

7 Leon Faucher, *Manchester in 1844*, [1844], p. 146.

8 J. Aston, *A Picture of Manchester*, [1816], p. 228.

9 An earlier MacIntosh mill in Chorlton-on-Medlock was destroyed by fire in August 1838, with the loss of three lives.

10 Edwards, *Growth*, p. 188.

11 Andrew Ure, *The Philosophy of Manufactures*, 1835, p. 32.

12 William Pole, ed., *The Life of Sir William Fairbairn, Partly Written by Himself*, 1877, p. 115.

13 Fairbairn was President of the Institution of Mechanical Engineers in 1854. He was awarded the Royal Society Gold Medal in 1860, became President of the British Association in 1861, gained an honorary LL.D. from Edinburgh in 1860 and another from Cambridge in 1862. He declined a knighthood in 1861, but accepted a baronetcy in 1869. His publications included: *Report of William Fairbairn, Esq. C.E., on the Construction of Fireproof Buildings*, Liverpool, 1844; *On the Application of Cast and Wrought Iron to Building Purposes*, London, 1854; *Treatise on Mills and Millwork*, two volumes, London, 1861–65; *Iron: its History, Properties and Processes of Manufacture*, Edinburgh, 1861.

14 A history of the firm can be found in D. R. Bellhouse, *David Bellhouse and Sons, Manchester*, 1992.

15 D. Bythell, *The Handloom Weavers*, 1969, p. 82.

16 Figures taken from the *Manchester Historical Recorder*, 1875, p. 107.

17 Figures from Alan Kidd, *Manchester*, 1993, pp. 41, 42, and from W. Cooke Taylor, *Notes of a Tour in the Manufacturing Districts of Lancashire*, [1842], pp. 9, 10.

18 Ure, *Philosophy*, p. 18.

19 James Phillips Kay, *The Moral and Physical Condition of the Working Classes employed in the Cotton Manufacture in Manchester*, [1832], p. 10.

20 Ure, *Philosophy*, p. 301.

21 Henry Morley, 'Ground in the Mill', *Household Words*, 22 April 1854.

22 Taylor, *Notes of a Tour*, p. 25.

23 Both quoted in L. Ettlinger, 'A German Architect's Visit to England in 1826', *Architectural Review*, 97, May 1945.

24 Roger Lloyd-Jones and M. J. Lewis, *Manchester and the Age of the Factory*, 1988, pp. 31, 32.

25 For a discussion of the economics of nineteenth-century warehousing see Stanley Chapman, 'The Commercial Sector', in Mary B. Rose, ed., *The Lancashire Cotton Industry*, 1996, p. 76.

26 Quoted in Lloyd-Jones and Lewis, *Manchester*, p. 33.

27 T. Swindells, *Manchester Streets and Manchester Men*, Series III, [1906–08], p. 105.

28 Aston, *Picture*, p. 221.

29 Swindells, *Manchester Streets*, Series III, pp. 96–9.

30 J. T. Slugg, *Manchester Fifty Years Ago*, [1881], pp. 10, 16.

31 Quoted in Swindells, *Manchester Streets*, Series I, p. 204. The text is probably based on the account given in John Morley, *The Life of Richard Cobden*, London, 1903, p. 22. George Hole is probably a misprint for George Hoyle.

32 Benjamin Love, *Manchester as it is*, [1839] 1971, p. 200.

33 'Fragments of a Provincial Tour', *Architectural Magazine*, 5, 1838.

CHAPTER 3   HOUSING IN THE NINETEENTH CENTURY

1 A close survey of John Street, Irk Town, is published in Jacqueline Roberts, *Working Class Housing in Nineteenth Century Manchester*, undated.

2 Friedrich Engels, *The Condition of the Working Class in England*, [1844], p. 82. Engels was the eldest son of a mill owner from the Wuppertal, sent to England aged twenty-two, ostensibly for twenty months, to finish his commercial training in the Ermen & Engels mills near Pendleton and in the firm's offices in Newmarket Buildings, Market Street. Engels travelled around the lanes and courts of Manchester on foot, accompanied by Mary Burns, an illiterate Irish factory girl with whom he lived until her death in January 1863. He returned to Barmen in the autumn of 1844, and met Karl Marx in Paris on his way home. They became friends for life. *The Condition of the Working Class* was written at his father's house in Barmen, and published in English in 1887.

3 James Phillips Kay, *The Moral and Physical Condition of the Working Classes employed in the Cotton Manufacture in Manchester*, [1832], p. 10. Sir James Kay-Shuttleworth (the name was adopted after his marriage), after studying medicine in Edinburgh, practised in Manchester, and went on to become the first Secretary of Whitehall's Education Department.

4 Kay, *Moral and Physical Condition*, p. 21.

5 Engels, *Condition*, p. 72.

6 John Burnet, *A Social History of Housing, 1815–1970*, 1978, p. 9.

7 Kay, *Moral and Physical Condition*, pp. 23, 24.

8 *The Cotton Metropolis*, [1849–50], pp. 5, 6.

9 Kay, *Moral and Physical Condition*, p. 34.

10 W. Cooke Taylor, *Notes of a Tour in the Manufacturing Districts of Lancashire*, [1842], p. 134.

11 Engels, *Condition*, p. 79.

12 Maurice Spiers, *Victoria Park, Manchester*, 1976, gives a full description of the Park and its chequered history.

13 Quoted in Michael Kennedy, *Portrait of Manchester*, 1970, p. 48. His great-great-grandfather was James Kennedy, the cotton magnate of Ancoats. His great-aunt Amy married into the Worthington family. Michael Kennedy worked for many years on the *Daily Telegraph*, as its Manchester music critic from 1950 and as northern editor from 1960.

14 A. P. Simon, *Manchester Made Over*, 1936, p. 28.

15 Leon Faucher, *Manchester in 1844*, [1844], p. 26.

16 *The Cotton Metropolis*, p. 7.

17 For a more detailed account of Manchester's water supplies see Tom Quayle, *Reservoirs in the Hills*.

18 E. M. Brockbank, *The Book of Manchester and Salford*, 1929, p. 185.

19 *Manchester Guardian*, 31 October 1934.

20 J. N. Tarn, *Working-Class Housing*, 1971, p. 25.

21 Address from the Right Reverend Dr Fraser, Bishop of Manchester, to the twenty-third Annual Congress of the National Association for the Promotion of Social Science. Quoted in the *Builder*, 4 October 1879, p. 1114.

22 *Transactions of the National Association for the Promotion of Social Science*, twenty-third annual meeting, Manchester, October 1879, pp. 18, 19.

23 David Rubinstein, *Victorian Homes*, 1974, pp. 139–42.

24 Thomas Worthington, *The Dwellings of the Poor*, 1893.

25 Anthony Pass, *Thomas Worthington*, 1988, is indispensable for an understanding of the architect's social commitment.

26 Spalding, with Cross, also designed the Technical School (UMIST) in 1895–1912.

27 H. Spalding, 'Block Dwellings: The Associated and Self-contained Systems', *Journal of the Royal Institute of British Architects*, VII, 1900, p. 254.

28 For a fuller discussion of the building of flats in nineteenth-century Lancashire see S. Martin Gaskell, 'A Landscape of Small Houses' in A. Sutcliffe (ed.), *Multi-storey Living*, 1974, pp. 88–121.

29 For more information see M. Kaufman, *Housing of the Working Classes and of the Poor*, 1975, pp. 36–9, 54.

30 From census returns quoted in T. W. Freeman, *The Conurbations of Great Britain*, 1959, p. 140.

31 T. Swindells, *Manchester Streets and Manchester Men*, Series V, [1906–08], p. 198.

32 J. N. Tarn, *Five per cent Philanthropy*, 1973, p. 178, n. 143. Tarn, strangely, ignores almost all Manchester's early attempts to alleviate the conditions of the poor, even though Manchester banned back-to-back housing earlier than most towns and its Improvement Act of 1867 set a national standard.

33 Quoted in J. Barry Cullingworth and Vincent Nadin, *Town and Country Planning in Britain*, 1995, p. 2.

CHAPTER 4 THE COMING OF THE RAILWAYS

1 Surprisingly, Liverpool merchants invested in 50 per cent of the shares, Manchester in only 2 per cent.

2 In 1784 Rennie had helped Boulton & Watt design and build machines at the Albion Flour Mills at Southwark, Birmingham, but became better known as a designer of bridges – Kelso, Waterloo (dem. 1938) and Southwark (dem. 1920). His London Bridge was removed stone by stone to the United States in 1967, the purchaser erroneously believing he had bought Tower Bridge.

3 Professor Simmonds points out in *The Victorian Railway*, 1991, p. 104, that Sir John Rennie had been involved in twelve railway schemes by 1844 but had not been made responsible for the execution of any of them.

4 For an account of the opening ceremony see Steve Little, 'The Opening of the Station', in C. E. Makepeace, ed., *Oldest in the World*, 1979. This very readable book has a series of essays telling the story of the station and its site from its earliest days through the struggles to get it accepted as the site of the Museum of Science and Industry.

5 A detailed account of the building and its construction, and that of the station buildings, can be found in R. S. Fitzgerald, *Liverpool Road Station, Manchester*, 1980.

6 The Liverpool & Manchester, the Grand Junction and the London & Birmingham Railways (both the latter running on payment of a toll) operated from Liverpool Road (in 1846 all three were amalgamated into the London & North Western Railway); the Manchester & Leeds Railway ran from Oldham Road and later from Victoria; the Manchester & Bolton from New Bailey Street, Salford, and then from Victoria with the Manchester & Leeds; the Manchester & Birmingham (also absorbed into the L&NW) and Sheffield Ashton-under-Lyne & Manchester Railways (which ran on toll) from Store Street (London Road); the Midland Railway, Great Northern Railway and the Manchester Sheffield & Lincolnshire Railway (as the SA&M became) formed the Cheshire Lines Committee into Central Station.

7 Leon Faucher, *Manchester in 1844*, 1844, p. 15.

8 *Builder*, 15 November 1845, p. 547.

9 Their history is given in R. L. Hills, *Beyer, Peacock, Locomotive Builders of Gorton, Manchester*, 1982.

10 J. T. Slugg, *Manchester Fifty Years Ago*, [1881], pp. 8, 9.

11 W. Cooke Taylor, *Notes of a Tour in the Manufacturing Districts of Lancashire*, [1842], p. 256.

12 Quoted in Simmons, *Victorian Railway*, p. 374.

13 J. F. C. Harrison, *Early Victorian Britain, 1832–51*, 1979, p. 64.

14 References to Sir Booth Gore developing the area around Grosvenor Square are inaccurate. The Chorlton Hall estate had been sold by Roger Aytoun to three developers in the 1790s. For details of the development of the area see Derek Brumhead

and Terry Wyke, *A Walk round All Saints*. Chorlton Hall now lies under the Mancunian Way.

15 John R. Kellett, *The Impact of Railways on Victorian Cities*, 1969, p. 290.

16 *Ibid.*, p. 326.

17 Quoted in *ibid.*, p. 346.

18 The 'Cheap Trains Act' of 1883 compelled the railway companies to offer cheap workmen's fares, and was designed to ease the migration of the working classes out of the cities and into the suburbs.

19 The details of the construction of Central Station are taken directly from Jack Bogle's essay, 'Greater Manchester Exhibition and Event Centre', in John Parkinson-Bailey, ed., *Sites of the City*, 1996.

20 David George, 'Turning the goods around: an introduction to railway warehouses', in Robina McNeil and A. D. George, eds, *The Heritage Atlas 3: Warehouse Album*, 1997. The *Engineer*, 2 September 1898, pp. 224–6, carried details of the opening ceremony.

CHAPTER 5 1840–60: THE ARCHITECTURE OF COMMERCE

1 T. Swindells, *Manchester Streets and Manchester Men*, Series II, [1906–08], p. 296.

2 Both Henry McConnel and William Fairbairn bought important collections of pictures from Agnew's. For more information on their collections see Elizabeth Conran's informative article 'Art Collections' in J. H. G. Archer, ed., *Art and Architecture in Victorian Manchester*, 1985.

3 For a detailed account of the commission see M. H. Port, *Six Hundred New Churches*, 1961.

4 Gunn House, Liverpool Road, was the former Sunday school of St Matthew's, 1825. It is Grade II listed.

5 V. A. C. Gatrell, quoted in D. Fraser, ed., *Municipal Reform and the Industrial City*, 1982, p. 22.

6 Gary Messinger, *Manchester in the Victorian Age*, 1985, p. 8.

7 See Michael Port, 'Francis Goodwin: an Architect of the 1820s', *Architectural History*, 1, 1958, pp. 61–72.

8 Solon was judged by many to be the father of democracy for his reforms in Athens in 594 BC; appropriately he persuaded those who could not earn enough money from farming to take up commerce, and thus stimulated trade. Alfred was not ony the first king of a united country, but the one who promoted education among his people and enacted the first laws which did not differentiate between the English and the Welsh. John Locke, the seventeenth-century philosopher, argued that sovereignty resided with the people. Sir Matthew Hale, the seventeenth-century statesman and jurist, though a Parliamentarian, helped in the restoration of Charles II to the throne and attempted to reconcile the opposing parties.

9 According to E. Delaire, *Les Architectes élèves de l'Ecole des Beaux Arts 1793–1907*, Paris, 1907, p. 311. The author is indebted to Peter Ferriday for this source.

10 By 1900 Slater's *Directory* listed 164 architects, of whom sixty-nine were Fellows and fifty-five were Associates of the Manchester Society of Architects.

11 The building is illustrated in Cecil Stewart, *The Stones of Manchester*, 1956, p. 21.

12 Alfred Darbyshire, *An Architect's Experiences*, 1897, p. 21.

13 Quoted in Cecil Stewart's article, 'MSA: a Brief History', in Dennis Sharp, ed., 'Manchester Buildings', *Architecture North West*, 1966.

14 *Builder*, 6 November 1847, p. 526.

15 For details of the founding of the RMI see Stuart Macdonald's essay, 'The Royal Manchester Institution', in John Archer, ed., *Art and Architecture in Victorian Manchester*, 1985.

16 Quoted in Marcus Whiffen, 'The Architecture of Sir Charles Barry in Manchester and Neighbourhood', in John Archer, ed., *Art and Architecture in Victorian Manchester*, 1985, pp. 52, 53.

17 Quoted in James Wheeler, *Manchester: its Political, Social and Commercial History*, 1842, p. 410. Wheeler also gives details of the institution's accounts at this time.

18 A history of the School of Art can be found in David Jeremiah, *A Hundred Years and More*, 1980, and of the Manchester Metropolitan University in Alan Fowler and Terry Wyke, *Many Arts, Many Skills*, 1993.

19 For a detailed account of Barry's work in and around Manchester see Whiffen, 'The Architecture of Sir Charles Barry'. The Brook Street Chapel, incidentally, is falling rapidly into a state of extreme decay in spite of its Grade II* listing. Would any other city allow a work of Barry's to perish so?

20 Wheeler, *Manchester*, p. 416.

21 For a discussion of the design of Italian *palazzi* see Peter Murray, *The Architecture of the Italian Renaissance*, London, Thames & Hudson, 1969, pp. 63–104.

22 Georgina Masson's *Italian Villas and Palaces*, London, Thames & Hudson, 1959, plate 96, illustrates the Palazzo dei Diamante.

23 Though this *soirée* was actually held in the Free Trade Hall. In the late 1930s the Athenaeum was acquired by the city as an enlargement of the City Art Gallery. The land at the rear of both buildings was cleared in 1975 ready for an extension, which has only taken twenty-three years to come to fruition!

24 The meeting took place in March 1832, according to Walters's obituary in the *Builder*.

25 It is often recorded that Walters retired after having failed to get the commission for the Assize Courts in 1858, but the list of his buildings supplied by his successors for his obituary show him working until 1865. The list is given in the *Builder*, 16 March 1872, pp. 199–200.

26 Richard Tattersall had earlier designed a warehouse for George Faulkner behind the Royal Infirmary, but this building was demolished, and no detailed record survives. He also designed a number of mills, including one for Peter Dixon & Co., the Shaddon Mill, Carlisle, of 1835–36 which was, at 224 ft by 58 ft and 83 ft high, then the largest cotton mill in Britain. But it had little embellishment. The mill is illustrated in Edgar Jones, *Industrial Architecture in Britain, 1750–1939*, 1985, p. 59.

27 As suggested by Steve Little in 'Flamboyant Façade and a very plain Rear', in Robina McNeil and A. D. George, eds, *The Heritage Atlas 3: Warehouse Album*, 1997.

28 This description, and an elevation drawing of the warehouse, are given in the *Builder*, 29 August 1868, pp. 641, 642.

29 Plan and elevation are shown in *ibid.*, 4 April 1874, pp. 288, 289.

30 Thomas Cubitt (1788–1855), a master carpenter by trade, was one of the largest property speculators in the country. At its peak his firm permanently employed over 1,000 workmen, and had eleven acres of workshops in Pimlico. Apart from speculative housing which provided much of Belgravia, Bloomsbury, Pimlico and Brighton, he helped the Prince Consort to design Osborne House on the Isle of Wight, the house to which Victoria retired after Albert's death. On his death Cubitt left over £1 million and the then longest will ever made, covering thirty pages of parchment.

31 *Builder*, 6 November 1847, p. 526.

32 *Ibid.*, 10 March 1849, p. 114, and 14 April 1849, p. 172.

33 W. H. Barlow, engineer of the Midland Railway, had been sent to Constantinople to superintend works for Messrs Maudslay. From that time a lifelong friendship developed between Walters and Barlow. In 1860 they were working together on the Midland Railway, Barlow laying out the line between Ambergate and Manchester, Walters designing the stations: Buxton, Bakewell, Longstone, Miller's Dale, Rowsley and

Hassop. Barlow is perhaps best known as the designer, with R. M. Ordish, of the train shed of Paddington Station (1865–68).

34 *Builder*, 16 March 1872, p. 199.

35 The dates of these buildings are taken from the list provided by Barker & Ellis (his partners and successors) for Walters's obituary in the *Builder*, 16 March 1872, pp. 199–200.

36 Asa Briggs, *Victorian Cities*, 1968, p. 119.

37 Peter Mathias, *The First Industrial Nation*, 1980, p. 301.

38 For details about this infamous incident, in which eleven people were killed and 600 were wounded, see M. and W. Bee, 'The Casualties of Peterloo', *Manchester Region History Review*, III, 1, 1989, pp. 43–50. Robert Walmsley, in *Peterloo: The Case Re-opened*, Manchester, 1969, gives an alternative view, and fewer casualties.

39 Quoted in Michael Kennedy, *Portrait of Manchester*, 1970, p. 96.

40 See Michael Kennedy, *The Hallé, 1858–1983*, 1982, and Michael Kennedy, ed., *The Autobiography of Charles Hallé*, 1972.

41 Older are Berlin, Leipzig and Chicago.

42 A. H. Layard, 'The Manchester Exhibition', *Quarterly Review*, July 1857, pp. 165–6.

43 Thomas Fairbairn owned Holman Hunt's painting *The Awakening Conscience* (Tate Gallery), which he loaned to the exhibition. He asked Hunt to repaint the face of the woman, as he found it too painful to live with.

44 When the Victoria and Albert Museum was redesigned by Captain Francis Fowke in the 1860s the 'boilers' were moved to Bethnal Green in east London – they now form the Museum of Childhood.

45 A full discussion of the exhibition is given in Ulrich Finke's 'The Art Treasures Exhibition' in J. Archer, ed., *Art and Architecture in Victorian Manchester*, 1985.

46 According to John Cassell, *Art Treasures Exhibition*, 1858, preface.

47 The figures come from the *Builder*, 13 February 1858, p. 9, and *The Century's Progress* of 1892, reprinted as *Good Value and No Humbug*, edited and published by Neil Richardson, Swinton, undated, pp. 10, 11.

48 See Elizabeth Adburgham, *Shops and Shopping*, 1964, pp. 18–21.

49 *Builder*, 17 October 1868, p. 759.

50 *Building News*, 7 June 1861, p. 473. The doorway is illustrated in Jones, *Industrial Architecture*, [47].

51 His drawings up to the competition for the Town Hall in 1867 are signed Salomon, and from then on Salomons. The author is grateful to David Hilton, Plankeeper, City Architect's Department, for poring over many of Salomon's original drawings.

52 *Builder*, 17 October 1868, p. 760.

53 *Ibid.*, 31 October 1868, p. 806.

54 Thanks are due again to David Hilton for his time and effort in helping to unravel this story.

55 British Jews were enfranchised in 1835; by 1914, at 35,000, Manchester had the largest Jewish population outside London.

56 *Builder*, 13 February 1858, p. 98.

57 Details of Manchester's nineteenth-century synagogues can be found in Bill Williams, *The Making of Manchester Jewry, 1740–1875*, 1976, pp. 253–6 and 323. The Great Synagogue is illustrated in plate III. See also Edward Jamilly, 'An Introduction to Victorian Synagogues', *Victorian Society Annual*, 1991, pp. 22–35.

58 Anthony Pass, *Thomas Worthington*, 1988, p. 32.

59 *Builder*, 12 May 1855, p. 222, carries Gregan's obituary.

60 These anecdotes are quoted in Leo H. Grindon, *Manchester Banks and Bankers*, 1878, pp. 133, 134.

61 *Builder*, 31 August 1861, p. 590. Atkinson, having started as a bricklayer's labourer and quarryman, became a stone carver and acted as clerk of works for Basevi at St Thomas's, Stockport.

62 *Ibid.*, 15 November 1845, pp. 546, 547.

63 The authoritative work on Cockerell is David Watkin's *The Life and Work of C. R. Cockerell*, 1974. E. M. Dodd, 'Charles Robert Cockerell', in P. Ferriday, ed., *Victorian Architecture*, 1963, also has a good discussion of the architect.

64 Cecil Stewart, in *The Stones of Manchester* (p. 43), says surprisingly, 'the list of his architectural achievements is very small'. But Colvin's *Biographical Dictionary of British Architects* lists thirty-eight public buildings and thirty-three domestic ones, as well as the considerable honours bestowed upon him.

65 *Builder*, 16 March 1872, p. 199.

66 The Manchester & Salford Bank later became Williams Deacon's Bank, and then, via Williams & Glyn's, part of the Royal Bank of Scotland.

67 Royle appears in directories from the 1820s as a land agent and architect. The bank's façade is shown in W. Westall and T. Moule, *Great Britain Illustrated*, 1830.

68 Illustrated in the *Builder*, 7 November 1896, plate following p. 380.

69 R. H. Pickard, 'Manchester and Cotton', in W. H. Brindley, ed., *The Soul of Manchester*, 1929, p. 213.

70 *Builder*, 17 October 1874, p. 859.

CHAPTER 6   1860–90: CONFIDENCE AND CIVIC PRIDE

1 Asa Briggs, *Victorian Cities*, 1968, p. 94.

2 Quoted in J. Mordaunt Crook, *The Greek Revival*, 1972, p. 129.

3 Thomas Rickman, *An Attempt to Discriminate the Styles of English Architecture*, 1862, p. 44.

4 *Contrasts*, published in 1836 and 1841; *The True Principles of Pointed or Christian Architecture*, 1841; *The Present State of Ecclesiastical Architecture in England*, 1842 (which illustrated the design for his St Wilfrid, Hulme); *An Apology for the Revival of Christian Architecture in England*, 1844.

5 Pugin had converted to Catholicism in 1835, and saw Christianity and pointed architecture as synonymous. Cardinal Newman said, 'The canons of Gothic architecture are to him points of faith, and everyone is a heretic who would venture to question them.'

6 Pugin, *The True Principles*, pp. 1, 2.

7 There really are only two books which deal well with Pugin the architect: B. Ferrey, *Recollections of Pugin*, 1861, and Phoebe Stanton, *Pugin*, 1971.

8 Georg Germann, *Gothic Revival in Europe and Britain*, 1972, is particularly informative on the Gothic Revival's European dimension.

9 Quoted in Crook, *Greek Revival*, p. 130.

10 Alfred Darbyshire, *An Architect's Experiences*, 1897, p. 21.

11 In a lecture, 'Traffic', given at Bradford on 21 April 1864.

12 Kenneth Clark, *The Gothic Revival*, 1962, p. 209.

13 Quoted in Colin Cunningham and Prudence Waterhouse, *Alfred Waterhouse, 1830–1905*, 1992, p. 35.

14 Joseph Kinneard, 'G. E. Street, the Law Courts and the Seventies', in Peter Ferriday, ed., *Victorian Architecture*, 1963. This book contains a number of very readable articles, e.g. E. M. Dodd on C. R. Cockerell, H. S. Goodhart-Rendell on Victorian public buildings, Alexandra Gordon Clark on Pugin and Peter Fleetwood-Hesketh on Barry. It was probably the first book which brought together essays on then undervalued architects.

15 A decent picture of the Assize Courts is shown in Eric Krieger, *Manchester in Times Past, 1900–1935*, 1987, p. 7.

16 In 1990, following a major riot, the prison was extensively refurbished by Austin-Smith:Lord, John Brunton Partnership and J. R. Harris. Details can be found in the

Northern Builder and Engineer, June 1992, pp. 20–5. Strangeways is now called the Manchester Prison.

17 Cecil Stewart, *The Stones of Manchester*, 1956, p. 76. The building is illustrated on p. 75.

18 *Building News*, 20 January 1861, p. 67.

19 Illustrated in Anthony Pass, *Thomas Worthington*, 1988, p. 44.

20 Sir George Gilbert Scott, *Personal and Professional Recollections*, 1879, quoted in Pass, *Worthington*, p. 45.

21 Details of the extensive restoration work are given in the commemorative booklet, *The Restoration of Manchester's Albert Memorial: a Report of the Albert Memorial Appeal Committee*, 1979.

22 *Manchester Guardian*, 12 November 1909, Worthington's obituary.

23 As reported in the *Builder*, 16 February 1867, p. 116.

24 Letters to the *Builder*, 16 November 1867, pp. 839–40. The MSA was founded only in 1865; the MAA was founded in 1861.

25 *Builder*, 16 March 1867, pp. 185. The competition is extensively covered in this volume, and in vol. 26, 1868. Waterhouse's design is shown on pp. 317–19, and Speakman & Charlesworth's on pp. 336, 337.

26 *Builder*, 30 March 1867, p. 223.

27 *Ibid.*, 7 September 1867, p. 660.

28 A copy of Street and Donaldson's 'Report to the New Town Hall Committee' was reproduced in *ibid.*, 14 March 1868, p. 190.

29 *Ibid.*, 14 March, 1868, p. 190.

30 *Ibid.*, 14 March, 1868, p. 190.

31 *Manchester Examiner and Times*, 13 March 1868.

32 *Builder*, 21 March 1868, p. 249.

33 Shown in *ibid.*, 9 May 1867, pp. 336, 337.

34 Paragraph XXXVIII, 'The Nature of Gothic', *The Stones of Venice*, Vol. 2, [1853] 1907, p. 163.

35 Robert Furneaux Jordan, *Victorian Architecture*, 1966, p. 153.

36 A full and perceptive description of the Town Hall is given in John Archer's essay, 'A Classic of its Age', in John Archer, ed., *Art and Architecture in Victorian Manchester*, 1985. Details of the building are given in *An Architectural and General Description of the Town Hall*, ed. William Axon, 1878.

37 For details of the murals see Julian Treuherz's essay, 'Ford Madox Brown and the Manchester Murals', in J. Archer, ed., *Art and Architecture in Victorian Manchester*, 1985.

38 Statistics from the *Builder*, 18 April 1874, p. 339.

39 *Times*, 14 September 1877.

40 Quoted in J. M. Golby, *Culture and Society in Britain*, 1986, p. 295.

41 Robert H. Kargon, *Science in Victorian Manchester*, 1977, p. 155.

42 Quoted by Vincent Knowles in 'The University of the Future', in C. F. Carter, ed., *Manchester and its Region*, 1962, p. 244.

43 A history of the Victoria University of Manchester is given in H. B. Charlton, *Portrait of a University, 1851–1951*, 1951.

44 In 1926 'Solway House', a warehouse for Messrs Stewart Thomson & Co., by Charles Clegg & Son, was erected on the site of the earlier buildings. Illustrated in the *Builder*, 30 April 1926, pp. 752–4.

45 Figures culled from *ibid.*, 11 January 1873, p. 34, and 3 June 1871, pp. 420, 421.

46 *Ibid.*, 7 November 1896, p. 371. This issue of the *Builder* has an article, 'The Architecture of our large Northern Towns', II, 'Manchester', pp. 369–80. It shows, incidentally, on p. 374, the Church of the Holy Name, Oxford Road, before its tower was built.

47 *Ibid.*, 29 August 1874, p. 737.

48 One of the most readable books on the Queen Anne Revival is Mark Girouard, *Sweetness and Light*, 1977.

49 Quoted in Stewart, *Stones*, p. 134.

50 Probably from the terracotta works at Ruabon.

51 See D. A. Farnie, *John Rylands of Manchester*, 1993. As Farnie points out, in spite of his achievements, Rylands is ignored in most of the histories of Manchester and the cotton trade, perhaps because Rylands himself eschewed public office and did not participate in either local or national politics.

52 Quoted in Stewart, *Stones*, p. 126.

53 Darbyshire, *Architect's Experiences*, p. 44.

54 *Ibid.*, p. 305.

55 Apart from his autobiography, the only account of Darbyshire's life is found in Terry Lockett's brief 'Alfred Darbyshire', in *Three Lives: It Happened round Manchester*, 1968, pp. 24–45, which also lists his works.

CHAPTER 7   1890–1940: AMBITION — FROM THE SHIP CANAL TO WORLD WAR II

1 Adamson, the head of a major engineering firm, lived in 'The Towers', designed by Alfred Waterhouse.

2 S. Reece, *Guide to Manchester and Salford*, 1948, p. 111. Though it must be noted that this ranking applies to the value of goods transported; in terms of tonnage, the docks ranked only tenth.

3 D. A. Farnie, *The Manchester Ship Canal*, 1980, p. 31.

4 Its weekly publication was *Cotton*. It established central selling rooms in the Royal Exchange on 19 December 1927, to serve as a spot market. The association ceased operations in 1968 on the closure of the Royal Exchange.

5 For Heathcote's obituary see the *Manchester Guardian*, 29 January 1938, and the *Builder*, 4 February 1938, p. 263.

6 C. H. Reilly, *Some Manchester Streets and their Buildings*, 1924, pp. 28, 29.

7 Kerry Downes's *English Baroque Architecture*, London, 1966, lavishly illustrates the buildings which so appealed to the builders of the Wrenaissance.

8 Biographies of these architects can be found in A. Stuart Gray, *Edwardian Architecture*, 1985. Alastair Service, *Edwardian Architecture*, 1977, gives a useful account of building in the period, though very much London-based.

9 The *Builders' Journal* started in 1895, subtitled *An Architectural Review*. In 1896 the *Architectural Review* appeared as a separate monthly. The *Builders' Journal* became the *Builders' Journal and Architectural Record*, then, in 1906, the *Builders' Journal and Architectural Engineer*, and in 1910 the *Architects' and Builders' Journal*. In 1919 it assumed its present title, the *Architects' Journal*.

10 C. H. Reilly, *Representative British Architects of the Present Day*, London, 1931, p. 61. Sir Charles H. Reilly (1874–1948) was trained by his father, C. T. Reilly, and John Belcher. In 1904 he was appointed Roscoe Professor of Architecture at Liverpool University, the first university school of architecture in the country, where he remained until 1934. He was knighted in 1944.

11 Robert Macleod, *Style and Society*, 1971, p. 120.

12 Reilly, *Some Manchester Streets*, p. 104. This publication was based on a series of articles written for the *Manchester Guardian*.

13 Leeds Fireclay of Burmantofts were responsible for most of the brown and buff terracotta in Manchester, though toward the end of the century much came from Shaw's of Darwen and the Bispham Hall Brick & Terracotta Works. For more information see Michael Stratton, 'The Terracotta Revival', *Victorian Society Annual*, 1982–83.

14 For more details see R. F. Bonner and J. Dwan, *The Finest Fire Station in this Round World, Manchester*, undated.

15 Gavin Stamp, 'London 1900', *Architectural Design*, 48, 5–6, 1978, p. 310.

16 Reilly, *Some Manchester Streets*, pp. 118–19.

17 Quoted by Nicholas Taylor in 'Sir Albert Richardson: a Classic Case of Edwardianism', in Alastair Service, ed., *Edwardian Architecture and its Origins*, 1975, p. 453. Taylor seems not to have noticed that the Manchester building was Richardson & Gill's first major commission.

18 H. Clay and R. Brady, eds, *Manchester at Work*, 1929, p. 131.

19 From a Lloyd's Packing Warehouse publicity brochure, mid-1940s, quoted in William Whittam, *Fairhursts Architects*, 1986, p. 8.

20 His obituary is given in the *Builder*, 13 April 1945, p. 287.

21 Further details in Adrian Wilson, 'Labelling the Pieces: an Introduction to Cotton Trade Marks', in Robina McNeil and A. D. George, eds, *The Heritage Atlas 3: Warehouse Album*, 1997.

22 According to Asa Briggs, *Friends of the People*, 1956, p. 106. The dates of Lewis's are difficult to unravel. Briggs adds to the confusion (p. 77) by stating, 'Until the building of the new Lewis's in 1929–33, there were few further structural changes,' yet elsewhere lists only the Birmingham and Glasgow stores as being built at that date. Philip Atkins's *Guide across Manchester*, 1987, p. 28, gives 'major extensions of 1908 and 1929'.

23 Details of Britain's decline in the world market can be found in B. Bowker, *Lancashire under the Hammer*, 1928, pp. 49–51.

24 Sir Raymond Streat, *Manchester Guardian*, 3 December 1957, quoted in L. P. Green, *Provincial Metropolis*, 1959, p. 72.

25 Figures from R. H. Pickard, 'Manchester and Cotton', in W. H. Brindley, ed., *The Soul of Manchester*, 1929, pp. 203, 204.

26 Sir William Himbury, of the British Cotton Growing Association, in E. M. Brockbank, *The Book of Manchester and Salford*, 1929, pp. 222, 223.

27 C. H. Reilly, 'The Pace of Manchester', in W. H. Brindley, ed., *The Soul of Manchester*, 1929, p. 106.

28 The cladding is shown in a perspective drawing by Ted Adams, in the possession of Fairhursts.

29 The author is obliged for this snippet to John Sheard of Cruickshank & Seward, who as a child was seated at Adams's drawing board by his father when Adams was working on the Rylands building.

30 *Building for Bankers: Sir Edwin Lutyens and the Midland Bank, 1921–1939*, 1980, p. 21. The author is indebted to Peter Ferriday for this source. The bank is also illustrated in *Architect and Building News*, 30 August 1935, pp. 241–4.

31 From 1929 to his death in 1944 Lutyens was engaged on the design of Liverpool Cathedral. Although his building wasn't continued above the level of the vaults, these are well worth visiting and give an indication of the enormous scale of the intended building. The model, held in the cathedral, is a wonder.

32 *Architect and Building News*, 16 February 1934, p. 218.

33 *Ibid.*, p. 219.

34 Ian Nairn, *Architectural Review*, August 1960, p. 117. Gordon Cullen also deals with the solid geometry of buildings in *Townscape* – the whole book provides, through sequences of photographs, a fascinating insight into how the urban landscape can be read.

35 J. M. Richards, *An Introduction to Modern Architecture*, 1940, p. 27.

36 M. J. Pullen and B. R. Williams, 'The Structure of Industry in Lancashire', in C. F. Carter, ed., *Manchester and its Region*, 1962, p. 147.

1 Raymond Unwin, *Nothing Gained by Overcrowding!* 1912.
2 E. D. Simon, *The Anti-slum Campaign*, 1933, p. 11.
3 J. Barry Cullingworth and Vincent Nadin, *Town and Country Planning in Britain*, 1994, p. 3.
4 Osbert Lancaster, *Here, of all Places*, 1959, an amusing and barbative caricature of suburban housing.
5 E. D. Simon and J. Inman, *The Rebuilding of Manchester*, 1935, p. 90.
6 Alfred P. Simon, *Manchester Made Over*, 1936, p. 13.
7 Simon, *Anti-slum Campaign*, p. 25.
8 E. M. Brockbank, *The Book of Manchester and Salford*, 1929, p. 126.
9 Simon and Inman, *Rebuilding*, p. 18.
10 Simon, *Anti-slum Campaign*, p. 88. Simon noted that Sheffield had 16,000 back-to-backs, Birmingham 40,000 and Leeds 72,000, though Birmingham had built 40,000 new dwellings between 1921 and 1931, and, unlike all the other large cities, including London, was considerably reducing its slum population.
11 *Manchester Guardian*, 29 July 1933, cited in Simon, *Anti-slum Campaign*, p. 124.
12 Quoted in Simon and Inman, *Rebuilding*, pp. 60, 61.
13 *Ibid.*, p. 62.
14 *Ibid.*, p. 66.
15 Sir Ernest Simon's father had founded the great engineering firms of Henry Simon Ltd and Simon Carves Ltd. He was one of the three businessmen who founded the Hallé Concerts Society. Ernest Simon was MP for Withington from 1923–24 and Chairman of the Council of the Victoria University from 1939; it was he who encouraged the building of Jodrell Bank radio telescope. He was Chairman of the BBC from 1947 to 1952. Shena Simon was a graduate of the London School of Economics, and joined her husband on the City Council in 1924, becoming Chairman of the Education Committee in 1932. In 1964 she was made a freeman of the city.
16 Abercrombie was the leader in founding the Council for the Preservation (later Protection) of Rural England in 1926. He wrote about *feng-shui* as early as 1926.
17 Parker, cited in Peter Hall, *Cities of Tomorrow*, 1988, p. 110.
18 These were based on the Radburn system, which Parker had discussed with its creators in 1924. A smaller scheme already existed in Manchester, in Burnage Garden Village, by J. Horner Hargreaves, 1906.
19 Quoted in D. Deakin, *Wythenshawe*, 1989, p. 58.
20 See Ann Hughes and Karen Hunt, 'A Culture Transformed? Women's Lives in Wythenshawe in the 1930s', in Andrew Davies and Steven Fielding, eds, *Workers' Worlds*, 1992.
21 Michael Kennedy, *Portrait of Manchester*, 1970, p. 124.
22 R. Nicholas, 'Planning the City of the Future' in C. F. Carter, ed., *Manchester and its Region*, 1962, p. 257.
23 Hall, *Cities of Tomorrow*, p. 111.
24 Quoted in Lionel Esher, *A Broken Wave*, 1981, pp. 28, 29.
25 Simon and Inman, *Rebuilding*, p. 94. A detailed discussion of Birmingham's policy toward flat building is given in Anthony Sutcliffe's essay 'A Century of Flats in Birmingham, 1875–1973' in A. Sutcliffe, *Multi-storey Living*, 1974, pp. 181–206.
26 Simon and Inman, *Rebuilding*, pp. 94, 95.
27 *Ibid.*, p. 106.
28 *Architect and Building News*, 20 September 1935, pp. 326–9.
29 Sutcliffe, *Multi-storey Living*, p. 124.

1 R. Nicholas, *City of Manchester Plan, 1945*, 1945, p. 184. Permission to quote from the plan has kindly been given by the Department of Environmental Development, Manchester City Council.

2 *Ibid.*, p. 1.

3 *Ibid.*, p. 185.

4 *Ibid.*, p. 202.

5 *Ibid.*, p. 104.

6 *Ibid.*, p. 199.

7 *Ibid.*, p. 196.

8 *Ibid.*, p. 205.

9 C. M. Law, 'Post-war Employment Changes', in H. P. White, ed., *The Continuing Conurbation*, 1980, p. 41.

10 John Singleton, *Lancashire on the Scrapheap*, 1991, p. 231.

11 Figures from David M. Smith, *Industrial Britain: The North West*, 1969, pp. 142–70.

12 B. Bowker, *Lancashire under the Hammer*, 1928, p. 127.

13 The Act followed the recommendations of the Barlow Report, published in 1940. The Royal Commission, chaired by Sir Anderson Montague-Barlow, was tasked to 'consider what social, economic or strategic disadvantages arise from the concentration of industries or of the industrial population in large towns or in particular areas of the country; and to report what remedial measures if any should be taken in the national interest'. For more details see J. Barry Cullingworth and Vincent Nadin, *Town and Country Planning in Britain*, 1994, p. 6.

14 H. B. Rodgers, 'Manchester Revisited: a Profile of Urban Change', in H. P. White, ed., *The Continuing Conurbation*, 1980, p. 31.

15 Brian Rodgers, 'Manchester: Metropolitan Planning by Collaboration and Consent; or, Civic Hope Frustrated' in G. Gordon, ed., *Regional Cities in the U.K., 1890–1980*, 1986, p. 49.

16 Smith, *Industrial Britain*, p. 139.

17 By 1977 Stanlow was the largest oil refinery in Britain. Pipelines link Stanlow with the chemical plants at Partington and Carrington, and seventy-six miles away with Amlwch in Anglesey, where the largest oil tankers can berth. Six pipelines link Stanlow with Heysham for the transport of crude oil.

18 Ministry of Labour figures, quoted in Smith, *Industrial Britain*, p. 194.

19 C. M. Law, T. Grundy and M. L. Senior, *Comparative Study of Conurbations Project*, 1984, p. 124. (By 1978 Regional Development Grants were only £3 million for projects costing a total of £57·6 million. *Manchester and Salford Inner Area Study*, 1978, p. 14.)

20 Law *et al.*, *Comparative Study*, p. 124.

21 P. Lawless and C. Raban, eds, *The Contemporary British City*, 1986, p. 51.

22 R. D. P. Smith, 'The Changing Regional Hierarchy', *Regional Studies*, 2, 1968, pp. 1–19, quoted in Gordon, *Regional Cities*, p. 6.

23 More details of the rebuilding are given in *Manchester Free Trade Hall: Issued on the Occasion of the Re-opening of the Reconstructed Hall, November 1951*, 1951.

24 Colin Amery and Dan Cruickshank, *The Rape of Britain*, 1975, p. 11.

25 The author is beholden to John Sheard of Cruickshank & Seward for this anecdote. His colleague John Seward died, unfortunately, in 1998.

26 Malcolm MacEwen, *Crisis in Architecture*, 1974, p. 21.

27 Nikolaus Pevsner, *The Buildings of England: South Lancashire*, 1969, p. 297.

28 Quoted in MacEwen, *Crisis*, p. 35.

29 Rod Hackney, *The Good, the Bad and the Ugly*, 1988, p. 8.

30 Quoted in Kenneth Hudson, *The Fashionable Stone*, 1971, p. 76.

31 *Architectural Review*, August 1960, p. 112.

32 Nikolaus Pevsner, *The Englishness of English Art*, 1964, p. 184. These ideas are given more form in Kevin Lynch, *The Image of the City*, 1986.

33 *Architect and Building News*, 15 June 1960, p. 759.

34 R. Nicholas, 'Planning the City of the Future', in C. F. Carter, ed., *Manchester and its Region*, 1962, pp. 254, 259.

35 A. P. Simon, *Manchester Made Over*, 1936, p. xii.

36 Nicholas, 'Planning the City of the Future', p. 262.

37 *Manchester and Salford Inner Area Study*, 1978, p. 12.

38 Rogers, 'Manchester Revisited', p. 29.

39 'Manchester Reunited', *Architectural Review*, August 1962.

40 'Comment', *ibid.*

41 Ian Nairn, in *Architectural Review*, August 1960, p. 115.

42 MacEwen, *Crisis*, p. 14.

43 Phill Bamford, *Manchester: Fifty Years of Change*, 1995, p. 26. More details are given in Ken Childs, 'Reclaim the Roads', *Manchester Forum*, December 1997.

44 See H. A. Tripp, *Town Planning and Road Traffic*, London, Edward Arnold, 1942, and his earlier *Road Traffic and its Control*, London, Edward Arnold, 1938.

45 Colin Buchanan, *Traffic in Towns*, 1963.

46 *Architects' Journal*, 23 June 1960, p. 948.

47 John Sheard worked for Wilson & Womersley in the 1960s and went on to become a senior partner in Cruickshank & Seward. His proposals for the city centre were conceived as part of his town planning thesis. He was aware, of course, that Manchester already had an underground system of basements and canals. His scheme was featured not only in the *Architectural Review*, 16 June 1960, but as a banner on the front page of the *Manchester Evening News*, 15 June 1960.

48 Robert Home, *Inner City Regeneration*, 1982, p. 77.

CHAPTER 10   HOUSING IN THE POST-WAR PERIOD

1 R. Nicholas, *City of Manchester Plan, 1945*, 1945, pp. 4–5.

2 Quoted by Derek Senior in 'Manchester Redevelopment', *Architects' Journal*, 16 June 1960, p. 907.

3 A full account of the public inquiry is given in L. Keeble, *Town Planning at the Crossroads*, 1961, pp. 63–7.

4 C. F. Carter, ed., *Manchester and its Region*, 1962, p. 179.

5 R. Nicholas, 'Planning the City of the Future' in C. F. Carter, ed., *Manchester and its Region*, 1962, pp. 256, 257.

6 Brian Rodgers, 'Manchester: Metropolitan Planning by Collaboration and Consent; or, Civic Hope Frustrated', in G. Gordon, ed., *Regional Cities in the U.K., 1890–1980*, 1986, p. 48.

7 Senior, 'Manchester Redevelopment', p. 905.

8 John English, Ruth Madigan and Peter Norman, *Slum Clearance*, 1976, p. 30.

9 A list is given in M. Glendinning and S. Muthesius, *Tower Block*, 1994, p. 359.

10 Quoted in *ibid.*, p. 256.

11 For an account of the effect of the inner-city policies of the 1960s and 1970s see Susan Laurence and Peter Hall, 'British Policy Responses', in Peter Hall, ed., *The Inner City in Context*, 1981.

12 Colin Buchanan, *The State of Britain*, 1972, p. 78.

13 Rod Hackney, *The Good, the Bad and the Ugly*, 1988, p. 40. The first community architecture in the country was the Black Road scheme in Macclesfield (1972–74), where residents, led by Rod Hackney, fought the council to preserve their early

nineteenth-century terraced housing, and won. Reviled then as a 'builder' by some of his colleagues, Dr Hackney went on to become President of the RIBA in 1987.

14 'Views from the Crescents', Hulme Views Project, *Hulme News*, 1991.

15 *Ibid.*

16 See Hugh Wilson and Lewis Womersley, *Manchester Education Precinct: The Final Report of the Planning Consultants, 1967*, 1967, and *Manchester Education Precinct: A Review of the Plan, 1974*, 1974.

17 From his obituary in the *Architectural Review*, November 1990.

18 Quoted by Hackney in *The Good, the Bad and the Ugly*, p. 21.

19 Phill Bamford, *Manchester: Fifty Years of Change*, 1995, p. 39.

20 Quoted in 'Views from the Crescents'.

21 M. Middleton, *Cities in Transition*, 1991, p. 26.

22 *Hulme Study – Stage One: Initial Action Plan*, Department of the Environment, HMSO, London, 1990, p. 13.

23 *Architects' Journal*, 20 April 1994, p. 16.

24 *Manchester and Salford Inner Area Study*, 1978, p. 40.

25 *Ibid.*, p. 45.

26 *Ibid.*, p. 45.

27 *Ibid.*, p. 36.

28 Figures quoted in Alan Kidd, *Manchester*, 1993, p. 220.

29 Figures from *Poverty in Manchester: The Third Investigation*, Manchester City Council, 1988, quoted in Kidd, *Manchester*, p. 222.

30 'Residents Play a Part in Making Hulme Habitable', *Architects' Journal*, 20 April 1994.

31 Hulme Regeneration, *Rebuilding the City*, 1994, p. 15.

32 For more information see George Mills, 'Homes for Change/Work for Change', in J. Parkinson-Bailey, ed., *Sites of the City*, 1996, pp. 111–14.

33 *Architects' Journal*, 20 April 1994, p. 10.

34 Quoted in 'Residents Play a Part in Making Hulme Habitable'.

35 *Manchester: Making it Happen*, Planning and Environmental Health Handbook, Manchester City Council, 1996/97, p. 1.

CHAPTER 11   THE 1970S: DEVELOPERS AND DEMOLITION

1 P. Ambrose and B. Colenutt, *The Property Machine*, 1975, p. 37.

2 A full set of figures and discussion is given in C. M. Law, T. Grundy and M. L. Senior, *Comparative Study of Conurbations Project*, 1984, pp. 86–101.

3 *Service Sector Employment in Manchester, 1971–1976*, City of Manchester Planning Department, Manchester, 1978, p. 18.

4 Ambrose and Colenutt, *Property Machine*, pp. 63, 64.

5 Quoted by Stephen Gardner in the *Observer*, 25 February 1973.

6 Richard Sheppard, 'In Search of the Unique', *RIBA Journal*, June 1973.

7 All the gory details are given in Raymond Fitzwalter and David Taylor, *Web of Corruption*, 1981.

8 Patrick Nuttgens, 'Towards the Future', in Barbara Goldstein, ed., *Architecture: Opportunities, Achievements*, 1977, p. 97.

9 John Millar, Manchester City Planning Officer and President of the Royal Town Planning Institute, 1972–73, in *The Times*, 12 November 1972, quoted in Malcolm MacEwen, *Crisis in Architecture*, 1974, p. 16.

10 *Manchester's Architectural Heritage*, 1974, p. 1. A Department of Environment survey of the city took place in 1973, with a list of 600 buildings issued in October 1974. A survey in the early 1990s by the Department of National Heritage resulted in 960 buildings being listed in 1993, 50 per cent of which were in the city centre. There is

no specific provision for conservation, but the city spent about £3·5 million between 1988 and 1993 on conservation-related matters. It may be noted that even in the 1980s Liverpool had 2,300 listed buildings.

11 Under the terms of the Planning (Listed Buildings and Conservation Areas) Act of 1990, local authorities are now required to identify areas of special architectural or historical interest, the character or appearance of which it is desirable to preserve or enhance, and to designate them as conservation areas. In Manchester, twenty-eight such areas have already been designated, with others to follow.

12 Randolph Langenbach in Marcus Binney *et al.*, *Satanic Mills*, p. 12.

13 Extract from Minutes of the Town Hall Committee, July 1971.

14 Colin Amery and Dan Cruickshank, *The Rape of Britain*, 1975, p. 11.

15 John Betjeman, foreword to *ibid.*, p. 7.

16 Nikolaus Pevsner, *The Buildings of England: South Lancashire*, 1969, p. 295, [62].

17 The author is indebted to discussions with Malcolm Brown of Levitt Bernstein, the partner in charge of the design of the Royal Exchange Theatre.

18 John Millar, 'Planning for the Future', in H. P. White, ed., *The Continuing Conurbation*, 1980, p. 172.

19 Brian Rodgers, 'Manchester: Metropolitan Planning by Collaboration and Consent; or, Civic Hope Frustrated', in G. Gordon, ed., *Regional Cities in the U.K., 1890–1980*, 1986, p. 57.

20 Miles Wright and Paul Brenikov, 'Towards Urban Renewal', *Architects' Journal*, June 1960.

21 Michael Kennedy, *Portrait of Manchester*, 1970, p. 183.

22 The name 'Arndale' is derived from ARNold Haggenbach and Sam ChippinDALE, founders of the Arndale Property Trust in 1950. Haggenbach was a third-generation Swiss baker from Wakefield, Chippendale was an estate agent in Bradford. The firm began by building small shopping parades in Yorkshire, and later began buying up cheap land for speculative development. Their story is told in O. Marriott, *The Property Boom*, 1967.

23 Quoted by David Ward in 'Sales Pitch', *Guardian*, 10 October 1978.

24 *Ibid.*

25 *Ibid.*

26 Manchester City Council Planning Department, *The Arndale Development,* information sheet, Manchester City Council, January 1976.

27 Idris Walters, 'Arndale Approach', *Building Design*, 11 January 1974.

28 Ward, in 'Sales Pitch'.

29 *Ibid.*

30 Quoted in, *ibid.*

31 *Manchester Evening News*, 4 October 1974.

32 The author is indebted for this information to John Sheard, who, with John Seward, was one of the architects of the scheme.

33 The author is grateful to Peter Crockett, of Morrison Merlin, for his reminiscences and for digging into his archives for information. Peter Crockett was clerk of works on the G-MEX and Midland Hotel projects, and is Property Manager of the Great Northern Experience. A fuller discussion of the refurbishment of G-MEX is given in Jack Bogle's essay in J. J. Parkinson-Bailey, ed., *Sites of the City*, 1996. The Seminar Centre at the side of G-MEX is covered in Nicholas Bogle's essay in the same publication.

34 With 750 staff in Manchester, London, Sheffield, Glasgow, Belfast and Dublin, BDP are probably the country's largest multi-disciplinary practice.

CHAPTER 12   1980 TO THE MID-1990S: ENTERPRISE AND THE CMDC

1 Department of the Environment, *Policy for the Inner Cities*, 1997, quoted in Robert Home, *Inner City Regeneration*, 1982, p. 44.

2 *Policy for the Inner Cities*, quoted in N. Deakin and J. Edwards, *The Enterprise Culture and the Inner City*, 1993, p. 20.

3 Mark Dickinson, *Goodbye Piccadilly*, 1990, p. 76.

4 *Renaissance – North West*, 1987, pp. 81, 82.

5 *Ibid.*, p. 13.

6 Warren Marshall is the Urban Design and Conservation Officer. Excerpts from his personal and unofficial 'Design Guide to the City Centre' were published in *Urban Design Quarterly*, April 1994.

7 Quoted in the *Manchester Metro News*, 28 July 1995. The losing submissions are illustrated on p. 3 of the *Manchester Evening News*, 7 February 1995.

8 Quoted in the *Manchester Metro News*, 12 September 1997.

9 For a history of the Chinese community in Manchester see Yung Yung Buckley, *British Soil, Chinese Roots*, 1996.

10 *Renaissance – North West*, p. 24.

11 The author is obliged to Vic Basil of Holfords for this story. It is worth noting that one of Leach Rhodes Walker's alternative schemes for Heron House was for a mirror glass building.

12 Further details can be found in George Mills, 'New Headquarters for Siemens plc', in J. Parkinson-Bailey, ed., *Sites of the City*, 1996.

13 *Renaissance – North West*, pp. 86, 87.

14 The author is indebted to John Lynch of Fairhursts Designs for the detailed information on the Northern Gateway initiative. The report was published as Manchester and Salford Phoenix Initiatives *et al.*, *The Northern Gateway to Two Cities*, 1988.

15 Deakin and Edwards, *Enterprise Culture*, p. 39.

16 Doreen Massey, 'Local Economic Strategies', in S. MacGregor and B. Pimlott, *Tackling the Inner Cities*, 1991, pp. 256, 257.

17 Michael Middleton, *Cities in Transition*, 1991, p. 49.

18 Together with Teesside, Tyne and Wear, the Black Country and Cardiff UDCs.

19 Chris Law, 'Property-led Urban Regeneration in Inner Manchester', in P. Healy *et al.*, *Rebuilding the City*, 1992, p. 72.

20 *Trafford Park, Greater Manchester*, undated.

21 According to Mike Shields, ex-leader of Trafford Park Development Corporation, on BBC-2's 'Working Lunch', 6 March 1998.

22 Deakin and Edwards, *Enterprise Culture*, p. 4.

23 Quoted in *ibid.*, p. 31.

24 Teesside UDC was the largest at 11,260 acres, the Black Country next at 6,420, then London Docklands at 5,100, Trafford Park at 3,140, Merseyside at 2,370, Leeds at 1,330 and Bristol at 890.

25 Details taken from the CMDC's 'Opportunities' brochure, 1993.

26 Full figures are given in Rob Imrie and Huw Thomas, eds, *British Urban Policy and the Urban Development Corporations*, 1993, p. 17.

27 *Manchester Evening News*, 29 November 1991.

28 Law, 'Property-led Urban Regeneration', pp. 75, 76.

29 Figures from Berry Ritchie, *The Good Builder*, 1997, p. 179.

30 The building is discussed in detail in George Mills, 'Manchester Metropolitan University Library', in J. Parkinson-Bailey, ed., *Sites of the City*, 1996.

31 For more information see James Stevenson's essay 'Crown Courts, Minshull Street', in J. Parkinson-Bailey, ed., *Sites of the City*, 1996.

32 The *Manchester Plan*, 1992, p. 133.

33 *Acquisitions Monthly*, Manchester supplement, May 1996, p. 12.

34 Quoted by David Thame, 'The Manchester Follies', *Business*, December 1995, p. 39.

35 An essay by Nicholas Thompson of RHWL can be found in Parkinson-Bailey, *Sites*. An independent view of the Bridgewater Hall, together with a brief history of concert hall design, can be found in *RIBA Profile*, October 1996. Len Grant's *Built to Music*, 1996, is a wonderful collection of his photographs of the building of the hall.

36 The details of this scheme are taken from Robin Derham's essay in Parkinson-Bailey, *Sites*, p. 31.

37 'Fitzroy Robinson was here', *Building Design*, 3 November 1972.

38 For details of both the 82 King Street and 201 Deansgate buildings see Andrew Robson's essays in Parkinson-Bailey, *Sites*, pp. 77–85.

39 *City Pride*, 1994.

CHAPTER 13 THE 1990S: BIDDING FOR THE GAMES, AND A BOMB

1 Councillor Jack Flanagan, *Manchester Evening News*, 2 September 1998.

2 Beswick, Clayton and Openshaw are to benefit from a £25 million Beacons for a Brighter Future Partnership funding by 2007, and there are prospects of a further £67 million of public and private funding being generated. It is hoped that the government will announce a further £50 million ten-year funding in September 1999.

3 Figures from KPMG Management Consulting, quoted in *Manchester 2000: The British Olympic Bid*, 1993, pp. 4, 5.

4 A more detailed account of the Velodrome and the Arena can be found in J. J. Parkinson-Bailey, ed., *Sites of the City*, 1996.

5 *Manchester Metro News*, 29 July 1994.

6 Though the architects want to see the towers demolished as part of their master plan.

7 Gerry Boone of Deloitte & Touche in the *Financial Times*, 19 February 1998.

8 Ian Simpson, architect, in 'Good Enough for Manchester', *Manchester Forum*, December 1997.

9 The runner-up teams were: BDP, Donaldsons and Oscar Faber; R. James Chapman, Mills Beaumont Levey Channon, OMI, Gillespies, Ove Arup, Benjamin Thompson & Associates, Professor Ian Taylor, Salford University, and Professor Brian Robson, University of Manchester; Halliday Meecham with Richard Reed & Associates; Llewelyn Davies, Michael Hyde & Associates, JMP Consultants, Derek Lovejoy Partnership, Roger Tym & Partners, DTZ and Debenham Thorpe.

10 Sir Alan Cockshaw, Chairman of Manchester Millennium, in *Millennium*, spring 1997.

11 Originally named Kemsley House, the building was the headquarters of the *Daily Despatch* and the *Manchester Evening Chronicle*, and printed northern editions of the *Daily Telegraph*, *Empire News*, *Sunday Times*, *Sunday Graphic* and *Sunday Chronicle*. At Thomson House, as it was renamed in the 1980s, were printed the *Daily Telegraph*, *Daily Mirror*, *Sunday Times* and *Sporting Chronicle*. It was renamed Maxwell House by the ill-fated newspaper magnate Robert Maxwell, and from here the *Daily Mirror* and *Sunday Mirror* were printed.

12 *Manchester Metro News*, 25 July 1997.

13 *Ibid.*, 15 March 1996.

14 *Manchester Evening News*, 24 October 1995.

15 *Ibid.*, 18 August 1998.

16 *Great Northern Experience*, publicity brochure published by the development partners.

17 *Manchester Metro News*, 24 October 1997.

18 *Manchester Evening News*, 16 February 1998.

19 Quoted by Ray King, 'Towering Infernal, or Is it really a Blessing?', *Manchester Evening News*, 8 May 1998.

20 In July 1999 the City Council (working with English Heritage) announced the proposal for a new 200 bed hotel scheme for the Free Trade Hall but with the body of the hotel built as an extension on Windmill Street. The Council rejected schemes which would have provided a public space and bar on the ground floor with apartments and offices above; a mixture of shops, leisure and offices; and a world snooker centre.

21 *Piccadilly Regeneration Study*, Manchester City Council, June 1997.

22 *Manchester Evening News*, 11 August 1998. Lambert Smith Hampton have managed the property on behalf of the Arab Bank since 1994.

23 From a publicity brochure issued by the City Council, 1999.

24 Roger Stephenson, 'Learning to love the Plaza', *Architects' Journal*, 12 October 1995.

25 In 1998 the average office rental in Manchester was £210 per square metre for a central location in an office block erected in the previous ten years. Average retail rental was £1,000 per square metre in the town centre, going up to £2,500 per square metre in a prime position. Source: *Valuation Office Property Market Report*, spring 1998.

26 Details from *Manchester Metro News*, 28 August 1998.

27 The Trafford Centre had 26 million visitors in 1999.

28 Peel Holdings, the parent company of the Ship Canal Company, has assets of £700 million, mostly in the Manchester region, making it Manchester's largest private landholder. The chairman, John Whittaker, lives in tax exile, leaving deputy chairman Robert Hough in charge of Peel Holdings. Hough is also chairman of the Ship Canal Company, and under his guidance the payroll was reduced by 80 per cent and profits put up by 700 per cent in four years.

29 Quoted in N. Deakin and J. Edwards, *The Enterprise Culture and the Inner City*, 1993, p. 192. Chapter eight, 'Private enterprise alone', gives a full account of the planning enquiries and argues meaningfully in support of the Trafford Centre. One of the authors, Edwards, presented information to the planning inquiries on behalf of the Manchester Ship Canal Company.

30 'Bluewater' in Kent, even larger than the Trafford Centre, opened in spring 1999, and is likely to be the last such development – until the next one?

31 Martin Vickerman of Grimley, quoted in 'Reporting Britain 4', *Financial Times*, 19 February 1998.

32 A. P. Simon, *Manchester Made Over*, 1936, p. 47.

33 Quoted in *Manchester Metro News*, 17 October 1997.

34 Jonathan Glancey, 'Exciting, daring design? Not if we can help it', *Guardian*, 30 March 1998. The Cardiff Opera House scheme designed by Zaha Hadid was dropped in favour of a Wales Millennium Centre, designed by the Percy Thomas Partnership.

35 Peel Holdings put up £12·5 million, the European Regional Development Fund £8·2 million, English Partnerships £2·5 million, Trafford Council £2·5 million and the Imperial War Museum £2·5 million.

36 Source, *Marketing Manchester*.

37 *Manchester Metro News*, 28 January 1999.

CHAPTER 14   INTO THE TWENTY-FIRST CENTURY: A EUROPEAN CITY

1 Quoted in *Investors' Chronicle*, 26 September 1997, p. 8.

2 *Ibid.*, pp. 32, 62, 64.

3 Healy & Baker, *European Real Estate Monitor*, Europe's Top Cities, 1992.

4 Cited in Ian Taylor, Karen Evans and Penny Fraser, *A Tale of Two Cities*, 1996, p. 302.

5 According to a survey by international property consultants Healey & Baker, quoted in *Millennium*, No. 5, summer 1998.

6 Ian Nairn, *Britain's Changing Towns*, 1967, p. 45.

NOTES

7 *Ibid.*, pp. 45, 46. Although revised for the book in 1967, the essay on Manchester had originally been published in the *Listener* in September 1960.

8 Report, *Housing Land Supply*, Greater Manchester Research, 1999.

9 According to research by the Manchester Metropolitan University's Institute of Popular Culture.

10 In his introduction to the 1998 *Restaurant, Café Bar and Pub Guide to Greater Manchester*, published by City Life, an excellent and objective guide to food and drink in the Manchester area.

11 *Building Design*, 4 September 1998, has a well illustrated article on Quay Bar.

12 Jim Ramsbottom won the 1999 Manchester Civic Society Spirit of Manchester Award for his contribution to the regeneration of Castlefield.

13 A full account of the design of the bridge is given in Mark Whitby's article 'Merchants Bridge, Castlefield', in J. J. Parkinson-Bailey, ed., *Sites of the City*, 1996.

14 HRH the Prince of Wales, Urban Village Forum, Manchester, 14 July 1998.

15 For their history see Anthony Rea, *Manchester's Little Italy*, 1988.

16 For more information on the Ancoats vision see Paul Butler, David Tye and Ian Finlay, 'Ancoats Urban Village: Old Mills, New Homes', in J. J. Parkinson-Bailey, ed., *Sites of the City*, 1996.

17 The register covers 1,500 Grade I and II sites which have fallen into disrepair, and covers 198 properties in the north-west, eighteen of which are in Manchester.

18 'Reporting Britain: Manchester', *Financial Times*, 19 February 1998.

GAZETTEER

Page numbers are given for significant buildings described in the text
Other buildings are described here

ALBERT SQUARE

Town Hall. Alfred Waterhouse, 1867–77. Grade I. See p. 106

Albert Memorial. Thomas Worthington, 1862–67. Grade I. See pp. 103, 203

Fountain. Thomas Worthington, 1896–97. To celebrate the opening of the Thirlmere Viaduct.

Memorial Hall, 14 Lloyd Street. Thomas Worthington, 1863–66. Grade II*. See pp. 105, 106

Lloyd's House, corner of Lloyd Street and Southmill Street. Speakman & Charlesworth, 1867–68. Grade II. Headquarters of Manchester shipping offices and packing company. A poorer building than its neighbours, in brick with over-heavy stone decoration. The first bay on Lloyd Street and all the Southmill Street façade have windows in triplets like the Memorial Hall opposite. A huge corner turret is carried on pairs of Gothic columns which look far too frail to carry the weight above them. See p. 117

Albert Chambers, 16 Lloyd Street. Clegg & Knowles, 1866–68. Grade II. The first building after the Memorial Hall to be erected on the Lloyd Street side. The ground and first-floor arches follow the line of the arches of its neighbour, as do the sills and string courses. The upper, third-floor windows are debased Venetian Gothic. The roof line has Italianate swallow-tail crenellations. Darley Dale sandstone. There is a bust of Prince Albert over the entrance door. See p. 117

Bridgewater Buildings, 18 Lloyd Street. Clegg & Knowles, dated 1873. Grade II. Offices of the Bridgewater Canal Company. Little note seems to have been taken of the earlier adjoining buildings, but the third-floor windows are simplified versions of those on Albert Chambers, to the right. At each end of the building, below the cornice, are what can only be described as Gothic pilasters, but not wide enough to fill the wall space. See p. 119

St Andrew's Chambers, 20 Lloyd Street, corner of Mount Street. George Tunstall Redmayne, dated 1872. Grade II. Built as offices for the Scottish Widows Fund Life Assurance – hence the figure of St Andrew on the façade. Darley Dale sandstone, and in thirteenth-century Gothic like the Town Hall. See p. 00

Heron House, between Lloyd and Brazennose Streets. Leach Rhodes Walker, 1979–82. Four storeys and dormer windows over a ground-floor arcade, around four sides of a huge trapezoidal light well. All in brick, and replacing earlier brick buildings.

Commercial Union offices, between Brazennose Street and Tasle Alley. Kingham Knight Associates, 1983. Four storeys over an arcade and running down Brazennose Street. In a light-red brick, and window surrounds in sandstone-looking concrete. Fourth storey has oriels with round-headed dormers above. Like Heron House, the ground floor is used as a restaurant.

Liverpool London & Globe Insurance, between John Dalton Street and Tasle Alley. Percy Worthington, 1903. A narrow building, given some majesty by its Portland stone cladding and the four giant-order Corinthian pilasters carrying a deep entablature and heavy cornice.

Glasgow Assurance Building, corner of Cross Street (1–7 Princess Street). Pennington & Bridgen, 1877. Grade II. Red brick, white stone dressings, with pierced stone balconies and cut brickwork panels. Enormous variety in the window openings. Prominent gables and tall chimney stacks (the very tall stacks abutting the Northern Assurance Building next door were extended after that building was erected). The peculiar porched openings into the roof space look like a later addition but are original. See p. 119

Northern Assurance Building (9–21 Princess Street). Waddington & Dunkerley, 1902. Grade II. Free, Flemish style. Windows stepped back behind semicircular arches, Dutch gables. Portland stone and a grey granite infill which is picked up as the columns on the upper storeys. On the ground floor, Wippell's, one of the few shops where one can buy a bishop's mitre or a bow tie. See p. 119

ALL SAINTS AND ENVIRONS

All Saints Building. Gordon Taylor, 1978. Steel and concrete with red brick cladding, for Manchester Polytechnic, now the Metropolitan University's administration centre and main library, one of the best arts libraries in the provinces.

CAVENDISH STREET

Chorlton-on-Medlock Town Hall. Richard Lane, 1830–31. Grade II. See p. 61

School of Art. George Tunstall Redmayne, 1881. Grade II. Sandstone and Gothic Revival, 'but take the period details away and you have Mackintosh's School of Art, i.e. an ornate treatment of the centre, but otherwise all frankly large studio windows' (Pevsner, *Buildings of England: South Lancashire*, p. 313). Red brick extensions to the rear, J. Gibbons Sankey, 1898–1918. Now part of the Metropolitan University's Faculty of Art and Design.

LOWER ORMOND STREET

Bellhouse Building. 1832, home of David Bellhouse, Jnr. Converted by Thomas Worthington & Sons in 1910 to the Manchester Ear Hospital (until 1974). Only the street façade is original and is listed Grade II; behind is a reconstruction of the original house, now offices of the Metropolitan University.

St Augustine's Church. Desmond Williams & Associates, 1968. Load-bearing brick, and almost entirely roof-lit. Designed to seat 500, some of whom are in a gallery over the narthex. The altar is arranged so the celebrant of the Mass faces the congregation.

Ormond Building. Mangnall & Littlewood, dated 1881. Red brick with sandstone dressings. Generally Italianate, but a mixture of Classical and Flemish features (like the chimney stacks disguised as gables). Home to the Poor Law Guardians and a register office. Emmeline Pankhurst worked here.

Righton Building. 1905. Grade II. Terracotta and brick, built as a drapery shop for William Righton. In 1959, a shop for Till & Kennedy, ironmongers, until 1969, after which it became the Students' Union. Now the home of the Metropolitan University's Department of History of Art and Design. Internally, a top-lit gallery supported on cast-iron columns, around which is the benching on which cloth was measured.

The Grand. Was the A. Collie & Co. Warehouse, Mills & Murgatroyd, 1867.
 Grade II. Converted into the Grand Hotel in 1880. Converted into grand flats
 by Simpson Architects, 1988. See pp. 7, 69, 71, 283

College of Commerce. S. G. Besant Roberts, City Architect's Department, 1962. All
 concrete and rather grim, and relieved only by the Library, below. Now part of the
 Metropolitan University.

Manchester Metropolitan University Library Building. Mills Beaumont Leavey, 1994.
 White rain-screen cladding, like their Siemens Building. Note the *brise soleil* on the first
 floor to shade the computer suite. See p. 235

Crown Courts. Was the Police and Sessions Court. Thomas Worthington, 1867–73.
 Grade II*. Refurbished by Hurd Rolland Partnership, completed in 1996. See pp. 114, 237

BARBIROLLI SQUARE

Bridgewater Hall and offices. Renton Howard Wood Levin, 1990–96. See p. 238

BENGAL STREET

For mills in this street see Chapter Two

BLACKFRIARS STREET

Warehouse, between Deansgate and Chapel Street. F. H. Oldham, 1884. Queen Anne
 Revival.

Ramada Renaissance Hotel. See DEANSGATE.

BLOSSOM STREET

St Peter. Isaac Holden & Son, 1859–60. Grade II. Romanesque, red brick with white brick
 dressings. Deconsecrated.

Nos 29–33. A late nineteenth-century, four-storey ice building, used to store fish and
 meat, once attached to possibly the earliest ice-making factory in the north.

BOOTH STREET

No. 1, Greg's Building. Possibly J. E. Gregan, 1845. Grade II. For Robert Hyde Greg,
 son of Samuel Greg of Quarry Bank Mill.

No. 4. Royle & Bennett, 1880s. Grade II. Red sandstone, tall Jacobean pilasters.

No. 6, Massey Chambers. Edward Salomons (and John Ely?), 1879. Grade II. For
 Thomas Jepson, solicitor. Replaced the Buck Hotel (demolished in 1876). York stone.
 Arched windows on first storey with carved heads in the arch spandrels. Note the
 veiled head over the doorway and the *putti* supporting the gable.

No. 8, Manchester & Salford Trustee Savings Bank. Edward Salomons, 1872. Grade II.
 Darley Dale stone, Italianate windows on first storey with carved heads on their
 keystones.

BOOTLE STREET

Manchester City Police Headquarters. G. Noel Hill, City Architect, 1936. Ferro-concrete,
 Portland stone-clad. Central courtyard for parades, underground courtyard for service
 in emergencies.

BRIDGE STREET

Albert Bridge. Jesse Hartley, 1850. Grade II

Albert Bridge House. E. H. Banks, Ministry of Works, 1958–59. Offices for 800 tax officials. Eighteen storeys, concrete-framed, Portland stone-clad and sill panels of grey glass. Much liked by Ian Nairn, 'easily the best modern building in Manchester, and an outstanding example of what good proportions and straightforward design can do. There is no misplaced hankering after Corbusier here, just nineteen storeys, the windows gridded up into a giant frame, the lifts gathered together behind blank walls at one end' (*Britain's Changing Towns*, 1967, p. 45). See p. 175

Scottish Life House. Leach Rhodes Walker, 1965. Now Manchester House. See p. 171

Masonic Temple. Percy Worthington, 1929. Grade II. Portland stone-clad and, belied by its plain exterior, inside it is a monumental Neoclassical building, and its main hall, with a coffered barrel vault carried on Ionic columns, has a great sense of scale. It won for Worthington the RIBA Gold Medal in 1930.

No. 50, Manchester & Salford Street Children's Mission. Late 1880s. Tall and elegant yet simple. Glazed faience, and heads at the base of the gable.

No. 64, Rational Chambers. Samuel Davidson, 1879. Brick and over-heavy stone, terracotta panels.

Nos 66–76, Bridge Street Chambers. Bramald & Smith, 1898. Note how the windows and pilasters continue round the corner into Deansgate on the façade of the Sawyer's Arms, but all in glazed terracotta.

No. 83, Kenworthy's Buildings. Bramald & Smith, dated 1902. Italianate but banded brickwork and a huge arched gable – note the mask.

BRIDGEWATER VIADUCT

Congregational Chapel (actually 378 Deansgate). Walters, 1858. Grade II. Now a recording studio.

Quay Bar. Stephenson Bell, 1998. Manchester Civic Society, Victorian City Award, 1999. See p. 288

On the left, in Knott Mill, 104 new apartments for Crosby Homes. Stephenson Bell, 1999. See p. 291

BROWN STREET

Nos 24–30, St James's Court. Fairhursts, mid-1980s. Red brick.

Nos 46–8, Lombard Chambers and Brooks's Bank. George Truefitt, 1868. Grade II. York stone. A mixture of Gothic and Italian. Tall, round-headed windows light the banking hall. Above, deep corbelled string courses act as sills for the windows. Dormer windows are gablets, and have Gothic colonettes. Spiky metal cage over corner tower. See p. 93

No. 55, Chancery Building, see CHANCERY LANE

CAMBRIDGE STREET, CHORLTON-ON-MEDLOCK

Chorlton New Mill. For Birley & Co., 1814–45. Grade II. Only the walls are left, and these are being repaired. See p. 23

CANAL STREET

Manto's. Benedict Smith Associates, 1989. The first bar on the street. Brick and steel with windows across the width of the façade to see out, and to be seen. A rooftop restaurant, the Sarasota. See p. 285

Corn and Produce Exchange. Ball & Elce, 1889–90, Potts Son & Pickup, 1904–14, in a staged building programme. Grade II. Replaced Richard Lane's building. Now 'The Triangle'. See p. 261

CASTLEFIELD

Merchants' Warehouse. The oldest extant canal warehouse in Manchester, 1827–28. Grade II. Conversion by Simpson Associates, 1996, into offices and studios. See pp. 16, 289

Middle Warehouse. 1831. Restored (AMEC design and build) 1992, into offices and flats. Now Castle Quay. See pp. 17, 289

Britannia Mills. 1810s. Conversion to loft apartments by Urban Splash, 1998. See p. 00

Eastgate Building. 1810s. Conversion by Stephenson Bell, 1992. Was Gail House, Lamb's furniture manufactory. 1993, won Civic Trust award for outstanding contribution to the quality and appearance of the environment.

Dukes 92. Conversion of Merchants' Warehouse stables into public house. Stephenson Bell, 1992, for Jim Ramsbottom, the first person to see the potential of Castlefield. See p. 289 Extension, OMI Architects, 1998.

Youth Hostel, on Potato Wharf. Halliday Meecham, 1995. A 154 bed hostel with licensed café, games room, self-catering kitchens and laundry. Popular and inexpensive.

CATALAN SQUARE

Barça. Harrison Ince, 1996, for Mick Hucknall. A two-storey café bar tucked under the railway arches. See p. 289

Merchant's Bridge. Whitby & Bird, 1996. A torsion structure designed by engineers and selected for a Millennium Product Award. See p. 290

CATEATON STREET

No. 14, Mynshull's House. William Ball and Thomas Brookes Elce, 1890. Grade II. Jacobean revival, in red sandstone and terracotta. Carvings by J. Jarvis Millson.

CHANCERY LANE

Chancery Building. Hamilton Associates, 1995–96. Replaces a nineteenth-century warehouse. Note façade of original building on Brown Street, Grade II, and a replica wall on Chancery Lane.

CHAPEL WHARF, SALFORD

Trinity Bridge House. Leach Rhodes Walker, 1998–99. Private Finance Initiative building for the Inland Revenue. Fast-track design and build. Linked to Manchester by Calatrava's Trinity Bridge (see ST MARY'S PARSONAGE). See p. 276

CHARLOTTE STREET

No. 10, Charlotte House. Edward Walters, 1857. Grade II. Could easily be mistaken for a gentlemen's club. Nine bays of brick but the window surrounds and the whole of the ground floor in sandstone. The second storey is marked out as the *piano nobile* by the use of corbelled window sills and pediments above the windows. Note the ground-storey stressed keystones, a feature of most of Walters's buildings. See p. 73

Nos 14–16. Edward Walters, 1860. Grade II. Brick with sandstone dressings like No. 10. Note the prominent chimneys, on the office face of the building – insurance companies would not permit fireplaces in the warehouse areas.

No. 32, Hanover House. Spratley & Cullearn, 1983. A modern *palazzo*-style office block in brick.

No. 34, Manchester Associated Mills. Edward Walters, 1855. Grade II. Functional brick building with minimal sandstone dressings. Large stone entrance portal set asymmetrically in the fourth bay. All the floors are given equal treatment, and there is no indication of a *piano nobile*. See p. 73

No. 36, Fraser House. Corner of Portland Street. Walters, *c*. 1855. Grade II. Brick with stone dressings.

CHEETHAM HILL ROAD

No. 19, *c*. 1840. Grade II. Was a Methodist chapel, then a synagogue. Two storeys above a basement. Classical front.

Crumpsall and Cheetham District Library. Henry Price (City Architect), 1909–11. Grade II. Baroque Revival, red brick and sandstone dressings.

No. 107, Cheetham Town Hall. Thomas Bird, 1856. In the palazzo style, at present neglected.

No. 190, synagogue. Edward Salomons, 1873–74. Grade II*. For the Sephardic community. Now the Manchester Jewish Museum, and well worth a visit. See p. 85

St Luke. Thomas Witlam Atkinson, 1836. Grade II. Sadly, only the tower remains.

CHEPSTOW STREET

Oxford Court. Leach Rhodes Walker, 1987. See p. 233

Canada House. William G. Higginbottom, 1909. Grade II. Five storeys and an attic clad in buff terracotta, the second and third storeys as oriels set back behind the building line. The cast-iron frame of the building is revealed on the rear elevation. A fine Art Nouveau gate.

Chepstow House (Sam. Mendel Warehouse). Speakman & Charlesworth, 1874, then Speakman Son & Hickson. Grade II. See p. 71

Peveril of the Peak, public house, *c*. 1820, altered *c*. 1900. Grade II.

CHESTER STREET

Victoria and Albert Warehouses. 1843. Grade II. Large arched openings on street side and covered wharves facing river. The last extant riverside warehouses in Manchester. Converted by BDP, 1992, for Granada Theme Parks & Hotels, to a 132 bedroom four-star hotel. On each of the four upper storeys a concrete floor slab is supported on the original cast-iron and wood structural frame to provide fire and acoustic separation.

CHORLTON STREET

Arthur House. Cruickshank & Seward, 1963, for Central & District Properties. A clean and simple building of seven storeys in reinforced concrete. Each floor is self-contained for letting, accessed by the end staircase, the ground floor given over to car parking. Was in scale with surrounding warehouses.

Boulton House, between Bloom Street and Major Street. E. Kirby & Son, 1973. A modern interpretation of a Victorian warehouse.

Car park and bus station. Leach Rhodes Walker, 1963. Part of St Andrew's House complex. Reinforced concrete floors and pre-cast concrete panels.

Freemasons' Hall. William Mangnall, 1863. Grade II. Stone-clad, with pilasters and
engaged columns. Note the sculptures of Prudence, Fortitude, Temperance and Justice.
Home of the Freemasons until the building of the Masonic Temple, Bridge Street, 1929.
Now home to 'Oscar's'.

Corporation Street

Marks & Spencer. Building Design Partnership, 1997–99. See p. 258
Bridge, over. Hodder Associates and Ove Arup & Partners, 1999. See p. 263
Urbis. Simpson Architects, 1999–2000. See p. 262
CWS Building, corner of Hanover Street. F. E. L. Harris, dated 1906. Baroque revival
in red and grey granites, red brick and sandstone. Its twin demolished 1977 for the
Co-operative Bank, below.
Co-operative Bank, corner of Balloon Street. CWS architects, 1980. Four storeys in red
brick, and three more floors in the deep, grey, metal-clad roof.
CWS Building, corner of Hanover Street. W. A. Johnson, chief architect to the CWS,
1928. Grade II. Classical with attached, square Corinthian columns over rusticated base.
All in sandstone.

Cross Street

Arndale Centre. Wilson & Womersley, 1972–79. See p. 209
Royal Exchange. Bradshaw Gass & Hope, 1914–21. Grade II. See pp. 141, 206
Royal Exchange Theatre, Levitt Bernstein Associates, 1974 and 1998. See pp. 206, 257
Nos 11–15, Commercial Chambers. Walters Barker & Ellis, 1867–68. Grade II. Four
storeys and attic, in the *palazzo* style, but with arched windows and Gothic colonettes.
Praised by the *Builder*. Now Sabre House, refurbished and rebuilt by Fairhurst's.
The Observatory. Holford Associates, 1995–96. Incorporates the Cross Street Chapel on
the ground floor. L-shaped to fit the site. See pp. 4, 244
Nos 28–34, Alliance House, corner of St Ann's Street. Heathcote & Rawle, 1901.
Grade II. Stone-clad. Round-headed arches, and colonettes dividing the windows –
but not Classical. A profusion of gables replicating the shapes of the second-storey
windows (reminiscent of the Palazzo Corner-Spinelli, Venice). A large corner lantern
tower.
Nos 33–5, Lloyds Bank, corner of King Street. Heathcote, 1915. Grade II. Heathcote at his
most excessive, exuberantly Baroque. Statuary and decoration, Earp Hobbs & Miller.
Inside, a glazed coffered vault over the banking hall. See p. 129
No. 36, Hanover House (National House), corner of St Ann's Street. Horton & Bridgford
and Robert A. Walker of London, 1875. Grade II. Salomons received equal first
premium, but not the contract. Segmental-arched windows with broken-bed pediments.
A pediment over classicising details, and a convex entablature forming a balcony, all on
St Ann's Street. A strange mixture, perhaps due to two firms combining in the design.
Was the Conservative Club.
No. 37, Northern Rock Insurance, corner of King Street. Charles Heathcote, 1895.
Grade II. Flemish renaissance. Tall gables mark the corners. Note the sculptural
decoration above the central colonettes of the first-storey windows. See p. 129
No. 42, Mr. Thomas's Chop House. Dated 1901. Grade II. Three small storeys and gable.
Glazed terracotta.
Nos 56–60, Ottoman Bank, corner of King Street. Mills & Murgatroyd, c. 1889. Red brick
and notable corkscrew chimneys.

No. 68, Eagle Insurance, between King Street and South King Street. Charles Heathcote, 1911. Grade II. Giant Ionic corner pilasters, blocked columns at first floor, huge semicircular gables, especially on South King Street. See p. 129

Nos 70–6, Steam Packet House, corner of South King Street. Grace & Farmer and Frank Oakley & Gerald Sanville (son of Salomons), 1910s. Clad in Portland Stone; restrained, with decoration only between second and third storeys.

No. 86, Anglia House, corner of John Dalton Street. Charles Heathcote, dated 1904. Grade II. Baroque in polished brown granite, red sandstone.

CROWN SQUARE

Courts of Justice. Leonard C. Howitt, City Architect, 1960–62. Grade II. Steel-framed, Portland Roach cladding, with a façade of huge plate-glass panels held between thin stone piers. The canopied ceremonial entrance is no longer used, for security reasons. Inside, the public concourse runs the length of the building, providing access to the six court rooms. On the upper three floors are rooms for the judiciary, counsel and administration. Entrance extension by the Property Services Agency, 1986. See p. 183

Magistrates' Court. Yorke Rosenberg & Mardall, 1971. Interior public spaces faced with Travertine marble. This building will shortly be demolished for the Crown Square developments. See p. 184

Cumberland House, Crown Square/Spinning Fields. Leach Rhodes Walker, 1965–67. Education offices, *Manchester Evening News* offices, works, precinct, all soon to go. See p. 183

DALE STREET

Stone-built warehouse, of 1806, corner of Dale Street and Back China Lane. Grade II*. William Crossley. Belonged to Rochdale Canal Company and later Carver's Warehouse. 'Weather-shot' millstone grit. Four storeys and attic. Straddles canal arm off Piccadilly basin with two arched shipping holes, flanked by two smaller arches for road access. East and south elevations have loopholes. Ground floor has six millstone grit piers grouped in pairs, upper floors have cast-iron columns supporting timber joists. Attic housed the hoists originally powered by a 'breast-shot' water wheel (of 1824) situated in the southernmost part of the building. Hydraulic power, supplied by Manchester Corporation, powered the hoists from about 1895. A water tunnel (constructed in 1830) runs off to the waterwheel of the (demolished) 1822 warehouse which stood next to Dale Street lock. Sadly neglected.

Langley Buildings, corner of China Lane. R. Argile, 1908. Grade II. Five storeys and three bays on Dale Street, all in deep brown glazed terracotta, and fifteen bays running down China Lane.

Industry House, corner of Back China Lane. W. Longworth, 1913. Grade II. Five storeys and five bays on Dale Street, and a decorative corner entrance. Buff glazed terracotta.

DANTZIC STREET

No. 29, Dantzic Building. W. A. Johnson, 1937–42. Grade II. Streamlined and modernist. Cream bricks laid as stretchers, and bands of metal Crittall windows, curving round the corners. Farther along, the Redfern Building is similar.

DEANSGATE

Renaissance Manchester Hotel. Cruickshank & Seward, 1960s, as an office, Fairburn House. Later converted into the hotel. Refurbishment by EGS Designs (1999–2000) will open the reception area to daylight. See p. 182

Speakers' House. Douglas Stephen & Partners, 1963. First on the left before Barton Arcade. Concrete-framed, of seven storeys over a two-storey coarse aggregate and brick podium.

Barton Buildings and Barton Arcade. Corbett Raby & Sawyer, 1871. Grade II*. One of the first buildings to be erected on the newly widened Deansgate. The Barton Buildings have Italianate details, but are not in the *palazzo* style. The Arcade is three storeys of iron and glass, mass-produced by Macfarlane's Saracen Foundry in Glasgow. Not built to the scale of Matcham's arcades in Leeds, but elegant and light, and the proportions and detailing make it a treasure.

Nos 83–93, Waterstone's. Kendal Milne's original building, rebuilt by E. J. Thomson, 1873. Italianate but not a palazzo. See p. 80

Nos 95–103. See King Street, Nos 8–14

Nos 98–116, Kendal Milne's. J. S. Beaumont, 1938, but not opened until after World War II. Grade II. See p. 151

Nos 111–13, Queen's Chambers, corner of John Dalton Street. Pennington & Bridgen, 1876. Grade II. Another government office; note the royal arms above the corner entrance and Victoria's statue high on John Dalton Street. On the two major façades are a variety of window shapes, pointed, ogival and square-headed, but almost all with mullions and transoms. Battlemented balconies, buttresses and gables, all in a whitish sandstone. Note the gargoyles. It looks as though there should have been gables on John Dalton Street; as it is, that façade appears very truncated. See p. 119

Nos 118–24, corner of King Street West. Queen Anne Revival, of four storeys, red brick and simple stone detailing. Mullioned and transomed windows (plate glass has replaced the glazing bars) and gables over the second and fourth bays. Of the late 1870s, architect unknown. Now Daisy & Tom's toy shop.

Nos 126–8. Dated 1868. *Palazzo* style, red brick, white stone detailing.

No. 136, Halifax House, corner of Bridge Street. Turner Lansdown Holt, 1983. Above the ground floor are two over-sailing storeys and a slated roof with dormer windows. Apart from the roof, all is in brick, including the huge piers which run up to the roofline. Immensely thick, and the deep-set windows are almost lost in the sea of brickwork.

No. 138, Sawyer's Arms, corner of Bridge Street. Grade II. A rebuilding of a narrower pub (probably from 1777). It continues the style of Bridge Street Chambers, Bramald & Smith, 1898, and is obviously by them.

No. 140, Old Gas Board Office. Edward Salomons & Alfred Steinthal, 1880s. Stone with Jacobean details and a gable.

No. 144, Rylands Library. Basil Champneys, 1890–99. Grade I. Note on the side elevations the mythical creatures supporting the rainwater pipes. See p. 122

No. 127, Lincoln House, corner of Brazennose Street. Holford Associates, 1986. The first all-glass building in Manchester. Now occupied by Pannone's. See p. 225

No. 129, Centurion House, corner of Brazennose Street. Leach Rhodes Walker, 1977. Part of the landscaping of Brazennose Street. See p. 207

No. 182, Northcliffe House. Waddington Son & Dunkerley, 1904, and later additions by J. W. Beaumont, late 1920s (which must include the tower). Was offices for Associated Newspapers. This site is due to be developed. See p. 267

No. 184, Inland Revenue Office. Dated 1896. Grade II. Another Italianate building, for the Inland Revenue, now the County Court.

No. 151, Elliot House, between Lloyd Street and Jackson's Row. Royle & Bennett, dated 1888. Extended 1904 and 1914. Grade II. Was the School Board Office. Pink sandstone on ground floor and two storeys of red brick above. Sandstone surrounds and decorations, and terracotta panels. Jacobean pilasters and small dormers. Beautifully carved sandstone cartouches with *putti* surround the windows on the angled corners of the ground floor. It became the Register Office until the 1990s, and is now home to Simply Heathcote's. See p. 119

No. 201. Holford Associates, 1996–97. See p. 246

No. 202, **Royal London House**, corner of Quay Street. Heathcote, 1904. Grade II. Baroque revival in Darley Dale stone. Replaced the Scottish Panorama.

Nos 205–9, **Onward Buildings**. Heathcote, 1903–05. Grade II. Red brick and yellow terracotta. Was the Band of Hope building.

Nos 223–95. The longest Victorian frontage in the country. Built at the same time as the Great Northern Railway Company's Goods Warehouse – their offices were above the ground-floor shops. See p. 265

Great Northern Railway Company's Goods Warehouse. Designed by A. Ross of the GNR, consulting engineer W. T. Foxlee, 1896–98. Grade II*. Of hard, industrial blue brick on the lower two floors and red brick above. The walls are eight bricks thick at the three entrances, carrying decorated steel lintels, and the centres of the lintels are supported by steel columns. Internally, upright steel stanchions carry riveted wrought-iron beams and each stanchion is capable of carrying a load of 650 tons. 267 ft long, 217 ft wide and 75 ft high. See pp. 55, 265

Great Northern Initiative. Masterplan, SOM. Leslie Jones Architects, 1998–. See p. 264

No. 246, **Deansgate Court**. Henry Lord, 1900. Was Congregational Church House, built at cost of £20,000 on a site given by Mrs Rylands.

No. 298, **Sovereign House**. Small two-storey, four-bay Queen Anne Revival building tucked into the front of a modern brick building between Camp Street and Tonman Street. Red brick with sandstone banding and stone dressing to the tall, pedimented first-storey windows. Above the front rises a large shaped gable with a window set into its face.

Nos 322–30, **Library and Market Building**, corners of Tonman Street and Liverpool Road. George Meek & Allison, 1882. Grade II. Designed partly as a library and partly as an improved entrance to the Upper Campfield Market. Ground floor of sandstone, above which was the first-storey library, which had double windows to keep out the noise of traffic on Deansgate. Above, the fenestration is a very free interpretation of a Venetian opening. Figures in the arched pediment represent Commerce, Industry, Peace and Trade. The upper floor now contains the Urban Studies Centre, and on the lower floor are Dimitri's restaurant and Jowata, the first African restaurant in Manchester.

No. 376, **Atlas Bar**. Simpson Architects, 1994. Part-owned by the architect and Nick Johnson. Built into the railway arches, and at the rear is a small terrace designed by Landscape Projects. Manchester Civic Society Shop Window Award, Commendation, 1999. Opposite, at No. 343, is their delightful Delicatessen. See p. 288

DICKINSON STREET

North West Electricity Board Headquarters. H. S. Fairhurst & Son, 1963. Steel-framed, glass curtain wall, all set on a difficult L-shaped site.

FAULKNER STREET

Nos 41–3. Thomas F. Taylor, 1846. Grade II. Was a warehouse. Darley Dale stone, giant-order Doric columns over a deep rusticated base, and more rustication between the cornice and pediment.

Nos 52–4. Warehouse. Said to be Clegg & Knowles, 1876. Grade II. Four storeys of plain red brick.

No. 55, corner of Nicholas Street. Warehouse, Clegg & Knowles, 1870. Grade II. Similar to Nos 52–4.

No. 56. Warehouse. Said to be J. Feer, 1868. Grade II. Three storeys red brick, second and third storeys have very narrow paired windows.

Cathedral. Originally the Collegiate Church of St Mary, St Denys and St George, designated a cathedral in 1847. Grade I. The 'Angel Stone' is suspected to have come from the Church of St Mary which allegedly stood near the site and was mentioned in the Domesday Book. Lady Chapel, 1350; Ely Chapel, 1515; St John's Chantry, 1513. The choir stalls were described by Pevsner as 'the finest in the North of England'. Alterations carried out by John Palmer (1785–1846) in 1814–15. In 1864 the west tower was demolished and another one, 6 ft higher, erected in its place. The south porch was demolished, to be replaced by a two-storey one, and the clerestory was rebuilt in 1871. A new porch was added on the north side in 1872; the Fraser Chapel added in 1890; Baptistery added in 1892. J. S. Crowther was the diocesan architect. Victoria Porch by Basil Champneys; organ case by George Gilbert Scott; font by George Truefitt. Lady Chapel, Ely Chapel and St John's Chantry demolished 24 December 1940 by a land mine. Main beams of nave severely damaged, and nave was in danger of collapse. Damage worse than in any cathedral except Coventry. Restoration by Hubert Worthington and James Brown of Wilmslow, completed by 1963.

FOUNTAIN STREET

Royal & Sun Alliance. See YORK STREET

York House. See YORK STREET

Guardian Royal Exchange, corner of York Street. 1990s. Large, banded stone and brick, polychromatic on the corner. Rectangular windows with stone sills. No reveals, so the huge eaves are useful for keeping the rain off the walls.

Barnett House. Cruickshank & Seward, 1959–61. Concrete piers and sills of polished marbles. Set back over a deep podium, ready for the intended road widening.

No. 46, Overseers' and Churchwardens' Office. Thomas Worthington, 1851–53. Upper storeys added 1857–58. Grade II*. See p. 85

No. 50, offices. Fairhursts, 1980. For Barclays, extending into the warehouse on the corner of Spring Gardens. See WAREHOUSE, below.

Warehouse, corner of Spring Gardens. Stone, *palazzo*-style. Grade II. Given as Waterhouse, 1888–91, but stylistically very unlikely for architect or date. More likely to be Salomons or Clegg & Knowles, and dated around the 1870s. No. 50 is extended into this building behind the retained walls.

No. 60, offices. Spratley Cullearn & Philips, 1990s. Simple and elegant stone-clad evocation of a Victorian warehouse. Tall ground-floor windows, and the entrance corner marked by a plain column. Above is a deep, curved cornice.

No. 68, Fountain Court. Fairhursts, 1990s. Metal, and boxed-out windows with reflecting glass. Roofline battered in like a smaller version of Casson's NatWest building on King Street (*q.v.*).

Warehouse, corner of Booth Street. Dated 1868, and probably by Edward Salomons. Grade II. Red brick and stone and polychrome arches in the Venetian Gothic style.

81st on Fountain. Holford Associates, 1990s. Ground and mezzanine clad in polished figured marble, upper floors framed in deep rectangles of white stone, and convex on the middle bay. Top storeys cut back in stages.

GEORGE STREET

Chinatown arch, 1987. See p. 223

No. 34. Rutherford House. Ministry of Public Buildings and Works, 1967. Concrete-framed with stone cladding. A telephone exchange, it is a product of the Cold War, and is built over nuclear bunkers and the nuclear bomb-proof Guardian exchange.

GRANBY ROW

Granby House, Granby Row. G. H. Goldsmith, 1911. Grade II. Part of Halliday Meecham's Granby Village for Wimpey Homes, 1989–95. See p. 282

Nos 65–6, Orient House. G. H. Goldsmith, 1914. Grade II. White glazed façade, dominated by fluted and decorated Ionic columns. Greek key-pattern frieze, acroteria on door pediments. Rear and side elevations unadorned, metal windows. Glass and concrete box at rear.

GRAND ISLAND SITE

British Gas Building. Building Design Partnership, 1992. See p. 231

GRAPE STREET

Bonded warehouse. 1867–69, for the London & North Western Railway. 200 ft long and 100 ft wide, of five storeys and a basement, with arched doorways on the viaduct side. Possibly the earliest three-way iron frame structure in the country. Columns at 24 ft centres, ground-floor cruciform cast-iron columns carry riveted wrought-iron beams running lengthways, supporting wrought-iron cross-beams from which spring brick jack arches. The floor boards are of $2\frac{1}{2}$ in. thick redwood. See p. 50 Restoration work by Building Design Partnership, 1982–83. The exterior was to be used as a film backdrop, so walls were repaired with matching bricks overpainted with household soot. Replica steel windows on upper three floors. Internally the original, lower, railway sidings were jacked up to raise the sidings to the same level as the adjacent floor. Outside is the Sherlock Holmes' Baker Street set. See p. 216

GREAT ANCOATS STREET

Brownsfield Mill. 1820s. See p. 00

Daily Express **Building**. Sir Owen Williams, 1935–39. Grade II*. Glass and black Vitrolite panels. Rescued by Express Printers. Now owned by Carol Ainscow's Artisan H, and planned for flats and a restaurant. See pp. 151, 293

Piccadilly Village. Halliday Meecham, 1990–94. See p. 283

GREAT BRIDGEWATER STREET

Lee House. H. S. Fairhurst, 1928–31. Grade II. For Tootal Broadhurst Lee & Co., as an extension of the Tootal Building. Steel-framed, concrete floors, brick walls and bronze frames around the windows. Originally intended to be seventeen storeys high, and stone-clad all the way up. See p. 145

GROSVENOR STREET

Adult Deaf and Dumb Institute. John Lowe, 1877. Grade II. Gothic Revival, and in York stone. Above the door is a carving of a hand on a book, the badge worn in the nineteenth century by the deaf.

HANOVER STREET

Holyoake House (the Co-operative Union). F. E. L. Harris, dated 1911. Grade II. Neo-baroque in a light blue and cream faience.

For mills in this street see Chapter Two

HYDE ROAD

Nicholls's Hospital School. Thomas Worthington, 1877–80. For Benjamin Nicholls, as a memorial to his son, as a school to educate 100 poor boys whose parents were needy, honest, hard-working and Protestant. Brick with stone dressings, and erected faithfully to the perspective drawing prepared for Nicholls before his death. Five bays on either side of a 130 ft high central tower. Corner tourelles and a steep-pitched roof reminiscent of Worthington's design for the Town Hall. The attic, behind gabled dormer windows, housed the school dormitories. Subsequently the Ellen Wilkinson High School.

JACKSON'S ROW

Synagogue. P. Cummings & E. Levy, 1952. A plain brick building, and the first new Manchester building after World War II.

JOHN DALTON STREET

No. 16, Trinity Court. Stephenson Bell, 1993. Possibly one of the best interiors in Manchester behind the retained façade of what was once Prince's Chambers, Lamb's furniture showrooms (Edward Salomon, 1865). Further storeys added above the original building, but set back so as to be unobtrusive. See p. 235

St James's House, St James's Square. Fairhursts, 1997. Red brick with stone for the ground floor and for the many convex bays (large on the John Dalton Street and on the corner; smaller on St James's Square). Arched openings at ground storey carried on attached columns.

KENNEDY STREET

City Arms and the Vine. Both originally Georgian town houses. Both Grade II.

Nos 26–36, warehouses. See p. 270

Manchester Law Library. Thomas Hartas, 1885. Grade II*. 'Perpendicular' Venetian Gothic tracery in sandstone.

KING STREET

Nos 8–14 c. 1860s. Grade II. Four storeys and seven bays (and five bays on Deansgate with a large central gable). *Palazzo*-style in York stone. For S. & J. Watts, with their initials entwined over entrance, together with allegorical figures of arts and crafts and textile manufacture.

No. 35. 1736, residence of Dr Peter Waring. 1772, Jones & Co. bank. Later, NatWest Bank. Refurbished Leslie Jones, 1997. Grade II*. See p. 271

Nos 41–3. Buttress Fuller Alsop, 1994. See p. 271.

No. 56. Town house, c. 1700. Grade II. First-floor front room with fielded panelling and Ionic pilasters; rear room with plastered frieze with animal decorations. Linked by corridors to No. 41 South King Street.

No 62. Pennington & Bridgen, 1877. York stone, with pink sandstone framing around the centre three bays – these have ogival arched windows.

Nos 76–80, Prudential Assurance. Alfred Waterhouse, 1881. Grade II. Accrington brick and red terracotta. Round-headed windows, some with transoms. String course with diaper-work decoration is supported on a corbel table. Centre of the building and the corner bays supported on brick columns with stiff-leaf foliage. Door porches have dog-tooth mouldings, Romanesque rather than Gothic. Tower and gables removed, and ground floor granite-clad when it became a Barclays bank in 1975. Was home of the Manchester Stock Exchange, now Jigsaw and DKNY. The conversion to a shop, by Buttress Fuller Alsop Williams, won the Manchester Civic Society Shop Window Award, 1999. See p. 121

No. 55, National Westminster Bank. Casson Conder & Partners, 1966–69. Sold by NatWest to Orbit Developments, March 1999. See p. 177

Pall Mall Court. Lionel Brett & Pollen, 1969, for Sun Alliance. See p. 178

Norwich Union. 1960s. Curtain wall over steel frame.

Manchester (Reform) Club. Salomons with John Philpot-Jones, 1870–71. Grade II*. See p. 117

Bank of England. C. R. Cockerell, 1845. Grade I. Huge blocks of deeply channelled stone. Tall windows for the banking hall (the entrance on King Street was a later addition). Six giant-order Tuscan Doric columns carry a Doric frieze with triglyphs. Second-storey pilasters carry a central pediment, broken into by a thermal window carried on small Doric columns. Inside, four cast-iron columns support the double-height barrel vaults and a saucer dome carried on pendentives. The bank furniture has been stripped out and the banking hall is now somewhat bleak. See p. 91. Behind is:

No. 82. Holford Associates, 1996, for Friends' Provident, 1996. See p. 244

Nos 84–6, Sun Fire & Life Office. Given (wrongly) in the listed buildings index as *c.* 1910. Stylistically, and in size, much closer to 1840s or 1850s. Grade II. On the site of the Manchester & Salford Savings Bank. Stone, with a tall rusticated ground-floor arcade – could it have lit a banking hall? Above are two storeys of square-headed windows linked by giant-order Doric pilasters. The deep frieze is decorated with wreaths, reminiscent of Lane, but the architect is unknown.

No. 96, Ship Canal House. H. S. Fairhurst, 1924–26. Grade II. On the site of first Bank of England. See p. 144

Atlas Assurance Company, corner of Brown Street. Michael Waterhouse, grandson of Alfred, 1929. See p. 145

Midland Bank. Edwin Lutyens with Whinney Son & Austen Hall, designed from 1929, erected 1933–35. Grade II*. See p. 147

LEVER STREET

GPO Sorting Office. H. G. Swann, Ministry of Public Buildings and Works, 1965–68. Ten storeys of frosted glass and deep bands of coarse concrete aggregate. Decorated panels on the Hilton Street end. Bleak.

Nos 69–77. A row of restored houses, 1787. Grade II. See p. 8

LIVERPOOL ROAD

Liverpool Road Station. Grade I. On the corner of Water Street is the Agent's House, brick with a hipped roof and a Doric porch. The large windows are from its later conversion into a shop. Next are the 1830 railway buildings, banded rustication at ground floor but stuccoed brick above. A parapet conceals a hipped roof. The two bays on either side of a semi-portico were the booking hall and waiting room for first-class passengers; tacked on to the right-hand side is the second-class passenger doorway. The next two bays with an asymmetrically placed doorway were for the booking hall of the Grand Junction Railway, rebuilt in 1837. A pilaster running through both floors marks the junction of the buildings. To the right are the goods office and shops of

1831. The first-floor façades are only a screen concealing accommodation for rail coaches. See pp. 49, 215

1830 Goods Warehouse, Liverpool Road. Grade I. 320 ft long and 70 ft deep. Three floors and a basement on the carriers' side off Water Street, and two storeys on the railway side. Upper floors supported on timber posts, basement supports of cast iron. Building curved to meet the railway lines, and six sets of tracks originally ran into the building via turntables. Loopholes alternate with arched wagon entries on both the rail side and the street side of the building. By 1831 increased storage space had been created by the addition of an extra floor inserted into three bays. An engine house was added to the west elevation for steam power applied to some hoists. See p. 49 Two bays are now the National Electricity Gallery of the Museum of Science and Industry, and a further six bays are being converted at cost of £8 million as a display area for the goods handling, communications and food technology industries.

Higher Campfield Market Hall. Mangnall & Littlewoods, 1877–78. Grade II. Iron and glass, replacing an open hay and straw market. There was strong opposition to the building of the Market Halls because this had been the site of the Acres Fair since 1823.

Lower Campfield Market Hall. Mangnall & Littlewoods, 1877–78, opened in 1880. Grade II. Now the Air and Space Gallery of the Museum of Science and Industry. In World War II barrage balloons were made here.

LONDON ROAD

Piccadilly Station. W. R. Headley, succeeded by R. L. Moorcroft, British Rail Regional Architects, 1959–66. Replaced London Road Station, Mills & Murgatroyd, 1862. First stage development was the ten-storey office, housing all the railway staff in one block. The two-storey passenger concourse in front of the 1880s train shed was completed in 1966, just in time for the electrification of the west-coast main line, then the most up-to-date railway in the country. In process of being refurbished.

Gateway House, Station Approach. Richard Siefert & Partners, 1969. Serpentine block, as a speculative building, part of the general facelift of the station.

Police and Fire Station. Woodhouse Willoughby & Langham, 1904–06. Grade II*. See p. 134

LONG MILLGATE

Chetham's College. Grade I. Founded in 1653 by Humphrey Chetham, a merchant, and incorporated by royal charter in 1655. The long and low buildings, of local red Collyhurst sandstone, had been the homes of the Gresleys and the de la Warres. A schoolroom was built in 1878, a manual training department for instruction in wood and metal in 1888, and in 1898 a large swimming bath was added. It is the oldest Bluecoat school in the country. It provided, free of cost, maintenance, clothing and education for ninety-four boys aged between six and ten who were the legitimate children of respectable parents. Chetham's library is housed in what used to be the priests' dormitories of the Collegiate Church, partitions having been removed to provide one long room, and the narrow windows enlarged. Recent renovation work by Thomas Worthington & Sons.

Old Manchester Grammar School. Alfred Waterhouse, 1870. Grade II.

LOWER BYROM STREET

Warehouse, 1880, for the Great Western Railway. Grade II. Four storeys with huge square openings at rail level. Ground floor similar to the Grape Street warehouse but, on the first floor, cast-iron columns support wrought-iron girders. On the rail side are three sets of loopholes. Now the Education, Conference and Archive Centres of the Museum, and a Granada Television building masks the rear. See p. 216

Market Street

Lewis's. J. W. Beaumont & Sons, 1929. On the site of the Royal Hotel. See p. 141
Rylands (Debenham's). P. Garland Fairhurst, 1929–32. Grade II. See p. 146
Arndale Centre. Wilson & Womersley, 1972–79. See p. 209

Miller Street

Co-operative Insurance Society Building and New Century House. G. S. Hay of the CWS and Sir John Burnet Tait & Partners, 1962. Grade II. Twenty-five storeys over a five-storey podium. See p. 181

Mosley Street

Lewis's extension. J. W. Beaumont & Sons, 1929.
No. 10, Manchester & Salford Bank, corner of Marble Street. Richard Tattersall, 1836. Grade II. York stone. Above the tall rusticated ground storey is a portico of giant-order Corinthian columns framing the upper two storeys. See p. 89
No. 16, Harvest House. Walters, 1839. Grade II. Walters's first warehouse for Richard Cobden. The ground floor has been modified. See p. 69
No. 32, Colwyn Chambers, corner of York Street. J. Gibbons Sankey, 1898. Was the Mercantile Bank. Grade II. Portland stone. Tall ground floor with banded rustication. Attached Ionic half-columns couple the first and second floors. Above these another storey under a very deep cornice. Refurbished by Fairhursts, and an extension added at the rear, for Orbit Developments.
Nos 38–42, Manchester & Salford Bank, corner of York Street. Walters, 1861–62. Grade II*. York stone and gorgeous. Tall ground-floor banking hall with banded rustication over a vermiculated base. Window lights divided by thin and elegant cast-iron tracery. The walls take the form of Doric pilasters, and above minimal capitals is an entablature with a decorated frieze and modillions supporting a semi-cornice which also provides the base for the upper two storeys. Pedimented first-storey windows and, above, rectangular and garlanded second-storey windows. The corners of the upper storeys are marked by pilasters carrying a deep cornice. Behind the balustrade is an attic storey. The adjoining building (No. 44) by Barker & Ellis, 1880s. It is in matching York stone, and has subtle variations from the original; the ground-floor windows actually light two floors, the second-storey windows are cut back, and there are no pilasters. Internally, gutted and refurbished by Fairhursts for Williams & Glyn's Bank. Now the Royal Bank of Scotland. See p. 91
Nos 46–54, Williams & Glyn's Bank. Fairhursts, 1968–72. Now Royal Bank of Scotland. Monumental; large blocks of sandstone cut back to provide articulation, and all the lines and openings reflect the banks next door. This replaced Walters's Schwabe Warehouse, 1845.
No. 45, Williams Deacon's Bank Headquarters Building, corner of York Street. H. S. Fairhurst & Son, 1965 (now Royal Bank of Scotland). Built as the headquarters of the bank, with provision for the board, general management, intelligence and controlling departments. Composite steel and reinforced concrete. Clad in polished granites. Floors with high loading capacity for fireproof rooms designed for the safekeeping of documents. Designed to give as much light as possible into the offices,

so the six-storey main block stands on its own above a first floor which connects with the neighbouring building, and is the only office block in Manchester with trees on its roof. See p. 175

Nos 47–51, Barclay's Bank. Fairhursts, 1980s. York stone-framed lower storeys, the upper storeys glazed across the width of the building, and stepped back – did memories stir of Harry Fairhurst's demolished York House?

No. 57, Portico Library. Thomas Harrison, 1802–06. Grade II*. Major refurbishment of the library in the 1990s by Thomas Worthington & Sons. See pp. 11, 12

Nos 54A–70, Eagle Star House. Cruickshank & Seward, 1973. Originally for Royal London Assurance. A large block, which replaced the equally large Milne Building of *c.* 1845, its long bands of concrete and windows were an attempt to answer the bulk of the bank farther up the road. The open space at first storey was intended for deck access. See p. 205

Nos 59–61, Woolwich House, corner of Charlotte Street. H. S. Fairhurst & Son, 1965, for the Woolwich Building Society. Clad in Portland stone but the ashlar blocks, with windows punched through, give a visual impression of being load-bearing. Cutting back the corner angle not only marks out the different number of storeys on the two main façades, it also gives an impression of bulk to the building (though the give-away is the thin piers of the ground-floor banking hall). See p. 175

No. 75, Commercial Union Assurance, corner of Nicholas Street. H. A. J. Darlow of Watney Eiloart Inman & Nunn, 1964–66. Now Companies House. Six storeys over a podium base set back from the street line, except for its supporting piers. Its boxed-out concrete windows provide articulation and bulk. Concrete-framed, clad with a coarse, shelly Portland Roach. Replaced the Union Club, Richard Lane, 1836. See p. 175

Royal Manchester Institution (City Art Gallery). Charles Barry, 1829–35. Grade I. See pp. 64, 278

Mount Street

ABC Television House, corner of Peter Street. J. E. Beardshaw & Partners, 1959–60. Ten storeys of steel frame clad in matt grey-brown and glazed black ceramic tiles. Fifteen bays on Mount Street and a narrower building extending back twelve bays between Peter Street and Bootle Street. Site of the old Gaiety Theatre.

Friends' Meeting House. Richard Lane, 1828–30. Grade II. See p. 62

Lawrence Buildings, corner of Central Street. Pennington & Bridgen, 1874. Grade II*. For the Inland Revenue. Five storeys, of Darley Dale stone, the style is a florid fourteenth-century English Gothic. The public room (51 ft long by 20 ft wide by 14 ft high) was entered by the canted doorway under the two-storey oriel window on the corner of Central Street. Above the doorway are shields of the chief towns of the six northern counties; the entrance is flanked by pedestals bearing the lion and the unicorn. A life-size statue of Queen Victoria in a decorated niche on the Mount Street façade. Separate entrances and loading ways allowed parts of the sub-basement and upper rooms to be let out as offices. See p. 119

Mulberry Street

St Mary (R. C.), 'Hidden Gem'. John Gray Weightman & Matthew Ellison Hadfield, 1848. Grade II. Hadfield's scheme for a Byzantine church had been published in *The Rambler* and so enraged Pugin that he published a tract entitled *Some Remarks on the Articles which have recently Appeared in the 'Rambler' relative to Ecclesiastical Architecture and Decoration*. The design, according to Pugin, had 'all those features which would be considered objectionable in a pointed building, without any of its beauties . . . As regards the external appearance of the building, it is even below the ordinary run of nondescript churches . . . It only shows into what depths of error even good men fall when they abandon the true thing and go whoring after strange styles.' Pugin objected especially to the 'German' spire. 'Not that these remarks ruffled the temper of the peccant architect – a smile, with a good-humoured verbal protest, was the reply. The design was afterwards carried out, with some modifications, in the church at Mulberry-street, Manchester' (*Builder*, 11 April 1885, p. 512).

New Bailey Street

Aldine House. Leach Rhodes Walker, 1967. A phased development for the Land Commission, between the Irwell and Salford railway viaduct. Three similar interlocked blocks – Aldine House, Delphine House and Cloister House – clustered round a court to provide a sense of community. Each block of five storeys is of reinforced concrete with an exposed aggregate finish, which helps to reduce the effects of staining. The architects' own offices were built here in 1975, two storeys, clad in polished black granite – no bare concrete for them. Internally, oak-panelled and gentlemanly.

Nicholas Street

No. 16. Alfred Waterhouse, *c*. 1870. Grade II. Five storeys and attic over a semi-basement in red brick and sandstone, Elizabethan revival.

Norfolk Street

Northern Stock Exchange. Bradshaw Gass & Hope, 1907. Grade II. Portland stone, Baroque Revival.

Offices, corner of Brown Street. Briggs Wolstenholme & Thornley, 1909. Grade II. Portland stone. Almost an imitation Norman castle.

Oldham Road

Tenement. Spalding & Cross, 1889. Grade II. See p. 43

Oldham Street

Dry 201 (interior). Ben Kelly, 1989. The earliest revitalisation of the street after the blight of the Arndale Centre. See p. 285

Smithfield Building. Stephenson Bell, 1998. For Urban Splash. Was part of Affleck & Brown's empire, and in the 1960s British Home Stores, until they moved to the Arndale. See p. 292

Oxford Road

Oxford Road Station. W. R. Headley, British Rail Regional Architect, 1960. Grade II. Awkward triangular site bridged by three conoid shells of nailed and glued timber boards carried on laminated wood arches. The dynamic shape comes from the designs by Max Glendinning (project architect) as concrete shells. Restored 1998.

BBC Building. Fairhursts, late 1970s. Concrete and bands of brick cladding. The BBC moved here from 33–5 Piccadilly.

National Computing Centre. Cruickshank & Seward, 1964. See p. 172

Grosvenor Picture Palace. Percy Hothersall, 1913–15. Grade II. Green and white faience, and muted Baroque. Once holding 1,000 cinemagoers, it is now the Film and Firkin pub.

Manchester Metropolitan University Humanities Building. Sheppard Robson, 1994–96. A high-energy-efficiency concrete-framed building clad in red brick and glass. Inside, a large atrium provides generous circulation space; three floors of staff and teaching rooms, and lecture theatres in the basement and ground floors.

Blackwell's Bookshop. Fairhursts, 1995. Blackwell's have moved to the Precinct Centre.

Manchester Pool 50. FaulknerBrowns, 1999–2000. See p. 253

Royal Northern College of Music. Bickerdicke Allen Rich & Partners, 1968. All concrete, and with deck access at first storey. Rear extension, Mills Beaumont Leavey Channon, 1998

Federated Business School. ORMS, 1997–98. Red sandstone, metal and glass in the new Manchester vernacular. A new footbridge connects with below.

Precinct Centre. Wilson & Womersley, 1970s. All the buildings were to be concrete-faced, but were redesigned with a brick cladding.

University of Manchester Owens Building. Waterhouse, 1870–98. Grade II*. See p. 114

Church of the Holy Name of Jesus. Joseph Aloysius Hansom, 1869–71. Grade I. Thirteenth-century French in style. Warwick Bridge stone; internally, vaults of hollow hexagonal terracotta blocks. Cost over £30,000. Stained windows added in 1907. It was intended to have tower and spire 240 ft high. West tower added 1926–28 as a memorial of Fr Bernard Vaughan, SJ, at a cost of £19,000, after designs by the brothers Sir Giles Gilbert and Adrian Gilbert Scott. Terracotta interior by Gibbs & Canning, who also did the terracotta decoration of the Natural History Museum, London. Hansom invented the eponymous cab in 1834, sold his rights in it for £10,000 but never received the money. He was the founder of the *Builder* in 1842.

Whitworth Art Gallery. J. W. Beaumont, 1895. Grade II. John Bickerdicke, interior refurbishment, 1964.

Royal Eye Hospital. Pennington & Bridgen, 1884–86. Grade II. Brick and stone and restrained, in the manner of R. N. Shaw.

Royal Infirmary. E. T. Hall and John Brooke, 1905–08. Grade II. Brick and stone, Baroque Revival.

St Mary's Hospital. Watkins Grey Associates, 1966–70. Concrete. Refurbished and white rain-screen clad, Fairhursts, 1990.

University of Manchester buildings

Arts Library, Sir Hubert Worthington, 1935–37.

Electrical Engineering, J. S. Beaumont, 1953.

Union, J. S. Beaumont, 1953–56.

Williamson Building, H. S. Fairhurst & Son, 1957–66.

Simon Engineering Laboratories, H. S. Fairhurst & Son, 1957–66.

Arts Faculty, H. S. Fairhurst & Son, 1957–58.

Joint Examination Board, Playne & Lacey, 1960s.

Refectory, J. S. Beaumont, 1960–65.

Mobberly Tower, J. S. Beaumont, 1960–65.

Staff House, J. S. Beaumont, 1960–65.

Humanities Building, Building Design Partnership, 1961–67.

Roscoe Building, Cruickshank & Seward, 1964.

Physics and Chemistry Building, H. S. Fairhurst & Son, 1966, Schuster Laboratories.

Social Science and Economics Building, Cruickshank & Seward, 1966–67.

Mathematics Building, Scherrer & Hicks, 1967–68.

University Theatre, BDP, late 1960s.

Computer Building, BDP, 1972.

Medical School, Fairhursts, 1972–74, Stopford Building.

Information Technology Building, BDP, 1994.

Christie Library, inserted into Owens Building, BDP, 1997–98.

Biological Sciences Incubator, Fairhursts, 1998–99.

OXFORD STREET

Paramount Cinema. Verity & Beverley, 1930. Became the Odeon in 1938.

The Circus. Leslie Jones, 1999–2000. See also 106–18 PORTLAND STREET. See p. 280

Portland Buildings, corner of Portland Street. P. Nunn, 1860. For Louis Behrens & Sons. See p. 81

Prince's Building. I. R. E. Birkett, 1903. Cream brick and buff terracotta, and on the terracotta the Art Nouveau shapes are worth a close look. Prominent chimneys are connected by semicircular parapets. Only the front wall (Grade II) remains, the offices behind were redeveloped by Leach Rhodes Walker, 1987, together with Oxford Court (1987–89). See p. 233

Offices on either side. Leach Rhodes Walker, 1989. See p. 233

The Picture House. 1911, for Provincial Cinematograph Theatres. Now a Macdonald's.

St James's Building. Clegg Fryer & Penman, 1912. Grade II. For the Calico Printers' Association. Portland stone, Baroque Revival. 1,000 rooms. See p. 137

Tootal Building. Joseph Gibbons Sankey, 1898. Grade II*. For Tootal Broadhurst Lee & Co. In the 1930s and 1940s artists of the design department exhibited their work in the ground-floor windows. Now Churchgate House. See p. 133

Palace Theatre. Alfred Darbyshire and F. Bennett Smith, 1889. Altered 1913, Bertie Crewe, London. Restructured and tiled 1956. See p. 124

Refuge Building. Alfred and Paul Waterhouse, 1891, 1910. Grade II*. See p. 133

Cornerhouse. Mullard Partnership and Fletcher Priest Architects, 1985. Converted from Shaw's furniture shop and warehouse into an exhibition centre and cinema. An early sign of Manchester's cultural renaissance.

Cornerhouse Cinema. Opened in 1910 as the Kinemacolor Palace. Refurbished, David Chipperfield, 1998.

PETER STREET

YMCA (St George's Building). Woodhouse Corbett & Dean, 1909. Grade II. The first structural use of reinforced concrete in Manchester. Clad in henna and straw-coloured terracotta. Now a modern office block, conversion by Austin Strzala Turner with Ove Arup & Partners, 1993. Note the copy of Donatello's St George over the main entrance. See pp. 130, 235

Theatre Royal. Irwin & Chester, 1844. Grade II. Remodelled 1875, Edward Salomons & John Ely. Became Royales Discotheque 1989. See p. 13

No. 49. Mills Beaumont Leavey, 1992. Clad in polished granites and cleverly bridges two dissimilar buildings either side. Organised around a full-height glazed atrium. See p. 235

Free Trade Hall. Walters, 1853. Grade II*. See pp. 75, 266

No. 47, Lancashire House, c. 1870. Grade II.

No. 37, Harvester House. Clegg & Knowles, 1868. Grade II. For Ralli Bros. See p. 83

No. 44. Fairhurst's, 1988–90. Tall, reflective glazing panels stressed by stone mullions. On the fifth floor is a 'pediment' spanning three bays – a simple but effective postmodern interpretation of a Classical portico. Ground-floor reveals mirror the arcade of the Free Trade Hall, and the top storey is set back to show the Hall's frieze, which rounds the corner at this point. A Mansard roof contains offices and hides the heating and ventilation plant from the street. The rear of the building is brick-clad like the rear of the Free Trade Hall. See p. 231

Nos 29–35, **Petersfield House**. Howitt & Tucker, 1965. For Scottish Mutual Assurance. Five upper floors over a ground-floor showroom (now the Armed Forces Recruitment Centre). Expensive stonework cladding (Derbyshire spar and Sicilian marble), but visually hard to spot, and could as well have been made entirely of concrete. The right-hand bays, a second phase, span Marron Place and replaced No. 35 (Walters Barker & Ellis, 1868). See pp. 84, 175

No. 27, **Albert Hall and Aston Institute**. W. J. Morley of Bradford, 1910. Grade II. Was the Methodist Hall, built for the Manchester and Salford Weslyan Mission at a cost of £55,000. Granite and terracotta. Included large hall with galleries, seating 2,000 with organ, and reading and class rooms. Converted to leisure use as a Brannigans, 1999.

PICCADILLY

Piccadilly Plaza complex. Covell Matthews & Partners, 1959–65. Refurbishment by Leslie Jones Architects, 1999–. See pp. 184, 269

No. 1, corner of Tib Lane. James Lynde, 1879. Grade II (in 1987 the only listed building on Piccadilly). Canted bays, panelled bands, pilasters and dormers all brightly painted.

No. 5. Refurbishment of interior, and cladding over an earlier brick building, as a showroom for Norweb, D. Y. Davies, c. 1990.

Nos 7–9. Charles H. Heathcote & W. A. Thomas, 1910. Moorish in style, for the Kardomah Coffee Company, then the State Café of Joe Lyons. All in a grey-white glazed faience. Had little Moorish turrets and looks truncated without them. See p. 130

Nos 9a–13. Percy Hothersall, 1922. Beaux Arts classicism in white matt-glazed faience. From 1922 to 1937, the 'Piccadilly', a super-cinema with long bar and café, then a Littlewood's until their transfer to the Arndale. On the site of the Mosley Hotel.

No. 17, corner of Oldham Street. Royle & Bennet, 1881. Grade II. York stone and Italianate. Was Saqui & Lawrence offices, then Yorkshire Building Society.

Nos 19, 21, corner of Oldham Street. 1928. Portland stone. Was Woolworth's, which moved here from Oldham Street. On the site of the Albion Hotel.

Nos 33–5, **Manchester & County Bank**. Given as Mills & Murgatroyd, 1928 (but Mills died 1905, and the elder Murgatroyd in 1894, so it must be the son, A. Murgatroyd). Grade II. Portland stone. Ionic pilasters on ground floor, with lions guardant on the entablature. Note also the lions' heads on the cornice. Was Imperial Hotel, then home to the BBC, now NatWest Bank.

No. 49. William G. Higginbottom, 1892. Grade II. *Palazzo*-style in brick and stone. Now a Wetherspoon's pub.

No. 51–3. William G. Higginbottom, 1904. Grade II. This, like Nos 59–61, Flemish Revival; both in stone with tall gables, and matching building lines and cornice heights. It looks as though a similar-size building was intended to be built between them.

Nos 55–7. 1880s. Red sandstone palazzo with dormers set behind a balustrade. Was Manchester Corporation Transport Department. Now Gardens Hotel.

Nos 59–61, **Clayton House**. William G. Higginbottom, dated 1907. See No. 51–3.

Nos 63–5, **St Margaret's Chambers**, corner of Newton Street. 1890s. Grade II. Elizabethan Revival with huge gables, and a finely decorated one on Piccadilly. Beautiful decorated panels over first-floor windows.

No. 67, **Prince of Wales Building**, corner of Newton Street. Simple Italianate warehouse, c. 1850s. Brick and stone, rendered and painted.

Nos 71–5, **Hall's Buildings**. 1870s, in the style of Clegg & Knowles. Grade II. York stone. Now the 'Goose on Piccadilly'.

Nos 77–83. Clegg & Knowles, 1877. Grade II. Rendered brick and stone *palazzo*. Decorated frieze above third-storey windows, and a corbelled-out bartizan at second storey. Note the seated men supporting the balustrade, like bookends, either side of the corner turret.

No. 97, **Brunswick Hotel**. Eighteenth-century, Grade II.

No. 107, **Sparrow Hardwick & Co. Building**, corner of Lena Street. C. H. Heathcote, 1898. Grade II. Baroque Revival in banded red sandstone and brick. Deep rustication on ground floor with blocked columns and piers. Corner turrets, gables and a circular attic. As idiosyncratic as Heathcote got. Behind, on Lena Street, a matching building, Horrocks Crewdsen & Co. Warehouse. Grade II. See p. 130

Rodwell Tower. Douglas Stephen & Partners, 1965–66. Eighteen-storey tower over podium. Eight huge piers carry it over the Rochdale Canal. The concrete has not lasted well. See p. 174

No. 12, **Barclays Bank**. Thomas Worthington & Sons, 1911. Grade II. Portland stone *palazzo*-style. Was Union Bank of Manchester.

Joshua Hoyle Building (now the Malmaison), corner of Auburn Street. J. W. Beaumont, 1904–06. Grade II. Converted to the Malmaison by Darby Associates, 1998. Manchester Civic Society, City Award, Phoenix Award and Renaissance Award, Commendations, 1999. The Imperial Hotel, birthplace of the Football Association, was demolished for the stone-clad extension. See p. 268

PORTLAND STREET

No. 1. Steel-framed, curtain wall of bronze glass. Twelve bays, and half a bay at each end to terminate the building. The set-back roof storey with plant towers on top relates to the scale of Nos 3–5 next door. Replaces the Queen's Hotel of 1845.

Nos 3–5, **E. & J. Jackson Warehouse**. Walters, 1858. Grade II. Yorkshire stone. Four storeys, six bays. Each floor higher than No. 7. Tall and elegant arcade with decorated arch spandrels. Second-storey windows carry arched pediments, and the entablatures run on the line of the minor cornice of No. 7. Over the main cornice a walled balustrade, like central part of No. 9's, brings the building to the height of No. 7's cornice. An assured building. Nos 3–9 now all the Thistle Hotel. For this and Nos 7 and 9 see pp. 74, 75

No. 7, **Kershaw Leese & Sidebottom Warehouse**. Walters, 1852. Grade II. Yorkshire stone and all ashlar except quoins. Seven bays, six storeys, and ground and basement contained under a transomed and arched arcade with decorative wreaths in the spandrels. First-floor windows with arched pediments. Minor cornice over second storey supported by rusticated quoins. Deep cornice over fourth storey at the height of the balustrade of No. 9. The sixth storey looks to be an addition; it is likely that the cornice would have finished the building, and it is unlikely Walters would have done anything so clumsy.

No. 9, **Brown & Son Warehouse**. Walters, 1851–52. Grade II. Yorkshire stone. Four storeys, and ground and semi-basement as one under round-headed arched arcade, a transom divides them. Rusticated ground floor and ashlar above, with stressed quoins. Segmental arches on first and second storeys, and second-floor windows pedimented. Deep cornice and balustrade, later modified on the Aytoun Street façade. Seven bays on Portland Street, twelve on the cheaper Aytoun Street side. The attic floor is concealed behind a balustrade. The attic windows on the Aytoun Street elevation were added later.

Bank of England Northern Headquarters. Fitzroy Robinson & Partners, 1971. The twelve-storey Bank House, with bronze glazing and black and white cladding, and the Portland stone-clad banking hall are both set over a podium of concrete and polished black granite cladding. The Bank of England has moved out. See p. 201

No. 11, corner of Aytoun Street. Fitzroy Robinson & Partners, 1973. Was GMC County Hall. Six storeys over ground-floor podium Bands of brick, concrete and glass, all with a concrete lid over set-back sixth storey. Ground floor improved and opened out. See p. 211

Nos 35–47, S. & J. Watts Warehouse. Travis & Mangnall, 1855–58. Grade II*. Now the Britannia Hotel. See pp. 78, 206

No. 53, St Andrew's House (now the Portland Tower). Leach Rhodes Walker, 1962, for Scottish Widows. Twenty-one storeys over a two-storey podium. The core was cast by means of a continuously climbing shutter. The Car Park and Bus Station, Chorlton Street, also Leach Rhodes Walker, 1963, were part of the complex. See p. 171

No. 55, Telephone House. E. Norman Bailey & Partners, 1959–61. An early curtain-walled building. See p. 171

Nos 70, 72, corner of Nicholas Street. Pennington & Bridgen 1873. Five-storey *palazzo* in York stone.

No. 101, Pickles Building, corner of Princess Street. Clegg & Knowles, 1870. Grade II. Now the Princess Hotel. See p. 83

Nos 106–18, all Grade II and becoming part of The Circus, Leslie Jones, 1999–2000 (Nos 110–14, Shaw & Webster, 1866). See p. 280

No. 125, Beaver House, corner of Dickinson Street. 1920s. Once a Lloyd's Packing Warehouse.

Nos 127–33, Behrens's Warehouse. P. Nunn, 1860. Grade II. See OXFORD STREET.

PRINCESS STREET

Nos 1–7, Glasgow Assurance Building. See ALBERT SQUARE.

Nos 9–21, Northern Assurance Building. See ALBERT SQUARE.

Nos 14, 16, corner of Mosley Street. Warehouse, 1860s. Grade II. Red brick and sandstone dressings and balustrade.

Nos 18–24, Princess Buildings. Warehouse, 1860s. Grade II. Sandstone, becoming white brick on Back George Street.

Nos 65–71. Row of four town houses, late eighteenth-century. Grade II.

Nos 73, 75, corner of Cooper Street, *c.* 1870s. Grade II. Ten bays, mostly red brick, with banding, diaper-work and some arch voussoirs in blue brick. Stone as base of first storey, for window heads, for capitals on second storey and colonettes on third. Looks Venetian but only from its polychromy. Ground floor is a new office.

No. 81, Athenaeum. Charles Barry, 1836–39. Grade II*. See p. 66. Extension of City Art Gallery/Athenaeum, Michael Hopkins & Partners, 1999–2001.

No. 83, corner of George Street. Warehouse. Travis & Mangnall, 1847–48. Grade II. Red brick, and sandstone ground floor.

Nos 87–91. A row of three town houses. Late eighteenth-century. Grade II.

No. 101. Clegg & Knowles, 1869. Grade II. Red brick and sandstone dressings, pedimented windows on first floor.

No. 103, Mechanics' Institute. J. E. Gregan, 1854. Grade II*. The building is now the National Museum of Labour History. See p. 85

Nos 105–7, Brazil House, *c.* 1860s. Grade II. Pair of warehouses in yellow brick with sandstone dressings.

No. 109. Clegg & Knowles, 1863. Grade II. Brick with stone detailing round the windows – stilted arches over the first and second floor, and round-headed over the top floor – and the corners of the building are visually strengthened with stone quoins. Refurbished for apartments, Stephenson Bell, 1998. Manchester Civic Society, Phoenix Award, Commendation, 1999. See p. 83

No. 111, New Union Hotel, corner of Canal Street. Grade II.

No. 74, Central House, corner of Whitworth Street. Corsen & Aitken, 1880. Grade II. All brick, in the Scottish Baronial style. Converted into the Dominion Hotel in the 1980s and subsequently into apartments. See p. 87

No. 82, Asia House. H. S. Fairhurst, c. 1900–10. Grade II. Three floors of banded rustication in brown sandstone. Above, three floors in pinkish brick coupled by giant-order Ionic pilasters in sandstone, and another floor above the cornice.

No. 86, Manchester House. Probably I. R. E. Birkett, 1900s. Grade II. Brown sandstone and pinkish brick, rusticated base and Ionic pilasters, all very similar to Asia House, but who copied whom?

QUAY STREET

Overseas House. Leach Rhodes Walker, 1970s. Concrete with revealed structure and a brown brick facing. Seven storeys, with twelve bays on Quay Street and five on Deansgate.

Sunlight House. Joseph Sunlight, 1932. Grade II. See p. 147

Opera House. Richardson & Gill and Farquharson, 1912. Grade II. See p. 136

No. 15, offices. Stephenson Bell, 1992. An exercise in street, contextual architecture. Civic Trust Award Commendation 1993; RIBA Regional Award, 1994. See p. 235

Hospital for Skin Diseases. T. Worthington & Son, 1903–06. Baroque Revival. It had its origins in a small house in Dale Street in 1884, removing to a large house in Quay Street in 1895, with beds for six in-patients and an out-patient department. The hospital was demolished late 1999. See p. 135

Cobden Building, corner of Byrom Street, 1750s. Grade II*. Was Cobden's House, then Owens College. See p. 113

Quay House. H. S. Fairhurst & Son, 1964–65. Seven floors above a ground-floor podium. A building with a large footprint (the façade on Quay Street has thirty-eight bays), but the bulk is reduced by forming three distinct bays of twelve, fourteen and twelve windows separated by staircases which are cut back into the façade. Huge concrete cladding panels, each almost a floor high. The fifth floor has concrete transoms to its windows; the upper storey has more solid than void – a modern version of the cornice? The yacht-like steel canopies are of recent date – a rash of these has sprung up in the city in recent years.

Granada Television Centre. Ralph Tubbs, 1956–66. See pp. 169, 170

REDHILL STREET

For the mills on this street see Chapter Two.

SACKVILLE STREET

Institute of Technology (UMIST). Spalding & Cross, 1895–1912. Grade II. French Renaissance style. Accrington brick and terracotta, roof of Tilberwaite green slates. Six storeys on a plot of 6,400 square yards. Entrance hall 4,000 ft² laid in marble tiles and once had examples of antique sculpture. Great hall for examinations and public lectures. Cost over £300,000. See also Whitworth Street.

UMIST buildings

Renold Building, Chandos Hall, Mathematical and Social Sciences, Students' Union, Chemistry Building, Wright Robinson Hall. All by Cruickshank & Seward, 1962–68.

Chemical Engineering Pilot Plant, Civil Engineering, Chemistry Building, Mechanical Engineering, Jackson Street Mill conversion, Paper Science. All by H. S. Fairhurst & Son, mid to late 1960s.

Joule Library, BDP, 1987.

Conversion of existing warehouse buildings, Sackville Street, Stephenson Bell, 1996–97.

No. 55, corner of Fountain Street. 1990s. The wondrous Daniel Lee & Co. warehouse, Edward Salomon, 1856, was demolished for this.

Nos 54–72, **W. R. Callender Warehouse**, between Fountain Street and West Mosley Street. Walters, 1851. Grade II. Red brick, stone dressings, clumsy corner windows.

No. 60, **Commercial Buildings, now Gan House**, corner of Chancery Lane. Waterhouse, 1882. Grade II. Stone-clad, three storeys of square-headed windows above a rusticated ground floor. Dormer windows above a corbelled cornice, and turrets to stress the corners in the Manchester manner. Leach Rhodes Walker, refurbishment behind retained façades, late 1980s. See p. 121

Warehouse, Spring Gardens/Concert Lane/Fountain Street. See 50 FOUNTAIN STREET.

No. 47, **Commercial Union Buildings** (later Martin's Bank), corner of Concert Lane. Heathcote, 1881–82. Grade II. Stone-clad, with square-headed windows with mullions and transoms. Ground-floor windows flanked by Doric pilasters, decorated with fluting and lozenged panels, more Jacobean than Classical. Attached composite half-columns on the first storey, but thin and frail-looking. Three roof turrets, the two left-hand ones with complex interlacing. The apsidal corner to Concert Lane is a simplification of the Spring Gardens façade. See p. 121

Nos 43–5, **Lancashire & Yorkshire Bank**, termination of King Street. Heathcote & Rawle, 1890. Grade II. Two storeys of mullioned and transomed windows for the banking hall, within deeply rusticated stone. The piers are simplified square Doric columns, carrying an entablature. Huge asymmetrical doorway within rusticated voussoirs. Above rises a tower with a tall drum and cupola. Second-storey aedicular windows are bracketed by paired Corinthian columns. Above all rises a huge gable, with Corinthian columns and supported by side scrolls – reminiscent of an Italian Baroque church. Now Rothwell's. See p. 121

No. 41, **National Provincial Bank**, corner of York Street. Waterhouse, 1888–90. Grade II. Effectively a two-storey banking hall at ground level, with windows flanked by giant-order Doric pilasters; the ground floor was a later modernisation. First and second storeys coupled by giant-order Ionic pilasters on tall decorated bases. Scrolled pediments with a flange above (reminiscent of Borromini) form both hoods to the lower windows and sills for the upper ones. At roof level are small gabled windows. On the King Street face, two doorways, with open curved pediments, above which are triangular pediments, each carried by three large curved brackets. Above these, at second storey, are two balconies each carried by three huge sculpted consoles from behind which the first-storey windows peep out. Above all is a two-storey decorated gable. This was the early headquarters of the Manchester Ship Canal Company. See p. 122

Parr's Bank, corner of York Street (1–3 York Street). Heathcote, 1902. Grade II*. Red sandstone. Large arched windows of the banking hall are flanked by giant paired Doric columns standing on huge rusticated pedestals. On top of each column is a deep shield and a scroll bracket which supports absolutely nothing. The doorway, canted on the corner, is flanked by columnar drums which rise the height of the building, and on top of each of these are a finial and paired colonnettes carrying a pediment. A drum and cupola top off the lot. Internally the supporting columns, of Pyrenean marble, shipped as entire columns, are just as huge. Now the Athenaeum Bar. See p. 122

St Andrew's Street

Parcel Post Office. H. G. Swann, Ministry of Public Buildings and Works, 1966–68. Concrete, and grim.

ST ANN'S PASSAGE

Old Exchange (Lady Bland's Assembly Rooms). Grade II. See p. 6

ST ANN'S SQUARE

St Ann's Church. 1709–12. Grade I. In the Wrennian manner, architect unknown but probably John Barker (1668–1727) of Rowsley in Derbyshire. Two storeys of round-headed windows between paired pilasters. The tower originally had a cupola, removed in 1777 and replaced by a spire, later removed. Restoration of the church and remodelling of the interior took place in 1837. Waterhouse restored the church again in 1886–91, and enclosed the chancel with oak screens, thus creating vestries and the chapel. The chancel and sanctuary were raised above the level of the nave. Internally galleried, the upper Tuscan Doric columns are original, the lower ones remodelled by Waterhouse. Originally all white glass, the stained glass windows of the apse are by Frederick Shields, 1886–91, and the nave windows of later date. Further restoration of the church in 1904, 1912 and 1973. The church is built of local Collyhurst sandstone, the chief building stone of early Manchester, and the patchwork appearance is due to restoration with a variety of other sandstones – yellowish-grey from Darley Dale, pinkish from Hollington in Staffordshire, dark red from Runcorn and pale brown from Parbold in Lancashire. See p. 4

Old Bank Chambers, corner of Old Bank Street. H. S. Fairhurst & Son, 1920s. For Manchester Liners, with a ship's prow carved on the corner. Narrow but nicely proportioned and in Portland stone.

Royal Exchange. See CROSS STREET.

Barton Arcade. See DEANSGATE.

The Gardens. Was Royal Insurance Company, H. S. Fairhurst & Son, 1959. Expensive building in granite and Westmorland stone, costing £365,000. Overlaid by David Backhouse's postmodern building, The Gardens, 'Manchester's Unique Shopping Experience', in 1986. At the rear a small sloping atrium. The ground floor now given over to a Disney shop.

ST ANN STREET

Heywood's Bank. J. E. Gregan, 1848. Grade II*. Large arched windows on ground floor, set in deep rustication. First-floor offices are marked by aedicular windows. Deeply overhanging cornice. The attached building, connected by a stone arch, in a similar style, but of brick with stone dressings, and slightly lower, for the chief clerk. T. Worthington & Sons (1988) restored the banking hall back to its original design for the Royal Bank of Scotland, and repaired the external stonework. See p. 87

Nos 28–32, Pearl Assurance Building. J. W. Beaumont, 1901. Four storeys and attic. Granite, red brick and terracotta.

ST MARY'S PARSONAGE

Arkwright House. H. S. Fairhurst, 1927. Grade II Portland stone. Once headquarters of the English Sewing Cotton Company. See p. 144

National Buildings. H. S. Fairhurst, 1905–09. Grade II. Baroque Revival. Nine bays, seven storeys, in red brick and mostly pink terracotta. Rusticated lower floors and banding on the corners runs all the way up to the two towers. Note the lions' heads above the fifth-storey cornice. For the National Boiler & Generator Insurance Company (later the Vulcan Insurance Company).

National Boiler Extension (Century Buildings). Fairhursts, 1968. Originally six storeys over a podium, and a set-back seventh storey under a deep concrete lid. In 1999 a partial brick cladding, and the addition of two more storeys (Assael Associates of London), for the most expensive apartment in Manchester.

Blackfriars House, corner of Blackfriars Street. H. S. Fairhurst, 1923. Bleachers' Association building. Ground floor and mezzanine in channelled rustication, and the rustication becomes the arch voussoirs, all Hawksmoor-like. Five storeys of ashlar topped by a cornice, then another storey. See p. 143

Trinity Bridge, off St Mary's Parsonage. Santiago Calatrava, 1994. His only bridge in the UK. Pylon and cable stays support a triangular box-section footbridge. Formally opened on 25 September 1995 by the Lord Mayors of Salford and Manchester, symbolising a new link between the two cities. Paid for by Salford. See p. 274

ST PETER'S SQUARE

Midland Hotel. Charles Trubshaw, 1898–1903. Grade II*. Now the Crowne Plaza Midland Hotel. See p. 133

Peter House, 2–34, Oxford Street. Amsell & Bailey, 1958, for the Clerical Medical & General Life Assurance Company. Twenty-eight bays and eleven storeys above a podium, all gently curved on the street line. Two five-storey pavilions on the front, and rearward extensions. Windows gridded up between Portland stone sills and piers. Big with a sense of *gravitas*. On the site of the Prince's Theatre (Salomon, 1860, blitzed).

Elizabeth House. Cruickshank & Seward, 1959–60. Four (and a set back fifth) storeys over a two-storey podium. Was meant to be stone-clad, but the money ran out. See p. 177

Cenotaph. Sir Edwin Lutyens, 1924. Grade II*.

St Peter's Cross. Marks site of old St Peter's Church, James Wyatt, 1788–94. Tower and spire added by Goodwin 1824, all demolished 1906–07. Extensive vaults, with their coffins, remain. The organ of 3,728 pipes was, until 1872, the largest in England, and the twin of the one in the Free Trade Hall (destroyed in the blitz). Organ removed to St Bride's Church, Old Trafford (demolished), then rescued to a warehouse in Lincolnshire, present whereabouts unknown.

Central Reference Library. E. Vincent Harris, 1930–34. Grade II*. See p. 148

Town Hall Extension. E. Vincent Harris, 1934–38. Grade II*. See p. 150

Century House, corner of Dickinson Street. 1934. Portland stone, and immured columns over entrance. This building stopped the development of the square in 1934. See p. 149

STANLEY STREET (SALFORD)

Ralli Quays. Fairhurst's, 1991–93. For HM Customs and Excise. One of the first buildings to look on to, rather than turn its back on, the Irwell.

TARIFF STREET

Hall & Rogers Warehouse. Dale Street basin, 1836. Grade II. Red brick, five storeys, twelve bays. Small round-headed windows, stone sills. Cast-iron columns. Loopholes and catheads at ends of building. Canal arm filled in, but double-arched barge entry can still be seen.

Salt Warehouse, 1817. Stone, arched bays on canal side, now bricked up.

UPPER BROOK STREET

Unitarian Chapel. Charles Barry, 1836–39, and said to be the first Gothic Nonconformist chapel. In danger in spite of its Grade II* listing.

UPPER STANLEY STREET

Rochdale Canal Company Warehouse, 1836. Grade II.

VICTORIA BRIDGE STREET

Highland House. Leach Rhodes Walker, 1966. Twenty-three storeys over a ground-floor podium. The central core, cast by a climbing shutter, carries in-situ floor slabs and pre-cast, fair-faced concrete panels. The ends of the building and the service tower are sprayed in a patent black and white paint finish. The windows, described by Pevsner as 'funnel holes', are of stove-enamelled steel. The building is actually in Salford.

VICTORIA STATION APPROACH

Victoria Station. George Stephenson, 1844; enlarged, William Dawes, 1909; internal changes and MEN Arena, Austin-Smith:Lord, 1992–96 (Arena design, DLA Ellerbe Beckett). See pp. 50, 250

WHITWORTH STREET

India House. H. S. Fairhurst, 1905. Grade II. See p. 139
Lancaster House. H. S. Fairhurst, 1909. Grade II. See p. 139
Bridgewater House. H. S. Fairhurst, 1912. See p. 139
UMIST Extension. Bradshaw Gass & Hope, 1927. Grade II. Not finished until 1957, by which time the style was considerably out of date. Red brick, yellow terracotta, Norman Shaw gables. Cost £250,000. The land for the gardens opposite had been bought by the Corporation in the 1880s at the prompting of the Education Committee, which wanted nothing to spoil view of the original Institute of Technology (see SACKVILLE STREET).
Sheena Simon School. Potts Son & Pickup, 1900. Grade II. Was Central School, then Mather College.

WHITWORTH STREET WEST

Ritz Dance Hall, 1927. Grade II.
Barclay's Textiles. H. S. Fairhurst, 1920s. White faience.
Deansgate Station. Grade II.

WINDMILL STREET

G-MEX. Original train shed, Sacré, Johnson and Johnson, 1880. Refurbishment, Essex Goodman & Suggitt, 1982–86. Grade II*. See pp. 54, 213
International Convention Centre. Stephenson Bell, 1999–2000. See p. 267

WITHY GROVE

Kemsley House (later Thomson House, then Maxwell House, now The Printworks). Arthur Rangely, in-house architect, 1929– . The site grew organically. By the 1940s the largest newspaper headquarters and printing works in Britain, in which were produced the *Daily Despatch*, the northern edition of the *Daily Telegraph*, the *Sunday Empire News* and northern editions of the *Sunday Times*, *Sunday Chronicle* and *Sunday Graphic*. Weekly output was more than 11 million copies of newspapers and periodicals. See p. 263

York Street

Royal & Sun Alliance (Clock House), corner of Fountain Street. Cassidy & Ashton of Preston, 1996. Red brick and stone bands. Ground and first storeys clad in stone. On York Street, stone piers rise to support a pediment on the sixth storey – a postmodern interpretation of a portico?

York House, corner of Fountain Street. Leach Rhodes Walker, 1975. For Abbey National. Ten storeys over a podium. Piers of dark brown brick alternate with cream tiles running the height of the building. Set back, not for road widening but to create a grassed area at ground level. See p. 207

No. 26, Telephone Buildings. L. Stokes and J. W. Beaumont, 1909. Grade II. Red brick with cream faience banding and dressings. The quoins have blue brick banding.

GLOSSARY

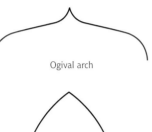

Ogival arch

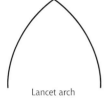

Lancet arch

Basket arch

191] Arches

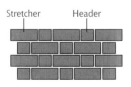

Stretcher   Header

Flemish bond

English bond

192] Brickwork

Aedicule. An opening, usually a window or door, framed by columns or pilasters and a pediment; hence *aedicular*

Apse. Part of a building that is semicircular in plan; hence *apsidal*

Arcade. A range of arches

Arch. See [191]

Architrave. The lowest element of an **entablature**

Archivolt. A continuous moulding following the shape of an arch

Ashlar. Stones cut into regular and rectangular blocks

Atrium. An open area; in modern architecture usually glazed over

Attached. See **engaged**

Baluster. A small column

Balustrade. A series of **balusters** supporting a line of coping stones or a handrail

Barrel vault. A semi-circular **vault**

Bartizan. A small battlemented **turret** projecting from the angle of two walls

Basket arch. See **arch**

Batter. The vertical inclination of a wall

Bay. The external or internal division of a building marked by columns, piers or other features

Bay window. A projecting window which comes down to ground level. If only on upper floors, an Oriel window

Bracket. A small supporting piece of stone, sometimes fancy See **console**

Brickwork. See [192]

Brise soleil. A screen, usually of metal strips, to keep sunlight off, usually, windows

Buttress. A mass of brick or stonework built up to and projecting from a wall to give it support

Cartouche. An ornate carved frame

Cathead. Small pitched roof over a **loophole**

Coffering. Cutting back of a vault in a polygonal pattern

Colonnade. A range of columns

Column. Upright member of a classical order, comprising base, shaft and capital. See **orders**

Console. A decorative **bracket**, usually with a curved or shaped outline

Corbel. A block of stone supporting a projecting element of a wall

Corbel table. A series of corbels in a continuous row

Corinthian. See **orders**

Cornice. The upper section of an **entablature**. More often a projecting feature at the top of a wall, used in warmer climes to keep sun from the wall surface

Crenellation. A parapet with a series of indentations, also *battlement*. E.g. *swallow-tail crenellation*, a parapet with the upper parts shape like a swallow's tail

Crocket, crocketing. Flame or leaf-like decorative elements, usually on a sloping element such as a spire or gable

Cross-window. A window with one **transom** and one **mullion**

Cupola. A domed turret

Curtain wall. A non-load-bearing wall

Darley Dale sandstone. A Millstone Grit sandstone (grains of sand or quartz with some feldspar, cemented together with silica) from quarries around Bakewell and Matlock. Yellow-brown when quarried, tending to become darker with weathering

Dentils, dentillation. One of a series of blocks of stone supporting an entablature. From the Latin for 'tooth', hence like a row of teeth

Doric. See **orders**

Dormer window. Window placed vertically in a sloping roof

Dripstone. Moulding over a window to shed rain. Also *hoodmould*

Engaged (columns). Of a column that is attached to a wall and not free-standing

English bond. See **brickwork**

Entablature. The horizontal member above, and carried by, classical columns, comprising **architrave**, **frieze** and **cornice**. See [**193**]

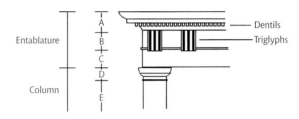

193] The order showing entablature

A cornice

B frieze

C architrave

D capital (Doric)

E shaft

Faience. Glazed ceramic tiles or decorative panel

Fenestration. Arrangements of windows in a building

Ferro-concrete. See **reinforced concrete**

Finial. (Usually decorative) top of a pinnacle or gable

Flemish bond. See **brickwork**

Fluting. Channelling of the shaft of a column

Foil, foiled. A lobed opening, usually an arch or circular element of a window; hence *trefoil*, a three-lobed opening, *quatrefoil*, a four-lobed opening, *cinquefoil*, five-lobed, etc

Foliated. Having leaf shapes. Usually of a capital

Freestone. A stone capable of being carved in all dimensions

Frieze. The middle element of an **entablature**. Also as a decorative band

Gable. Triangular upper part of a wall at the end of a pitched roof. Also as a free-standing decorative element at roof level. A Dutch gable has curved sides

Giant order. Columns which rise through more than one storey

Header. See **brickwork**

Hoodmould. See **dripstone**

Intercolumniation. The distance between columns, usually dictated by the column diameter, but not always adhered to in Victorian architecture

Ionic. See **orders**

Jamb. The upright side of a door or window

Label. A decorative panel below a window

Lancet (windows). Tall, narrow, pointed-arched windows

Lantern. Circular or polygonal turret

Lintel. Horizontal member above a door or window

Loophole. Loading bay rising the height of a building with doors at each floor level

Lunette. A semicircular opening, usually of a window

Metope. A panel, often decorative, between the **triglyphs** of the Doric order

Ionic capital

Corinthian capital

194] Capitals of two
types of order

Mezzanine. A half-floor inserted between two major floors

Modillion. A small bracket supporting, e.g., a cornice. If in a continuous row, a *modillion frieze*

Mullion. A vertical element dividing a window into lights. See also **transom**

Narthex. An enclosed vestibule at the entrance to a church

Ogee. See **arch**

Orders. See [194]

Oriel. See **bay**

Palladian opening. See **Venetian opening**

Parapet. A low wall

Pargeting. Incised or, more usually, raised plasterwork decoration

Pediment. A, usually, triangular element above a portico, windows or doors. Normally supported on one of the classical orders. Straight-sided or segmentally curved. Broken-bed and broken-apex pediments where the base or top has, respectively, a gap

Pendentive. A concave **spandrel** leading from the angle of two straight walls to the base of a dome

Piano nobile. The major floor of an Italian Renaissance *palazzo*, or the major floor of a Victorian Italianate warehouse. Usually denoted by additional decoration or larger windows

Pier. A solid masonry or brick support where there is no classical column. Also the mass of supporting material between windows

Pilaster. A decorative feature taking the form of one of the classical orders, usually rectangular and projecting slightly from the wall

Pilotis. Piers which raise a building to first-floor level, leaving the ground floor open

Plinth. Projecting base of a column or wall

Podium. A discrete and continuous structure at the base of a tower building

Porte cochère. A porch large enough to admit wheeled vehicles

Portico. A covered entrance to a building usually with a pediment supported on classical columns: *prostyle*, if projecting from the building; *in antis*, if in line with adjoining walls

Portland stone. An oolitic limestone from Portland in Dorset. Cream or buff when quarried, Portland stone becomes whiter when exposed and rain-washed. Larger blocks can be obtained, though generally in blocks 10 ft long by 5 ft wide and 4 ft 6 in. deep. The finest grained stone is the Whitbed from the middle bed, or the similar Basebed. More textural, with the indentation from the shells of sea creatures, is the shelly Roach, from the topmost bed. In this the fine granules of ooliths (rounded granules of carbonate of lime) and fragments of shell can often be seen

Quatrefoil. See **foil**

Quoins. Dressed stones at the corner angle of a building, often laid in alternate large and small stones

Reinforced concrete. Concrete strengthened by the addition of steel rods or mesh

Rendering. Plastering of a wall

Reveal. The part of a **jamb** which lies between a door or the glass of a window and the outer wall

Roach. See **Portland stone**

Rustication. Masonry cut into blocks and separated by deep channels

Sandstone. Compressed and cemented particles of quartz, with other minerals such as feldspar and mica, eroded from older rocks. In the north, most sandstones are cemented together with silica, hence *siliceous* sandstones

Sill (sometimes **Cill**). Horizontal member below a window opening

Soffit. Underside of an arch or lintel. Under an arch also called an *archivolt*

Spandrel. Triangular surface between two arches

Stiff-leaf (foliage). Foliage of a botanically indeterminate form, generally of the twelfth century

Stretcher. See **brickwork**

String course. A horizontal (often decorated) band on, or projecting from, a wall

Terracotta. Literally 'baked earth'. Fired clay which is often moulded or sculpted into decorative shapes before firing. When glazed is almost impervious to weathering

Thermal (window). See **lunette**

Tourelle. A turret corbelled out from a corner

Tracery. Intersecting ribs of stonework, usually in windows, occasionally decoratively in blank arches on walls or on vaults

Transom. Horizontal member across a window opening, often in conjunction with **mullions**

Trefoils. See **foil**

Triglyph. A panel or block of three vertical grooves, used in a Doric frieze. See also **metope**

Turret. A very small tower

Tympanum. The space enclosed by a **pediment**, and the space between a lintel and an arch above it

Vault. An arched ceiling in stone (usually), wood or brick

Venetian window. A three-light window with a wide central arched opening supported on columns, flanked by two rectangular and narrower openings. Also known as a Palladian opening, or a Serlian opening

Vermiculation. **Rustication** with a texture like worm holes

Voussoir. Wedge-shaped stone forming part of the construction of an arch

York stone. A generic name for the light-brown to yellow, and even-grained, sandstones from quarries around Halifax and to the south of Leeds and Bradford

SELECT BIBLIOGRAPHY

Abercrombie, P., *Town and Country Planning*, London, Thornton Butterworth, 1933

Abrams, Charles, *Housing in the Modern World*, London, Faber & Faber, 1964

Albert Memorial Appeal Committee, *The Restoration of Manchester's Albert Memorial, 1977–8*, Manchester, Manchester City Planning Department, 1979

Aldrich, M., *Gothic Revival*, London, Phaidon, 1994

Allaun, F., *No Place like Home: Britain's Housing Tragedy*, London, André Deutsch, 1972

Allen, R. J., *The Manchester Royal Exchange, 1729–1921*, Manchester, Manchester Royal Exchange, 1921

Allsopp, Bruce, *Towards a Humane Architecture*, London, Frederick Muller, 1974

Ambrose, Peter, and Colenutt, Bob, *The Property Machine*, Harmondsworth, Penguin Books, 1975

Amery, Colin, and Cruickshank, Dan, *The Rape of Britain*, London, Paul Elek, 1975

Archer, J. H. G., ed., *Art and Architecture in Victorian Manchester*, Manchester, Manchester University Press, 1985

Ashmore, Owen, *Industrial Archaeology of Lancashire*, Newton Abbot, David & Charles, 1969

Ashton, T. S., *The Industrial Revolution, 1760–1830*, London, Oxford University Press, 1947

Ashworth, W., *The Genesis of Modern British Town Planning: A Study in Economic and Social History of the Nineteenth and Twentieth Centuries*, London, Routledge & Kegan Paul, 1954

Aston, Joseph, *A Picture of Manchester*, Manchester, E. J. Morten [1816] 1969

Atkins, Philip, *Guide across Manchester*, Manchester, Civic Trust for the North West, 1976

Axon, William E. A., *An Architectural and General Description of the Town Hall, Manchester*, Manchester, City of Manchester, [Abel Heywood & Son, 1878] 1977

Axon, William E. A., *The Annals of Manchester*, Manchester, John Heywood, 1886

Bamford, Phill, ed., *Manchester: 50 Years of Change*, London, HMSO, 1995

Banham, Reyner, *The Architecture of the Well-tempered Environment*, London, Architectural Press, 1969

Barker, W., ed., *Your City: Manchester, 1838–1938*, Manchester, Manchester Municipal Officers' Guild, 1938

Bellhouse, D. R., *David Bellhouse and Sons, Manchester*, London, Ontario, published by the author, 1992

Benevolo, L., *The Origins of Modern Town Planning*, London, Routledge & Kegan Paul, 1967

Berry, Fred, *Housing: the Great British Failure*, London, Charles Knight, 1974

Bethell, H., 'At the Free Trade Hall, of course!', in *Manchester Free Trade Hall: issued on the Occasion of the Re-opening of the reconstructed Hall, November 1951*, Manchester, Manchester City Council, 1951

Binney, Marcus, *Our Vanishing Heritage*, London, Arlington Books, 1984

Binney, Marcus, et al., *Satanic Mills: Industrial Architecture in the Pennines*, London, SAVE Britain's Heritage, undated

Black, Jeremy, *An Illustrated History of Eighteenth Century Britain, 1688–1793*, Manchester, Manchester University Press, 1996

Blowers, A., *et al.*, *The Future of Cities*, Milton Keynes, Open University Press, 1974

Bonner, R. F., and Dwan, J., *The Finest Fire Station in this Round World: A History of London Road Fire Station, Manchester*, Manchester, GMC Public Relations Unit, undated

Bowker, B., *Lancashire under the Hammer*, London, Hogarth Press, 1928

Bradshaw, L. D., *Origins of Street Names in the City Centre of Manchester*, Swinton, Manchester, Neil Richardson, 1985

Briggs, Asa, *Friends of the People: The Centenary History of Lewis's*, London, Batsford, 1956

Briggs, Asa, *Victorian People*, Harmondsworth, Penguin Books, 1965

Briggs, Asa, *Victorian Cities*, Harmondsworth, Penguin Books, 1968

Brindley, W. H., ed., *The Soul of Manchester*, Manchester, Manchester University Press, 1929

Brockbank, E. M., *et al.*, *The Book of Manchester and Salford: Written for the Ninety-seventh Annual Meeting of the British Medical Association in July 1929*, Manchester, George Faulkner & Sons, 1929

Brockman, H. A. N., *The British Architect in Industry, 1841–1940*, London, Allen & Unwin, 1974

Brooks, Ann, and Haworth, Bryan, *Manchester 'This Good Old Town': An Illustrated Anthology*, Preston, Carnegie Publishing, 1997

Brooks, Chris, and Saint, Andrew, eds, *The Victorian Church: Architecture and Society*, Manchester, Manchester University Press, 1995

Brothers, Alfred, *Manchester as it is: A Series of Views of Public Buildings in Manchester*, Manchester, E. J. Cornish, 1878

Brotherston, Isabel, and Windmill, Charlotte, *Bridging the Years: A History of Trafford Park and Salford Docks as Remembered by those who Lived and Worked in the Area*, Salford, Salford Quays Heritage Centre, 1992

Brumhead, Derek, and Wyke, Terry, *A Walk round All Saints*, Manchester, Manchester Polytechnic Publications Unit, undated [1987]

Brumhead, Derek, and Wyke, Terry, *A Walk round Castlefield*, Manchester, Manchester Polytechnic, 1989

Brumhead, Derek, and Wyke, Terry, *A Walk around Manchester Statues*, Manchester, Walkround, 1990

Brunskill, R. W., *Brick Building in Britain*, London, Victor Gollancz in association with Peter Crawley, 1997

Brunskill, Ronald, and Clifton-Taylor, Alec, *English Brickwork*, London, Ward Lock, 1977

Buchanan, Colin, *Traffic in Towns* (the Buchanan Report), London, HMSO, 1963

Buchanan, Colin, *The State of Britain*, London, Faber & Faber, 1972

Buckley, Yung Yung, *British Soil, Chinese Roots*, Manchester, Countyvise, 1996

Burnett, John, *A Social History of Housing, 1850–1970*, Newton Abbot, David & Charles, 1978

Bythell, D., *The Handloom Weavers*, Cambridge, Cambridge University Press, 1969

Carley, Michael, *Housing and Neighbourhood Renewal: Britain's New Urban Challenge*, London, Policy Studies Institute, 1990

Carter, C. F., ed., *Manchester and its Region: a Survey prepared for the Meeting held in Manchester, August 29 to September 5, 1962*, Manchester, Manchester University Press for the British Association, 1962

Cassell, John, *Art Treasures Exhibition: containing Engravings of the Principal Masterpieces, etc.*, London, W. Kent, 1858

Chandler, G., *Victorian and Edwardian Manchester from old Photographs*, London, Batsford, 1974

Charles, HRH the Prince of Wales, *A Vision of Britain*, London, Doubleday, 1989

SELECT BIBLIOGRAPHY

Charlton, H. B., *Portrait of a University, 1851–1951*, Manchester, Manchester University Press, 1951

Cherry, Gordon E., *The Evolution of British Town Planning*, London, Leonard Hill, 1974

Cherry, Gordon E., *Cities and Plans: The Shaping of Urban Britain in the Nineteenth and Twentieth Centuries*, London, Edward Arnold, 1988

Cherry, Gordon E., ed., *Pioneers in British Planning*, London, Architectural Press, 1981

City Centre Land Use Surveys, Manchester, Manchester City Planning Department, 1977

City Pride: A Focus for the Future, Manchester, Manchester City Council, 1994

City Pride Baseline Study, Manchester, Manchester City Planning Department, Planning Studies Group, 1994

Clark, Kenneth, *The Gothic Revival*, third edition, London, John Murray, 1962

Clarke, Basil Fulford Lowther, *Church Builders of the Nineteenth Century: A Study of the Gothic Revival in England*, Newton Abbot, David & Charles, 1969

Clay, Henry, and Brady, Russell, eds, *Manchester at Work: A Survey*, Manchester, Sherratt & Hughes for the Manchester Civic Week Committee, 1929

Clayre, Alasdair, ed., *Nature and Industrialisation: an Anthology*, Oxford, Oxford University Press in association with the Open University Press, 1977

Clifton-Taylor, Alec, *The Pattern of English Building*, London, Faber & Faber, 1972

Coleman, Alice, *Utopia on Trial: Vision and Reality in Planned Housing*, London, Hilary Shipman, 1985

Colvin, Howard, *A Biographical Dictionary of British Architects, 1600–1840*, London, John Murray, 1978

Cooke Taylor, W., *Notes of a Tour in the Manufacturing Districts of Lancashire*, second edition, London, Frank Cass, [1842] 1968

Corbusier, Le, *Towards a New Architecture*, London, Architectural Press, [1927] 1946

Corbusier, Le, *The City of Tomorrow and its Planning*, London, Architectural Press, [1929] 1947

Corbusier, Le, *The Radiant City*, London, Faber & Faber, [1933] 1967

Cotton Metropolis, The: Manchester in 1849, Manchester, R Shipperbottom, [published in the *Morning Chronicle* 1849–50] 1972

Crawford, David, *A Decade of British Housing, 1963–1973*, London, Architectural Press, 1975

Creese, W. L., *The Search for Environment: The Garden City Before and After*, New Haven CT, Yale University Press, 1966

Crook, J. Mordaunt, *The Greek Revival*, London, John Murray, 1972

Croston, J., ed., *Old Manchester: A Series of Views of the More Ancient Buildings in Manchester and its Vicinity, as they appeared Fifty Years Ago*, Manchester, J. E. Cornish, 1875

Crowe, Timothy D., *Crime Prevention through Environmental Design*, London, National Crime Prevention Institute, 1991

Crowther, J. S., *An Architectural History of the Cathedral Church of Manchester, dedicated to S. Mary, S. George and S. Denys*, Manchester, J. E. Cornish, 1893

Cullen, Gordon, *Townscape*, London, Architectural Press, 1961

Cullingworth, J. Barry, and Nadin, Vincent, *Town and Country Planning in Britain*, eleventh edition, London, Routledge, 1994

Cunningham, C., *Victorian and Edwardian Town Halls*, London, Routledge & Kegan Paul, 1981

Cunningham, Colin, and Waterhouse, Prudence, *Alfred Waterhouse, 1830–1905: Biography of a Practice*, Oxford, Clarendon Press, 1992

Curl, James Stevens, *Victorian Architecture: its Practical Aspects*, Newton Abbot, David & Charles, 1973

Curl, James Stevens, *An Encyclopædia of Architectural Terms*, London, Donhead, 1993

Curl, James Stevens, *Victorian Churches*, London, Batsford, 1995

Dannatt, Trevor, *Modern Architecture in Britain*, London, Batsford, 1959

Darby, H. C., ed., *Historical Geography of England before 1800*, Cambridge, Cambridge University Press, 1936

Darbyshire, Alfred, *An Architect's Experiences: Professional, Artistic and Theatrical*, Manchester, J. E. Cornish, 1897

Davies, Andrew, and Fielding, Steven, eds, *Workers' Worlds: Cultures and Communities in Manchester and Salford, 1880–1939*, Manchester, Manchester University Press, 1992

De Motte, Margaret, *A Municipal Palace: A Select Bibliography on the Construction and Opening of the new Town Hall, Manchester, 1877*, Manchester, City of Manchester Cultural Services, 1977

Deakin, D., *Wythenshawe: The Story of a Garden City*, Chichester, Phillimore, 1989

Deakin, Nicholas, and Edwards, John, *The Enterprise Culture and the Inner City*, London, Routledge, 1993

Defoe, Daniel, *A Tour through the Whole Island of Great Britain*, Harmondsworth, Penguin Books, [1724–26] 1971

Derry, T. K., and Williams, Trevor I., *A Short History of Technology from the earliest Times to A.D. 1900*, London, Oxford University Press, 1960

Dickinson, Mark, *Goodbye Piccadilly: The History of the Abolition of the Greater Manchester Council*, Poynton, Intercommunication Publishing, 1990

Dixon, Roger, and Muthesius, Stefan, *Victorian Architecture*, second edition, London, Thames & Hudson, 1985

Dobbin, A. M., *et al.*, *This is your City: Manchester*, Holmes McDougall [Manchester, c. 1971]

Dunleavy, Patrick, *The Politics of Mass Housing in Britain, 1945–1975*, Oxford, Clarendon Press, 1981

Dyos, H. J., and Wolff, Michael, eds, *The Victorian City: Images and Realities*, two volumes, London, Routledge & Kegan Paul, 1973

Eastlake, Charles L., with an Introduction by J. Mordaunt Crook, *A History of the Gothic Revival*, Leicester, Leicester University Press, 1970

Edwards, Michael M., *The Growth of the British Cotton Trade, 1780–1815*, Manchester, Manchester University Press, 1967

Engels, Friedrich, *The Condition of the Working Class in England*, Oxford, Oxford University Press, [1844] 1993

English, John, Madigan, Ruth, and Norman, Peter, *Slum Clearance: The Social and Administrative Context in England and Wales*, London, Croom Helm, 1976

Esher, Lionel, *A Broken Wave: The Rebuilding of England, 1940–1980*, London, Allen Lane, 1981

Evans, S., and Treuherz, J., *Manchester: Three Architectural Walks*, Victorian Society Walks No 3. London, Victorian Society, 1980

Fairbairn, W., *The Application of Cast and Wrought Iron to Building Purposes*, London, John Weale, 1854

Farnie, D. A., *The English Cotton Industry and the World Market, 1815–1896*, Oxford, Clarendon Press, 1979

Farnie, D. A., *The Manchester Ship Canal and the Rise of the Port of Manchester, 1894–1975*, Manchester, Manchester University Press, 1980

Farnie, D. A., *John Rylands of Manchester*, Manchester, John Rylands University Library of Manchester, 1993

Faucher, Leon, *Manchester in 1844: its Present Condition and Future Prospects*, London, Frank Cass, [Manchester, Abel Heywood, 1844] 1969

Felstead, Alison, Franklin, Jonathan, and Pinfield, Leslie, *Directory of British Architects, 1834–1900*, London, Mansell, 1993

Ferrey, Benjamin, *Recollections of A. N. Welby Pugin, and his Father Augustus Pugin*, London, Stanford, [Aldershot, Scolar Press, 1978] 1861

Ferriday, Peter, ed., *Victorian Architecture*, London, Jonathan Cape, 1963

Fitzgerald, R. S., *Liverpool Road Station, Manchester: An Historical and Architectural Survey*, Manchester, Manchester University Press in association with the RCHM and GMC, 1980

Fitton, R. S., and Wadsworth, A. P., *The Strutts and the Arkwrights*, Manchester, Manchester University Press, 1973

Fitzwalter, Raymond, and Taylor, David, *Web of Corruption: The Story of John Poulson and T. Dan Smith*, St Albans, Granada Publishing, 1981

Fowler, Alan, and Wyke, Terry, *Many Arts, Many Skills: The Origins of the Manchester Metropolitan University*, Manchester, Manchester Metropolitan University Press, 1993

Frampton, Kenneth, *Modern Architecture: A Critical History*, London, Thames & Hudson, 1985

Frangopulo, N. J., *Rich Inheritance: A Guide to the History of Manchester*, Manchester, Manchester Education Committee, 1962

Frangopulo, N. J., *Manchester*, London, Blond Educational, 1967

Frangopulo, N. J., *Tradition in Action: The Historic Evolution of Greater Manchester County*, Wakefield, EP Publishing, 1977

Fraser, D., ed., *Municipal Reform and the Industrial City*, Leicester, Leicester University Press, 1982

Freeman, T. W., *The Conurbations of Great Britain*, Manchester, Manchester University Press, 1959

Garrigan, K., *Ruskin and Architecture: His Thought and Influence*, Madison WI, University of Wisconsin Press, 1973

Gauldie, E., *Cruel Habitations: A History of Working Class Housing, 1780–1918*, London, Allen & Unwin, 1974

Germann, Georg, *Gothic Revival in Europe and Britain: Source, Influences and Ideas*, London, Lund Humphries, 1972

Girouard, Mark, *Sweetness and Light: The 'Queen Anne' Movement, 1860–1900*, Oxford, Oxford University Press, 1977

Girouard, Mark, *Return to Camelot: Chivalry and the English Gentleman*, New Haven CT and London, Yale University Press, 1981

Girouard, Mark, *Cities and People: A Social and Architectural History*, New Haven CT and London, Yale University Press, 1985

Glendinning, Miles, and Muthesius, Stefan, *Tower Block: Modern Public Housing in England, Scotland, Wales and Northern Ireland*, New Haven CT and London, Yale University Press, 1994

Gloag, J., and Bridgwater, D., *A History of Cast Iron in Architecture*, London, Allen & Unwin, 1948

Golby, J. M., *Culture and Society in Britain, 1850–1890: A Source Book of Contemporary Writings*, Oxford, Oxford University Press, 1986

Goldstein, Barbara, ed., *Architecture: Opportunities, Achievements* (report of the RIBA annual conference, 1976), London, RIBA Publications, 1977

Goodhart-Rendell, H. S., *English Architecture since the Regency: An Interpretation*, London, Constable, 1953

Gordon, George, ed., *Regional Cities in the U.K., 1890–1980*, London, Harper & Row, 1986

Gouldman, H., ed., *Manchester Great Synagogue, Cheetham Hill Road, Manchester 8, 1858–1958*, Manchester, The Synagogue, 1958

Grant, Len, *Built to Music: The Making of the Bridgewater Hall*, Manchester, Manchester City Council, 1996

Gray, A. Stuart, *Edwardian Architecture: A Biographical Dictionary*, London, Duckworth, 1985

Greater Manchester Structure Plan: Draft Written Statement, Manchester, Greater Manchester Council, 1978

Green, Edwin, *Buildings for Bankers: Sir Edwin Lutyens and the Midland Bank, 1921–1939*, London, Midland Bank, 1980

Green, L. P., *Provincial Metropolis: The Future of Local Government in South East Lancashire*, London, Allen & Unwin, 1959

Grindon, Leo H., *Manchester Banks and Bankers*, second edition, Manchester, Palmer & Howe, 1878

Guide to Development in Manchester, Manchester, Manchester City Council, 1997

Guppy, H., and Vine, G., *A Classified Catalogue of the Works on Architecture and the Allied Arts in the Principal Libraries of Manchester and Salford with Alphabetical Author List and Subject Index*, Manchester, 1909

Hackney, Rod, *The Good, the Bad and the Ugly: Cities in Crisis*, London, Frederick Muller, 1988

Hadfield, Charles, and Biddle, Gordon, *The Canals of North West England*, two volumes, Newton Abbot, David & Charles, 1970

Hague, Graham, and Hague, Judy, *The Unitarian Heritage: An Architectural Survey of Chapels and Churches in the Unitarian Tradition in the British Isles*, Sheffield, P. B. Godfrey, 1986

Hall, Peter, *Cities of Tomorrow: An Intellectual History of Urban Planning and Design in the Twentieth Century*, Oxford, Blackwell, 1988

Hall, Peter, *Urban and Regional Planning*, third edition, London, Routledge, 1992

Hall, Peter, ed., *The Inner City in Context: The Final Report of the Social Science Research Council Inner Cities Working Party*, London, Heinemann, 1981

Harries, J. G., *Pugin: an Illustrated Life of Augustus Welby Northmore Pugin, 1812–52*, Aylesbury, Shire Publications, 1973

Harrison, J. F. C., *Early Victorian Britain, 1832–51*, London, Fontana, 1979

Healey, Patsy, *et al.*, eds, *Rebuilding the City: Property-led Urban Regeneration*, London, Spon, 1992

Hersey, George L., *High Victorian Gothic: A Study in Associationism*, Baltimore MD and London, Johns Hopkins University Press, 1972

Hills, R. L., *Beyer, Peacock, Locomotive Builders of Gorton, Manchester: A Short History*, Manchester, Greater Manchester Museum of Science and Industry, 1982

Hitchcock, Henry-Russell, *Early Victorian Architecture in Britain*, two volumes, London, Trewin Copplestone, 1954

Hitchcock, Henry-Russell, *Architecture: Nineteenth and Twentieth Centuries*, London, Penguin Books, 1990

Home, Robert K., *Inner City Regeneration*, London, Spon, 1982

Horsfall, T. C., *The Improvement of the Dwellings and Surroundings of the People: The Example of Germany*, second edition, Manchester, Manchester University Press, 1905

Howe, Anthony, *The Cotton Masters, 1830–1860*, Oxford, Clarendon Press, 1984

Hudson, Kenneth, *The Fashionable Stone*, Bath, Adams & Dart, 1971

Hulme Regeneration, *Rebuilding the City: A Guide to Development in Hulme*, Manchester, Hulme Regeneration and Manchester City Council, 1994

Hussey, Christopher, *The Life of Sir Edwin Lutyens*, London and New York, Country Life, 1953

Hutchinson, Maxwell, *The Prince of Wales: Right or Wrong?* London, Faber & Faber, 1989

Imrie, Rob, and Thomas, Huw, eds, *British Urban Policy and the Urban Development Corporations*, London, Paul Chapman, 1993

Jackson, Anthony, *The Politics of Architecture*, London, Architectural Press, 1970

Jackson, Frank, *Sir Raymond Unwin: Architect, Planner and Visionary*, London, Zwemmer, 1985

Jencks, Charles, *The Language of Postmodern Architecture*, New York, Rizzoli, 1981

Jencks, Charles, *The Prince, the Architects and New Wave Monarchy*, London, Academy Editions, 1988

Jeremiah, David, *A Hundred Years and More*, Manchester, Manchester Polytechnic, 1980

Jones, Edgar, *Industrial Architecture in Britain, 1750–1939*, London, Batsford, 1985

Jones, G. B. D., and Rhodes, D., *Historic Castlefield*, Manchester, no publisher given, 1979

Jordan, Robert Furneaux, *Victorian Architecture*, Harmondsworth, Penguin Books, 1966

Kargon, Robert H., *Science in Victorian Manchester: Enterprise and Expertise*, Manchester, Manchester University Press, 1977

Kaufman, Moritz, *Housing of the Working Classes and of the Poor*, Wakefield, EP Publishing, 1975

Kay, James Phillips, *The Moral and Physical Condition of the Working Classes employed in the Cotton Manufacture in Manchester*, Shannon, Irish University Press, [1832] 1971

Keeble, Lewis, *Town Planning at the Crossroads*, London, Estates Gazette, 1961

Keith, Michael, and Rogers, Alisdair, eds, *Hollow Promises: Rhetoric and Reality in the Inner City*, London, Mansell, 1991

Kellett, John R., *The Impact of Railways on Victorian Cities*, London, Routledge & Kegan Paul, 1969

Kennedy, Michael, *Portrait of Manchester*, London, Robert Hale, 1970

Kennedy, Michael, *The History of the Royal Manchester College of Music, 1893–1972*, Manchester, Manchester University Press, 1971

Kennedy, Michael, *The Hallé, 1858–1983: A History of the Orchestra*, Manchester, Manchester University Press, 1982

Kennedy, Michael, ed., *The Autobiography of Charles Hallé, with Correspondence and Diaries*, London, Paul Elek, 1972

Kidd, Alan, *Manchester*, Keele, Ryburn Publishing, 1993

Kidd, Alan J., and Roberts, K. W., *City, Class and Culture: Studies of Social Policy and Cultural Production in Victorian Manchester*, Manchester, Manchester University Press, 1985

Krieger, Eric, *Manchester in Times Past, 1900–1935*, Chorley, Countryside Publications, 1987

Lancaster, Osbert, *Here, of all Places: The Pocket Lamp of Architecture*, London, John Murray, 1959

Land Availability in Manchester, Manchester, Manchester City Planning Department, 1977

Law, C. M., Grundy, T., and Senior, M. L., *Comparative Study of Conurbations Project: The Greater Manchester Area*, Manchester, Greater Manchester Council, 1984

Lawless, Paul, *Britain's Inner Cities*, second edition, London, Paul Chapman, 1989

Lawless, Paul, and Raban, Colin, eds, *The Contemporary British City*, London, Harper & Row, 1986

Leach, Penny, *St Mary's Hospital, Manchester, 1790–1990*, Manchester, no publisher, undated

Lee, C. H., *A Cotton Enterprise, 1795–1840: A History of M'Connel & Kennedy, Fine Cotton Spinners*, Manchester, Manchester University Press, 1972

Lloyd-Jones, Roger, and Lewis, M. J., *Manchester and the Age of the Factory: The Business Structure of Cottonopolis in the Industrial Revolution*, London, Croom Helm, 1988

Lockett, T. A., *Three Lives: It Happened round Manchester*, London, University of London Press, 1968

Love, Benjamin, *Manchester as it is: or, Notices of the Institutions, Manufactures, Commerce*, Manchester, E. J. Morten, [Love & Barton, 1839] 1971

Lutyens, Mary, *Edwin Lutyens*, London, John Murray, 1980

Lyall, Sutherland, *The State of British Architecture*, London, Architectural Press, 1980

Lynch, Kevin, *The Image of the City*, Cambridge MA and London, MIT Press, 1986

Macaulay, James, *The Gothic Revival, 1745–1845*, Glasgow, Blackie, 1975

McCarthy, Michael, *The Origins of the Gothic Revival*, New Haven CT, Yale University Press, 1987

M'Connel & Co., *A Century of Fine Cotton Spinning, 1790–1906*, Manchester, M'Connel & Co., 1906

MacEwen, Malcolm, *Crisis in Architecture*, London, RIBA Publications, 1974

Macfadyen, D., *Sir Ebenezer Howard and the Town Planning Movement*, Manchester, Manchester University Press, 1933

MacGregor, Susanne, and Pimlott, Ben, eds, *Tackling the Inner Cities: The 1980s Reviewed, Prospects for the 1990s*, Oxford, Clarendon Press, 1991

Macleod, Robert, *Style and Society: Architectural Ideology in Britain, 1835–1914*, London, RIBA Publications, 1971

McNeil, Robina, and George, A. D., eds, *The Heritage Atlas 3: Warehouse Album*, Manchester, Field Archaeology Centre, University of Manchester, 1997

Magnel, Gustave, *Prestressed Concrete*, second edition, London, Concrete Publications, 1950

Makepeace, Chris E., *Manchester as it was*, six volumes, Nelson, Hendon Publishing, 1972–77

Makepeace, Chris E., *Science and Technology in Manchester: Two Hundred Years of the Lit. and Phil.*, Manchester, Manchester Literary and Philosophical Publications, 1984

Makepeace, Chris, ed., *Oldest in the World: The Story of Liverpool Road Station, Manchester*, Manchester, Liverpool Road Station Society and Manchester Region Industrial Archaeological Society, 1979

Maltby, S., MacDonald, S., and Cunningham, C., *Alfred Waterhouse, 1830–1905*, London, RIBA Heinz Gallery, 1983

Manchester and Salford Inner Area Study, Manchester, Department of the Environment, 1978

Manchester and Salford Phoenix Initiatives *et al.*, *The Northern Gateway to Two Cities*, Salford, City of Salford for the Northern Gateway Working Party, 1988

Manchester City Centre Local Plan, Manchester, Manchester City Council, 1984

Manchester City Planning Handbook, London, Pyramid Press, 1994

Manchester Economic Facts, Manchester, Central Manchester Development Corporation, 1993

Manchester Historical Recorder, The, Manchester, John Heywood, [1875]

Manchester, Making it Happen: Planning and Environmental Health Handbook 1996/7, third edition, Wallington, Burrows Communications, 1997

Manchester Plan, The: The Unitary Development Plan for the City of Manchester, Deposit Draft, Manchester, Manchester City Council, 1992

Manchester Plan, The: The Adopted Unitary Development Plan for the City of Manchester, Manchester, Manchester City Council, 1995

Manchester's Architectural Heritage: A List of Buildings of Special Architectural or Historic Interest in the City of Manchester, revised edition, Manchester, City of Manchester Planning Department, 1993

Marcus, Steven, *Engels, Manchester, and the Working Class*, London, Weidenfeld & Nicolson, 1974

Markus, Thomas A., *Buildings and Power: Freedom and Control in the Origin of Modern Building Types*, London, Routledge, 1993

Marriott, Oliver, *The Property Boom*, London, Hamish Hamilton, 1967 and 1989

Mason, Tim, *Inner City Housing and Urban Renewal Policy: A Housing Profile of Cheetham Hill, Manchester and Salford*, London, Centre for Environmental Studies, 1977

Mathias, Peter, *The First Industrial Nation: An Economic History of Britain, 1700–1914*, London, Methuen, 1980

Messinger, Gary S., *Manchester in the Victorian Age: The Half-known City*, Manchester, Manchester University Press, 1985

Metrolink 2000, Manchester, Greater Manchester Passenger Transport Authority, [1994]

SELECT BIBLIOGRAPHY

Metrolink in East Manchester and Tameside, Manchester, Greater Manchester Passenger Transport Executive, 1996

Middleton, Michael, *Cities in Transition: The Regeneration of Britain's Inner Cities*, London, Michael Joseph, 1991

Midwinter, E. C., *Victorian Social Reform*, Harlow, Longman, 1968

Muthesius, Stefan, *The High Victorian Movement in Architecture, 1850–70*, London, Routledge & Kegan Paul, 1972

Muthesius, Stefan, *The English Terraced House*, New Haven CT and London, Yale University Press, 1982

Nairn, Ian, *Outrage*, London, Architectural Press, 1955

Nairn, Ian, *Britain's Changing Towns*, London, British Broadcasting Corporation, 1967

Nasmith, J., *Recent Cotton Mill Construction and Engineering*, Manchester, John Heywood, 1909

National Consumer Council, *What's wrong with Walking? A Consumer Review of the Pedestrian Environment*, London, HMSO, 1987

Newman, Oscar, *Defensible Space: People and Design in the Violent City*, London, Architectural Press, 1973

Nicholas, R., *City of Manchester Plan, 1945*, Norwich and London, Jarrold & Sons, 1945

Office Development in Manchester, 1996/7, Manchester, Manchester City Planning Department, 1997

Oliver, Paul, Davis, Ian, and Bentley, Ian, *Dunroamin: The Suburban Semi and its Enemies*, London, Barrie & Jenkins, 1981

Owen, David, *Canals to Manchester*, Manchester, Manchester University Press, 1977

Owen, David, *The Manchester Ship Canal*, Manchester, Manchester University Press, 1983

Pacione, M., *Britain's Cities: Geographies of Division in Urban Britain*, London, Routledge, 1997

Parker Morris Report, *Homes for Today and Tomorrow*, London, Department of the Environment, 1961

Parkinson-Bailey, John J., ed., *Sites of the City: Essays on Recent Buildings by their Architects*, Manchester, Manchester Metropolitan University, 1996

Pass, Anthony J., *Thomas Worthington: Victorian Architecture and Social Purpose*, Manchester, Manchester Literary and Philosophical Publications, 1988 (special subscription edition)

Pawley, Martin, *Architecture versus Housing*, London, Studio Vista, 1971

Percy, Clayre, and Ridley, Jane, eds, *The Letters of Edwin Lutyens to his Wife Lady Emily*, London, Collins, 1985

Perkins, T., *The Cathedral Church of Manchester: A Short History and Description of the Church and of the Collegiate Buildings now known as Chetham's Hospital*, London, George Bull, 1901

Pevsner, Nikolaus, *The Buildings of England: South Lancashire*, Harmondsworth, Penguin Books, 1969

Pevsner, Nikolaus, *The Englishness of English Art*, Harmondsworth, Penguin Books, [London, Architectural Press, 1956] 1964

Pevsner, Nikolaus, *A History of Building Types*, London, Thames & Hudson, 1976

Pickles, W., *Our Grimy Heritage*, Fontwell, Centaur Press, 1971

Plumb, J. H., *England in the Eighteenth Century*, Harmondsworth, Penguin Books, 1975

Port, M. H., *Six Hundred New Churches: A Study of the Church Building Commission, 1818–1856, and its Church Building Activities*, London, SPCK, 1961

Powell, K., and Fieldhouse, J., *Manchester: the Disappearing Cathedral Conservation Area*, Hebden Bridge, Victorian Society Manchester Group, 1982

Power, Anne, *Hovels to High-rise*, London, Routledge, 1993

Procter, R. W., *Memorials of Manchester Streets*, Manchester, Thomas Sutcliffe, 1874

Procter, R. W., *Memorials of Bygone Manchester*, Manchester, Palmer & Howe, 1880

Pugin, A. W. N., *Contrasts: or, A Parallel between the Noble Edifices of the Middle Ages, and Corresponding Buildings of the Present Day; Shewing the Present Decay of Taste*, second edition, London, Charles Dolman, 1841

Pugin, A. W. N., *An Apology for the Revival of Christian Architecture in England*, London, John Weale, 1843

Pugin, A. W. N., *The Present State of Ecclesiastical Architecture in England*, London, Charles Dolman, 1843

Pugin, A. W. N., *The True Principles of Pointed or Christian Architecture: Set Forth in Two Lectures delivered at St Marie's, Oscott*, London, Henry Bohn, 1843

Quayle, Tom, *Reservoirs in the Hills*, Glossop, Mopok Graphics, for North West Water, undated

Ramwell, Robert, and Saltburn, Hillary, *Trick or Treat? City Challenge and the Regeneration of Hulme*, Manchester, North British Housing Association and Guinness Trust, 1998

Rea, Anthony, *Manchester's Little Italy: Memories of the Italian Colony of Ancoats*, Manchester, Neil Richardson, 1988

Reach, Angus Bethune, *Manchester and the Textile Districts in 1849*, ed. C. Aspin, Helmshore, Helmshore Local History Society, 1972

Reade, E. J., *British Town and Country Planning*, Milton Keynes, Open University Press, 1987

Redford, A., and Russell, T. S., *The History of Local Government in Manchester*, London, Longmans Green, 1940

Reece, S., *Guide to Manchester and Salford*, second edition, London, John Sherratt, 1948

Rees, Gareth, and Lambert, John, *Cities in Crisis: The Political Economy of Urban Development in Post-war Britain*, London, Edward Arnold, 1985

Reilly, C. H., *Some Manchester Streets and their Buildings*, London, Hodder & Stoughton, and Liverpool, Liverpool University Press, 1924

Renaissance – North West: A Plan for Regional Revival, Manchester, North West Civic Trust, 1987

Retail and Leisure Development in Manchester, 1996/7, Manchester, Manchester City Council, Technical Services (Planning) Department, 1997

Richards, J. M., *An Introduction to Modern Architecture*, Harmondsworth, Penguin Books, 1940

Richards, J. M., *The Functional Tradition in Early Industrial Building*, London, Architectural Press, 1958

Rickman, Thomas, *An Attempt to Discriminate the Styles of English Architecture, from the Conquest to the Reformation*, sixth edition, London, John Henry Parker, 1862

Ritchie, Berry, *The Good Builder: The John Laing Story*, London, James & James, 1997

Roberts, Jacqueline, *Working Class Housing in Nineteenth Century Manchester: The Example of John Street, Irk Town*, Swinton, Manchester, Neil Richardson, undated

Robson, R., *The Cotton Industry in Britain*, London, Macmillan, 1957

Rolt, L. T. C., *Victorian Engineering*, London, Allen Lane, 1970

Rose, Mary B., ed., *The Lancashire Cotton Industry: A History since 1700*, Preston, Lancashire County Books, 1996

Ross, M., *Planning and the Heritage*, London, Spon, 1991

Rubinstein, David, *Victorian Homes*, Newton Abbot, David & Charles, 1974

Ruskin, John, *The Seven Lamps of Architecture*, London, Longmans Green, 1849

Ruskin, John, *The Stones of Venice*, three volumes, London, J. M. Dent [Longmans Green, 1851–53], 1907

Ryan, Rachel, *A Biography of Manchester*, London, Methuen, 1937

Sanders, John, *Manchester*, London, Rupert Hart-Davis, 1967

Scott, George Gilbert, *A Plea for the Faithful Restoration of our Ancient Churches*, London, J. H. Parker, 1850

Scott, Robert D. H., *The Biggest Room in the World: A Short History of the Manchester Royal Exchange*, Manchester, Royal Exchange Theatre Trust, 1976

Service, Alastair, ed., *Edwardian Architecture and its Origins*, London, Architectural Press, 1975

Service, Alastair, *Edwardian Architecture: A Handbook to Building Design in Britain, 1890–1914*, London, Thames & Hudson, 1977

Service Sector Employment in Manchester, 1971–1976, City of Manchester Planning Department, Manchester, 1978

Sharp, Dennis, *Manchester*, London, Studio Vista, 1969

Sharp, Dennis, ed., 'Manchester Buildings', *Architecture North West*, No. 19, October–November 1966, special commemorative issue.

Sharp, Thomas, *English Panorama*, London, Dent, 1936

Shaw, W. A., *Manchester Old and New*, three volumes, Manchester, Cassell, 1894

Simmie, J., *Power, Property and Corporatism*, London, Macmillan, 1981

Simmons, Jack, *The Victorian Railway*, New York, Thames & Hudson, 1991

Simon, Alfred P., *Manchester Made Over*, London, P. S. King & Son, 1936

Simon, E. D. (Sir), *The Anti-slum Campaign*, London, Longmans Green, 1933

Simon, E. D. (Sir), and Inman, J., *The Rebuilding of Manchester*, London, Longmans Green, 1935

Simon, Sheena D., *A Century of City Government: Manchester 1838–1938*, London, Allen & Unwin, 1938

Simpson, I. M., and Broadhurst, F. M., *A Building Stones Guide to Central Manchester*, Manchester, University of Manchester, 1975

Singleton, John, *Lancashire on the Scrapheap: The Cotton Industry, 1945–1970*, Oxford, Oxford University Press, 1991

Skyrme, Thomas (Sir), *History of the Justices of the Peace*, three volumes, Chichester, Barry Rose Law Publishers, 1991

Slugg, J. T., *Reminiscences of Manchester Fifty Years Ago*, Shannon, Irish University Press [1881], 1971

Smelser, N. J., *Social Change in the Industrial Revolution*, London, Routledge & Kegan Paul, 1959

Smith, David M., *Industrial Britain: The North West*, Newton Abbot, David & Charles, 1969

Spiers, Maurice, *Victoria Park, Manchester: A Nineteenth Century Suburb in its Social and Administrative Context*, Manchester, Chetham Society, 1976

Stamp, Gavin, 'London 1900', *Architectural Design*, Vol. 48, Nos 5–6, 1978

Stanton, Phoebe, *Pugin*, London, Thames & Hudson, 1971

Stewart, Cecil, *The Stones of Manchester*, London, Edward Arnold, 1956

Stollard, Paul, *Crime Prevention through Housing Design*, London, Chapman & Hall, 1991

Summerson, John, *Architecture in Britain, 1530–1830*, Harmondsworth, Penguin Books, 1953

Summerson, John, *The Turn of the Century: Architecture in Britain around 1900*, W. A. Cargill Memorial Lectures in Fine Art, Glasgow, University of Glasgow Press, 1976

Sutcliffe, Anthony, ed., *Multi-storey Living: The British Working-Class Experience*, London, Croom Helm, 1974

Swindells, T., *Manchester Streets and Manchester Men*, five volumes, Manchester, [J. E. Cornish, 1906–08] Morten, undated

Tann, J., *The Development of the Factory*, London, Cornmarket Press, 1970

Tarn, John Nelson, *Working-class Housing in Nineteenth-century Britain*, London, Architectural Association, 1971

Tarn, John Nelson, *Five per cent Philanthropy: An account of Housing in Urban Areas between 1840 and 1914*, Cambridge, Cambridge University Press, 1973

Taylor, Ian, Evans, Karen, and Fraser, Penny, *A Tale of Two Cities: Global Change, local Feeling and everyday Life in the North of England. A Study in Manchester and Sheffield*, London, Routledge, 1996

Taylor, Nicholas, *Monuments of Commerce*, London, RIBA Publications, 1968

Tetlow, J., and Goss, A., *Homes, Towns and Traffic*, London, Faber & Faber, 1965

Thompson, Paul, *William Butterfield*, London, Routledge & Kegan Paul, 1971

Town and Country Planning Summer School, *Report of Proceedings*, London, Town Planning Institute, 1968

Towndrow, Frederic, *Architecture in the Balance: An Approach to the Art of Scientific Humanism*, London, Chatto & Windus, 1933

Trafford Park, Greater Manchester, Manchester, Trafford Park Development Corporation, undated

Unwin, Raymond, *Nothing Gained by Overcrowding! How the Garden City Type of Development may Benefit both Owner and Occupier*, London, P. S. King, 1912

Ure, Andrew, *The Philosophy of Manufactures: or, An Exposition of the Scientific, Moral and Commercial Economy of the Factory System of Great Britain*, London, Charles Knight, 1835

Ward, C., *When We Build Again: Let's Have Housing that Works*, London, Pluto Press, 1985

Ward, J. T., *The Factory System*, Newton Abbot, David & Charles, 1970

Watkin, David, *The Life and Works of C. R. Cockerell*, London, Zwemmer, 1974

Wheeler, James, *Manchester: its Political, Social and Commercial History, Ancient and Modern*, Manchester, Simms & Dinham, and London, Simpkin Marshall, 1842

Whiffen, M., *The Architecture of Sir Charles Barry in Manchester and Neighbourhood*, Manchester, Manchester University Press, 1956

White, H. P., ed., *The Continuing Conurbation: Change and Development in Greater Manchester*, Farnborough, Gower, 1980

White, James, *The Cambridge Movement: The Ecclesiologists and the Gothic Revival*, Cambridge, Cambridge University Press, 1962

Whittam, William, *Fairhursts: The History of a Manchester Practice*, Manchester, Department of History of Art and Design, Manchester Polytechnic, 1986

Wilkinson, Stephen, *Manchester's Warehouses: Their History and Architecture*, Manchester, Neil Richardson, 1981

Willan, T. S., *Elizabethan Manchester*, Manchester, Chetham Society, 1980

Williams, Bill, *The Making of Manchester Jewry, 1740–1875*, Manchester, Manchester University Press, 1976

Williams, Mike (with D. A. Farnie), *Cotton Mills in Greater Manchester*, Preston, Carnegie Publishing, for the Greater Manchester Archaeological Unit and the Royal Commission on the Historical Monuments of England, 1992

Wilson, Hugh, and Womersley, Lewis, *Manchester Education Precinct: The Final Report of the Planning Consultants, 1967*, Manchester, Manchester University Press, 1967

Wilson, Hugh, and Womersley, Lewis, *Manchester Education Precinct: A Review of the Plan, 1974*, Manchester, Manchester University Press, 1974

Winter, John, *Industrial Architecture: A Survey of Factory Buildings*, London, Studio Vista, 1970

Wolfe, Tom, *From Bauhaus to our House*, London, Jonathan Cape, 1982

Wyke, T., *A Hall for all Seasons: A History of the Free Trade Hall*, Manchester, Charles Hallé Foundation, 1996

Yorke, F. R. S., and Gibberd, Frederick, *The Modern Flat*, London, Architectural Press, 1937

Zukin, Sharon, *Loft Living: Culture and Capital in Urban Change*, London, Radius, 1988

INDEX

Note: General buildings, e.g. offices, warehouses, and those distinguished by number only, appear as the name of the street on which they appear. Named buildings appear as entries in their own right. Gazetteer page numbers appear in **bold**. Photographs and illustrations appear in *italics*.